LEADERS IN THE SHADOWS

The Leadership Qualities of Municipal Chief Administrative Officers

In most municipalities across Canada, the top public servant is the chief administrative officer (CAO) or city manager. Compared to elected politicians such as the mayor and the council, the work of a CAO is often overlooked and not well understood. In *Leaders in the Shadows*, David Siegel brings the CAO into the limelight, examining the leadership qualities of effective municipal managers.

Using the examples of five exceptional CAOs who have worked in municipalities of varying sizes across Canada, Siegel identifies the leadership traits, skills, and behaviours that have made them successful. Interweaving the stories of his subjects with insights drawn from leadership theory, Siegel offers an engrossing account of how CAOs must lead "up, down, and out" in order to succeed. Offering well-rounded accounts of the challenges and opportunities faced by public servants at the municipal level, *Leaders in the Shadows* is a valuable resource for academics and practitioners alike.

DAVID SIEGEL is a professor in the Department of Political Science at Brock University.

IPAC The Institute of
Public Administration of Canada

IAPC L'Institut d'administration
publique du Canada

The Institute of Public Administration of Canada Series in Public Management and Governance

Editors:

Peter Aucoin, 2001–02
Donald Savoie, 2003–07
Luc Bernier, 2007–09
Patrice Dutil, 2010–

This series is sponsored by the Institute of Public Administration of Canada as part of its commitment to encourage research on issues in Canadian public administration, public sector management, and public policy. It also seeks to foster wider knowledge and understanding among practitioners, academics, and the general public.

For a list of books published in the series, see page 325.

Leaders in the Shadows

The Leadership Qualities of Municipal Chief Administrative Officers

DAVID SIEGEL

UNIVERSITY OF TORONTO PRESS
Toronto Buffalo London

© University of Toronto Press 2015
Toronto Buffalo London
www.utppublishing.com
Printed in the U.S.A.

ISBN 978-1-4426-4925-5 (cloth)
ISBN 978-1-4426-2665-2 (paper)

Printed on acid-free, 100% post-consumer recycled paper.

Library and Archives Canada Cataloguing in Publication

Siegel, David, author
Leaders in the shadows: the leadership qualities of municipal chief administrative officers / David Siegel.

(Institute of Public Administration of Canada series in public management
and governance)
Includes bibliographical references and index.
ISBN 978-1-4426-4925-5 (bound). – ISBN 978-1-4426-2665-2 (pbk.)

1. City managers – Canada – Case studies.   2. Municipal government by
city manager – Canada – Case studies.   3. Leadership – Canada – Case
studies.   I. Title.   II. Series: Institute of Public Administration of Canada
series in public management and governance

JS1710.S53 2015   352.23'2160971   C2014-907067-5

This book has been published with the help of a grant from the Federation
for the Humanities and Social Sciences, through the Awards to Scholarly
Publications Program, using funds provided by the Social Sciences and
Humanities Research Council of Canada.

University of Toronto Press acknowledges the financial assistance to its
publishing program of the Canada Council for the Arts and the Ontario
Arts Council, an agency of the Government of Ontario.

 Canada Council   Conseil des Arts
for the Arts   du Canada

ONTARIO ARTS COUNCIL
CONSEIL DES ARTS DE L'ONTARIO
an Ontario government agency
un organisme du gouvernement de l'Ontario

University of Toronto Press acknowledges the financial support of the
Government of Canada through the Canada Book Fund for its publishing
activities.

Contents

Foreword

This fascinating book sheds a new light on public sector leadership, a topic we need to be talking about a lot more. Chief Administrative Officers – the peaks in the administrative hierarchy of most municipalities in Canada, large and small – are called upon today to go far beyond the vital tasks of orchestrating the planning, organizing, staffing, directing, coordinating, reporting, and budgeting (the ageless POSDCORB activities that were itemized by Luther Gulick and Lyndall Urwick in the 1930s). Today, CAOs are leaders in their own right, called upon to model the noblest ethics of public service as they bring a rigorous and thoughtful approach to ensuring that districts, regional governments, cities, and towns deliver expected services *and* anticipate future needs. They form the glue that, if they perform effectively, will ensure that municipal councils and municipal bureaucracies will work together in a common direction. CAOs are the butter between the two proverbial slices of bread of politics and administration: the indispensable ingredient that makes the two stick together to form government and make governance as palatable as possible.

This subject is not entirely new to the Institute of Public Administration of Canada (IPAC). In 1994, IPAC published T.J. Plunkett's *City Management in Canada: The Role of the Chief Administrative Officer*. After carefully examining the growing trends in the relations between municipal councils and city managers, and scrutinizing the functions of CAOs over the 1980s, Plunkett came to the conclusion that "the role was in transition." Twenty years later, it can safely be said that the transition is over and that CAOs are solidly anchored fixtures in the administration of municipalities. Both municipal councils and the bureaucracy greatly depend on the individual who holds that position.

David Siegel brings a focus on the qualities of the people who are charged with the dual responsibilities of making bureaucracy accountable to mayors and municipal councils but also of finding the magic words and techniques that will translate the (sometimes contradictory) wishes of the people's representatives to a bureaucracy that is constantly adapting to changing technologies. To capture the work of these critical change agents, Siegel followed men and women whose experiences put the position and its context in perspective. He sees them asking the difficult questions, working hard to convince entire bureaucracies to adapt to changes in the environment, in accountability, and in performance management. The evolution in the approach, from Plunkett's necessary structures and rules to Siegel's case study method, is in its own way a clue to how the CAO's position has changed and gained importance.

This is the fourth volume in the IPAC Series in Public Management and Governance to focus on leadership. My own *Searching for Leadership: Secretaries to Cabinet in Canada* (2008) united scholars from across Canada who combined structural, theoretical, and biographical approaches to a subject that heretofore had not been explored. The key message of the book was that secretaries to cabinet had evolved so much over the past decades that their leadership deserved to be scrutinized. Robert Wardhaugh also used a biographical approach to understanding leadership with his *Behind the Scenes: The Life and Work of William Clifford Clark* (2010). That book explored the work of a key deputy minister in Ottawa during the Depression and Second World War. In 2014, Jacques Bourgault and Christopher Dunn edited *Deputy Ministers in Canada: Comparative and Jurisdictional Perspectives*, a massive 15-chapter volume that scrutinized as never before the opportunities and constraints of this key position in the federal and provincial governments. Together, and now with the addition of the volume that is in your hands, these works provide essential nourishment for a reflection on public sector leadership in Canada.

David Siegel is so well suited to this task. A deeply respected student of public administration for decades, he has long taken an active interest in the problems of managing the local level of government and in understanding the perspective of rank and file public servants. He brings the informed eye of a forerunner himself, having long served Brock University in a variety of leadership positions, not least as Dean of Social Sciences. His insatiable curiosity and background of impressive accomplishments, in combination with exquisite scholarly skills, position him as the ideal guide to exploring how the role of CAO is performed in Canada today.

Patrice Dutil
Editor, IPAC Series in Public Management and Governance
Ryerson University

Acknowledgments

It was a real pleasure to write this book for a number of reasons. It tells the story of an important, but much underrated group of people: senior managers of municipalities. I have always had a great deal of respect for the important work these people carry out, and I hope this book does justice to this important group of professionals by telling their story more widely than it is currently known. It was also a pleasure to be able to go across the country and meet so many people who were directly involved in or interested in municipal management. I hope I have captured the excitement I felt from those people.

Although I enjoyed writing the book, I could not done it without the cooperation and involvement of many others. The Social Sciences and Humanities Research Council provided funding to hire research assistants and to undertake the travel required. This infusion of funds came after I had received some valuable seed money from the dean of the Faculty of Social Sciences at Brock University. Such grants are essential to doing this kind of project.

An earlier version of Chapter 1 was published in 2010 in *Canadian Public Administration* under the title "The Leadership Qualities of Municipal Chief Administrative Officers." The feedback I received on this article was very helpful in the framing of this book.

I owe a more personal debt to many other people. The five senior managers who are the subject of this research gave their time generously and provided many insights into their profession. They also opened up their personal and professional lives to more light than public servants are accustomed to. They traditionally live in the shadows behind their political masters, and I know that becoming involved in a project like this was difficult for them. I thank them deeply for taking

the risk inherent in this kind of project, and for entrusting their stories to a well-meaning non-member of their profession. Michael Fenn
deserves special mention because he not only agreed to be a subject;
he also read the manuscript carefully and provided valuable advice at
various stages.

This book is the product of over 100 interviews with people involved
in some way with municipal government. Their voluntary contributions were absolutely essential to capture the full story of the work
of the five subjects of the research. Since I promised them anonymity,
I cannot name them, but this book would not have been possible without their involvement.

I also need to recognize the contribution of the many students I have
taught over the years both at Brock University and at the University of
Western Ontario. I have learned a great deal about municipal administration from them, and they have helped stimulate my interest in what
a municipal manager does. I hope that future generations of students
will find this work of some value to them.

Some individuals deserve a special mention. Nigel Bellchamber, a
well-respected municipal CAO and general manager of the Ontario
Municipal Administrators' Association, was supportive of this work
from its inception. He gave me many good ideas, and many opportunities to try out my ideas with real live managers. Gordon McIntosh has
had a distinguished career in municipal management and consulting,
and was completing his PhD thesis while I was working on this project.
I was fortunate to be able to draw on his encyclopedic knowledge of
municipal administration across the country. Ken Cameron, a retired
planner but still-active researcher and writer, discussed my ideas early
on and reviewed some parts of the work. The late Tom Plunkett also
encouraged me in this project, and taught me a great deal about municipal administration over our long lunches at the Kingston Brew Pub.
Finally, I owe the catchy title of this work to my collaborator on a number of projects and my colleague from Brock University, Erin Sharpe.

I was particularly fortunate to have two excellent research assistants.
Mai Nguyen was very helpful as my first research assistant, who worked
on the chapter on Michael Fenn. Jack Lucas was my research assistant
for the second part of the project. He provided excellent assistance in
the heavy sledding of wading through newspapers and other sources,
but he also played a valuable role in helping me to formulate many of
my ideas. This book would not have been nearly as good without the

involvement of these two young scholars, who have excellent careers in front of them.

Finally, I would like to thank the two anonymous reviewers contracted by the University of Toronto Press to review the manuscript. They did a thorough and conscientious job, and their comments improved the finished product considerably. I also thank my freelance copy editor, Barry Norris, as well as Wayne Herrington and Daniel Quinlan at the University of Toronto Press. Wendy Feldman of the Institute of Public Administration of Canada also provided encouragement and advice at key times.

Having implicated all these other people in this work, I need to do what authors always do in these situations and to acknowledge that, despite all the assistance I received, I still might have made some errors or misinterpretations, for which I take full responsibility.

LEADERS IN THE SHADOWS

**The Leadership Qualities of Municipal
Chief Administrative Officers**

Introduction

Two things seemed pretty apparent to me. One was, that in order to be a [Mississippi riverboat] pilot a man had got to learn more than any one man ought to be allowed to know; and the other was, that he must learn it all over again in a different way every twenty-four hours.

– Mark Twain, 1875

Municipal chief administrative officers (CAOs)[1] are men and women in the shadows.[2] Indeed, in the trade there is a tacit understanding that a CAO whose name is in the media frequently is probably in some kind of trouble. In municipal administration, things that work well are invisible; the media take an interest only when things go wrong. Although usually invisible, municipal CAOs are important cogs in the machinery of government and, like Twain's riverboat pilots, they must navigate some difficult and constantly changing waters.

CAOs can make a mayor and council look exceptionally good (or bad). They can be a source of great pride and motivation among the staff of the municipality (or not). They can be an important conduit in the two-way flow of information between community organizations and the municipality (or not). A tremendous amount hinges on how well a CAO carries out her or his responsibilities.

The purpose of this book is to identify the leadership qualities that a successful CAO needs. I draw on lessons from Canadian municipal CAOs who have been identified as successful leaders to produce an analysis of the traits, skills, and behaviours required to be a good leader in municipal government. A great deal has been written about leadership, ranging from evidence-based academic research to folksy advice columns. Barbara Kellerman points out that there has been a huge increase in the number of books about leadership in the past thirty years, but she laments that much of it tends to be fairly generic, and assumes that leadership is leadership, regardless of the type of organization.[3] In the realm of public administration, quite a bit has been written about the leadership role of senior public servants, and there is also a considerable literature on the role of deputy ministers in federal and provincial governments.[4] Very little has been written, however, that specifically addresses the leadership role of chief administrative officers in Canadian municipalities.

The city manager system originated in the United States, and a great deal has been written about it there.[5] It grew out of a variety of circumstances related to what has generally been called the "turn of the century reform movement." As is sometimes the case, the early history is a bit murky, but the first city manager was appointed either in Ukiah, California, in 1904 or in Staunton, Virginia, in 1906.[6] The system arrived in Canada considerably later, however, and much more tentatively. Two of the first comprehensive textbooks on municipal government in Canada, written by Horace L. Brittain[7] in 1951 and Kenneth Grant Crawford[8] in 1954, barely mention the city manager system. In fact, Crawford made it clear that the normal method of administration then involved chairs of council committees working directly with department heads.[9] But by the time Thomas J. Plunkett wrote his 1968 text, the council-manager system was deemed worthy of an entire, though relatively short, chapter.[10] Around 1973, Paul Hickey produced an encyclopedic report for the Ontario government that discussed the pros and cons of virtually every possible configuration of local government in Canada and in selected other countries as well. He found that, prior to 1970, the Ontario Municipal Act did not provide any general authority to appoint a CAO, but seven municipalities had sought specific enabling legislation, beginning with Chatham in 1921.[11] Even though he concluded that "the CAO [had] yet to make an impact" in Ontario,[12] his recommendation was quite clear: "The council of every municipality in Ontario should be required to appoint a CAO."[13]

Hickey was speaking from a position of influence since he was an assistant deputy minister at the time, but his timing was also excellent. A major reorganization of Ontario municipalities was then occurring with the creation of regional governments. The legislation establishing these new units of government permitted the appointment of CAOs in all cases, except in Sudbury, where it was actually required. This certainly gave the concept of the CAO a boost.

A unique Canadian administrative structure developed in western Canada – the council/commissioner system.[14] This system was similar to the city manager system except that administrative power was vested in a three-to-five-member board of commissioners instead of one manager. The board consisted of a chief commissioner and several commissioners, each of whom had line authority over municipal departments. This group, sometimes controversially including the mayor, formed a board of commissioners that collectively made decisions about the administrative side of the municipality. This system was found at different times in Edmonton, Calgary, Saskatoon, Regina, Winnipeg, and in smaller places, but has now died out, replaced in most cases by the CAO system.[15]

As the field of municipal management has matured, the literature about it has become more analytical. Donald Rowat provides an interesting analysis of why the US form of city manager system is not needed in Canada, but some form of chief administrative officer would be beneficial.[16] The useful works of W. George R. Vance, Trevor Price, and Plunkett[17] provide a broad overview and some interesting insights, but they are based on general surveys and so do not provide much depth of information about how individual CAOs work. Gordon McIntosh's recent excellent PhD thesis is also based on broad survey data, but provides much more in-depth analysis than earlier works.[18] Eamon O'Flynn's recent MA thesis does an excellent job of updating Plunkett's work and of providing an overview of how the profession has changed in the twenty-five years since Plunkett's book was published.[19]

This is a good time to be writing about the role of the municipal CAO because the number of municipalities using the position has grown rapidly over the years. The plan was first used in Canada in Westmount, Quebec, in 1913. By 1952, 34 Canadian cities had a CAO, and by 1989 the number had grown to 170.[20] There seems to be no recent systematic count, but observation suggests that, by the dawning of the twenty-first century, a high proportion of municipalities in Canada had some type of chief administrative officer.

As described throughout the book, the role of the chief administrator has also changed over time. In the past, many municipalities tried to "sneak up" on the CAO system by retitling the clerk as the clerk/administrator.[21] In many cases, this position was a department head just like the others. The clerk/administrator did not have line authority over other department heads, but did have a somewhat closer working relationship with council. This constituted a tentative movement toward a CAO system without making a real commitment to adopt it in whole. Most municipalities, however, have now moved to a real CAO system in which the CAO is the only official who reports directly to council and has line authority over all department heads.

In the United States, James Svara has written extensively on council-staff relations in a manner that emphasizes the importance of leadership,[22] but his work, although quite valuable, requires some translation to be relevant in the Canadian context. In the 1990s there was a major comparative project under the auspices of the Union des Dirigeants Territoriaux de l'Europe (UDTE) which surveyed 4,000 managers in 14 countries (not including Canada). This produced some important publications on which I will draw,[23] but this book supplements these earlier surveys with a more in-depth analysis of the activities of specific leaders.

I use the still-developing but well-grounded narrative approach to research. Simply put, narrative is about storytelling, but storytelling with a purpose. It uses stories as a method of bringing order to a complex sequence of events.[24] As Sonia Ospina and Jennifer Dodge explain, "[n]arrative inquiry is a research orientation that directs attention to narratives as a way to study an aspect of society. It is not, however, just about studying texts, whether written or visual. It is about finding meaning in the stories people use, tell, and even live ... What distinguishes narrative inquiry ... is the focus on narratives and stories as they are told, implicitly or explicitly, by individuals or groups of people, not on texts that are independent of the tellers or institutions where they are scripted."[25]

More particularly, this book reflects a stream of the narrative approach that draws on the biography of leaders. Boas Shamir, Hava Dayan-Horesh, and Dalya Adler ague that "the leader's biography is an important source of information from which followers and potential followers learn about the leader's traits and behaviours, that the leader's life story provides the leader with a self-concept from which he or she can lead, and that telling the biography is an important leadership behaviour."[26]

I use a number of components that are widely recognized as part of the narrative approach. First, this book is an implicit partnership between the author and the public servants whose stories I tell here.

This is an attempt to break down the practitioner-academic barrier that sometimes exists in public administration research. Practitioners sometimes feel that out-of-touch academic research "does not produce meaningful, actionable knowledge"[27] that is helpful to practitioners. Practitioners recognize the complexity of problems, and they prefer to hear from participants with a number of different perspectives on a problem rather than just one version.[28] This book lets practitioners tell their own story.

Second, the book is informed by the idea of polyphony, a musical term that literally means "many voices." In each chapter the CAO is the central character, but her or his story is told through both the CAO's own words and those of people all around the CAO. I took a great deal of care to find a number of diverse people who were able to comment on the CAO.

Third, the context of the story is important. Surveys typically ask people to tick a particular box without delving into the back story of why the respondent ticked that particular box. Narrative inquiry brings out not only the person's immediate actions, but the broader context of why the person took the action that he or she did. As Steven Maynard-Moody and Michael Musheno note, "[s]tories offer insights into how actors make choices, understand their actions, and experience frustrations and satisfactions. Stories give research a pungency and vitality often absent from mainstream social science because they give such prominence to individual actions and motives and the human condition."[29]

Finally, the narratives draw on the biographies of leaders to enlighten why and how they became leaders – through natural process, struggling and coping with difficulties, self-improvement through learning, and finding a cause – and how they developed their relationships with followers.[30] I do not engage in a psycho-social analysis of these leaders, but I use their life stories to a certain extent to determine the context of their leadership.

Although the narrative approach is beneficial in terms of the context and richness it provides, it can also create problems in terms of the selective memory or the accuracy of the memory of interviewees. In some cases, I asked people to reach back twenty or more years, and some interviewees frankly admitted they just could not remember certain events very well. To deal with this problem, I used the principle of triangulation: if I did not obtain a roughly similar story from two or three sources, then it did not find its way into the book. Newspaper and other documentary accounts were useful for this purpose because they were usually written at the time the event occurred.

The narrative approach has been used in a number of different ways. The genesis of this book owes much to Eugene Lewis's *Public Entrepreneurship*,[31] although I later found an equally good book edited by Jameson Doig and Erwin Hargrove that employs a similar style.[32] Mark Moore also uses the technique of employing specific people and the situations they face to illustrate points in his two excellent books on public value.[33] Lewis focuses on three US public servants who were widely viewed as public entrepreneurs. The value of his book is in the final chapter's conclusions about the characteristics of public entrepreneurs and in the thick case studies that illustrate many of the positive (and some negative) activities of the public entrepreneur. Lewis's book is both an outstanding academic work and a source of practical advice for public servants.

Although the books by Lewis, Moore, and Doig and Hargrove are my prime models, many other books approximate this style of reasoning from case studies about individuals or individual organizations to more general findings. *Leader-Managers in the Public Sector: Managing for Results*, by Michael Dukakis and John Portz, is similar in focusing on the leadership qualities of seven exemplary public sector managers.[34] James MacGregor Burns's acclaimed book, *Leadership*,[35] draws extensively on case studies of individual leaders throughout, and Melvin Holli's book on mayors uses the same technique to identify the shared characteristics of the ten best mayors in the United States.[36] There are also some examples of this style of research being employed in the early years of the city management system in the United States. In 1927 Leonard D. White presented case studies of a number of managers before writing in a learned manner about the current state of the profession.[37] Harold A. Stone, Don K. Price, and Kathryn H. Stone participated in an even more ambitious project that involved case studies of forty-eight manager cities, documented in several books that supported their excellent book-length review of the state of the profession in 1938.[38] Barbara Kellerman's *Bad Leadership*[39] employs the same approach in a different direction to examine the characteristics of bad leaders and their followers.

The case study approach has much in common with what has been called the observational approach.[40] This approach can be seen in Henry Mintzberg's seminal book, *The Nature of Managerial Work*, which begins with in-depth reviews of the activities of five managers.[41] Tony Watson's *In Search of Management*[42] is the product of extensive analysis of one company. Melville Dalton's *Men Who Manage*[43] reviews four companies. The strength of the observational approach is that it does not rely on vague recollections that could be coloured by a variety of events over many succeeding years. I chose to use the case study approach, however, because it gave me a broader view of the qualities of the leaders as seen from their perspective as well as from the perspective of those around the leader. It also allowed me to examine more leaders than I could have with the labour-intensive observational method, including some leaders who were retired.

Both of these approaches have been characterized as interpretive approaches, to distinguish them from the explanatory approach frequently seen in the natural and social sciences. Thus, I do not engage in rigid hypothesis testing or statistical probabilities that would allow me to make statements such as "if A occurs, then B will follow." Employing a sample size of five makes this approach impossible anyway. Interpretive research, however, has a rich tradition of its own. As Jay White notes, "[i]nstead of seeking causal explanations of behavior, interpretive research enhances our understanding of, among other things, the beliefs, meanings, feelings, and attitudes of actors in social situations."[44] White goes on to explain how the interpretive approach is a powerful research technique that is used in all types of research, including the natural sciences.

The main purpose of this book is to describe the contemporary role of the municipal chief administrative officer, with special emphasis on the leadership qualities expected of someone in this position. This role has changed much over time as both the role of municipal government and the role of senior managers in any public service organization have changed.

A related purpose is to demystify the idea of leadership. Too many highly capable people believe they could never be leaders because they lack some mythical set of qualities with which only a select few are born. We will see that the leaders discussed in this book are truly exceptional, but they are exceptional because they have developed a particular set of traits, skills, and behaviours that anyone is capable of developing.

Another purpose of this book is to tell the stories of some heroes whose job it is to labour quietly in the shadows while ensuring that others obtain credit. There was space in this book to tell only five stories, but there are many more where these came from. Private sector leaders have never been shy about singing their own praises, and in most cases they are quite justified in doing so, and, as Sandford Borins has argued, "[c]learly, there is in American public sector narratives a strong heroic fable."[45] That tradition, however, has not carried over to Canada, where first-hand accounts of the position by CAOs, in particular, are relatively rare.[46] Most high-profile Canadian media stories of public servants focus on misdeeds rather than on accomplishments. This creates the false impression that public servants have no positive stories to tell. In this book, I want to set the record straight by telling the stories of heroes who are too well socialized as public servants to take credit for their own accomplishments.

This book is a product of the usual academic research, but it also reflects what I have learned from numerous discussions with senior administrators and from teaching a number of mid-career public servants. In the municipal management field, the "usual academic research" must rely fairly heavily on sources from the United States, as we are still developing our own Canadian literature in this field. This is another reason the involvement of mid-career public servants was essential to this project. In my discussions with them, I frequently found that they were receptive to the foreign literature, but they were quick to insert Canadian perspectives when necessary.

I have identified five CAOs who have been recognized by their peers and others in the municipal field as successful leaders in their positions. In examining the careers of these five CAOs, I aim to determine the leadership qualities they exhibit and, by inference, the qualities those who aspire to become municipal CAOs should develop. A chapter about each of these individuals has been derived from background research and from interviews with both the person and people around her or him. The purpose of the case studies is to identify the characteristics that caused the individual to be recognized as a successful leader. The concluding chapter then ties together the findings from the individual case studies to identify the characteristics of a successful CAO. This book follows in a long and rich tradition of drawing on the administrative behaviour of particular individuals to infer the sorts of traits that are desired in an administrative position.[47]

As rich as the tradition of case study research is, there are frequent conflicts between that approach and broader quantitative approaches to determine which conveys the real truth. I prefer to see the two styles as complementary rather than conflicting. At about the same time that I was doing the research for this book, Gordon McIntosh was writing his PhD dissertation at the University of Victoria, which involved a quantitative analysis of questionnaires submitted by hundreds of CAOs, supplemented by a large number of interviews.[48] The research approaches of our works could not have been more different, but I found his to be tremendously helpful in my research. I have also benefited from Eamon O'Flynn's and George Vance's theses, which take more of a middle ground between broader quantitative analysis and qualitative interviews.[49] I suggest our works should be read together to get a full understanding of the field.

I do not plan to wade into a full-fledged defence of the case study method because that issue has been treated well elsewhere,[50] but I offer some words of explanation about why I chose this approach. Works such as those of McIntosh, O'Flynn, and Vance are tremendously useful because they use a rich representative random sample of CAOs to give us a broad overview of the field. My research does not involve a random sample; on the contrary, my subjects were hand-picked precisely because they stood out. I wanted to focus on the best and brightest in the field. My approach allows us to determine why these people are so well-respected in their field.

Although it might seem that I have employed "only" five case studies, in fact the background research and the interviews for each CAO have produced a significant number of observations in each case.[51] A variety of techniques can be used to organize all of these observations to allow meaningful analysis to be done. Process tracing has been used in international studies mainly to trace events in a chronological fashion,[52] but I have used it here implicitly to identify the reasons interviewees felt that a particular person is a good leader. This study has also lent itself well to a typological approach because the comments of interviewees have clustered into clear "pathways"[53] that indicate the characteristics that a manager needs to manifest in order to become a good leader.

Since I have picked for analysis five people who have been identified as good leaders, it might appear that I have selected on the dependent variable, which is always cautioned against because it provides no point of comparison. The interviewees around the leaders provided as much information about the characteristics of poor leaders, however, as they did about good ones. After all, the reason these interviewees identified the subjects of this research as good leaders is that they have had exposure to some not-so-good leaders in the past. The people around the leaders told me a great deal not only about the individuals I chose, but also about how they differ from other managers with whom they had worked. Thus, the five case studies in fact draw on information from many more situations.

This raises the question of sample selection. Choosing just five out of the large number of exceptionally good municipal administrators with which Canada is blessed was not an easy task. I do not contend that these five are the best CAOs in Canada; indeed, I have no idea how such a determination could ever be made. It was quite clear from the comments of many knowledgeable observers, however, that all five are exemplary members of their profession who exhibit positive leadership traits.

My method of selection was careful and conscientious, but admittedly not particularly scientific. The early gestation period of this book was quite lengthy, as I undertook the usual search for research funding. This allowed me to have many informal conversations with astute observers from all ten provinces and one territory about the people they regarded as successful leaders. Over time I consulted with senior members of the profession, mayors and councillors, staff of municipal associations, officials of provincial departments of municipal affairs, academics, and journalists. I also reviewed awards presented by professional associations such as the Canadian Association of Municipal Administrators, the Canadian Urban Institute, and the Institute of Public Administration of Canada.

I deliberately did not develop a definition of a leader in advance – after all, the purpose of this project is to provide such a definition. If I had started with a definition, I would have been guilty of the logical fallacy known as affirming the consequent: having chosen my research subjects on the basis of a specific set of qualities, I would then have discovered that they all possessed those qualities. When Holli asked experts to identify the ten best US mayors, he found that he generally obtained the same result whether he specified the qualities he was seeking or allowed respondents simply to respond to the adjective "best."[54] In the same way, I wanted the experts I consulted to respond to the word "leader" and to identify for me the people in their field who are most widely regarded as effective leaders. Interestingly, the people I was conversing with seldom asked for such a definition because the idea of leadership is quite well understood, whether people are relying on a specific definition or not.

I did set out a few broad stipulations. My intent was not to focus on leadership demonstrated in one critical event, such as an economic crisis or natural disaster. I was more interested in career achievements, likely through positions in a number of different organizations. I was also searching for leaders who were, in Kellerman's terms, both effective and ethical.[55] In other words, I wanted leaders who were not only able to attract and guide a significant cadre of followers, but who also took those followers in a desirable and ethical direction. I was searching for people who had a fairly lengthy career as a CAO, who had worked in more than one municipality or in the same municipality for long enough that they had interacted with several mayors and councils – in effect, who had successfully plied their trade in different situations over a period of time. It is not really a test of leadership abilities to work well with a particular mayor and council for three or four years – that could be just coincidence or luck.

I was pleased that, in my search for successful leaders, I was able to find a good variety of people. One is from British Columbia; one is from Alberta, although he spent part of his career in British Columbia; two are from Ontario; and one made his name in the Maritimes, but migrated to Ontario shortly before the chapter about him was written. Two worked in large urban areas, one in mid-sized jurisdictions, and two in smaller places. Only one is a woman. I would have been happy to have more, but a recent national survey found that about 25 per cent of CAOs are female,[56] so my 20 per cent representation is not far off.

I drew the raw material for this book from three sources. My long-time interest in the general literature on leadership, especially as it pertains to the role of municipal CAOs, resulted in an article for the journal *Canadian Public Administration*,[57] which I reproduce here in a considerably revised form as Chapter 1. From that general background, I then moved on to do research on the individual CAOs.

The second strand of research involved reviewing the relevant newspapers and undertaking an extensive search of Web sources related to the subjects of the case studies.

The third strand was the interviews my research assistant and I undertook with each subject at both the beginning and the end of the process. Between those bookends we interviewed a number of people at 360 degrees around the subject. We tried to interview all of the heads of council and a good sample of councillors for whom the CAO worked. We also sought out staff members who had worked closely with the person. Finally, we interviewed community members who had worked with the person or had special knowledge. We sought out journalists, in particular, although they frequently did not have much knowledge of administrators. We also interviewed people associated with local chambers of commerce, business people, people active in community organizations of various kinds, union representatives, and peers in other municipalities and the provincial government. These people were very cooperative in giving us their time and forthright in sharing their opinions. They were promised anonymity when interviewed, however, so except in a few cases where they agreed to be identified, they are not named.

The outline of the book is straightforward. The first chapter is an overview of the literature on leadership generally and the role of municipal CAOs more specifically. It also sets out the framework I use to analyse the multiple roles of the CAO of leading down, leading up, and leading out. In leading down, CAOs must function as the supervisor of their staff in the usual managerial way. In leading up, they need to inspire the confidence of their political masters on council and so work together to achieve their joint goals. This is a particularly difficult form of leadership because it requires the subordinate, who in many cases will possess expert knowledge, to guide her or his superiors, many of whom will have somewhat less substantive knowledge but well-developed egos. Finally, good CAOs must lead out in their dealings with residents' groups, the media, and so forth, over which they have no authority. Their behaviour, however, must inspire the confidence of these groups to be guided in a particular direction. Leading in each direction requires somewhat different skill sets, but the truly effective CAO must possess all three.

After the introduction, the next five chapters tell the stories of the five selected CAOs. All of these chapters are organized in a similar fashion. They begin with an overview of the person's career and some personal discussion of their early development. This is followed by a more in-depth narrative of their activities as CAOs in their municipalities, with particular emphasis on their accomplishments and the problems they have handled. Some of these people had significant careers outside the municipal sector, but, without wanting to diminish those accomplishments, I have focused quite specifically on the municipal portion of their careers. The final section of each chapter then analyses their careers in terms of leading down, leading up, and leading out.

These five case studies lay the groundwork for the final chapter, which draws lessons from the five individuals to identify the leadership qualities that a successful CAO needs. This chapter follows Henry Mintzberg's advice that, "If You're Not Serving Bill and Barbara, Then You're Not Serving Leadership."[58] Mintzberg argues strongly that leadership research needs to be conducted and written in such a way that it provides advice to leaders; he is sharply critical of researchers who develop elaborate theories for the benefit of one another. This final chapter does not attempt a grand theory of leadership; rather, it is a simple statement of the various traits, skills, and behaviours that the five CAOs in the case studies have in common, coupled with advice to several audiences about how to use this information.

The book was written with several audiences in mind. I have been blessed with a number of engaged and interested students over the years, both young students in the process of choosing a career and mid-career public servants climbing the ladder of their profession. I hope that this book will have an influence on younger students who are contemplating a career in the tremendously interesting and rewarding field of municipal government. I also hope it will give the mid-career contingent some insights into the kinds of traits, skills, and behaviours they need to develop to climb the ladder.

The book is also directed at heads of councils, councillors, and councils collectively. Hiring the right CAO is probably the most important single decision that any council makes. It will affect the overall well-being of the municipality for many years into the future. I hope that the information in this book will provide heads of council and councillors some ideas about the qualities they should seek in a CAO. One lesson discussed in this book is that there is no such thing as a one-size-fits-all "best" CAO. Any candidate for CAO will possess a variety of strengths and weaknesses. The first task in hiring a new CAO is to look at your own organization, determine its needs at that time, then find a CAO who matches those needs.

Finally, but most important, this book is addressed to all the residents of municipalities in Canada who benefit from the good work of municipal public servants. Captains of industry in the private sector are not shy about trumpeting their leadership qualities in all sorts of books and speeches. Public servants, in contrast, are socialized to work in the shadows behind their political masters, and are much less comfortable boasting of their achievements. This creates the false impression that all the good leaders are in the private sector and that nothing of interest is happening in the public sector. In fact, Canada has benefited from some excellent municipal leaders over many years, and we should celebrate them more than we do. I am sorry that I had room to tell the stories of just five of these people; there are many more stories like these out there. I hope, however, that highlighting their accomplishments will help to overcome the perception that the public sector lacks high-quality leaders. A former councillor interviewed for this work said it well: "A city manager is a very valuable commodity because ... [c]ouncil gets the publicity and gets the TV coverage, but when you think about it, [the city manager] sets the tone around city hall with her staff. They were ambitious, [they] knew they were going to get a fair shake ... That's a big commodity. That's a good asset."[59]

This book is dedicated to all those public servants who labour quietly in the shadows and make sure that our streets are safe, our garbage gets picked up, our recreation programs are delivered, and all sorts of other services are provided. They make our lives safer and more livable every day, and they do it in such a way that we seldom even think about it.

1 The Leadership Role of the Municipal Chief Administrative Officer

A great deal has been written about leadership.[1] However, very little has been written that specifically addresses the leadership role of chief administrative officers (CAOs) in municipalities. This book fills that lacuna by arguing that the municipal CAO occupies a unique position with regard to the leadership skills required of the incumbent.

I begin this chapter by describing the differences between local government and parliamentary systems that prevent leadership lessons from flowing freely between the two types of entities. The second section reviews some of the relevant literature on leadership to identify what is expected of leaders in general. The next three sections analyse the three roles of the municipal CAO as leader: leading down, leading out, and leading up. The conclusion then ties this together by using contingency theory to argue that the successful municipal leader must be able to shift gears and demonstrate different types of leadership skills in different situations.

The Unique Character of Municipal Government

Much has been written about the role of senior managers in public organizations. Some of this is relevant to municipal CAOs, but much misses the mark. This stems mainly from the fact that the structures of municipal governments differ sufficiently from those of parliamentary systems that lessons do not travel well between the two types.

As the highest-ranking appointed person in the municipal hierarchy, the CAO plays a significant role with regard to the linkage between the political arm of government (the mayor and councillors) and the administrative arm of government (the appointed public service).[2] There are some similarities between this position and a secretary to cabinet in a parliamentary system,[3] but the operation of a municipal government differs from a parliamentary system in ways that are significant for the role of the CAO.[4]

First, parliamentary systems have an executive branch in the form of a cabinet with a first minister who is usually described as *primus inter pares*. Policies are made by cabinet as a body and are implemented in accord with the concept of collective ministerial responsibility. This means that cabinets always show a unified front to the outside world. Of course, insiders can be keenly aware that at times there are serious rifts within a cabinet. However, the convention of collective ministerial responsibility means that it is in the interest of all participants to maintain a public veneer of unity.

A municipal government is headed by a council that consists of the head of council (usually called the mayor) and elected councillors. The mayor is not analogous to a first minister in a parliamentary system in that the mayor has no control over other councillors.[5] Most Canadian municipalities do not have party systems to structure and unify council, and even where there are party systems, they are not disciplined parties in the same manner as in parliamentary governments. Compared to a first minister in a parliamentary government, a mayor has relatively few prestigious appointments at her or his disposal to maintain discipline.

Therefore, a municipal government is not unified in the same sense as a parliamentary government. Although a secretary to cabinet works for an entity that is either united or at least maintains an appearance of unity, a municipal CAO works for a group of councillors that can be severely and openly divided on a variety of issues. Each councillor is elected in a distinct geographic area by a distinct constituency. Even when councillors are elected at-large rather than by ward, it is frequently the case that they each rely for their election on the support of varying constituencies.[6] It is sometimes said (only half-jokingly) that a municipal council is a group of individual entrepreneurs held together by a common parking lot.

As well, municipal governments are much more open and transparent in their decision making than are parliamentary forms of government. One reason for this is that provincial legislation requires that municipalities conduct their business in the public eye. Even in the absence of such legislation, however, the structure of municipal government would make it more open than parliamentary systems. In parliamentary governments, the public service works for cabinet. The constitutional convention is that advice provided to cabinet by the public service remains confidential, and individual public servants remain anonymous with regard to that advice. Although this seems to be breaking down in practice,[7] it is still the governing convention. The public service is expected to be sensitive to the concerns and questions of opposition party members, but opposition members or even government backbenchers are not treated in the same manner as members of cabinet.[8] In municipal governments, all council members (including the mayor) have equal status, and must be treated in the same manner by public servants. It is an important principle of municipal government that all public servants work for council as a whole; they do not work for the mayor; they do not work for committee chairs; they do not work for individual councillors. In practice, this means that information provided to any one councillor must be provided to all councillors. Therefore, the provision of advice to any limited group of elected officials – such as the public service in a parliamentary system routinely provides to cabinet – is highly inappropriate. All advice must be provided equally to all councillors, and, with few exceptions, it must be provided in public.[9]

In a situation where a municipal council has significant divisions, this puts public servants in an awkward position. Even though public servants ought to be providing their best professional, administrative advice without regard to political considerations, that advice almost always will favour one side's position over others. The fact that this is done in public will exacerbate the situation because the group on the negative side of the advice will see themselves as put at a significant disadvantage, which they could well blame on the public service.

This procedure provides some insight into the chaotic world in which the municipal CAO works. Unlike the cabinet secretary, the CAO must work for a diverse group of people who sometimes have strong public disagreements with one another. Yet the CAO somehow must take direction from this fractured group and pass that direction on to municipal staff. And unlike in parliamentary systems, all of this happens in a very public venue that almost inevitably will add to the CAO's tensions. The CAO thus needs to develop particular leadership skills to deal with this challenging environment.

The fractured nature of most councils makes the private sector leadership literature somewhat problematic. In the memoirs of private sector leaders and other similar writings, the leader is viewed as a relative free agent operating her or his own company, or having a fairly broad mandate from a sometimes not particularly attentive board. In the former case the leader can do whatever he or she wants; in the latter case the leader typically has a fairly weak tether as long as the company continues to make money and does not do anything embarrassing.

The public sector leader is much more tightly tethered. He or she operates under the control of an attentive group of political masters that, in the case of a municipal council, frequently meets weekly. The public sector leader is seldom given a particularly broad or clear mandate analogous to the private sector's "maximize share price" or "increase market share." The nature of the political process dictates that mandates will be vague and likely to change frequently. This requires the public sector leader to exercise care in the single-mindedness with which he or she pursues mandates. Thus, the public sector manager is somehow held to the same leadership standards as her or his private sector counterpart, but will have a much more limited mandate for action. This poses a unique problem for the public sector manager.

What Is Leadership?

Leadership is one of those words that everyone understands in an ephemeral way, but can be difficult to define precisely. A part of the definitional problem is that the term "leader" is used to describe many different types of people. Leaders can be organizational managers who have legitimate formal authority over subordinates, or they can be charismatic individuals who lead by influence even though they have no formal authority over followers. One sees this latter type of leadership in voluntary associations such as religious groups, political parties, and criminal gangs.

The nineteenth-century historian Thomas Carlyle posited the "great man" theory of leadership. His classic work, *On Heroes, Hero-Worship, and the Heroic in History*, considered such people as Mohammed, Dante, Shakespeare, Cromwell, and Napoleon as great men. He explained:

[T]he history of what man has accomplished in this world, is at bottom the History of the Great Men who have worked here. They were the leaders of men, these great ones; the modellers, patterns, and in a wide sense creators, of whatsoever the general mass of men contrived to do or to attain; all things that we see standing accomplished in the world are properly the outer material result, the practical realisation and embodiment, of Thoughts that dwelt in the Great Men sent into the world; the soul of the whole world's history, it may justly be considered, were the history of these.[10]

For Carlyle, the study of leaders was really a by-product of his study of history. One of the first systematic approaches to the study of leadership as leadership was the traits approach: "The underlying assumption of trait theory was that *leaders have certain characteristics that are utilized across time to enhance organizational performance and leader prestige.* The notion was that traits affected behaviors and behaviors affected effectiveness. The hope was to identify a master list of traits ... that would prescribe the ideal candidate or ideal leader in action."[11]

Some of the traits of leaders that have been identified over time are age, height, physical or athletic prowess, physical appearance or style of dress, fluency of speech, intelligence, judgment and decision-making ability, and many more.[12] Over time the trait theory has moved in and out of favour,[13] and sometimes produced inconsistent results – for example, some studies found leaders to be older, while others found them to be younger.[14] The theory was sometimes seen as too mechanistic and biologically determinate (height, physical appearance). It also frequently generated a fairly long list of traits without determining clearly which are the most important. Recent scholars, however, have used the traits approach in a somewhat more nuanced manner. For example, Thomas Peters and Robert Waterman have identified certain traits of excellent organizations, although the understanding was that only leaders who possessed certain traits could create these organizations.[15]

By the twenty-first century, some complexities had been added to these early ideas of leadership. One is that modern leadership is more likely to be shared among a group than personalized in one individual. Modern, large, diverse organizations actually might need a team of leaders, rather than one great leader. Another idea was the concept of followership, which was introduced as important to understand the concept of leadership.[16]

Jim Collins introduced the idea of what he calls the "level 5 leader." These are leaders who have turned around Fortune 500 companies in a way that has sustained their performance over many years. These leaders are in some ways the opposite of Carlyle's great men in that they exhibit great personal humility, but channel intense professional will into their organizations: "Level 5 leaders channel their ego needs away from themselves and into the larger goal of building a great company.

It's not that Level 5 leaders have no ego or self-interest. Indeed, they are incredibly ambitious – *but their ambition is first and foremost for the institution, not themselves.*"[17]

Collins emphasizes that these people focus first on surrounding themselves with good people even before they decide where they want to take the organization: "[T]hey *first* got the right people on the bus (and the wrong people off the bus) and then figured out where to drive it."[18] His three-pronged rationale is: 1) it is easier to adapt to a changing world if you have the right people in place; 2) there are no real problems of managing and motivating the right people; and 3) the wrong people going in the right direction still will not make your company great.[19]

Others have focused on the concept of shared, or team,[20] or distributed leadership,[21] which "emphasizes interdependence, coordination and reciprocal influence,"[22] rather than individualized vertical leadership. The idea here is that leadership is a process[23] or activity,[24] rather than a quality vested in one individual, and that complex, modern organizations require the skills of a number of leaders, rather than one heroic leader. This is what Larry Terry calls a viable executive cadre,[25] although Terry's approach still seems to involve a somewhat hierarchical structure.

Shared leadership has been defined as

> a dynamic, interactive influence process among individuals in groups for which the objective is to lead one another to the achievement of group or organizational goals or both. This influence process often involves peer, or lateral, influence and at other times involves upward or downward hierarchical influence. The key distinction between shared leadership and traditional models of leadership is that the influence process involves more than just downward influence on subordinates by an appointed or elected leader. Rather, leadership is broadly distributed among a set of individuals instead of centralized in hands [*sic*] of a single individual who acts in the role of a superior.[26]

The concepts of distributed or shared leadership have developed several different meanings, depending on a number of characteristics, including whether the interactions are spontaneous, intuitive, or institutionalized.[27] There is some division in the literature about whether shared leadership involves a group of absolute equals or whether there can be a team in which everyone is treated as equal even though the organization chart shows a vertical leader.

The need for distributed leadership is based on the fact that leading a large, modern, complex organization is simply beyond the abilities of any one person no matter how heroic he or she might be. This concept might not fit well with some small or medium-sized municipalities, although large municipalities are as large as many large corporations. However, even small municipalities are quite complex as measured by the broad scope of services they deliver compared to the average manufacturing or retail enterprise. The scope of responsibilities of even small municipalities runs from hard services such as roads, bridges, and underground pipes, to soft social services, to planning, which involves knowledge of planning principles, softer citizen engagement processes, and detailed knowledge of highly arcane legislation. This leads to one of the main reasons for shared leadership: no one person ever has the detailed level of knowledge required over such a broad scope of responsibilities.

The members of the team must all be competent in their respective fields, but they must also have a shared view of their organization and a shared value set.[28] On the one hand, the team aspect might seem to limit the role of the leader. On the other hand, the nominal leader in fact has an important role in assembling the team, developing the skills of its members, managing the relationship between the team and the rest of the organization, and empowering the team with full authority to act.[29] One of the most important roles of this type of leader is "the development, mentoring, and unleashing of the capability of followers"[30] – in other words, "leading others to lead themselves."[31]

A good team will increase the quality of decision making through representation of a diversity of views, but it could also improve the speed of decision making, because team members who are confident that they share the values of other members of the team will not have to refer every decision to the full team. Individual members will be able to make their own decisions with confidence.

The second modern variation on Carlyle's individual heroic leader is the importance of followership. One of the first and most influential writers to focus on the importance of the relationship between leaders and followers was James MacGregor Burns. His seminal book, *Leadership*, compares transactional leadership with transformational leadership. Transactional leadership is the predominant leadership style. It is geared to accomplishing some agreed-upon goal, but it does little to elevate either leader or followers. It is described as an exchange relationship between a leader and followers when the leader offers followers something of value to them (money, position, prestige) in exchange for following.

The transformational leader is less common, but more inspiring. He or she works with followers to determine where they mutually want to go. This type of leadership elevates followers by appealing to the mutuality of goals between the leader and follower. As Burns notes, "[l]*eadership over human beings is exercised when persons with certain motives and purposes mobilize . . . institutional, political, psychological, and other resources so as to arouse, engage, and satisfy the motives of followers.* This is done in order to realize goals mutually held by both leaders and followers."[32]

Robert Greenleaf developed the idea of the servant leader, which focuses on the importance of followers in creating leaders. His view is that true leaders exist only when followers decide willingly to follow them: "A new moral principle is emerging which holds that the only authority deserving one's allegiance is that which is freely and knowingly granted by the led to the leader in response to, and in proportion to, the clearly evident servant stature of the leader. Those who choose to follow this principle will not casually accept the authority of existing institutions. *Rather, they will freely respond only to individuals who are chosen as leaders because they are proven and trusted as servants.*"[33]

This concept seems to have particular relevance to the public sector. Greenleaf distinguishes between the person who first aspires to be a top-down leader and the person who first aspires to be a servant and then is drawn to become a leader: "The difference manifests itself in the care taken by the servant-first to make sure that other people's highest priority needs are being served. The best test, and difficult to administer is: Do those served grow as persons? Do they, *while being served*, become healthier, wiser, freer, more autonomous, more likely themselves to become servants? *And*, what is the effect on the least privileged in society; will they benefit, or, at least, not be further deprived."[34] Greenleaf believes that this would have a significant impact on organizations because servant leadership creates a different and better type of organization: "The secret of institution building is to be able to weld a team of ... people by lifting them up to grow taller than they would otherwise be."[35]

Barbara Kellerman has been one of the strongest proponents of the importance of followership. She argues that leaders and their followers create "[w]ebs of leadership [that] are tangled, the strands – the leader, the followers, and the context – hard to separate one from the other."[36] The entire thrust of her book, *Bad Leadership,* is that leaders and followers have a responsibility to one another to keep themselves on the appropriate path away from the corruption, incompetence, and other horror stories that she recounts in her book.

In a later book, tellingly titled *The End of Leadership,* Kellerman argues that the historical trajectory has been "about the devolution of power – from those up top to those down below."[37] She traces this devolution from King John's signing Magna Carta, through the political philosophers Thomas Hobbes and John Locke, who provided a rationale for the power of the masses, to the American and French revolutions, which actually put power in the hands of the masses. She argues that, by the latter part of the twentieth century, both political and business leaders were under siege from the bottom up by people who had lost faith in the ability and even the honesty of leaders.

Kellerman argues that, because of the declining power of leaders, it is no longer appropriate to take a leader-centric approach; the role of followers is becoming much more important.[38] It seems difficult to disagree completely with this perspective, but in this book I still take a fairly unabashed leader-centric approach. Many of the problems that have resulted in the downgrading of leaders, such as political deadlock and ethical lapses, apply more on the political stage writ large than to individual organizations. Although some of the cynicism spills over throughout the system, if leaders were competent and ethical, they might not suffer from the downgrading Kellerman identifies.

One of the major components in developing a unified team and in stimulating followership is a strong organizational culture. Organizational culture is difficult to define, in part because the word "culture" has a variety of meanings.[39] This problem has been compounded by the recent introduction of the study of organizational discourse and organizational identity, although it is unclear if these newer concepts are really distinct from the older idea of organizational culture.[40]

Edgar Schein's definition of organizational culture is one of the most widely cited: "The culture of a group can now be defined as *a pattern of shared basic assumptions that was learned by a group as it solved its problems of external adaptation and internal integration, that has worked well enough to be considered valid and, therefore to be taught to new members as the correct way to perceive, think, and feel in relation to those problems.*"[41] Herbert Kaufman uses the phrase "organizational tone," but it is clear that he is referring to what we would call organizational culture: "By organizational tone, I mean a combination of morale, crispness of task performance, and policy consensus. Morale is the level of unity, pride, confidence, dedication, enthusiasm, conscientiousness, and industry displayed by an organization's members. Crispness is a comprehensive term for the speed, accuracy, efficiency, and competence with which the members do their jobs. Policy consensus means the absence of sharp divisions about the values emphasized in the organization's operations."[42]

John Kotter and James Heskett see organizational culture as operating at two levels. At the invisible level, it is a system of values – what people in the organization really care about (such as technological innovation, employee well-being). At the more visible level, it is patterns of behaviour or style (such as hard work, a friendly nature).[43] This strong organizational culture aligns an organization from top to bottom around the same values and behaviours. It allows top leaders to motivate "a large number of their middle managers to play a similar kind of leadership role in creating change for their own divisions, departments, and groups."[44] It is generally assumed that a consistent and strongly held organizational culture will improve the performance of the organization.[45] Many empirical studies tend to confirm that this view is generally accurate, although there are some caveats.[46]

Schein sees leadership and organizational culture as completely intertwined. He argues that there is an iterative process through which the leader creates a particular organizational culture, which, in turn, moulds future leaders of the organization, until some disjuncture occurs, at which point a new leader must emerge and reshape the organizational culture, which then becomes firm and moulds new leaders, and so it goes. This relationship between organizational culture and leadership is captured well in Schein's oft-quoted statement: "It can be argued that the only thing of real importance that leaders do is to create and manage culture; that the unique talent of leaders is their ability to understand and work with culture."[47]

A municipality is a complicated organization with a number of leaders at both the political and administrative levels, and it would be difficult to pinpoint one person who is responsible for creating an organizational culture in this context. It is clear, however, that one of the main roles of a good leader is to establish an organizational culture. This involves establishing values around integrity, respect, service to citizens, and all the other values that a modern public service organization must have. A successful CAO must take the lead in modelling these values and establishing the desired organizational culture.

In this book I work the broad middle ground between Carlyle's deification of one great leader and the idea of a group of equals all engaging in leadership or a web of leaders and followers. I argue that one person at the top of the organization can make a major difference in how that organization functions. Of course, in modern organizations, that person's leadership ability more likely will consist of assembling a strong team and developing a unified organizational culture than being a strong individual leader. It must be recognized, however, that this type of team building is an example of the great person as leader at work.

Within formal organizations, leadership is frequently viewed as an extension of the concept of management. A manager has power over subordinates based on her or his ability to wield legitimate authority. Subordinates comply with the manager's directives because the manager can impose discipline usually up to and including dismissal from the organization. Subordinates do not have to like the manager, they do not have to respect the manager, but they must comply with the manager's legitimate instructions or face the consequences.

Thomas Kent uses short, succinct language to make very clear distinctions between the leader and the manager:

- managers do things right; leaders do the right things;
- managing is an authority relationship; leading is an influence relationship;
- managing creates stability; leading creates change.[48]

Kotter makes a similar point in a slightly different manner:

> Leadership is different from management, but not for the reasons most people think. Leadership isn't mystical and mysterious. It has nothing to do with having "charisma" or other exotic personality traits. It is not the province of a chosen few. Nor is leadership necessarily better than management or a replacement for it.
>
> Rather, leadership and management are two distinctive and complementary systems of action. Each has its own function and characteristic activities. Both are necessary for success in an increasingly complex and

volatile business environment ... Good management brings a degree of order and consistency to key dimensions like the quality and profitability of a product.

Leadership, by contrast, is about coping with change.[49]

Kotter goes on to argue that a distinctive characteristic of leaders is that they use vision to align people within the organization. He emphasizes the importance of alignment, and argues that it goes well beyond organization and staffing. The essence of alignment is communicating with people and motivating them so that everyone associated with the organization sees the same vision.

Although seemingly clear conceptual differences can be drawn between leaders and managers, in practice it is unusual to find someone who unequivocally fills one or the other role. This is especially true in government organizations, where concepts such as vision and innovation are problematic. Of course, a good public servant should be both visionary and innovative, while also respecting the ultimate authority of her or his political masters.

A leader differs from a manager by achieving the compliance of followers through influence rather than raw power. Thus, a manager can be a leader in the sense that subordinates follow not only because he or she has legitimate authority, but also because of the respect that followers have for that person. Katz and Kahn refer to this as the "influential increment": "[W]e consider the essence of organizational leadership to be the influential increment over and above mechanical compliance with the routine directives of the organization."[50] A true leader is able to exact some increment of compliance from followers beyond what subordinates must provide to a manager under threat of discipline.

The concepts of leadership and influence become particularly important when a leader must deal with people over whom he or she does not have any legitimate authority. These could be stakeholders outside the organization or even be the leader's superiors within the organization. Organizations frequently depend on external stakeholders for their very existence or rely on them as partners for the delivery of services. Stakeholders are external individuals or groups that have no obligation to support the organization, but can be persuaded to do so if they are influenced by an appropriate leader. Some examples of such stakeholders are donors to charitable organizations, or recreation associations or immigrant settlement groups that assist local governments in the provision of services.

Officials also must sometimes exercise a leadership role with regard to people who are their nominal superiors. Canadian local governments take pride in the role of "part-time amateur politicians," a phrase that is not meant to be demeaning, but that refers to someone whose full-time occupation keeps her or him in close contact with the community, allowing politicians to ensure that the community perspective is reflected in any decision. Part-time amateurs, however, usually do not have the same level of technical expertise about how to build a bridge or handle a planning application as do full-time officials.

The public servant has no real power over superiors; instead, he or she must rely heavily on influence in dealing with them. External stakeholders or politicians frequently will listen carefully and accept the advice of a nominal subordinate if they have confidence in the ability of that subordinate. The exercise of influence in this way requires a great deal of what has come to be called emotional intelligence. It has long been recognized that intelligence is not one single concept: scholars now discuss such multiple intelligences as musical, bodily kinesthetic, logical-mathematical, spatial, and spiritual.[51] Although measuring the precise impact of different forms of intelligence on life success has proven controversial,[52] it seems clear that traditional measures of intelligence go only a certain distance toward determining likely career success. The psychologists who coined the term emotional intelligence define it as "the subset of social intelligence that involves the *ability to monitor one's own and others' feelings and emotions, to discriminate among them and to use this information to guide one's thinking and actions.*"[53]

Emotions and intelligence are sometimes cast as opposites in that emotions can be seen as overwrought, somewhat irrational, responses, while intelligence is cold, calm, and rational. In fact, emotions are powerful forces that can be used in a positive way to motivate people. As Peter Salovey and John Mayer explain, "[p]eople who have developed skills related to emotional intelligence understand and express their own emotions, recognize emotions in others, regulate affect, and use moods and emotions to initiate adaptive behavior."[54]

Daniel Goleman, one of the gurus of emotional intelligence, expands on this definition with his own five-part definition: 1) knowing one's emotions (self-awareness); 2) managing emotions (act appropriately; smooth out the extremes of emotion); 3) motivating oneself (self-control to direct yourself to the desired goal); 4) recognizing emotions in others (empathy, altruism toward others); and 5) handling relationships (social competence, managing emotion in others).[55] He also talks about "managing with heart,"[56] and argues that the former "jungle fighter" style of manager has been replaced by "the virtuoso in interpersonal skills,"[57] who must be good at recognizing that he or she is dealing with people who are diverse and have a broad range of emotions, and therefore must be dealt with somewhat differently. This is the idea of handling relationships, which leads Goleman to the idea that "the fundamental task of leadership is an emotional one."[58]

Being aware of one's own emotions does not mean keeping them bottled up. Rather, emotional intelligence encourages the idea of approaching a job with passion – not unbridled, irrational passion, but a passion that is controlled, like all emotions, and directed in a constructive manner. This is an important way of motivating oneself and those around the leader.[59]

In a subsequent work, Goleman, Boyatzis, and McKee extend the concept of emotional intelligence by developing the idea of the primal leader – a neurological basis for leadership through which a leader's attitudes infect others in the organization.[60] Leaders can be either resonant, meaning that they spread a positive mood through empathy, humour, and a generally positive attitude, or dissonant, in the sense of being openly abusive or at least of draining the happiness from an organization. Goleman, Boyatzis, and McKee tie the neurological and social aspects of leadership together very nicely in this quotation:

> The continual interplay of limbic open loops among members of a group creates a kind of emotional soup, with everyone adding his or her own flavor to the mix. But it is the leader who adds the strongest seasoning. Why? Because of that enduring reality of business: Everyone watches the boss. People take their emotional cues from the top. Even when the boss isn't highly visible – for example, the CEO who works behind closed doors on an upper floor – his attitude affects the moods of his direct reports, and a domino effect ripples throughout the company's emotional climate.[61]

A recent study by Martina Kotzé and Ian Venter laments that, although there have been many empirical tests of the relationship between effective leadership and emotional intelligence in the private sector, there have been few similar tests in the public sector. Their extensive study of public servants in South Africa, however, indicates a positive correlation between effective leadership and emotional intelligence.[62]

Janet Denhardt and Robert Denhardt also see an emotion-based aspect to leadership, but they view it as having aspects of an art form.

They admit that leadership has certain rational elements – understanding production processes, for example – but leadership also has an emotional element:

> Good leadership, like art, touches us. It stimulates not just our minds, but our emotions, and makes us come alive. Certainly we expect that leadership will help us to accomplish things we might not otherwise accomplish, and so we look for results. But leadership also touches us in more personal ways. Good leadership excites and activates us. Good leadership inspires and encourages us (that is, it gives us courage). Good leadership makes us feel better about ourselves. It is this emotional side of leadership that provides the energy to move and to change small groups, large organizations, and even whole societies.[63]

Denhardt and Denhardt compare good leaders to ballet dancers in that both must have a good sense of space and time; both need to have an understanding of and the ability to communicate with their audience; they need to employ creativity and improvisation; and they need to have a certain energy that pervades the entire organization and energizes other people. "The leader must touch not only the 'head' but also the 'heart.'"[64]

It should be clear by this point that leadership can mean many different things, and its meaning can shift in different circumstances. This now well-travelled contingency theory of leadership was developed by Fred Fiedler.[65] The theory has had many variants, but the general idea is that there is no one best leader who will function perfectly in all situations. Instead, the situation the organization faces will determine the type of leader it needs at that time.[66] Broadly speaking, contingency theory recognizes task-oriented leaders, as distinct from relationship or people-oriented leaders. The optimum leader in a given situation will depend on leader-member relations, task structure, and the strength of the leader's position power.[67] For example, a leader who works in a routinized, factory-type environment is more likely to focus on the task, and see people as one more tool to be used to accomplish that task. Conversely, a leader who manages a group of scientists in a laboratory where innovation is the goal is more likely to focus on maintaining a good environment for highly skilled people and to assume they will accomplish the task on their own.

Although there has been much discussion about the most relevant situational variables, the concept of task-oriented versus people-oriented leaders has had a great deal of staying power. Of course, it is understood that no leader is entirely oriented in only one direction – any leader must pay attention to both the task to be accomplished and the people in the organization – but some leaders do tend to lean in one direction or the other.

Much literature on leadership focuses on the relationship between leaders and followers, but Larry D. Terry reminds us that leaders also have an obligation to their organizations, particularly in the public sector, where the organization strives to embody the public interest. Terry argues that the public sector leader should be a conservator in the sense that *"the primary function of bureaucratic leaders is to protect and maintain administrative institutions in a manner that promotes or is consistent with constitutional processes, values, and beliefs."*[68] Although we do not typically talk about constitutional values with regard to local governments, Terry's principle is that bureaucratic leaders have an obligation to maintain the fundamental governing principles embodied in their institutions in the face of attempts on the part of others to violate those principles. He recognizes that, in some cases, this could require public servants to limit the power of their political masters: "Although public bureaucracies must occupy a subordinate yet autonomous role with respect to other democratic institutions and processes, the performance of this role does not mean that career civil servants should become passive participants in governance. Guided by classical constitutional theory and, in turn, the logic of a constitution, public administrators have a legitimate right to check the power of elected political leaders."[69] This might sound like a radical concept, but, in fact, it is a reminder that, although professional public servants have a certain obligation to serve their political masters, they also have an obligation to preserve the integrity of the foundational principles of government and to maintain and further the broader public interest. I discuss this concept in more detail below with regard to the concept of "leading up," but public servants need to remember that they will occasionally be required to engage in a difficult balancing act between pressures from their political masters and broader guiding principles.

This background thus prepares the ground for the formidable task of developing a working definition of the municipal CAO as leader. There has been much discussion in the literature of the difficulty of defining this concept; in fact, some have even suggested that it is better not to attempt a definition.[70] Joseph Rost notes, indeed, that many people who have written extensively about leadership have not defined the term.[71] He suggests that one former definition saw the leader as an extension of the manager: the manager and the leader sit on the same continuum, but the leader is an exceptionally good manager. Rost refers to this as the "industrial paradigm" of the twentieth century and earlier, and rejects it as no longer suitable.[72] He then develops a definition that he feels fits the twenty-first century: "*Leadership is an influence relationship among leaders and followers who intend real changes that reflect their mutual purposes.*"[73]

My specialized definition of the leadership role of the municipal CAO owes much to Rost's definition: *A municipal CAO who is a good leader has the ability to move the municipality forward by interacting in a mutually influential way with and motivating council, external stakeholders, and organizational subordinates.*

The first element of the definition emphasizes that leadership qualities reside in the individual. The point is frequently made in discussions of bureaucracy that authority resides in the position, not in the current incumbent. The opposite is true of leadership, which resides in the individual, and cannot be attached formally to a position. The second part of the definition deals with leadership's organizational aspect: leadership must move the municipality forward in a desired direction; a leader cannot be a mere caretaker who holds on to the status quo or guides the municipality in the direction in which it was fated to move anyway.

An emphasis on change is a common theme in discussions of leadership. John Kotter and James Heskett note the importance of leaders' being in tune with the organization's broader environment and ensuring that the organization changes to remain in alignment with that environment: "In the cases of successful change that we have studied, we have always found one or two unusually capable leaders on top. These individuals had track records for producing dramatic results ... They challenged the status quo with very basic questions ... These leaders then motivated a large number of their middle managers to play a similar kind of leadership role in creating change for their own divisions, departments, and groups."[74]

This definition, however, stops short of emphasizing such grand ideas as producing major change in recognition of the fact that good leadership must be situational. Sometimes a leader will arrive on the scene when the municipality is in need of a major change; a good leader must rise to that challenge. In other cases an organization might be recovering from some major shock and is in need of a period of consolidation and stabilization. A good leader recognizes this situation and does not attempt major change, but moves the organization ahead in a low-key and restrained manner.

The third part of my definition deals with the personal interaction aspect of leadership. It emphasizes that leadership is about mutual interaction. This draws on the idea by Katz and Kahn of the influential increment, but it also recognizes that a good leader listens carefully to her or his followers, and is influenced by them as much as the leader influences the followers. This also reflects the ideas developed earlier on shared leadership, servant leadership, and emotional intelligence. Leadership is a shared function, not unidirectional. But this is not interaction for the sake of it – the successful leader must be able to motivate followers in a particular direction to move the municipality forward.

The final part of my definition goes beyond the traditional idea that leaders interact only with organizational subordinates, and recognizes that a good CAO must lead in three directions. In addition to motivating subordinates, a good CAO must sometimes lead her or his political masters by helping them to make decisions that move the organization in a particular direction. Thus, a CAO might put a contentious or unpopular issue on the agenda and encourage councillors to solve a problem that they would have been more comfortable ignoring. In some cases, the CAO will also need to work with outside stakeholders who can be instrumental in helping achieve the goal, but over whom the CAO has no direct authority. This could involve putting together a partnership to further the economic development and tourism goals of the municipality. Leading up and out thus requires the CAO to use influence, rather than authority. The CAO does have legitimate authority to exercise control over subordinates, but the wise leader uses influence with subordinates to craft a particular approach to a problem and to ensure that subordinates buy into the leader's approach to the problem.

The study of leadership continues to evolve. Entire journals are devoted to it, and it has a significant presence in any management journal. Much of the literature, however, consists of testing hypotheses related to contingency theory or developing "new" theories of and approaches to leadership that, in fact, are amalgams of the theories listed above.[75] In the next section, I apply some of these broad theories of leadership to the role of the municipal chief administrative officer as leader.

The CAO as Leader

Like most managers, the municipal CAO must lead in three different directions,[76] although I argue that the job of the CAO is unique in the way in which this trifurcated leadership role must be handled. The

CAO must lead down, out, and up. *Leading down* refers to the traditional role of leading or managing subordinates within the organization, as illustrated in any standard organization chart. *Leading up* refers to managing the CAO's relationship with council. Note that the phrasing here refers to managing the *relationship* with council. It would be unseemly for a subordinate to refer openly to managing a superior, although in unguarded moments, one sometimes hears CAOs refer to how they manage their council. Finally, *leading out* refers to managing the relationship with stakeholders that are outside the municipal government structure, but are important players in the system nonetheless: the media, residents' groups, business interests, other governments, and so forth.

Leading down

Leading down refers to the usual type of supervision that a superior provides to subordinates. In the case of a municipal CAO, this means dealing with department heads – sometimes called commissioners in municipal governments. Leading down is usually the easiest of the three leadership directions – which is not to say that it is easy in an absolute sense. In a world of great sensitivity to participative management and empowerment, and a need for compliance with ever more complicated collective agreements, regulations with regard to health and safety, human rights, and so forth, leading down requires a great deal of care to ensure that human, financial and other resources are organized appropriately to attain cost-effectiveness with due regard to the various rules and regulations that must be followed.

It is not that it is easy to lead down, but CAOs usually come to their position well prepared to do so. Anyone who cannot manage down well at lower levels of the organization will not climb the hierarchy in the first place. When one starts climbing the bottom rungs of the hierarchical ladder, one can take all sorts of courses of varying length, depth, and seriousness with titles such as "supervisory skills," "motivating and empowering employees," "managing the modern organization," and so forth. As well, considerable informal mentoring goes on within organizations and professional associations to assist lower- and middle-level managers to develop the necessary skills to manage down.

Many of the rules for leading down are fairly firmly established. As much as some senior managers might complain about unions and collective agreements, the fact is that collective agreements can be very useful to management because they make the rules of the game clear and they bind both sides. Managers at all levels must learn how to manage subordinates and administer collective agreements. Thus, the CAO usually arrives at her or his position with considerable experience in managing subordinates.

The CAO's major leadership role in leading down, and a difficult one, is to integrate all of the municipality's separate units into one comprehensive whole. The first obstacle in this regard is the incredibly broad scope of municipal activity. Most organizations can define a specific core activity – manufacturing cars, providing entertainment, educating students. Municipal governments are responsible for a broad variety of tasks ranging from hard services, such as building roads, to people services, such as caring for seniors, to the highly ephemeral, such as place shaping. In all of this, the CAO is the only administrator who holds the broad corporate perspective; her or his role is to integrate the diverse departments responsible for all these activities into one corporate entity.

"Horizontality" is a relatively new word in the public administration lexicon that refers to the need to manage initiatives across the organizational hierarchy, rather than up and down the traditional silos.[77] It is a reflection of the fact that many contemporary "wicked" problems do not fit neatly into one of the traditional departments. For example, homelessness involves the departments of social services, public health, planning, and police, among others. These kinds of issues frequently are addressed by the use of interdepartmental task forces, which inevitably raises concerns about accountability and responsibility. One possible way of addressing these concerns is to designate one individual or one department as the lead. When problems arise, however, there is really only one person in the organization who can deal with interdepartmental issues. The more of these horizontal task forces that exist, the more hot potatoes that ultimately end up on the CAO's desk.

Most organization charts are pyramids with one senior person at the pinnacle. The organization chart of a municipality looks more like an hourglass, with a group of councillors at the top frequently pulling in different directions and a group of departments at the bottom, each with a different mandate, and some horizontal task forces thrown in for good measure. The pinchpoint in the hourglass, the place through which everything must flow, is the CAO. The role of each department head in this structure is to make sure that the interests of the department are properly represented to council and the CAO. The role of the CAO is to meld these disparate interests into one corporate perspective.

In sum, leading down is not easy, but most CAOs bring considerable experience in leading down to the office with them. The difficulty with leading out and leading up, in contrast, is that training grounds for developing these skills do not exist. CAOs frequently find that they must develop these skills after they have filled the position.

Leading out

Leading out refers to the CAO's relationship with individuals or groups outside the municipal structure, such as the media, residents' groups, business organizations, and other governments. These relationships are important because outsiders see the CAO, as the senior administrative official, as one of the key representatives of the municipality, and anything that the CAO says will be taken as the municipality's official position. The CAO must be a diplomat because any exchange is public, or could be made public if it is in the other party's interest to make it so.

New Public Management and the New Public Service have changed this portion of the CAO's job considerably in that both concepts focus heavily on the relationship between public servants and citizens, but in rather different ways.

New Public Management (NPM), developed in the 1970s and later,[78] focuses on introducing business principles into government. One catchphrase is separating steering and rowing, by which is meant that governments should continue to make policy decisions (steer), but not necessarily deliver services (row). Under NPM, words such as empowerment and entrepreneurial were used for the first time in government. This opened the door for alternative service delivery, including privatization, contracting out, partnerships, and other novel means. NPM has also increased the focus on moving from process accountability to a greater emphasis on achieving results (results accountability) and performance measurement. This reorientation has changed the role of the CAO considerably, opening the door for the CAO to be more entrepreneurial and flexible in the way that he or she manages the environment. CAOs now need to look outward more than before and make decisions about contracting out, partnerships, and so forth. This often involves working with the community to locate the best partners. Results accountability and performance measurement require the CAO to look at the service from the perspective of the user of the service, not just the provider.

New Public Service (NPS)[79] was meant to be a strong attack on NPM and an attempt to resurrect the value of the public service from the attacks implicit in NPM, but the two approaches have certain things in common. The catchphrase of NPS is serving, rather than steering, and is a clarion call that providing services to the public is a proud vocation. At the same time, it gives "service" a connotation beyond merely responding to the stated desires of the public. Under NPS, serving the public means working with the public as a facilitator and broker to assist citizens in articulating their needs, and working with contending groups to identify the broader public interest in a particular issue. Like NPM, this requires the CAO to move beyond the comfort of the municipal building to play a real role in working with the community.

In principle, it seems that most relationships with external groups should be handled through the mayor and councillors, and politicians do play a significant role in this area. As the volume and complexity of issues have increased, however, it has become clear that it is beyond the capability of part-time, amateur councillors to deal with the high number and wide range of sometimes highly technical issues that come up.[80] Managing the citizen engagement process is becoming both an important and a complex activity.[81] The New Public Service argues that citizen involvement in decision making needs to be an intrinsic part of the role of the public administrator. Not only will it result in better decisions, it will also promote the important concept of democratic citizenship.[82]

Frequently, council will not be able to anticipate issues or arrive at a united position on issues that are just at the development stage. Therefore, it will fall to the CAO to take the lead and determine what issues are likely to become contentious, and to develop a strategy to manage these issues. Municipalities must understand that it is counterproductive to have to respond to issues in a defensive manner. Rather, it is more beneficial to be proactive in managing an issue before it becomes contentious.

Council frequently will delegate responsibility for certain types of negotiations to the CAO. In an ideal world, the council would provide the CAO with a clear idea of what it wants the CAO to accomplish in the negotiations. Council might be divided, however, about how it sees an issue, and will be unable to give the CAO guidance beyond something like "do the best you can." One US city manager described how this worked in his city: "The elected officials quietly say to the managers, 'Negotiate that problem with those other three governments. When you get a solution, bring it back to me. If I like it – and I probably will – then we'll have a ceremony and a press conference, and I'll sign a document. It will be mine, but we'll all know that you did it.'"[83]

The CAO might have to deal with a broad range of difficult issues. For example, in the case of a proposal for a new subdivision or commercial development, council might like the general idea, but feel that it needs particular changes before accepting it. Or a recreation association might want a new facility or a major renovation of an existing facility. Again, council might like the idea, but will not want to proceed until other recreation groups and residents' associations in the affected area have been consulted. If the municipality needs a new landfill site, council might feel that the most cost-effective way of dealing with the issue is to enter into a partnership with a neighbouring municipality. This approach, however, would require negotiations with the other municipality, affected residents' groups, and the provincial agencies that must approve the site.

These are all political issues in which council must play an important role, but the practicalities of these situations generally will dictate that the full-time professional CAO, rather than the part-time amateur councillors, take the lead role in the negotiations. The CAO must act as a broker in these cases, identify all the relevant actors (not always an easy job), and bring them together for discussions at the right times, and (equally important) keep them apart at other times, with the ultimate goal a deal that both the external groups and council can accept. A 1980 publication of the International City Management Association that looked forward to 2000 predicted presciently that "brokering and negotiating may be the prime talents of the successful manager of tomorrow. Managers will be required to listen carefully, interpret ideas, empathize with many people, and defer personal ego needs. Managers will need great patience and great faith in people's ability to reach agreement and understanding."[84]

Obviously, these negotiations can be delicate. For example, in the case of a development proposal, the CAO must drive a hard bargain to ensure that the municipality benefits, but cannot be so difficult that the developer withdraws the proposal and goes elsewhere. There are all sorts of "how-to" books on negotiating, but much of the literature assumes that the negotiator is either negotiating on her or his own behalf or is working for one single-minded principal. Yet, the municipal CAO lives in a world of ambiguity. In undertaking the delicate negotiations necessary in many situations, the CAO is working for a group of principals who might be seriously divided among themselves, in which case the CAO is forced to handle two sets of negotiations simultaneously – one at the table with the developer, and one behind the scenes to develop a unified position among councillors.

If the CAO is to be a true leader and exercise concern for the appropriate development of the community, he or she must play some role in the policy-making process. Leading out will inevitably draw the CAO even more deeply into that process, but the CAO must be conscious of the limits of her or his involvement. The distinction Poul Mouritzen and James Svara make between the two senses in which the word "politics" is used can be useful to the administrator here.[85] They suggest that one use of the word focuses on the "politics of securing office" – the electoral process and related patronage issues, including the jockeying for position that goes on before and immediately after the actual election. Politically neutral administrators must steer clear of this form of politics. The other sense of "politics" Mouritzen and Svara identify "stresses the process by which society authoritatively allocates resources and values." This is the policy-making side of politics, which they call "the politics of governing society." It is impossible for a successful CAO to remain aloof from this aspect of politics.

The media also take a great interest in local government, so it is important to take a proactive position with the media. This means spending time with members of the media and ensuring that they understand fully initiatives coming from the municipality. There has been an increase in the number of media outlets operating in less traditional areas, such as weekly community newspapers, Web-based specialized newsletters, and even personal blogs. CAOs might be tempted to dismiss some of these as not attracting a significant audience or being too quirky, but there is a certain peril in doing that. Examples exist of contagions starting in exactly these kinds of quirky locations that have swept up people and produced a great deal of interest.

The need to deal with other governments is also becoming more important. Municipalities have always been concerned about dealing with provincial governments, but recently the federal government has become a player at the municipal level as well. Of course, some of these relationships with other levels of government are mediated through provincial and national municipal associations, but some municipalities have worked hard to maintain their own relationships with these other governments in addition to the mediation through associations. Almost all municipalities have certain unique characteristics that place them in a one-on-one situation with other spheres of government from time to time – proximity to a military base, location at an international border, the presence of an important tourist centre, a significant harbour or airport. The list is endless.

Municipalities also must manage their relationships with other municipalities and local special-purpose bodies. In the case of two-tier governments such as counties, regions, and regional districts, the sharing of responsibilities is part of the day-to-day management of the municipality, but this is only the tip of the iceberg. Partnerships have become much more common as a result of the NPM, but municipalities have long had agreements with one another for such things as landfill sites and water purification and sewage treatment facilities. These arrangements are becoming more important as the regulations and citizens' concerns associated with such major projects have increased the costs and complications of establishing and operating these facilities.

This brings us to the question of whether it is appropriate for the CAO to be a community leader beyond her or his role in the civic administration. This question has been the subject of much deliberation in the US literature. Writing in the 1950s, an early proponent of the city manager as community leader argued that this type of city manager

> accepts without question the role of city emissary to state and federal government organs, ... to state and national professional and civic associations, and to other municipal governments. To some he will express the city's point of view and with others he may negotiate for his city.
>
> He will pay particular attention to all organized groups in his community, partially as a means of making the acquaintance of the natural leaders of these groups. "It is the manager's job to provide facts, offer counsel, encourage, and tactfully guide community groups in the planning of worth while [sic] improvements." The telephone number of the executive directors of associations presuming to speak for the interests of commerce, health, welfare, education, industry, religion, labor, good government, and real estate, among others, ought to be readily at hand.[86]

As the quiet 1950s gave way to the more turbulent 1960s, this issue morphed into a question of whether the manager had an obligation to speak for the poor, the disenfranchised, and the unorganized who otherwise had no one to speak for them. Svara points out that the New Public Administration movement "sought to address the deficiencies in the policy process that result from unrepresentative legislative bodies and the uneven level of political organization and participation among citizens by expanding the role of professional administrators."[87] As one US city manager put it, "[i]t is the responsibility of managers in government to take the initiative to see that an individual's quality of life is not negatively affected solely because that person does not know how to use the system."[88] Few Canadian CAOs would feel comfortable going as far as addressing the deficiencies of "unrepresentative legislative bodies,"[89] but this way of thinking does raise an interesting question about the extent to which the CAO has a moral obligation to make sure that the position of unorganized interests (frequently low-income people and ethnic minorities) are considered properly in the formulation of public policies.

Of course, the CAO also faces a dilemma in the opposite situation when council is being pressured by a vocal, well-organized interest group to do something that benefits the group but is not in the broader interest of the entire community.[90] Can a professional, ethical CAO sit quietly and watch this happen?

Clearly, the CAO must be careful not to become more visible in the community than the mayor and councillors. This does not mean, however, that the CAO should abdicate any type of leadership role in the community – such a "shrinking violet" role would short change both the civic administration and the community. The CAO who takes the leading-out role seriously probably will be guided more by a desire to accomplish certain goals than by a concern about boundaries.

Although the CAO has an important role to play in leading out, the specific nature of that role can be quite ambiguous. The mayor and councillors should take a strong role here, and the CAO must be careful not to be too far out in front of her or his political masters. There are situations, however, in which it is appropriate for the full-time administrative expert to take the lead. In some cases, the nature of the issue could be highly technical; in other cases, council could be divided, and the CAO would have to engage in two-sided negotiations to arrive at an agreement with the outside interest that the majority on council will accept. The CAO thus must function as both a diplomat and a broker, and manage her or his relationship with council carefully, which brings me to the CAO's role of leading up.

Leading up

Leading up is probably the CAO's most difficult task. In the first place, there is a significant structural issue here. In a democracy, the phrase usually employed to describe the relationship between politicians and public servants is "politicians on top; experts on tap." It is clear that the mayor and councillors are in a supervisory position with regard to the CAO. Therefore, the important public service value of accountability indicates that the CAO must be accountable to the mayor and councillors. So, why should someone in a subordinate position, the CAO, need to lead those to whom he or she reports? How does one go about leading a group to whom one should be accountable?

Part of the answer can be found in the various descriptions of leadership discussed earlier. Leadership is not just about formal authority; leadership also recognizes power that flows from influence. This influence, in turn, flows from technical expertise or just the ability to inspire confidence in one's judgment. The stark truth is that, in the interest of good governance, the CAO sometimes must take a leadership role with regard to her or his political masters. Robert Behn states the imperative very well:

> [P]ublic managers have to lead. They need to articulate their organization's purpose and motivate people to achieve it. They have to keep their agency focused on pursuing its mission. They need to encourage people to develop new systems for pursuing that mission. Markets don't work perfectly. Neither do organizations. Without some kind of conscious, active intervention – without leadership – public agencies (like private and nonprofit organizations) will fail to achieve their purposes. The people best situated, best equipped to exercise this leadership are the managers of the agency.[91]

This coincides with Terry's view, discussed earlier, that public servants have an obligation to be conservators in the sense of preserving the basic constitutional principles of their organization even if their political masters try to circumvent them.[92] Michael Useem provides examples from many organizational spheres of situations where leading up saved the organization from failure, and some examples where a failure to lead up doomed it to failure.[93] In the public sector, the New Public Management exhorts managers to be entrepreneurial; the New Public Service sees the public servant as the guardian of the public interest.[94]

Since it is clear that councillors depend heavily on the expertise of administrators,[95] it would be irresponsible on the part of the CAO *not* to exercise a reasonable degree of leadership. In the words of a US city manager,

> [a]s strongly as I respect elected officials and representative government, they simply do not have the tools themselves to set policy and set the strategy for the city, and it is not enough for the manager to give a report or say, "Here is the information, let me know what you decide." The way I do my job, it is my job to help them decide, and candidly it is often my job to decide what I think is good for the city, to test that, not to be arrogant about that decision, and then to help the elected officials to reach that conclusion, and if I am wrong, we readjust. But I don't think the manager can sit by passively.[96]

Councillors and administrators also have different time horizons.[97] Our political system holds councillors accountable by requiring them to contest elections. It should not be surprising, therefore, that the average politician's time horizon starts at three or four years and grows shorter as the term of office progresses. The time horizon of administrators, however, stems from their professional values and the likelihood of their staying with the municipality for an extended period. These different time horizons can generate either synergy, as the two groups share views about both the short and the long term, or tension, as the two groups struggle with each another over their different perceptions.

In the federal and provincial governments, the winning party comes to power after an election on a fairly clearly articulated platform. These politicians also bring with them a party apparatus to assist them in developing the promises they made during the election campaign. Even if there is a change in government, some members of the new cabinet or some members of the partisan support staff will have had experience in government in one jurisdiction or another. Municipal politicians, in contrast, often arrive in office comparatively naked.[98] Most Canadian municipalities do not operate on a party political system, so each candidate runs on her or his own platform, which could be a single issue such as "stop development in my neighbourhood" or platitudes such as "better service" or "lower taxes." In most municipalities, councillors have no political staff to assist them. If they are lucky, they will be able to draw on the advice of a few friends who might or might not have any experience of governing.

Although federal and provincial politicians move into their new offices with a great deal of baggage, local politicians generally will not have a clear idea of what they want to do.[99] And even if some councillors do know what they want to do, they rarely have the cohesion that comes from party discipline. It is not that federal and provincial politicians are more intelligent or more politically savvy than local politicians, but more a matter of organization. To run an effective national or provincial campaign, a party apparatus must organize and coordinate activities among a large number of candidates. Candidates for municipal office generally run on a much more personal basis, without partisan affiliation or even much expert assistance, and they arrive in the council chamber as individuals, not as party members. In parliamentary systems, one speaks of the majority party forming "the government." There is no comparable term at the municipal level – for a very good reason.

The lack of political parties at the municipal level creates a particular dynamic in the relationship between politicians and the CAO. In parliamentary systems, the cabinet secretary has a reasonably clear idea of what a new government wants to accomplish based on the campaign rhetoric of the winning party as refined by the Speech from the Throne, the budget, and other pronouncements from the first minister. It is much more difficult for a municipal CAO to read the tea leaves. Even if the CAO knows what the mayor and various individual councillors would like to accomplish, there is frequently no unity among the group, so that the CAO has no way of knowing how the dynamic of the council will unfold over time. Both the cabinet secretary and the municipal CAO must function as leaders, but the cabinet secretary is generally given a reasonably clear mandate, while the municipal CAO inevitably must play a role in shaping the mandate that the mayor and councillors would like to pursue.

The CAO frequently also must take on the role of mediator when an impasse develops on council, and the mayor and councillors are hopelessly divided on an issue. Legally, the mayor and councillors are equal, although the mayor has a higher profile than councillors. Under the law in most Canadian municipalities, the mayor is not even *primus inter pares* like the first minister in a parliamentary system. In the event of deadlock, there is no one among the mayor and councillors who can step forward with a solution. With no political axe to grind, however, the CAO is sometimes in the best position to mediate among these equals.

In some cases, the CAO might want to act proactively before an impasse develops. In these situations, the CAO could seize on a policy that he or she feels is important for the municipality ("the politics of governing society") and try to find a coalition to support it. This is clearly not within the "politics of securing office," which would be a violation of political neutrality, but a CAO must proceed carefully whenever he or she is working with some councillors to the exclusion of others.[100] This strategy could produce excellent results, but it could also put the CAO in an awkward position with some councillors.

The politicians and the CAO must recognize that they each have different contributions to make in the policy-making process. But what are those contributions, and how do they fit together? Frequently, the distinction is seen as the separation of politics and administration, where politicians make policy decisions and administrators implement them. Peter Self suggests that an

> alternative distinction between politics and administration is in terms of process. We can envisage an arch with the left arc representing the political process and the right arc the administrative process. The junction at the top represents the critical point at which political will flows into and energises the administrative system: and it is also the point at which influences that have been generated *within* the administrative process flow back into the higher levels of the political process. There is thus, at the apex of the arch, a fusion of political and administrative influences which have been generated lower down the two arcs.[101]

Thus, Self envisages a separation between politicians and administrators, but one based on distinct processes and quite permeable at the junction of the two.

This fluidity makes it difficult to specify precisely the role of the CAO with regard to the mayor and councillors, despite attempts at great precision in by-laws or employment contracts. And even if the CAO's precise role could be so defined, on the day after the by-law or contract took effect both the organization and its surrounding environment would start changing so as to outmode such static documents. In particular, expectations might change quite significantly after an election, when a new mayor and new councillors take office. Since it can be difficult to specify in writing what type of relationship is desired, the usual process is for the two sides to decide by trial and error what type of relationship they want. It is not a unilateral, once-and-for-all decision.

Robert Putnam has suggested that there are two polar types of public servants.[102] At one extreme is what he calls the *classical bureaucrat* who sees the public interest as a single-minded concept and all issues as technical issues that can be resolved by the application of the appropriate administrative technique. This type of bureaucrat has no use for the ambiguities inherent in the political process. In fact, he or she sees politics as an unnecessarily noisy and cumbersome process that interferes with achieving efficiency.

At the opposite pole is the *political bureaucrat* who has a "pluralistic conception of the public interest."[103] This official recognizes the legitimacy of the political process and the need to compromise and bargain to attain an acceptable (not perfect) resolution. As Putnam explains,

> [w]hereas the classical bureaucrat is "procedure-oriented" or "rule-oriented," the political bureaucrat is "problem-oriented" or "program-oriented." Whereas the classical bureaucrat views the politician as a troublesome or even dangerous antagonist, interfering with the efficiency and objectivity of government, the political bureaucrat sees the politician instead as a participant in a common game, one whose skills and immediate concerns may differ from his own but whose ultimate values and objectives are similar. The political bureaucrat understands and accepts the role of such institutions as parties and pressure groups. He is likely, as well, to understand and endorse the values of political liberty and equality.[104]

A good senior public servant should be able to orient him- or herself toward both poles. A good leader must ensure that the hierarchy is functioning properly, services are delivered, and rules are followed. In a well-functioning organization, however, the senior administrator should not need to spend a huge amount of time on this. As a US city manager is quoted as saying, "[i]t is not the job of the city manager anymore [*sic*] to make sure the streets get paved. The streets have to get paved, but if you have to be the one to make sure it happens, it is a misuse of your resources."[105] The main role of policy-oriented public servants is to work with their political masters to shape the policy agenda of the municipality. The political bureaucrat embodies the idea of leading up. The CAO is in the delicate position of needing to exercise some level of leadership with regard to her or his superiors despite not having legitimate authority over them, by inspiring confidence in her or his ability to provide sound advice and to carry out the work.

A significant complicating factor is that CAOs typically take up their positions with relatively little experience of working with the mayor and councillors in an intensive fashion in situations where they must make trade-offs and consciously manage the relationship. Actually, local governments are small enough that most middle- and senior-level officials have sporadic contacts with the mayor and councillors, but these interactions tend to be highly focused on a specific event (a new park, street repairs in a particular neighbourhood). Self suggests that interactions between politicians and public servants tend to decline in intensity as one moves down the hierarchy because "[a]dministrators down the line are primarily concerned with getting policies or rules effectively applied, without bothering overmuch as to how or why they were formulated."[106] It is this distinction between implementing established policies and becoming involved in formulating new policies that distinguishes the role of the CAO from other staff members. As Mouritzen and Svara note,

> [i]t is obvious from the existing literature and observation of local affairs that [chief administrative officers] interact extensively with elected officials. They are more than just the providers of information and recipients of instructions from elected officials. [CAOs] bring certain values and norms with clear political significance to their position. They are committed to neutrality between parties and candidates, but they are committed to acting on the basis of expertise. Rather than barring them from taking political stands, "expertise" viewed as a bundle of specialized knowledge, experience and familiarity with governmental practices, and professional values may support distinctive perspectives on policy … Furthermore, they are more or less extensively involved in communications with community groups and officials in other governments and are, therefore, potentially community leaders and "representatives" of citizens as well as administrative directors.[107]

Leading up involves the subtle ability to work with a diverse and sometimes divided group of councillors to further the interests of the municipality and its residents. This requires the CAO to be able to mediate among these diverse groups and to use the strength of her or his administrative expertise to attempt to mould action to move forward. The CAO must be policy oriented, but not political. He or she must be a leader without being out in front of the mayor and council. This is obviously a difficult role to play.

Putting It All Together

The great difficulty facing the CAO is the requirement to lead in three directions simultaneously, compounded by the need for a different skill set for each direction. Henry Mintzberg illustrates the concept of leading up, down, and out by describing the activities of three different managers in a national park, each of whom specializes in managing in one direction. He allows that none "of these three managers was free of the edges faced by the other two,"[108] but he makes it clear that there was a specialization of labour – no one of his managers was obligated to face in three directions at the same time, a luxury the municipal CAO does not have.

The seemingly impossible task of facing in three directions at once is further complicated by the speed at which events occur. The size of most municipal governments is such that most CAOs do not have the insulation that senior managers in larger organizations enjoy. Whether an issue is coming down, up, or in, it reaches the CAO very quickly without having to pass through many other layers of management. Many municipal CAOs talk about spending no more than ten minutes on any one task before moving on to another.

The contingency theory of leadership holds that there is no "one best way" to lead; rather, leadership is situational. It is possible that a leader can be highly effective in one situation but completely dysfunctional in another. The municipal CAO's situation puts a new wrinkle in the contingency theory of leadership. The usual prescription of contingency theory is that an organization must find the type of leader that fits its current needs, but the theory does not address the municipal CAO's need to take three different orientations at the same time. This difficulty ought to have an impact on the way councillors view the position of CAO and on the recruitment and selection process. Rather than focus on any one aspect of leadership, the selection process for a CAO should consider the candidate's ability to change direction and the speed with which the change can be accomplished.

Table 1.1 lists the different characteristics needed for the different roles, and indicates the great variety of hats the successful CAO must wear.

In addition to the complication of managing in three different directions, the CAO sometimes can experience tensions among the different directions. An obvious case is when a CAO must convey a message from council to staff that staff members do not want to hear (services must be reduced, administrative deficiencies must be corrected). The

Table 1.1. Different Roles of the Municipal CAO

Leading Down	Leading Out	Leading Up
Classical bureaucrat	Political bureaucrat	Political bureaucrat
Concern for production	Concern for people	Concern for people and production
Power through authority	Power through influence	Power through influence
Manager	Broker	Mediator
Knowledge of employment rules	Interpersonal skills	Interpersonal skills
Focus on motivating staff	Diplomat	Inspire confidence
Substantive knowledge	"Politics of governing society"	"Politics of governing society"

CAO must be loyal to a council that wants a particular message delivered, but the CAO must do this in such a manner that he or she does not seem disloyal to staff. What does the CAO do when a small, vocal group has convinced council to do something that is not in the best interests of the broader community? The traditional ethical and value frameworks do not help much here. According to the "Statement of Values" of the Canadian Association of Municipal Administrators, "the chief function of a municipal manager at all times is service to his/her employer and the public."[109] But what is the manager to do when there is a conflict between service to the employer and service to the public? If CAOs start to see their role more broadly as community leaders, then conflicts such as these are likely to occur more frequently.

Conclusion

The job of chief administrative officer of a municipality is a difficult one, a truism that no lengthy academic tome is needed to support. Instead, the purpose of this chapter has been to pull the job apart into its various components to obtain a better understanding of *why* it is so difficult. The first reason is that the scope of municipal government activities is very broad, and becoming broader all the time. Second, the CAO's position is unique in that he or she sits at the pinchpoint of the hourglass. The CAO sometimes must look up and exercise a leadership role with regard to a political executive that can be very divided. The CAO then must take sometimes-ambiguous direction from this divided executive and provide leadership to a group of senior administrators responsible for a broad range of services. Equally important, the CAO also must lead out in working with a diverse group of other governments, community groups, and media representatives. This is a precarious position from which to lead, and is complicated by the fact that leading requires a different set of skills for each direction and a different approach to the position.

Dealing with this conundrum requires us to rethink the values that typically have been associated with the position of CAO. The rigid dichotomy of politics and administration was jettisoned long ago, although aspects of it remain. A distinguished former federal public servant once described the role of the Privy Council Office as "nonpartisan, operationally oriented yet politically sensitive."[110] The municipal CAO's position could be characterized in a similar manner. The CAO must steer clear of the "politics of securing office," while taking a leadership role with regard to dealing with operational issues and the "politics of governing society." The contemporary municipal chief administrative office must remain separate from electoral politics, but operationally oriented, politically sensitive, and definitely involved in the politics of governing society.

In the next five chapters, I describe how some highly successful CAOs have balanced these difficult issues.

2 The Leader-Generalist: Michael Fenn

"I was one of the most fortunate mayors in the province of Ontario." Mayors and councillors like to think of themselves as important, strong, decisive people who make a real difference in their communities. In truth, intelligent, savvy politicians know they are only as good as the people around them. So it was not surprising to hear Walter Mulkewich refer to himself as one of the most fortunate mayors in Ontario because, when he became mayor of Burlington in 1991, he inherited Michael Fenn as the city's chief administrative officer (CAO).

Fenn began his professional career in the Ontario Ministry of Municipal Affairs and Housing, and worked his way through progressively more responsible positions there. He also spent some time in the municipal sector as assistant clerk for the County of Peel (just before it became the Regional Municipality of Peel) and deputy-administrator in Kapuskasing, a small northern Ontario municipality. He became a CAO in 1987 in Burlington, where he served until moving to the Regional Municipality of Hamilton-Wentworth in 1995. He served there until 1998, when he became deputy minister of municipal affairs and housing, and later held a number of other senior appointments in the Ontario government.

During his career, Fenn has been recognized as an outstanding leader by virtually every professional association in his field. In 1997, he was awarded the Lieutenant Governor's Medal of Distinction in Public Administration for Ontario by the Institute of Public Administration of Canada. He has received the highest awards for career achievement from two of Ontario's major municipal management organizations: the Association of Municipal Managers, Clerks and Treasurers of Ontario and the Ontario Municipal Administrators' Association. He has also

Table 2.1. Interviews about Michael Fenn

	Burlington, ON	Hamilton-Wentworth, ON	Total
Councillors	4	1	5
Staff	5	2	7
Others	2	2	4
Total	11	5	16

received the Award for Program Excellence in Citizen Involvement from the International City/County Management Association and the "Canada 125 Medal" for community service to Burlington. There seems no doubt that Fenn qualifies as a successful leader.

The raw material for this chapter is drawn from two sources. The first strand of research is a detailed review of the newspaper accounts of municipal politics during Fenn's career. A research assistant and I spent many hours reviewing the *Hamilton Spectator* for the period from 1987 to 1998.[1] The second strand is eighteen interviews. Fenn was interviewed at the beginning and end of this project. Between those bookends, I interviewed sixteen people at 360 degrees around him, as summarized in Table 2.1.

The picture all these people and the newspaper accounts of Fenn's career paints is remarkably consistent. In doing this kind of research, one sometimes experiences difficulty in piecing together the *real* story because of conflicting accounts from different people. This was not the case for Fenn. Everyone told the same, remarkably positive story of Fenn's career and his approach to leadership.

Career Path

Michael Fenn was born in Toronto in 1949, and grew up in the Riverdale area of downtown Toronto. His grandfather was a butcher by trade who made the Fenn name well known in the area. His father worked at a Dickensian-type job (Fenn's description) in the insurance industry, but was very active in his church and in local community organizations. He was an important member of the Riverdale Community Organization, one of the first and most active of community groups that did much to change the style of local politics in Toronto in the 1960s.[2] Fenn describes his mother as not being a feminist, but she was obviously quite progressive and industrious in that she worked full time outside the home as a medical stenographer while raising six children.

Fenn followed in his father's footsteps in terms of community activity. He grew up in a time of Saul Alinsky–type community organizing, so it was not surprising that he was attracted to a political career in municipal government. To further his political aspirations, he pursued the study of local government while doing two bachelor's degrees, one in administration and one in political science, at York University.

Fenn seems to be an example of that rare person who makes a career decision fairly early in life and does not deviate significantly from it, although there were some adjustments along the way. Originally drawn to the political-activist side of local government, his first job after university, in the Sudbury field office of the Ministry of Municipal Affairs and Housing, opened his eyes to the possibilities inherent in a career in municipal administration. He decided that he wanted to be a CAO in a medium-sized municipality. He was aware, however, that the deck was stacked against a young generalist graduate in political science, as CAO jobs seemed to go to older, more experienced people with backgrounds in engineering and finance. He knew he had to manage his career carefully to attain his goal.

He recognized that starting his career in the field office of the Ministry of Municipal Affairs and Housing in Sudbury (and subsequently moving to a similar position in London) was a good opportunity to obtain a broad range of experience quickly. Staff members in these field offices get to see the workings of a number of municipalities, and they frequently are called upon to help clean up problems. Such experience is broader than one could obtain working in a single municipality, and it is closer to the real working environment of municipal government than one would experience in the head office of a ministry.

Fenn speaks positively of a number of the people he worked with in the ministry. He used his time there to learn about municipal government, but he was also conscious of honing more mundane, but important, skills such as writing and communication. He was always open to mentoring opportunities, and he consciously took the opportunity to learn a great deal from his only slightly older colleagues in the ministry.

After spending some time in the two field office postings in Sudbury and London, Fenn's next move was into the municipal sector. His perceptive eye and his travels around the province allowed him to see the value in a position that others would undervalue, and he became deputy-administrator in the small northern mining town of Kapuskasing.

Others might see this as a dead end, but Fenn viewed it as an opportunity to learn the trade from Matt Rukavina, the town's CAO, who was held in high regard across northeastern Ontario.

Fenn's next step was back to the Ministry of Municipal Affairs and Housing, into a new entity called the municipal boundaries unit. This unit was established to assist municipalities in voluntarily restructuring so as to avoid the cost and uncertainty of an annexation proceeding before the Ontario Municipal Board. Fenn and his colleagues were trained as facilitators for the negotiations that would take place among municipalities. This was a further opportunity to travel around the province and learn more about how municipalities operate. It also provided an opportunity to learn a new skill set: facilitator of negotiations.

Along the way, Fenn also advanced his academic background by obtaining a diploma and a master's degree in urban/regional public administration from the University of Western Ontario. He later completed the Program for Senior Executives in State and Local Government at the Kennedy School at Harvard University. Throughout his career, Fenn has combined his communications skills with his academic background to allow him to be a frequent contributor to professional publications and academic journals.[3] This has allowed him to play a greater role in a variety of organizations beyond his current employment.

With this kind of background, Fenn now felt he was ready to move his career exactly where he had hoped for some time. He wanted to become the CAO of a medium-size municipality.

Burlington, ON (1987–95)

Burlington, Ontario, is a medium-sized, middle-class, relatively affluent community. In 1986 (just before Fenn arrived), it had a population of 116,675; in 1996 (shortly after he had moved on), it had risen to 136,978.[4] To describe the city as unremarkable is both praise and social commentary. It is frequently viewed as a bedroom community for families wanting to escape Toronto's high housing prices, although it has a significant number of jobs in the light manufacturing, retail, and services sectors. Indeed, by encouraging new start-ups, Burlington has tried not to become just another bedroom community. As one drives through it, Burlington looks like many new suburban municipalities: neat shopping centres, big box stores, and a few chrome-and-glass high-rise office buildings at the highway interchanges, surrounded by nearly new subdivisions of single-family homes. It also has a core of long-time residents living in some lovely pockets of homes in the centre city and along the shore of Lake Ontario. Geographically, Burlington probably can be seen as in transition from a traditional bedroom community to a so-called edge city.[5]

The politics of the place reflect its calm and unremarkable geography. Councillors are generally full-time professionals and businesspeople and part-time politicians fulfilling their civic duty to give back to their community. The style of debate in the council chamber is polite and respectful, and oriented more to providing the best quality of services than focused on grand political issues. There are disagreements around the council table, of course, but they tend to be more on the merits of the issue at hand and less on the venality of personal politics. The middle-class character of Burlington's residents and the growth of development in the community mean that financial constraints are considerably less pronounced here than in other Ontario municipalities.

This is what Burlington looked like in 1987 when Fenn was hired as its second CAO.[6] If this sounds like a dream situation for a young municipal administrator taking on his first assignment, Michael Fenn would agree. He sees himself as lucky to start his career as a CAO in such an environment. He professes some surprise, however, that he was hired. He describes himself as having been a young, inexperienced kid of thirty-seven coming into a fairly sophisticated, medium-sized city, and feels that some people in Burlington took a real chance on him.

The people doing the hiring remember the situation a bit differently. Some internal candidates for the position were well known, well respected, and quite capable of doing the job, and there was some sentiment that it was time to hire an insider, and some initial trepidation about bringing in a relatively inexperienced person from outside. The recollection of some of those who were involved in the hiring process, however, is that their concerns were quickly eliminated by a candidate who interviewed exceptionally well.

Those on the hiring committee recall meeting a candidate who exuded a certain quiet confidence flowing from both his own personality and the fact that he was exceptionally well prepared for the interview. By all accounts, he made a strong impression. In particular, he seemed to meet the needs of Burlington at that time. He was coming directly from having spent several years in the boundary negotiations unit of the Ministry of Ministry Affairs and Housing, which meshed nicely with Burlington's current involvement in some delicate negotiations to keep out a proposed regional landfill site. More important, however, was the idea that Fenn was a contrast to the previous CAO, whose style was described as high-profile and rather top-down. Fenn was viewed as more low-key and likely to be participatory in his approach. The mayor and council felt that Fenn's style was what Burlington then needed.

One of Fenn's positive recollections of his time in Burlington was working with Mayor Roly Bird, a well-known local insurance agent before he entered municipal politics. Bird was a popular mayor and well-respected community leader. Fenn talks about learning about the importance of integrity from Bird, who had an "absolutely unbendable sense of civic ethics. It won him no friends sometimes, but they always knew where he stood ... He was unassailable ... He had definite views about being more businesslike."

Michael Fenn and Burlington was a match that worked well. Even fifteen years later, Walter Mulkewich said (half-jokingly) that he was angry at his friend Terry Cooke in Hamilton-Wentworth for stealing Fenn away from Burlington.

Hamilton-Wentworth, ON (1995–98)

In 1995 Fenn was appointed CAO of the Regional Municipality of Hamilton-Wentworth. Geographically Burlington and Hamilton are separated by a small, calm body of water referred to alliteratively as either Burlington Bay or Hamilton Harbour, depending on where you stand. In terms of both political culture and general environment, however, the separation between the two is more like several million kilometres. Where politics in Burlington is middle class, polite, respectful, and non-partisan, in Hamilton it is proudly working-class, rough-and-tumble, bare-knuckles, partisan brawling.

Hamilton councillors are generally full-time politicians who frequently have an eye on moving to the next political level as much as serving in their current positions. Therefore, they are as interested in attracting media attention as they are in governing well. All of the ambitious councillors were aware of the presence of cable TV and the impact it could have on their future careers.

The feisty attitude among Hamilton's councillors carried over to their relationship with staff. There is a tradition in Hamilton of councillors managing the details of administration. This frequently manifested itself in their making personal attacks on individual staff members in public meetings. One observer of the local scene suggested that being a city manager is "probably one of the toughest jobs in any city, particularly in the city of Hamilton, where politicians tend to play with live ammunition. And there's always a tendency ... for politicians to try to blame anything that goes wrong on city staff and of course the buck stops with the city manager." In fact, a few years before Fenn came on the scene, the region had hired a CAO from outside the area who came in, looked around, spent just a few weeks in the job, and left. That's how attractive this job was.

Hamilton's culture is exemplified by the story of council's overturning a CAO's recommendation for a senior appointment in order to appoint someone who did not make the short list.[7] Obviously, council has a right to do this, but it is indicative of the relationship between council and senior staff in that city. It also suggests that senior staff appointments are evaluated more on the basis of political criteria than of administrative ability. Since this kind of discussion occurs in closed council sessions, it is impossible to verify the accuracy of this story, but the fact that it is oft-repeated says a great deal about the political culture of the area.

An additional complication at this time flowed from the restructuring issue. The Regional Municipality of Hamilton-Wentworth was an upper-tier municipality consisting of six municipalities, with the City of Hamilton by far the largest. Since the creation of regional governments in the early 1970s to replace the previous county structures, regional governments have always been the governments that Ontarians love to hate. This is compounded in the case of Hamilton-Wentworth by a dynamic of distrust and sometimes open hostility between the raucous, working-class big kid in the centre and the middle-class, genteel suburban municipalities.[8] In 1994 Terry Cooke was elected regional chair (head of council) on a platform of municipal restructuring, which clearly meant amalgamation of all the municipalities in the region into one large local government.[9] This had been discussed for some time, but Cooke made it a campaign issue with the intention of bringing it to a head if he were elected.

Hamilton-Wentworth was everything that Burlington was not. Fenn had quickly established a very good reputation in Burlington and, after eight years there, he seemed to be settled in a growing and dynamic, but also polite and manageable, city. Many wondered why anyone would want to leave this environment for a place with as difficult a reputation for administrators as Hamilton-Wentworth. Fenn always speaks fondly of his time in Burlington, but he also says that, in eight years, he had learned and done about as much as he could do there, and he wanted to move on. He was fully aware of the difficulties awaiting a senior administrator in Hamilton-Wentworth, but he felt up to the challenge. Hamilton-Wentworth, with a population in 1996 of 467,799,[10] is larger than Burlington and it had its own TV station and newspaper. With due respect to Burlington, this was a promotion.

Mac Carson retired from the CAO position shortly after Terry Cooke was elected regional chair. The selection of a new CAO is always a decision of the full council, but Cooke made it clear that he would take a strong role in the selection process because he needed a CAO who would support him in his major plans for the region. Contrary to what some believe, both Cooke and Fenn say they did not know each other prior to the selection process, although they allow that the geographic proximity of their cities meant they probably had said hello and shaken hands at some civic function.

Cooke embarked on the selection process by inquiring informally within the municipal community about who were some of the best and brightest senior municipal managers. His inquiries kept bringing him back to this guy who had made a very positive reputation for himself in a neighbouring municipality. The selection of Fenn seemed to follow a similar pattern to that in Burlington. Fenn, operating in his quiet, but self-confident manner, quickly convinced people that he would be a good choice, even though there were strong internal candidates. In addition to Fenn's general background, Cooke was pleased that he had worked for the Ministry of Municipal Affairs and Housing in the early 1970s, when regional governments were being created. Cooke felt this experience would be helpful in the restructuring he hoped to undertake in Hamilton-Wentworth.

Fenn remained the CAO of Hamilton-Wentworth until 1998, when he moved to the provincial government as deputy minister of municipal affairs and housing. He went on to hold several senior positions with the provincial government, and by all accounts had as illustrious a career at the provincial level as he had had at the municipal level.

The Leadership Role of the CAO

As noted, the successful CAO must lead in three directions: down, out, and up. Before I analyse the manner in which Michael Fenn led in each of these directions, I want to make some general statements about his personality and leadership style that will set the stage for the analysis.

General characteristics

The narrative approach suggests that one can learn a great deal about organizations from films and other forms of popular culture. In film, a typical leader is the John Wayne type – dominant, larger than life, quick to act, leading the troops over the hill in a demonstrative fashion. Less common is the leader like George Bailey in *It's a Wonderful Life* – the quiet, self-effacing type who never drew attention to himself and is always underestimated by those around him, a fact that he frequently uses to his advantage. George was slow to act, preferring to remain aloof while calmly assessing the situation and the people around him. In the final analysis, people like George quietly accomplish a great deal by moving deliberately but forcefully, and by always exercising impeccable judgment.

Michael Fenn is more George Bailey than John Wayne. At about six feet tall and of medium build, he is slightly above average height, but not in a way that dominates a room. In conversation, he would rather sit back and listen to others than control the room himself. But you always have the sense that his reserve is based not on a lack of interest, but on wanting to take the opportunity to learn and assess a situation. Those around him identified certain general traits they see as important to his leadership style.

ENERGY

Fenn exhibits a kind of quiet and reserved energy, as distinct from a more frenetic, out-of-control approach. Some of those interviewed used his e-mail messages at two or three in the morning to raise the question of whether he ever slept. One person suggested that, if he did sleep, he probably had a Blackberry on his chest for easy access.

PEOPLE SKILLS

The literature on leadership is highly varied, but it generally suggests that successful leaders must exhibit at least two orientations – task orientation and people orientation – and some writers add a third related to contextual thinking or vision. Writers generally make it clear that no leader is likely equally proficient in all orientations; most leaders exhibit one or two.

Fenn's view of himself is consistent with those around him: he and they see him as very people oriented, but the often-used phrase "people person" can have a number of connotations. Fenn is clearly not a people person in the mould of the extroverted glad-hander – interviewees used descriptions such as "aloof," "not someone you really warm to," and "not someone you go out and have a beer with." But if "people person" means someone who takes the time to get to know the strengths and weaknesses of the people around him, then Fenn is a people person extraordinaire.

As I discuss later, Fenn clearly has the vision and task orientation a leader needs, but he also recognizes the importance of working through people to realize the vision and tasks expected of a leader.

CONCEPTUAL SKILLS

Besides having people skills, there is no question that Fenn is also a strong conceptual thinker. As I discuss later, no one ever accused him of usurping the political role of council, but he was seen as perceptive about broad political issues, and he had a good sense of where the organization should go. One interviewee described this picturesquely: "He could have confidence in his plan because he had strategically thought it through. He has impeccable political instincts ... because he was fascinated and observed people, and process and patterns. He formed a strategy after he saw all that ... I always imagined Michael having this big map in his head, and he's slowly filling in the bits until the whole map is filled in, then he goes."

HUMOUR

Humour is not a quality one typically associates with someone who is described as aloof or formal, but a number of people referred to Fenn's dry, frequently self-deprecating sense of humour. He always had a sense of the proper time and place, and was never accused of making light of a serious situation, but several people noted that his sense of timing allowed him to use humour to take the edge off a difficult situation.

RESPECT

Respect is a word virtually every interviewee used to describe both Fenn's approach to those around him and the attitudes of his staff and colleagues toward him. One former staff member suggested that Fenn earned the respect of others by respecting others.

INTELLECTUAL CAPACITY

Virtually everyone interviewee commented on Fenn's exceptional intellectual capacity. His scope of knowledge is particularly broad. He was frequently described as a voracious reader, but he reads with a purpose.

His chosen fare is generally the latest books on management and administration in both the public and private sectors, and he always reads with a view to how he might use the information and how it could be applied within his organization. He credits *Reinventing Government*, by David Osborne and Ted Gaebler,[11] with stimulating his interest in performance measurement, which he has employed in his stops at both the municipal and provincial levels.

This intellectual curiosity carries over to his interest in travel, but the travelling, like the reading, has a purpose. He is always on the lookout for the next new thing, and in his travels he tends to seek out the movers and shakers and to learn as much as he can from them.

A RATIONAL STYLE

One would expect someone with a superior intellect to rely on a rational style in discussion and debate, and those around Fenn saw this as one of his hallmarks. In a political forum in which debate sometimes becomes highly emotional and intensely personal, Fenn always took the high road in presenting solid rational arguments. One interviewee tied the intelligence, respect, and rationality together in this manner:

> He's a very intelligent man. He's also I believe got very good political radar. He's got a nice style about him ... If he's got a point to make, he doesn't pound on the table in a real vocal dynamic way ... I think he gets his points across by ... [the fact that] people come to respect him ... [and] his demeanour. He comes across as knowledgeable. He comes across as having done his homework. He comes across as having thought this through, not like very emotional, reactive. I don't know if I'd say he was soft-spoken, but he's not loud and boisterous, so people have to kind of lean in to get the whole [story] ... For whatever reason, people want to hear what he has to say.

Fenn was a CAO when Ontario municipalities were going through difficult times: the so-called Rae Days of the early 1990s and the Common Sense Revolution of the mid- to late 1990s. There is a sense that the municipalities he worked for came through those times in better shape than did other municipalities. Interviewees attributed this to the fact that, while other municipal officials took emotional positions and protested in the streets, Fenn went to Queen's Park armed with data and rational arguments about how his municipality should be treated. I discuss this approach in more detail later.

MODESTY

Many people with high intellectual capacity are not shy about making others aware of their prowess – we have all met such people "entertaining" others at gatherings of various kinds. Fenn's intellectual capacity, however, is matched by a certain level of modesty. He is sufficiently confident of his abilities that he does not need to flaunt them.

One interviewee explained why Fenn had little difficulty establishing himself as the new CAO in Burlington even though he was fairly young and in his first CAO position: "He came in and he wasn't brash. There was no brashness about him, no ego whatsoever, it just doesn't exist with that man. And yet the respect for him is so high which to me tells you a little tale about human nature … He came and I don't think he had any trouble at all because of this personality that he had and the way he approached things and people."

CONSCIENTIOUS AND CAREFUL

Many bright people consider themselves to be visionaries, and do not have time for ordinary day-to-day activities. Fenn was consistently described as being incredibly conscientious and careful in how he conducted himself and how he communicated with others.

In reflecting on his people skills and his communication abilities, one person said: "He led by example over and over and over again. Everything he did was absolutely top drawer – whether it was a speech, whether it was him writing a report, or a … memo. We were always impressed about how the man could express himself."

COMMUNICATION SKILLS

You would expect someone with good people skills and a superior intellect to be a good communicator, and Fenn fits that bill. He credits his communication skills to his time as a member of the debating team in high school, which he feels taught him to understand and frame issues for discussion. He also learned a significant amount about communication during his time as a facilitator for boundary negotiations, which required him to listen carefully to everyone and ensure that everyone understood everyone else's position. This is a skill that he has carried with him throughout his career.

Interviewees also saw him as an excellent writer, and commented how his writing was always clear and concise and took into account the audience's perspective. Without being patronizing, he could write so as to be understood by an audience that was not necessarily highly conversant with municipal jargon or practices.

Another aspect that came across in the interviews was Fenn's willingness to spend a great deal of time on the communications process. He relied to a significant extent on time-consuming one-on-one communication, which allowed him to build rapport with people and to obtain a clear idea of what the other person *really* wanted. This is a skill of an experienced facilitator.

Fenn describes how he tried to spend time with most councillors, particularly the mayor and committee chairs. He took the time to understand that each councillor had a unique set of interests, and in his discussions he tried to determine the three or four things that really interested the person or that the person wanted to accomplish during his term on council. He also tried to determine the three or four things that put "raspberry seeds under the councillor's dentures." This allowed him to frame issues in ways that attracted councillors, or at least minimized their irritation. This is a perfect example of his emotional intelligence, discussed earlier.

"COOL AS A CUCUMBER"

One interviewee described Fenn as "cool as a cucumber," a sentiment many others echoed. Being a CAO is a stressful job. A good one leads in three directions, but the inverse is that the CAO is also a target from three directions. No one recalls Fenn's ever losing his temper or appearing anything other than calm and in control of a situation, regardless of the temper of those around him. This instilled a great deal of confidence in him, and it also considerably enhanced his reputation for rationality. Even as those around him engaged in emotional personal invective, he would quietly and calmly present the facts. At the end of the day, it is clear which style evokes the greater level of confidence.

INTEGRITY

A characteristic that ties all of the other attributes together is absolute integrity, another of Fenn's traits to which virtually every interviewee referred. For example, "[h]e was the consummate city manager ... because he lived and worked his principles all the time ... He didn't let up on his principles. There was never any thought that Michael Fenn would do anything other than what was totally the right thing to do."

These are the broad, basic skills that Fenn used in his leadership as a CAO, and which he applied in a variety of different ways, depending on whether he was leading down, up, or out.

Leading down

Fenn did not climb the municipal ladder in the conventional fashion of moving through the hierarchy of a line department. He was by both training and temperament a generalist who developed a broad understanding of municipal government, but he readily admits that he does not have a good understanding of the nuts-and-bolts of operations in municipal departments. He is not defensive about it – in fact, he sees it as almost a benefit because it prevents him from interfering in activities better left to the experts. His approach is that the job of a senior manager is to work through other people. His major goal was to ensure that he surrounded himself with the right people so that he did not need to concern himself much with the details.

When he came to Burlington, there was a sense that he deliberately sat back and watched the people who worked there and the city's organization for about a year. Then, "his alarm went off at the end of his first year and he started to put his own focus on the organization." Fenn laughs when asked about this clever strategy on his part. Looking back he admits that this "clever strategy" was born of necessity: he was simply unsure of what he should do, but felt that his best course of action was to watch others and learn from them.

The lesson he took from this is that it is dangerous to move too quickly and act too decisively until you have taken the time to assess the entirety of the organization. A leader must be aware of both the formal and informal organization. In Fenn's picturesque language, "if you haven't grown up with the organization, you'll get clotheslined on that informal stuff." However, he was not paralysed. Over time, he initiated some fairly major changes, which I discuss later. As a reminder that leaders must always be aware of the specific environment in which they are working, interviewees indicated that Fenn did not engage in a wait-and-see approach when he went to Hamilton-Wentworth; he simply did not have that luxury in the difficult environment there.

His management style has two complementary elements: be sure that the right person is in the right place, then "don't dig in the weeds," as one of his former subordinates described it. Fenn is conscious of the need to surround himself with good people. A number of interviewees used expressions such as "he doesn't suffer fools gladly." He is a competent person with high energy and a strong work ethic, and he expects the same of others. He has said himself that he is not a fan of reclamation projects: if a relationship is not working, it is better for both the individual and the organization to part company as soon as possible. He is not shy about dealing with difficult personnel issues, and several people commented how he acted quickly and did not allow difficult issues to fester. One person said "he didn't like people gaming the system."

Fenn's emphasis on people is clear when he describes how he handled a major reorganization in Burlington. The classic prescription for organization design is to define structures based on purpose, process, place, or clientele. As an avid student of the management literature, he is certainly aware of this stricture, but his approach in this case was to begin by selecting the three people he wanted closest to him on his management team, then to group duties around these three. This produced what some people saw as an unconventional grouping of responsibilities, but Fenn's view is that good people can manage whatever package of responsibilities is given to them.

Fenn made it clear to subordinates that he had a great deal of trust in them and in their ability to do their job well, and that he would not micromanage them as long as they performed well. Subordinates commented on the impact this management style had on them. For example, "[h]e was the kind of person you wanted to please so you went out of your way to help him accomplish his goals. And in doing so he recognized your effort and appreciated the efforts that everyone was making."

Some supervisors use a fear of verbal explosions or discipline to motivate people. In Fenn's case, the motivation subordinates described was both more subtle and more effective. "You didn't want to let him down … [there was a sense that] I've been given this faith and trust and I don't want to squander it." Because Fenn bestowed so much trust on subordinates, there was a feeling that failure on their part would be "letting Michael down," and because of the respect that everyone had for him, "letting Michael down" was feared more than any of the overt reprisals that more blustery managers might employ.

This avoidance of an intrusive style of management should not be equated, however, with the laissez-faire leadership style that is frequently criticized as leading to anarchy. His subordinates always felt that Fenn was there for support when he was needed. One manager described a series of decisions to initiate an innovative project involving locating space outside city hall so that his unit could co-locate with related federal and provincial agencies. The manager indicated that this was a complex, somewhat politically difficult manoeuvre, which could not have happened without the support of the CAO, and Fenn was very supportive throughout the process.

Subordinates also understood that their work was being monitored in a variety of ways: "He held you accountable. It was arm's length, but you had to be accountable." Although Fenn did not micromanage, managers did report being asked insightful and analytical questions about their activities. Fenn also cultivated contacts in the community, which served as another monitoring mechanism for service delivery. While rubbing shoulders with private sector managers, Fenn learned that they focused much more on staying close to their customers and on assessing customer satisfaction, whereas public sector managers focused on process accountability or top-down types of performance measurement. He found that focusing on customer satisfaction was a way of understanding the work of subordinates, but it could be used to manage his relationship with council as well:

> If you focus effectively on the customer and really understand what the customer's view is, that will trump professional opinion, it will trump political motivation, and all these kinds of things. If you can demonstrate to that audience that the end user wants this, it knocks down a lot of dominos. I've used that as a touchstone ever since. It works religiously. So you just go over the head of the politicians to the consumer ... If the politicians complain about something on the land use side, and a bunch of people from the community come in and say, "we like this proposal," then the temperature in the room goes down and everything is fine.

Subordinates knew that he was discussing the quality of service delivery with local people. Of course, this is the ultimate test of the quality of service delivery. Subordinates were pleased to avoid the excesses of intrusive management, but they also understood that this was not a laissez- faire environment; Fenn was well aware of what was going in their units.

Although Fenn never used the word "empowerment" in our interviews, it was clear that his actions involved empowering staff. As one noted, "[h]e was really interactive with the staff ... He was very respectful of other people's opinions. He encouraged other people's opinions. He was not afraid to hear from all sides, and figure it all out. So as a second-tier management position at that time, I felt like I was in an environment where I could say something." When Fenn came to Hamilton-Wentworth, he encouraged department heads to make their own case before council. Previously, virtually all information had flowed through the CAO. Department heads welcomed this change because they felt it indicated that he had confidence in them and that it empowered them.

Another important aspect of leading down is the ability to deliver significant benefits to staff. During Fenn's tenure in Burlington, the Rae government at Queen's Park imposed a number of financial stringency measures to deal with the province's serious financial issues. One of the highest-profile manifestations of this was the imposition on public sector organizations of "Rae days": unpaid leave days for employees to reduce public expenditures. In practice, since the workload remained the same (or increased), many people found themselves voluntarily working the same number of days, but not being paid for them. This obviously was not a popular measure. Fenn did not automatically accept the idea of Rae days for Burlington. He was in a strategic position because he led the Association of Municipalities of Ontario team that negotiated the implementation of various financial stringency measures with the provincial government. He was in this position because he was a highly respected municipal administrator and because he was seen as someone who knew his way around Queen's Park. Some people said that he was the first administrator from Burlington to make a mark at Queen's Park in this way.

Fenn recognized that, although municipalities were not required to impose Rae days, they still had to find a certain amount of savings, and for most places Rae days were the easiest route. He was able to use payroll-reducing productivity improvements, however, along with resignations and retirements, to deliver the required savings without having to impose Rae days. Fenn modestly dismisses this as "luck," but one wonders how many administrators would have taken the initiative to package this "luck" with some hard work to deliver a significant benefit to staff. Even people who were in the lower echelons of the organization when this occurred remember Fenn as the hero who helped Burlington avoid Rae days.

There is no question that Fenn was well respected by his staff. He saved them from the financial cutbacks of Rae days, he had the delicate touch to avoid micromanaging while still monitoring their performance in reasonable ways, and he handled a major reorganization in a manner that won him a great deal of praise.

Leading up

Leading down can be difficult, but a manager at the top of the hierarchy always has ultimate authority over those lower down. Dealing with one's political masters is considerably more complicated. Council obviously sets policy and makes important decisions affecting the municipality, but council is composed of full-time and part-time politicians whose contributions tap into the feelings of the community. The CAO is the full-time professional expert whose contribution involves employing the superior substantive knowledge that the CAO and staff have. This creates a particular dynamic between councillors and staff. Councillors see themselves as representatives of the interests of residents and protectors of the public purse, while they sometimes see staff as protective of the specific interests of their departments and a little too anxious to spend money to further those interests. Ideally, a healthy tension will result from this interaction. Sometimes councillors will bring new ideas to the table and staff will raise concerns about their viability, and sometimes positions are reversed. The point is that councillors should be a bit sceptical of staff's ideas and expect staff to prove the worth of these ideas.

One major quality that councillors respected in Fenn was his lack of political bias. He was viewed not as political but as an expert on administration and government, and on how to implement programs. Because he dealt with all councillors in the same way, and because he emphasized full and open communication, there was never a sense that he was trying to manipulate a political agenda. Instead, he drew on his intellect to ensure that his recommendations were firmly grounded in rationality. As one councillor said, "[y]ou would always get the straight advice from him – not tinged. He would give you his best advice and more often than not he would be right." Interviewees described Fenn as being protective of the interests of staff, and as making it clear that the role of staff was administrative, not political, but in a way that separated himself – and, by extension, staff – from the political cut and thrust. This was particularly significant in Hamilton-Wentworth, where there was a tradition of drawing staff into political conflicts.

In both cities, Fenn cultivated relationships with the mayor and every councillor that were firmly grounded in the idea that he and the staff worked for the mayor and all councillors collectively, not for the mayor alone or for any individual councillor. This relationship was built on respect and communication, not subservience or political exigencies. As is expected of a good communicator, however, he took time to learn the point of view of each individual councillor so that he was speaking from a position of knowledge: "Michael had a very respectful interchange with councillors. Michael paid attention to sensitivities within council and what was happening with certain councillors and their wards and the issues that were going on. He didn't cater to it, but he was very smart about it ... He didn't buddy up with people, [but he did understand what was happening in individual wards]." Fenn's style in dealing with council was to instil a sense of confidence in councillors that he and other staff members were knowledgeable about a particular area or were handling a situation appropriately. He succeeded not only because of his intelligence, but also because he was always well-prepared for council meetings. Interviewees spoke of him as having a sixth sense about what the controversial issues would be and being prepared for them.

It is necessary here to make a distinction between understanding the political, in order to optimize one's impact, and acting in a political manner. Fenn had a reputation of always making recommendations based on sound professional administrative principles, and of understanding not just what he was communicating to council, but also what impact his communications would have on the recipients. Because he knew what each councillor wanted to accomplish and what their irritants were, he knew how each would react to his recommendations. The lesson is: always ground your advice in the rational, but always understand and anticipate the political impact of that advice.

Fenn was conscious, however, of the need for balance in this relationship. A CAO needs to know the temperature of council, but should avoid becoming too closely allied with it. As Fenn explains,

I didn't resort to [councillors] regularly. I think they are uneasy about being lobbied or being finessed or being schmoozed. A lot of the staff that I've noticed will try to ingratiate themselves and that doesn't generally work. Politicians ... by their nature, they're not fundamentally loyal to staff; [politicians] don't see [staff] as their fundamental partners in the transaction ... so [when] things get tough they're not going to be necessarily with you. So I have always maintained a certain amount of professional detachment, proper kind of relationship, and they seem to prefer that. My experience was they liked cool detachment; they liked ... proper relations as opposed to warm or friendly relations because it made it awkward for them if they went against your point of view. Politicians are real "people people." They think that if I don't follow your recommendations, you're going to think less of me where they never had that view about me. They knew I was a hired gun.

The CAO must ensure that council has all the information it needs to make its decision. This can involve a certain amount of agenda setting. Council always makes the final decision, but the CAO can introduce new concepts and ideas so that council views an issue in a certain way. The CAO can also use the strategic nature of the position to mediate potential disagreements among councillors.

Fenn felt that Burlington would benefit from having a strategic plan, and he knew certain councillors also held this view to varying degrees. There had been two previous, unsuccessful attempts to develop such a plan, however, so there was clearly some division of opinion. Fenn mustered rational arguments in favour of a strategic plan, and visited every councillor to determine their position and what reservations they might have. This is the style of operation that Fenn learned while facilitating boundary negotiations. He was then able to introduce the concept of the strategic plan in such a manner that he built on the strengths of those who were in favour while dealing with the criticisms of those who had reservations. The result was the development of a strategic plan for the city – one of the first in the country.[12] This is an excellent example of what is involved in leading up. Fenn did not take complete charge of the situation; that would have been inappropriate. Instead, he worked with each individual councillor to determine the best way to achieve consensus so that council would arrive at the decision it collectively wanted.

Another quality that served Fenn well was his "cool as a cucumber" demeanour. Tensions can run high at council meetings. The role of staff in those situations is to provide dispassionate expert advice and let the politicians fight over political issues. Sometimes, however, there can be spillover, with councillors attacking staff or staff reports and even accusing staff of being politically motivated. This seems not to have happened often on Fenn's watch. He presented his cases in a calm, rational manner, and councillors respected that.

It would be interesting to be able to measure the amount of time an administrator spends on leading in each of the three separate directions. This would provide a proxy measure of how much importance an administrator attaches to each direction. Of course, this would be virtually impossible because managers do not think this way. CAOs are probably most comfortable, however, leading down. After all, being good at leading down is probably how most of them got where they are. CAOs can perceive that many of their problems come from issues within the organization, and there are precise rules and procedures that can be used to lead down, unlike the messy environment encountered when leading up.

My sense is that Fenn spent more time leading up than do most of his counterparts. Establishing the freedom to do this is likely one reason he chose to deal with the leading-down part of his job in the arm's-length manner that he did. One simple rule is that, if you are going to do anything properly, you must be willing to spend the appropriate amount of time doing it. Fenn seems to have had his priorities set clearly in that he spent more time dealing with council (a responsibility that he could not delegate), and less time managing the organization (a responsibility that he could delegate).

CAOs frequently are cautioned that they should not get too far out in front of their councils. Councillors (and others) frequently praised Fenn because he always seemed to be out in front of issues – to be able to anticipate what the next big issue would be before it became a full-blown concern. Several people commented on the manner in which he handled strategic planning and program budgeting in Burlington, and how he was out in front of most councillors in these areas. How did he do this and not just survive, but win praise for doing it?

The problem does not seem to be getting in front of your council, but what you do when you get there. It seems that some CAOs get in front of their councillors and then turn around and lecture them about how foolish and backward they are. Fenn moved his council forward by respectfully communicating to councillors that the interests of the municipality would be better served and they could do their jobs better as councillors if they had a strategic plan and a program budget. It was not about displaying how much more intelligent he was than they were; it was a matter of councillors, the CAO, and staff working together to create a better municipality. When the issue was framed in this way, councillors never seemed to resent the fact that Fenn was out in front on an issue.

Fenn did an excellent job of leading his councils in a completely appropriate manner. He expended a great deal of effort to get to know the hot and cold buttons of the mayor and each councillor. He used this knowledge to help his council move in a direction they wanted to go, and cleared obstacles along the road.

Leading out

Fenn claims that he did not emphasize the leading-out aspects of his position. As discussed earlier, he was not reticent about expecting his staff to take a strong and visible role, and this is one of the areas where he relied on his staff to take a lead. Some interviewees, however, remembered his taking a leading role in select areas.

Many of the qualities discussed above in conjunction with leading down or leading up carry over in dealing with community stakeholders. Fenn's communications skills were the basis of his ability to lead out. One interviewee emphasized that, even when you were not successful in your dealings with him, he still had a winning way about him: "He never made you feel that [you had lost] ... You saw the other side. He could make you understand and explain it to you in a laymen's language ... Sometimes that doesn't come across. Sometimes there are what I would call statements they make and they're the same every time for everything, and they mean nothing. It's gobbledegook, but not Michael ... You understood Michael ... and in very simple terms." He was seen as open and willing to meet with anyone, and he had a reputation of behaving in a fair and even-handed manner. "He talked to everybody just the same ... Everybody was treated the same; there were no favourites. There were no leanings. You couldn't pick a leaning with him ... His thoughts were very close to his chest."

Stakeholders talked about his communication skills and the impact of his personality. One interviewee described how he dealt with a room full of concerned stakeholders: "He was very calming. He could calm a room by walking into it. He has a knack. I don't know just what it is. You can't get angry with him ... He has a knack of keeping people calm." He dealt with stakeholders the same way he dealt with others, in that he always focused on reasoned, rational arguments.

When the Harris government implemented local services realignment – which municipalities referred to as "downloading" – and current value assessment at the same time, it was clear that there would be a significant impact on the business community in Hamilton-Wentworth, which already saw itself as more heavily taxed than in other cities. Fenn took the initiative to approach the Chamber of Commerce about this impending issue. The chamber then established a task force to work with the region's finance staff on the implementation of these initiatives. One consequence of this approach was that, within the next year or two, as some elements of the business community reacted negatively to the tax changes, the chamber actually defended the region's actions because, of course, it had had a role in crafting them. It makes the encouragement of citizen engagement look beneficial not just in its own right, but also as a brilliant tactical move to blunt a group that can be strongly opposed to some civic initiatives, especially with regard to taxation. In the words of one member of a community group, "[i]t demonstrated his ability to get things done by and through people, and his willing[ness] to listen collaboratively to outside people ... Obviously it's part of his job to implement the strategic direction of elected council, but he was able to do so in such a way as to ensure that the views of informed stakeholders were taken into account ... I genuinely felt that we were a partner to the exercise."

Fenn, in short, was as good at leading out as he was at leading up and leading down. And he used many of the same techniques to do so. He followed the rational road, and emphasized his communication skills. He instilled a high level of trust in everyone he dealt with, which cemented his ability to lead out.

Conclusion: Putting It All Together

In this chapter, I have described and analysed Michael Fenn's personal background and his approach to leadership as a CAO. What are some of the lessons that others wanting to follow in his footsteps might draw from this case study?

MANAGE YOUR CAREER

Most people do not have complete control over their career opportunities. You have to earn an income, so you take the best job available. It is beneficial, however, to have a particular goal in mind and to see jobs as stepping stones to the ultimate goal. This might involve taking opportunities that others eschew, such as deputy administrator in a small northern community.

USE MENTORS

It is important to identify and use mentors along the way to develop particular skills and to develop contacts. The importance of mentoring was illustrated in Fenn's relationship with people in the Ministry of Municipal Affairs and Housing and his work with Matt Rukavina in Kapuskasing. One way to choose a mentor is to identify someone who is currently where you would like to be in five or ten years, and model yourself after that person. Some people might have specific skills or knowledge that will be useful to you even if they are not in a position to which you aspire; in fact, most people you work with are likely to have something to teach you.

THINK OUTSIDE THE BOX

Think in an innovative way is trite and simplistic advice; it is also advice that is difficult to follow. Everybody pays lip service to "thinking outside the box," but how do you actually do it? In Fenn's case, he is a voracious reader and an avid traveller, but he has a particular motive in mind for both of these activities, which some would describe as leisure. He is always looking for new ideas in his readings and travels that he can apply in his work environment.

THERE'S LIFE OUTSIDE YOUR MUNICIPALITY

A great deal of what Fenn was able to accomplish came as a result of knowledge he obtained and contacts he made from involving himself outside his municipality. He had worked for the provincial government in different positions before entering the municipal field. This put him in a good position to be the chief negotiator for the Association of Municipalities of Ontario during the financially turbulent Rae years, which, in turn, made him recognize that he could take certain actions in Burlington to cushion the effects of those years. This experience also allowed him to move to the "Who Does What" task force in the Harris years, which also had ramifications for Hamilton-Wentworth. Getting involved in activities outside your own municipality increases both your points of contact and the number of people you know. This might not always pay off in immediate benefits, but it does put you in a significant strategic position as the future unfolds.

Fenn also used his communication skills to make a mark outside his community. He wrote articles in a number of professional and academic venues. He feels this helped to organize his thinking about management issues and political processes, and enhanced and spread a positive impression of the organizations with which he was associated. It also raised his profile among his peers.

It is also important to maintain a work-life balance. People who worked with Fenn saw him as highly work focused, sending e-mail at all hours of the day and night. In fact, he is close to and involved in his family, and although he does not talk about it much, he is an accomplished artist who takes pride in his painting skills.

DEVELOP PARTICULAR SKILLS

Fenn was hired in Burlington in part because the city needed someone with negotiating skills, and in Hamilton-Wentworth because he had been involved in government restructuring. This can be seen as the luck of being in the right place at the right time. Of course, there are all sorts of expressions about people who work hard or are well prepared being luckier than others. The point is to approach every new job as an opportunity to develop a new skill that could be useful in a later position.

DEVELOP TRANSFERABLE SKILLS

Of course, not all skills are equal; some possess greater transferability than others, although it might take some perception to see that. In Fenn's case, the skill of being a boundary negotiator has a fairly limited transferability, but he used his time as a boundary negotiator to develop his communication and facilitation skills – skills that are highly transferable. The lesson here is to recognize that some skills are highly transferable and to take advantage of opportunities to hone those skills.

LEADERS COME IN MANY DIFFERENT TYPES

When most people hear the word "leader," they probably think of a John Wayne–type leading troops into battle. John Wayne would have been a lousy CAO. The people interviewed for this book wanted a leader who was modest, "cool as a cucumber," rational, respectful, and possessed of many other traits not always associated with the stereotypical over-the-top kind of leader.

COMMUNICATION IS KEY

One of the strongest messages coming from virtually every interviewee was that Fenn's communication skills were instrumental in everything else he did. In his case, communication took on several dimensions. To communicate well, you must be able to listen well. You must know what sorts of things are important to the people around you, and what sorts of things will push their buttons, in both a positive and negative sense.

Many interviewees described Fenn as an exceptionally good writer. What they meant by this is that he writes in a clear fashion, with particular emphasis on a style and language that his audience would find appealing and understandable. The lesson here is to know your audience and be aware of their level of knowledge of the topic about which you are writing. Moreover, he excelled at explaining complex technical issues in a readily understandable way.

He also relied a great deal on one-on-one, face-to-face communication. We all know people whose style is to sit in their office and send lengthy e-mail messages to long distribution lists, and say, "there, I've communicated." On important issues, Fenn's style was to meet with everyone (both inside and outside the organization) who would play a key role in the decision to be made. Furthermore, by all accounts, he talked to people not to sell his ideas, although in a round-about way he might have had that in mind, but to discover their opinions, what they liked and did not like about a proposal. In this way, he learned what sorts of ideas would find acceptance and what ideas might have to be revised first. This is a classic illustration of emotional intelligence at work. He took the time to get to know each councillor, and he managed that relationship carefully. This took an incredible amount of time – probably more time than most administrators are willing to invest – but virtually all interviewees saw this as an important part of Fenn's success.

THE TRADITIONAL VIRTUES OF RESPECT, HUMILITY, AND INTEGRITY ARE STILL IMPORTANT

At some point in virtually every interview, the words "humility," "respect," and "integrity" were mentioned, frequently in conjunction with one another. Fenn rarely draws attention to himself; instead, he is quite willing to share or deflect the credit for accomplishments to others. This could be one reason he is greatly respected as a leader. Several people suggested, however, that he receives so much respect because he treats everyone else with respect. Interviewees also commented how he exuded integrity himself, and did not tolerate lapses in integrity in others.

Overall Assessment

Effective leaders play on their strengths and understand their weaknesses. Michael Fenn was a generalist with an academic background in administration and political science and work experience in the Ontario Ministry of Municipal Affairs and Housing when he took on his

> A municipal CAO who is a good leader has the ability to move the municipality forward by interacting in a mutually influential way with and motivating council, external stakeholders, and organizational subordinates.

first CAO position. He recognized the limitations of his background and adopted a low-key and learning approach in the first year in his new position. He then used his emotional intelligence to develop a team around him that could take charge of managing the municipality. With the management team in place, he put a great deal of effort into leading up. He worked with councillors, particularly in Burlington, to develop changes such as strategic planning and program budgeting that moved the municipality forward and had a real impact on its organizational culture. He expected his management team to handle most of the leading out, but he chose his spots, made a favourable impression, and had successes in leading out. Fenn's career shows what a team-oriented generalist with excellent people and communication skills can accomplish.

3 The Task-oriented Leader: Mike Garrett

[I]t was my watch, I'm the accountable party ... I was the Captain of the ship, and if something went wrong with that ship, I take full responsibility for that.
　– Mike Garrett, testimony before the Toronto Computer Leasing Inquiry

In an era when obfuscation has become a form of high art, Mike Garrett stood in the witness box of the Toronto Computer Leasing Inquiry (the so-called MFP scandal), one of the largest in the City of Toronto's history, and spoke a few clear words of simple truth. Even a decade later, virtually everyone who comments on Garrett's approach to leadership remembers those words. Others who testified before the inquiry stooped to implicating their grandmother in their wrongdoing or conveniently forgot important facts, but Garrett did what a leader does: he accepted responsibility for what happened on his watch. The MFP scandal tarnished or destroyed the careers of many people; Garrett was one of the few whose reputation actually was enhanced by the inquiry.

Mike Garrett served as chief administrative officer in three of the largest municipalities in the country over an eighteen-year period from 1989 to 2007. He had interacted extensively with municipalities when he worked for conservation authorities, but his first municipal appointment was as CAO of the Region of Peel. In 1989 Peel Region encompassed the urbanized but still rapidly growing city of Mississauga and the somewhat rural but urbanizing municipalities of Brampton and Caledon. In 1997 he won the coveted position of first CAO of the newly amalgamated City of Toronto, by far the largest city in the country. He held that position through the tumultuous amalgamation process until 2001. In 2002 he became CAO of the Region of York, extending from the

Table 3.1. Interviews about Mike Garrett

	Peel Region, ON	City of Toronto	York Region, ON	Total
Politicians	2	1	1	4
Staff	2	3	7	12
Total	4	4	8	16

northern boundary of Toronto to Lake Simcoe. When he arrived York Region's population was just under a million, but the region was one of the fastest-growing in the country, absorbing the spillover from a virtually built-out Toronto.

As CAO of two rapidly growing regions, Garrett oversaw some of the largest municipal infrastructure projects in the country. During his time there, York Region was recognized as one of the top one hundred employers in Canada.[1] The budgeting system developed while he was at Peel Region won an award for excellence from the Government Finance Officers Association. He was a leader in developing performance measurement systems in the municipal sector. This led him to be the prime mover in the establishment of the Ontario Municipal Benchmarking Initiative. He served as chair of the CAOs group of MARCO (Mayors and Regional Chairs of Ontario). He also served on a number of provincial-municipal committees. It is not surprising that virtually everyone who worked with him saw him as a successful leader.

The raw material for this chapter was drawn from two sources. The first strand of research was a detailed review of various background sources of information. This involved looking at the newspapers of record in the three places Garrett worked during his tenure as well as wide-ranging Internet searches. The second strand was eighteen personal interviews. Garrett was interviewed at the beginning and end of this project. Between those bookends, sixteen people at 360 degrees around him were interviewed (see Table 3.1).

Career Path

Mike Garrett was born and raised in Ottawa. His mother was a university graduate and a teacher, but she became a stay-at-home mom while raising a family. His father was not as well educated, and he watched better-educated people pass by him in the bank where he worked. His parents believed their children should have long-term goals and a purpose in life, and this meant a solid university education.

One of Garrett's first goals was met by his experience as a teenager working summers on his uncle's farm outside Ottawa. He enjoyed it, and set his sights on becoming a farmer. Like any Ontario youth with that ambition, he enrolled at the University of Guelph to learn the academic aspects of agriculture. In his first year there, however, he learned a valuable practical lesson about farming from some of his fellow students who were raised on farms: "If I wasn't going to inherit a farm, I probably wasn't going to be a farmer. There was a whole other aspect of farming I hadn't appreciated as a city kid."

This reality caused him to rethink his interest in pursuing agriculture as a career, but he wanted to stay at Guelph because he enjoyed the atmosphere there – he still speaks highly of the university. He saw its strengths at the time as being in biology-related sciences and agricultural engineering. Of the two, he felt his personality was more suited to engineering, so he embarked on the introductory program, which included a survey of the various fields of engineering. His interest was captured by professors who taught water resources, and this led him to a lifelong interest in that field. After completing his BSc in Engineering at Guelph, he moved directly to Queen's University in Kingston, Ontario, to take an MSc in coastal engineering, while spending two summers working shoreline surveys on the Great Lakes for the federal Department of Public Works.

Immediately after completing his second degree, he found his first professional job as a project engineer on the Toronto Waterfront Project. The project had been assigned to the Metropolitan Toronto and Region Conservation Authority (MTRCA) because it was an existing legislated vehicle that allowed municipal and provincial cost sharing. Conservation authorities are unique Ontario organizations created in the 1940s to manage watersheds. They are ambivalent organizations in that they were created by provincial legislation, but they operate at the local level in close connection with municipal governments. As well, the boundaries of conservation authorities follow the watersheds of major watercourses, which, of course, do not respect municipal boundaries. The MTRCA covered the area of the former Metro Toronto, but extended beyond into adjacent Peel, York, and Durham regions.

Garrett was a project engineer for the Lake Ontario waterfront from Clarkson on the west to Oshawa on the east, excluding the port of Toronto. Even though he did not have his future career mapped out at this point, this position was an excellent training ground for where his career ultimately took him. As a project engineer, he was responsible for arranging for the design and construction of the waterfront park system (Humber Bay, Ashbridges Bay, and Bluffers Park), but he was also responsible for the much more delicate work of negotiating with the various municipalities to win acceptance for the master plans and raising the money to pay for them. As he tells it, conservation authorities "don't have any taxing power, so you have to persuade people that your project's a good one. Typically you have to raise the money, you have to get the plans approved, then you have to implement them." As a by-product of this, he met a number of influential municipal politicians and staff in many of the municipalities in the Greater Toronto area.

After ten years in this position, he was seconded to another that would draw on both his engineering and his leadership skills. The South Nation River Basin, in eastern Ontario, was suffering from economic development problems grounded to some extent in water resource management issues. Again, Garrett's real work was managing a difficult and extensive public consultation process.

His time in the South Nation River Basin was difficult because his family had stayed in Toronto while he commuted there weekly. So, after two years, he was ready to take a more settled position with the provincial Ministry of Natural Resources in Toronto. He spent the years 1982 to 1989 climbing the hierarchy of the ministry, starting as director of water and conservation authorities, moving through executive director of lands and waters, then becoming an assistant deputy minister (ADM) in 1988.

A lasting mindset that he developed while he was in the provincial government was a focus on long-term strategic thinking. He was instrumental in developing two of the first provincial policies under the planning act: the floodplains policy, including stormwater management, and the aggregates policy. The floodplains policy, in particular, was close to his interest in water, and he still takes a great deal of pride in the way in which Ontario residents are better protected from flooding than residents of other jurisdictions. It was an important part of his professional formation that he brought this long-term strategic mindset into a municipal environment that is more inclined to focus on short-term service delivery issues.

As a relatively young ADM, he was on track to become a deputy minister. As he describes it, however, "I began to find that what turns me on was that I like challenge and change – maybe to a fault." He was also starting to chafe under the weight of the bureaucratic confines of Queen's Park. He wanted to return to where the action was, as he had been with the conservation authorities, and was quite interested when a headhunter looking to fill the position of CAO in the Region of Peel came calling.

Region of Peel, ON (1989–97)

When Mike Garrett arrived in 1989, the Region of Peel, situated immediately west of what was then called Metropolitan Toronto, was growing quickly – indeed, from 732,798 in 1991 (shortly after Garrett arrived), the population grew to 852,526[2] in 1996 (shortly before he left). The region had long been a bedroom community for Toronto, but it was rapidly becoming an edge city[3] with its own retail and commercial base. The region, created in 1974 as an upper-tier municipality encompassing Mississauga, Brampton, and Caledon, was confronting many of the issues that typically face high-growth communities, although the fact that almost all the development was greenfield eliminated much of the tension sometimes encountered in these situations.[4]

Importing a new CAO with no direct municipal experience might have seemed a risk for Peel. In fact, it was a carefully considered decision. Although Garrett had never worked directly for a municipality before, his extensive experience with two conservation authorities had given him considerable insight into the operation of the municipal sector. He had also favourably impressed some Peel councillors when he was working on the Toronto Waterfront Project.

Another important consideration in hiring Garrett was that the region wanted to build a stronger relationship with the provincial government. Some councillors felt that the provincial government looked on Peel as a wealthy, rapidly growing metropolis that did not need much provincial assistance. In truth, Peel's rapid growth was fuelled in part by immigration, which brought some financial and other issues with it. Peel was happy to get a new CAO who knew his way around Queen's Park.

From the perspective of a new CAO coming in, some aspects of managing a region like Peel were favourable, but there were bumps in the road. The region was governed by a twenty-two-person council consisting of a regional chair (selected by the councillors) and twenty-one indirectly elected councillors. For everyone except the chair, this was a part-time job. In fact, for some, it was an adjunct to their part-time job as a local councillor. This type of arrangement does not make for a particularly engaged or activist council. A straw was stirring the drink, however, in this case.

Regional governments are relatively new in Ontario, and they tend to draw a certain amount of criticism. A number of issues can cause tension between the region and area municipalities, and almost every region has been subject to some sort of "abolish the region" movement. Peel, however, has a particular dynamic because Mississauga is much larger by population and has a larger property tax assessment base than the other two municipalities. Brampton is smaller, but growing rapidly; Caledon is predominately rural with some small urban pockets and aspires to stay that way.

Regional governments do not have direct taxing authority; instead they impose a levy on area municipalities, which, in turn, pass it directly on to ratepayers. The total regional levy is allocated among area municipalities based on each municipality's share of the total property tax assessment. In Peel, this means that regional projects are funded largely by Mississauga, but many provide significant benefits well beyond Mississauga's boundaries. This would create tension in any case, but the presence of Hazel McCallion as the long-serving and outspoken mayor of Mississauga heightened the tension.

All these factors created a situation in which councillors were frequently less than fully engaged in regional affairs, except when Mayor McCallion took an interest in an issue and stirred up her fellow councillors and the local media. Garrett talks about how he sometimes had difficulty getting councillors interested in senior hiring decisions. Council's collective attitude seemed to be that the person being hired would be working for the CAO, so it was the CAO's decision. When an issue touched Mississauga directly, however – and all spending issues had an impact on Mississauga – Mayor McCallion could be counted on to be highly vocal. These specific concerns frequently spilled over into more general region-bashing.

Garrett responded to these adverse circumstances with an innovation he became known for wherever he went. As mentioned earlier, "abolish the region" movements are common across Ontario, and most regional officials have learned to grin and bear it. But Garrett was not so accepting. He felt that, if the attacks went unanswered, they would undermine the region's credibility and sap the morale of regional employees. He wanted to respond to the criticisms, but he knew that he could not attack a councillor openly, particularly with someone as strong as McCallion leading the charge. He needed to find a low-key, administrative way of proving that the region was not as inefficient as its critics claimed. His engineering background drove him more toward a rational, evidence-based approach to counter the critics' rhetoric.

Garrett had attended a number of national and international management conferences, and he knew that performance measurement was coming into use in a number of jurisdictions, although not widely in Canadian municipalities. He felt a performance measurement system would prove Peel Region was just as efficient, per road-kilometre, per file processed, per cubic metre of water treated, and so forth, as any other municipality. The system Garrett developed in Peel, one of the first in Canadian municipal government, is one of his proudest accomplishments. It served as a model for other municipalities, and made Garrett a much sought-after advisor to other jurisdictions. After twenty years, the Peel system has undergone a number of changes, but people currently at Peel still credit Garrett as the architect of the system.

In addition to the internal challenges facing the region, through the 1980s and 1990s there were several proposals to restructure the municipal system in the Greater Toronto Area. While these proposals always had a patina of economic efficiency, better planning, and so forth, one consequence of many of them would be to pool the high revenues flowing into Peel Region with those of Toronto, which spent its budget on other priorities. Garrett developed a reputation for defending his region strongly in the face of provincial downloading,[5] as well as leading the charge to defend Peel against any attempts at restructuring.[6]

By all accounts, Peel Region developed well during Garrett's tenure there. The rapid growth of both population and business activity required significant infrastructure construction, but also generated the necessary funds not only to pay for the new infrastructure but also to pay off accumulated debt.[7] As always in these situations, there were localized tensions, but considering the magnitude of what was going on, there were surprisingly few major regional ones.[8] Garrett led an administration that accomplished a great deal in terms of providing services in a growing municipality and installing a successful performance measurement system.

After eight years in Peel, however, the itch that had caused Garrett to leave the provincial government flared again when a headhunter asked if he would be interested in what was regarded as the premier position in Canada for any municipal professional: CAO of the newly amalgamated City of Toronto.

City of Toronto (1997–2001)

Toronto is the largest city in Canada, certainly by population and probably by expenditure as well. City officials are fond of pointing out that Toronto has a larger budget than six provinces. The population of the new city was 2,385,254 in 1996, shortly before Garrett arrived, and had increased to 2,481,494 in 2001 when he left.[9] In 2002, its operating expenditures were $6.5 billion.[10]

The Toronto area had been governed since 1954 by a two-tier system of government consisting of the Municipality of Metropolitan Toronto (Metro) as the upper tier and, in later years, six area municipalities. In a highly controversial move, the provincial government decided to amalgamate these seven governments into one "megacity," as it was called in the media, effective 1 January 1998.[11] The primary stated reason for the wave of amalgamations instituted by Progressive Conservative premier Mike Harris and his minister of municipal affairs, Al Leach, across Ontario at this time was the province's position that significant savings would be reaped by reducing the number of municipal governments, resulting in lower property taxes. This involved moving from two-tier governments, which had been predominant in Ontario, to larger single-tier units. Other reasons were related to supporting financially weak municipalities, improving the international profile of Ontario's cities (particularly that of Toronto), and rationalizing service delivery.

Garrett was hired in 1997 by the Toronto Transition Team even before the new municipality had come into existence.[12] The team was appointed by the provincial government to manage the transition until a new council took office after the November 1997 election. It consisted of a small group of municipal politicians who had decided not to run in the election. As a group, they were knowledgeable, but they did not have the legitimacy of having been elected, nor would they have any status after the new council took office. Despite this, they made a number of important decisions about the new municipality, including the appointment of its senior officials. By appointing a CAO, they even decided what its organization structure would be, even though a number of newly elected councillors expressed concern about this process.[13]

Some saw the presence of a CAO as controversial because the City of Toronto had always rejected the idea of having one.

Thus, Garrett was entering this difficult transition time with an awkward mandate.[14] In effect, he and four other senior staff, whom he had no role in appointing, were chosen by a transition team of dubious legitimacy to administer a vast new organization that had experienced a controversial birth. Garrett was the only one of the five who had not worked in pre-amalgamation Toronto. It was suggested that the CAO was appointed from outside because it would have been too contentious to appoint an "insider," But it also meant that Garrett, the outsider, would be working with four "insiders" who would bring with them alliances from their previous municipalities. This had important consequences, which I discuss later. Although the five appointments were confirmed by the newly elected council at its first meeting, this was a perfunctory decision. The five then had the responsibility of creating an administrative structure and populating that structure with staff from the seven amalgamated municipalities. The volume of work was immense, but hanging over all of these human resource decisions was the provincial commitment that significant cost savings would accrue from the amalgamation.

Garrett's task would have been difficult to accomplish if he had had the full support of the mayor and a united council, but the political environment he faced made his task even more difficult. The first mayor of the new megacity was Mel Lastman, the former long-time mayor of North York and one of the most vocal critics of amalgamation. The nature of council was also problematic, with its fifty-six councillors bringing to the table some strong biases and mistrusts from their former municipalities. One person described the aura around the council table as "shock and chaos." Supposedly, some even held out hope that, if they were obstreperous enough, the province would roll back its amalgamation decision.

It seems that Lastman and Garrett never warmed to each another. One interviewee described them as "chalk and cheese." Garrett is a quietly competent career public servant, whose engineering background shows through in his emphasis on seeking rationality in decision making. Lastman is a bombastic salesman type whose regime in North York Justice Denise Bellamy, who headed the inquiry into the MFP scandal, described negatively as a family affair, in the sense that many things were handled informally with a focus on "getting ... things done without worrying too much about how."[15] It was suggested that this approach can be positive for a family, but not so good for a large government with the responsibility of stewardship of taxpayers' funds. Garrett emphasizes that he attempted to adapt his style to Lastman's, noting that it is the responsibility of a professional public servant to adapt to the needs and style of the politician, not the other way around. He had been able to do this in the past, but this time the gap was too wide.

The relationship between the mayor and the CAO can be illustrated by the location of their respective offices, at least for the first year. In most city halls, the offices of the mayor and the CAO are immediately next to each other – frequently so close that they share some common staff. In Lastman's Toronto, the mayor's office was in the iconic Toronto City Hall, close to the council chamber; the CAO's office was in the former Metro Hall, about a ten-minute walk away from the real seat of city government.

Developing a close relationship with the new council was difficult, not only because of its size and because Garrett was new, but also because the demands of his administrative job during the transition were enormous. Garrett never developed a particularly close relationship with most councillors. From his perspective, the large size of council and the huge administrative task he faced made this difficult. Most councillors, however, had little interest in administrative activities at this point anyway; instead, they focused on the high politics of the council chamber and the media. In Toronto, activities in the city council chamber attract considerably more media attention than does the staid provincial legislature up the street. Councillors spent a great deal of time jockeying for position on prize committees and for attention in the media. The mundane aspects of service delivery were not high on their list of priorities.

The only aspect of administrative activity that some councillors did take an interest in was seeing how their favourite staff members from their former municipalities were faring in the competition for positions in the new municipality. This led to a cultural clash that Garrett had not experienced at Peel Region. There, Garrett made senior staff appointments with little political involvement – a system he was comfortable with as a result of his experience in the provincial government with its strong merit system. In some Toronto-area municipalities, however, it was customary for councillors to be heavily involved in the staff appointment process even several layers down. Garrett clashed particularly in this area with powerful former City of Toronto councillor Tom Jakobek,[16] but there would be other conflicts between the two.[17]

Every CAO must decide where to take a stand on matters of principle, and hiring on merit without political involvement is an important principle for Garrett. As CAO, he was willing to be held accountable for the actions of the administration, but the corollary was that he should be responsible for ensuring that staff appointments were made on the basis of merit. Political involvement in that process could weaken the efficiency of his administration and confuse the lines of authority and accountability in the organization. The fact that some of the senior appointments were made not by Garrett, but by the transition team, would come back to haunt Garrett very quickly.

Garrett set about creating an administrative structure with proper hierarchical relationships and appropriate spans of control. His goal was that no manager should have responsibility for more than six major functional areas. He first completed the senior staffing started by the transition team by putting in place the heads of the various departments. This group then collectively moved to fill staff positions down through the hierarchy. At the senior levels, for each service, there had been six or seven department heads in the pre-amalgamation municipalities, but only one was needed in the new municipality, which meant a large number of disappointed people. A system of bumping was created so that former senior managers who were not chosen for a comparable position in the new organization could move down a level and compete with people at that level. This was seen as a fair way of providing opportunities; it also increased the number of disappointed people as staffing proceeded down the ranks.

As if the task of identifying the right person for the right job in such a huge organization were not difficult enough, Garrett felt pressure from the provincial government, which wanted to prove that the amalgamation would save money, and from Mayor Lastman, who wanted to honour his campaign commitment of no tax increase. Since salaries and wages constitute 60–80 per cent of the total expenditure of a typical municipal government, the only way to make significant savings was by reducing the number of people in the organization. Even this understates the nature of the problem. Costs have a natural tendency to increase in amalgamations because both service levels and labour costs will rise to the level of the highest municipality. So the cascading hiring process described above could go on for some time, but in the end it had to result in significant reductions in staff to achieve any serious savings.

Eventually, the savings from management staff cuts and integrating technical systems were offset by migrating to higher service levels and higher rates of pay for remaining staff. The only way to have effected significant savings would have been to cut front-line staff, with concomitant reductions in service levels, and council was unwilling to do this. In the end, the Toronto amalgamation did not produce any savings. This should not be surprising since there is no evidence that any of the other large number of municipal amalgamations in Ontario at this time generated significant savings.

Garrett had to meld seven organizations with different organizational cultures and, in some cases, serious animosities between them into one. He had to do this while achieving significant savings, which could be accomplished only by reducing the staff complement by an estimated 1,600, most of which was unionized.[18] Therefore, he needed to maximize staff morale and productivity in an environment in which no one was assured of keeping her or his current position, or even any position, in the revised administrative structure.

Garrett soon learned, moreover, that he could not count on the loyalty of some of his senior staff. Wanda Liczyk was appointed commissioner of finance by the transition team at the same time it appointed Garrett CAO. Liczyk came from North York, where she had risen quickly through the ranks to be that city's commissioner of finance. This made her a member of the "family," to use Justice Bellamy's word, and as such she had a close working relationship with Mayor Lastman. In fact, Garrett's relationship with Lastman was such that Garrett sometimes had to rely on Liczyk to interpret Lastman's actions.[19] It then became well understood around city hall that Liczyk wanted to be the new municipality's CAO.[20] Several interviewees commented on times when she attempted to undermine Garrett – indeed, Justice Bellamy found that Liczyk had withheld important information from Garrett and had overstepped her signing authority in a number of situations.[21]

Cultural clashes pervaded the administrative reaches of the new organization, and the end result was more of a marble cake than a melding. Staff from particular municipalities seemed to predominate in certain departments and brought their culture with them. The heads of finance and parks and recreation came from North York, so those came to be seen as "North York" departments. The senior people in planning came from the old City of Toronto and the inner borough of East York, so planning came to be seen as a "city" department. This sometimes made it unclear where the real reporting relationships lay. In particular, department heads from North York seemed to have a close relationship with the new mayor from their time working together in the old municipality.

In sum, Garrett faced a serious constellation of problems. He had no real relationship with his mayor; there was considerable tension between him and Tom Jakobek, one of the most influential members of council; and he had no time to develop relationships with other councillors, who had had no real role in choosing him. On the administrative side, he was trying to create a huge organization in an environment of clashing cultures and a situation where he could not trust one of his key senior staff. And, by the way, this new organization was supposed to generate significant savings so as to honour the mayor's pledge of no tax increase and the provincial expectation of significant cost savings.

Earlier, it was suggested that this was the premier job in Canada for a municipal CAO; it was also probably the most difficult. A number of interviewees suggested that nothing in the relatively quiet confines of Peel Region prepared Garrett for the minefields of Toronto city hall. Many of these interviewees suggested that this would have been an exceptionally hard job for anyone, but a nice guy like Garrett would have found it even more difficult.

Indeed, the harder Garrett worked, the more difficult his job became. The large savings promised by the provincial government did not materialize. The relationship with Mayor Lastman and influential councillors such as Jakobek deteriorated from an already shaky beginning. With every staffing decision, a handful of former staffers, and their supporters on council, were disappointed. Finally, after Lastman had publicly criticized city staff, Garrett suggested that the mayor needed to make a public statement in support of city staff, but Lastman refused.[22] Garrett must have known what was coming next.

On 27 June 2001, council convened in an *in camera* session. The meeting resulted in a motion to rescind Garrett's appointment, which was passed by a vote of 28–14. The vote sparked considerable controversy. The newspaper stories tended to be more critical of the mayor who led the attack than of Garrett.[23] Councillor Michael Walker was quoted as saying, "I had full confidence in Mike Garrett. Who I don't have full confidence in is Mayor Mel Lastman."[24] Veteran *Toronto Star* city hall columnist Royson James wrote, "the fact that the megacity is still standing is a testament to the skills, hard work and commitment of Garrett and his staff. But Lastman and his council apparently want more."[25]

The strongest criticism of Garrett at the time was that he was too nice and not tough enough. This seemed to be code for his not producing the savings anticipated by the amalgamation. In fact, he did produce some savings,[26] and there was a suggestion that he had recommended additional budget cuts, but that these had not been acceptable to the mayor.[27] The only thing that seems certain is that the relationship between the mayor and the CAO had broken down irreparably.[28] Although some councillors likely would have been happier to keep the CAO and lose the mayor, that is never the way these things play out.

The rescinding of Garrett's appointment did not, however, end his involvement with the City of Toronto. A scandal erupted, related to a project to integrate desktop computing through the use of leases, at the centre of which was the financial services company MFP. Unfortunately, the scandal stands out as one of the most significant events of the early years of the amalgamated city. It happened on Garrett's watch, yet it seems not to have tarnished him; some suggest, in fact, that it produced one of his finest hours. How did this come about?

According to Justice Bellamy, who was asked to conduct an extensive inquiry into the events precipitating the scandal, the roots of the scandal began in late 1997 when officials in the computer and purchasing divisions of the old city were concerned about dealing with the feared Y2K computer bug and meeting the needs of a new, larger council. These concerns were going to be expensive to manage and would require a new way of handling computer and software acquisitions, and MFP was happy to provide its expertise. From 1997 until the scandal broke in 2001, the city undertook a significant program of hardware acquisition, software purchasing and development, and related purchases, spending millions of dollars and following some lax and questionable processes. The details of the scandal started to break in the spring and summer of 2001, shortly after Garrett's tenure as CAO had ended. What was his role?

Justice Bellamy and her investigators did a tremendous amount of sleuthing to determine who knew what and when about the events involving MFP. She was meticulous in her analysis and unstinting in her criticism of the culprits in the story. Garrett is one of the few who drew high praise from her: "Mike Garrett was an impressive, responsible, senior public servant who took the principles of public service seriously."[29] Justice Bellamy's report contains numerous examples of times when Garrett tried to obtain information about the computer situation, while those around him variously lied directly to him, misled him, hid conflicts of interest from him, and gave him incorrect information.

It is an important tenet of good management that senior managers take responsibility for the actions of their subordinates. To what extent should this principle apply, however, when subordinates engage in a virtual conspiracy to prevent the manager from discovering the truth? This question could keep groups of management students busy for years. In practice, in this case, Justice Bellamy was clear: in a report that did not pull any punches about allocating blame, she heaped high praise on Garrett. The report tarnished and even destroyed the reputations of many people, but served only to burnish Garrett's. Many interviewees referred in particular to one short passage in Garrett's four days of testimony before the inquiry to describe why they were so impressed by him:

> [I]t was my watch, I'm the accountable party. It gives me no pleasure to – assuming that these allegations are true – I'm not the least bit pleased that what seems to have happened, happened. I was the Captain of the ship, and if something went wrong with that ship, I take full responsibility for that. Now, I can tell you when that broke I had left the City, it was a month or two (2) after I had left, and frankly, I was sick about it. It reflects ... poorly on the whole organization, which is not deserved. An organization that worked extremely hard to have the City run under trying circumstances over the past three (3) or four (4) years, since the beginning of amalgamation, and for that reason in particular, I feel badly.
>
> The other comment I'd like to make ... is that as a leader, we have to belly up to the bar, so to speak, and take responsibility for our actions. And if there was a fault, then we need to learn from it, and correct it and carry on. And we need to get to the bottom of what the problem was and to take the necessary action that – that fixes the problem, so that it doesn't happen again.[30]

Thus, in a few words, Garrett accepts responsibility for what happened on his watch, praises the good people who worked hard for him, and recognizes that an important part of accountability and accepting responsibility is taking action to ensure that mistakes are not repeated. It is not surprising that interviewees frequently mentioned this passage as emblematic of Garrett's integrity and leadership style.

No manager who takes pride in his ability as a leader wants to part company with an employer the way Garrett did. Among those in the profession, however, there is little stigma attached to having an appointment "rescinded," to use the City of Toronto's euphemism. The relationship between a CAO and a mayor and council is a close and personal one, and sometimes the relationship breaks down. When it does, it is impossible to assign blame; the two sides must recognize that the current relationship is not working and move on. Many CAOs have had their appointments rescinded or have left voluntarily when they recognized the difficulty of such a situation. Interviewees who worked with Garrett maintain tremendous respect for him, and spoke positively about him years after the fact. They recognized that he was in an impossible situation, made even more difficult by his immense workload and the conspiring of some of those around him.

A brief respite

Even many years after, it is clear that Garrett still carries wounds from what happened in the City of Toronto. It is understandable that he would. Having worked incredibly hard to try to make a success of an impossible situation, he was rewarded by being let go and then being told that a small group of senior staff members were working behind his back to bring discredit to an organization he was trying to build.

It should not be surprising that his main desire at that point was to put municipal government permanently in his rear-view mirror. He always planned on retiring well before the age of sixty-five. He proudly points out that he went directly from school to a full-time job and has never had an extended time away from work since he started. He has also seen friends and relatives deal with health problems as they became older. He wanted to retire early enough that he could enjoy his other interests. Having worked in the public service without a break throughout his career, and having negotiated a settlement as a result of the Toronto situation, he was financially secure. Further, with his reputation he could do as much consulting work as he wanted to supplement his income or occupy his time. He had no burning desire to return to municipal government.

In the twelve years he was a CAO, however, Garrett had become a part of a select community that meets in formal organizations such as the Canadian Association of Municipal Administrators and the Ontario Municipal Administrators' Association, but that also has a strong informal network that allows CAOs to share advice and have candid discussions. He was not sure if he had much left to give, but his friends felt he did, and encouraged him to get back into the field. So, when a headhunter looking to fill the position of chief administrative officer for the Region of York approached him, he somewhat reluctantly agreed to let his name stand.

Region of York, ON (2002-07)

Garrett's appointment at York was roundly welcomed by virtually everyone there. In the words of one senior manager, "everyone thought it was a coup." Many had known him earlier in his career because Peel and York regions share a boundary and interact often. He was also well respected for his time in Toronto. Everyone knew that it had ended badly for him, but they were also aware that the people he had worked with there thought highly of him and that he had accomplished a great deal against heavy odds. One person described him as 'Mr. Efficiency,' which is exactly what they were looking for in York at the time. His testimony before the Bellamy inquiry did not occur until he had been at York for several months, but even after many years, virtually every interviewee remembered his accepting responsibility as captain of the ship. They all wanted to work for someone like him.

York had some things in common with Peel, but there were some differences as well. Like Peel, York (at least its southern tier) was becoming home to many people who worked in Toronto, but either could not afford or chose not to live there. Like Peel, York was moving from being a bedroom community to becoming a full-fledged edge city, but it was at an earlier stage in its development than Peel was when Garrett arrived. This meant that much more basic infrastructure work needed to be done.

York Region is one of the largest municipalities in Ontario, its population growing rapidly from 729,254 in 2001 (shortly before Garrett arrived) to 892,712 in 2006 (shortly before he left).[31] It is also one of the largest in terms of expenditures: when Garrett left in 2007, they surpassed $1.2 billion.[32] York's nine area municipalities are a collection of small, medium, and large urban areas – ranging from classic, rustic villages such as Kleinberg and Unionville to bustling core areas with office towers and shopping centres such as Richmond Hill and Newmarket – separated by cash-crop farms, horse farms, and other rural areas. The population is quite dense close to the southern boundary of the region with Toronto and becomes sparser moving north to Lake Simcoe. There is considerable retail trade in York, and some large job generators are developing, but there is a definite orientation toward Toronto for jobs, major shopping, and entertainment. Settlement and transportation patterns in the region are quite complex, which produced some of Garrett's major challenges.

One such challenge was the "big pipe": the twinning of a huge sewer to collect all the wastewater through various areas of York and bring it ultimately to a sewage treatment plant in Durham Region. The big pipe was essential to accommodate the huge amount of greenfield development that was planned for York. Developers and residents wanted it, and wanted it as quickly as possible. The tunnelling had been a staged design-build project, but practical issues arose from allegations that construction was dewatering some local wells. York Region, on the advice of a consultant, at first suggested this should have been the contractor's risk, but ultimately had to accept responsibility. There were also issues with regard to the exact placement of pipes. Although it was a very large project with some engineering complexities, they were not nearly as difficult to manage as the people problems associated with placement. Still, Garrett got the senior executives of all the major engineering companies to devise a plan to deliver infrastructure more competently and quickly. The project seemed to be in difficulty before he arrived, but the combination of his engineering skills and people skills got it on track.

Another product of the rapid development occurring in York was VIVA, a new mass transit system developed during Garrett's tenure. It was actually the vision of regional chair Bill Fisch, but, of course, it required the work of a number of staff members to bring it to fruition. As new greenfield development was expanding the need for more infrastructure, the region and its municipalities were constructing new roads to cope, but not quickly enough to keep ahead of growing traffic. Emerging environmental concerns were also feeding a desire for alternatives to the car. Fisch recognized the need for a transit system to take people to commuter rail stations and the Toronto subway and thus reduce the need for roads. There was considerable discussion about light rail versus buses, but it was finally decided to operate a fleet of modern, comfortable buses on existing roads and eventually to provide exclusive rights-of-way for them.

Two related issues would have to be dealt with to make the new transit system work. One was to create an innovative system that would entice people to forsake their cars. York wanted both more attractive rolling stock and better communication systems than older transit systems had. The other problem was cost: the upfront capital cost of developing any transit system, much less something so innovative, was beyond the ability of York.

Fortunately, York's plans for a transit system were unfolding at a time when there was great interest in public-private partnerships, so the region explored this innovative approach to development and financing.

York was able to obtain money from both the federal and provincial governments, where transit priorities were resonating. Private sector firms supply the buses, develop facilities, operate the service, and, most significantly, provide the funding. The private sector partners have assumed some of the risk and provided up-front funding that the region will pay off over time. The project likely never would have happened without a funding arrangement like this to spread the large up-front cost over future years.

A complex arrangement like this requires the cooperation of a large number of people in a large number of organizations. Bill Fisch was certainly one of the prime movers, and the project began under Garrett's predecessor, Alan Wells. Still, many interviewees also gave Garrett a great deal of credit for using his task orientation to drive the project. Several people also suggested that he learned from his experience with MFP in Toronto, and was careful about the nature of the partnership agreements that were developed. Some people apparently were frustrated with the delays caused by this caution, but Garrett insisted on a system of checks and balances that contributed to a highly acclaimed system operating without serious administrative problems.

Garrett's time at York was busy and productive, and certainly less stressful than his time in Toronto. By 2007, however, he had served in York for the term of his five-year contract and was approaching his sixtieth birthday, and he honoured his commitment to himself to retire while he could still enjoy life. He had been in government service for thirty-seven years. Everyone interviewed at York lamented his decision to leave, but conveyed the idea that the place was in good shape when he retired.

The Leadership Role of the CAO

I have already noted that a successful CAO must be able to lead in three directions at the same time. In this section, I analyse the manner in which Garrett led in each of these directions, beginning with some comments about his personality and leadership style.

General characteristics

TASK ORIENTED

It is a common theme in the leadership literature that leaders must exhibit some balance of task orientation, relationship or people orientation, and conceptual orientation, but this is how Garrett sees himself: "I'm task oriented; I'm not relationship oriented. That's my weakness. I'm driven to deliver a task and I'd like to think I'm not an unfriendly person, but I don't live for the relationships. I live for what problem have you got to solve … that's probably coming from my engineering background … So that's my weakness, and it's my strength." His task orientation comes through in interviews with those around him and in the way in which his career unfolded. He worked in two rapidly growing municipalities where there was a great deal of emphasis on infrastructure, and one city where the organization structure needed to be built from the ground up.

Those around him understood how he viewed himself as first and foremost a task-oriented person. As one noted, "[h]e did do the requisite socializing, but mostly with people he worked with directly. At the large "meet and greets" where senior managers must put in an appearance and speak, he made a positive impression with rank and file staff, but he was not the stereotypic people person who knew the names, pets, and favourite colours of every clerk and receptionist in the place. He was cordial and friendly with rank and file staff, but he spent most of his time with senior managers because that was where the work needed to be done."

GOOD PEOPLE SKILLS

When interviewees were told that Garrett defined himself as more task oriented than people oriented, virtually everyone suggested that he was being too hard on himself on his supposed lack of people skills. After some reflection, however, virtually everyone understood that what he meant was that he was first and foremost about getting the job done. At the same time, they described him as a likeable guy with a congenial personality whose people skills were, in fact, significant: "He's a tremendous people person, but he is definitely task related. When he's at work, he's very focused on the outcome, very focused on the task that needs to get done. He's definitely results driven, for sure, but he does have an engaging personality and he's very personable."

A GOOD COMMUNICATOR

Even though Garrett was not strong on idle chatter, everyone referred to him as a good communicator, although with a certain formality. Several people focused on his ability to make strong, clear presentations to groups. This was seen as part of his task orientation because the presentations would involve selling a project or idea (as he had learned to do at the conservation authorities), allaying concerns of councillors or others, or updating staff. By all accounts, people came out of the presentation with a clear understanding of the points he wanted to get across and confidence in his ability to move forward.

One aspect of being a good communicator is being a good listener and able to draw out other people's opinions. Garrett had a reputation for not dominating conversations and meetings, but listening to what others had to say: "He liked to brainstorm and to hear people's ideas ... as opposed to [coming] to the table with an idea and this is the way you're going to do it ... People felt they were getting a hearing." Sometimes it is difficult for senior people to resist being the centre of attention in discussions with subordinates. It seems that Garrett's personal style prevented that: "[He's a] personable enough guy, but [there's a] certain shyness there ... he's not 'Hi, I'm Mike Garrett. I'm better than you.' That's not him. It goes back to his view of himself as being task oriented ... It's not that he wasn't concerned about staff, because he was."

He actually worked hard to obtain views from people throughout the organization and not to rely only on the normal chain of command. In Toronto, he invited specific individuals from all areas of the organization and all ranks to an informal monthly lunch with the CAO. He took this as an opportunity to hear about what they did and how they saw the organization.

A RATIONAL THINKER

Garrett's communication skills were supported by his ability to think rationally, which he and those around him attributed to both his task orientation and his engineering training.

When he came to York, there was a great deal of new infrastructure being constructed, but he was concerned that the direction and timing of construction was too influenced by the immediate needs of developers. He made certain that an overall infrastructure plan was in place to reflect the interests of the region. This ensured that infrastructure was being developed in a rational and efficient manner, and not just based on the squeaky wheel.

His devotion to the concept of performance measurement was a clear outgrowth of his focus on rationality. He always wanted to know about the numbers for any proposal. Subordinates understood that he was open to new ideas and new ways of doing things, but he always wanted to hear the business case; he was not interested in emotional pleas. Sub-ordinates probably also became aware that one reason he liked per-formance measurement was that it gave him a way of evaluating the performance of his department heads. He was heavily involved in the Ontario Municipal Benchmarking Initiative (OMBI), a consortium of large Ontario municipalities working with performance measurements to provide a basis of comparison among them. He saw department heads as lobbyists for their service, and as a CAO he had a limited abil-ity to discern whether their budget request was justified. Performance measurement and benchmarking gave him a window into the level of performance of his staff.

CAREFUL AND CONSCIENTIOUS

Garrett's communication skills and rational thinking were supple-mented by a careful and conscientious approach. He was confident in his ability, but did not suffer from hubris. On the contrary, people who worked closely with him talked about the elaborate preparations and care he put into honing his presentation.

CHANGE ORIENTED

Garrett talks about being restless and looking for change. He was never satisfied with the status quo, but he also did not tinker for the sake of tinkering, and he was careful in the way that he went about question-ing the status quo. When he came into a new organization, he did not behave like a bull in china shop, as one interviewee put it. He took his time to assess the overall situation and the strengths and weaknesses of his senior staff. After he understood what he had inherited, however, he was not afraid to make changes to improve the organization.

His introduction of performance measurement in Peel Region is a good example of this. In many regional governments, politicians and senior managers come to accept that they will be the scapegoats for the system. Garrett did not accept that this had to be the case in Peel, so he developed the idea of performance measurement and benchmarking to prove that Peel was more efficient than other municipalities.

At the same time, he did not necessarily accept all the innovations available, but picked and chose carefully. He was not a fan of broad-based strategic planning exercises that included council. He recognized that such exercises were expected, but he was much more interested in what he called functional strategic plans – plans geared to the de-livery of a particular service such as solid waste management. He felt that broad-based plans were too broad to be effective and were not that helpful in ordering priorities, whereas narrower functional plans could be real guides to action.

THERE'S LIFE OUTSIDE YOUR OWN MUNICIPALITY

Garrett worked hard to be a leader in his own municipalities, but he also was involved in outside organizations. His role in MARCO was important to him: the position of CAO is lonely at best, and only exacerbated if one comes into it as he did. He explains how the CAOs' group within MARCO worked: "We relished meeting together, and fed off each other. We could phone any one of them and those people had different expertise … So if you had a problem to solve, you could deal in confidence because I think city manager's a lonely job and they all were in it and so you could relate to that." He learned about performance measurement through some national and international conferences he attended. He then was instrumental in establishing the OMBI. He clearly benefited from working with various outside groups, and in turn provided much to these groups. That reciprocal relationship is important.

INTEGRITY

Virtually every interviewee commented on Garrett's integrity, of which his position during and after the MFP situation was an excellent example. All sorts of inappropriate benefits were being passed out to strategic people, but the perpetrators seemed to have had a sense that there would be no point even approaching Garrett. Moreover, everyone around him understood that he did not just talk about integrity: "What he said he believed, and when he said it, he did it, and he acted on it and followed through … He was not a man who said one thing … and then did something entirely different."

"HE WAS JUST MIKE"

All of these qualities were rounded out with a pleasing and easy-going personality. Many people spoke in different ways about his straightforward and honest personal style, but one person describing a job interview said it best: "He was just Mike in that process. He was who he was. And I think that's my observation about Mike through the entire time that I've worked with him. He just is what he is. There's no subterfuge, there's no deceit, there's no kind of sense of an agenda that he's managing you, or he's manipulating you … I would put it down to just a fundamental sense of decency and integrity that I got from him, and an honesty about what was going on. He told me the truth."

People who worked closely with him commented that he was the same, level-headed person every day. He never outwardly showed anger, upset, or other negative emotions, no matter what was happening around him. This kind of self-awareness and self-control is a good example of emotional intelligence. This meant that people had a great deal of respect for him.

Leading down

Garrett applied these broad, basic skills in a variety of different ways, depending on whether he was leading down, up, or out. He did not climb the municipal ladder in the traditional fashion. He worked closely with municipalities early in his career while with the conservation authorities and to a lesser extent during his time with the provincial Ministry of Natural Resources. His background in water resource engineering gave him insights into one aspect of municipal operations, but he had no experience across the broad scope of municipal activity. This conditioned how he approached leadership in the municipality. He had a reputation for being careful and thoughtful; he did not act precipitously when he arrived in a new municipality. He did, however, develop a reputation for two organizational approaches wherever he went: breaking down silos and relying on performance measurement.

Peel and York are both high-growth jurisdictions, which affects virtually every department within their organizations. Proper handling of rapid growth requires departments to work together to ensure that transit, road construction, community services, and all the other myriad municipal services are developed in synch with one another.

When he came to Peel, Garrett recognized that he had inherited a good organization with good people in place. He felt, however, that there was too much emphasis on silo management, whereby individual departments manage in isolation from other departments – highly problematic in an environment of rapid growth where issues run from engineering, water and sewers, to social services. He dealt with the problem by creating interdepartmental task forces that tackled issues that cut across all the silos. People really appreciated the ability to work with others in a variety of departments. They also enjoyed the sense of accomplishment in solving a problem rather than in dealing with only one aspect of it.

The traditional way of handling interdepartmental issues in York was for each manager to drive the issue up the hierarchy, ultimately to the CAO's office, from which a decision would be passed back down through the hierarchy. This system works fine in a low-speed, low-volume operation, but Garrett realized that high growth and the complex decision making that went with it made this process too cumbersome. He therefore established a growth management committee with representation from all affected departments, an approach that fit with his task orientation. As one interviewee noted, "Mike was always results-driven ... He was less concerned about who did it than achieving the result, and he really insisted on bringing the people together to focus on the outcome as opposed to focus on the process."

Such an approach requires a leap of faith on the part of the CAO. The process of having everything pass through the CAO's office was cumbersome, but it allowed the CAO to be involved in every decision. Delegating decisions to an interdepartmental committee meant the CAO had to release his personal grasp on decision making. But Garrett seemed to have just the right feel for managing subordinates in a way that gave them scope to carry out their duties while still maintaining appropriate accountability. He recognized that, as the CAO, he was at some remove from actual operations, and therefore he needed to rely on his senior managers to be the "lead dog" on most issues. As Garrett says, "[t]he ... commissioner did most of the work ... He was lead. [He] was the key guy; not me, but you're involved as the CAO, with the money, and so is the treasurer ... I can't honestly say I was the lead dog. I was the supporting cast member. When you go to the CAO's job in a big place, ... you've got many different businesses you're overseeing. Whether you like it or not, you're the manager of a holding company."

One senior manager described Garrett's style this way: "You have to know the programs to a certain degree, but you also have to let people do their job and you have to hold people accountable. You've got to give them freedom, but at the same time you have to hold them accountable. You have to be able to say if you're running your program, I'm going to leave you alone unless you screw up, and I'm going to help you any way I can, but I'm going to let you run with it. Because that's what people thrive on."

Garrett's staff, however, never felt abandoned. He made it clear that he was there for them when they needed his support. He encouraged department heads to present their own reports to council – after all, they have more expertise in their area than a generalist like a CAO – but he did not use this approach as an excuse to shirk his responsibility to support subordinates. He recognized when certain types of reports needed to come from the CAO – for example, he generally presented the budget. When commissioners did present their own report, however, he was there for them in a variety of ways. If a report was likely to be contentious, he would introduce it by saying something like, "I have asked the commissioner to present this report to council," to make it clear that he supported the report. He respected commissioners' abilities by not intervening in their presentations, but interviewees recalled his doing so if councillors were asking interdepartmental questions that were beyond a commissioner's scope or if councillors were pursuing an unfair line of questioning.

A situation he faced in Toronto was particularly telling. Garrett felt compelled to write a memo to the mayor about the conduct of Councillor Jakobek that began:

> Further to our previous conversations, I am writing to express my concern with respect to the conduct of the Budget Chair [Councillor Jakobek] in interactions with staff of the City. As Chief Administrative Officer, it is my responsibility to bring to your attention issues which negatively impact on staff's ability to serve Council and the public in a professional and objective manner. I have been approached on numerous occasions by staff in recent months who feel that they are being subjected to behaviour that impugns their reputation, that questions their professionalism and performance, and that deliberately creates an unproductive and unhealthy corporate culture.[33]

Was this a simple misunderstanding between Garrett and Jakobek, or was Garrett being too sensitive in defending staff from the justified inquiries of a conscientious councillor? Throughout the inquiry into the MFP scandal, Justice Bellamy praised Garrett's professionalism, while she was equally unstinting in her criticism of Jakobek, referring to him as a liar[34] and bully.[35]

Garrett's memo is significant because it illustrates his concern about the welfare of his staff and his attempt to protect them from unfair attacks, but it also says something about the environment around city hall at the time. It is not unusual for a CAO to have to discuss the behaviour of a councillor with the head of council. Usually, this is handled in a private personal discussion. That Garrett felt it necessary not only to prod the head of council to take some action but also to document the conversation offers insight into the relationship between the mayor and the CAO.

Garrett also worked with subordinates in a positive way at a more personal level. Staff always knew where they stood with him. He was quick to praise a job well done, but he also made it clear when he was not satisfied with someone's performance. One manager contrasted this latter behaviour with that of another manager, who did not confront people with problems, but instead, "you would hear later through indirect means that he was not satisfied with something you had done."

Garrett was not shy about discussing unsatisfactory performance with people, but he did it in a way that made it a positive learning experience. First, the discussion always took place privately; he never embarrassed anyone publicly. Second, the tone of the discussion always focused on how to improve the situation and how Garrett and the manager could work together to resolve the problem. Again, managers never felt they were being hung out to dry.

Garrett says he sat down with managers once or twice a year and evaluated them based on five factors: fiscal prudence; customer service; organizational climate; public image; and anticipation of the future and strategic planning.

He clearly had an impact on the organizational culture of the municipalities for which he worked. One interviewee discussed how Garrett "grew the learning side of the organization" in York. This person clearly appreciated the fact that York offered a great range of learning opportunities for staff at all levels, and he attributed this approach to Garrett's time at the helm, although he tied this back to Garrett's task orientation. Learning is done not just for the sake of learning; Garrett emphasized learning because of the importance he attributed to succession planning.

Garrett was also an outstanding mentor. People who worked for him can be found as CAOs or senior staff all over York and more broadly. At the time of this research, four of the ten CAOs in York region had worked for Garrett at some point in their careers. One of those CAOs described his experiences with Garrett in this way: "What he was really good at and what I appreciated, and why I'm here today [as a CAO] is [his investing] trust in staff ... You never felt like you were going to be hung out to dry; you always felt supported, and you were always trusted. He wasn't afraid to let you know that you screwed up ... but you always felt that he had your back and you were going to do well. He really understood what it meant to help people be great."

Garrett clearly was adept at leading down. Whether despite or be-cause of his task orientation, he was able to make things happen. He also clearly had well-developed personal skills to go along with that task orientation. He was able to motivate and mentor staff in a positive manner.

Leading up

Leadership is situational. A good leader must recognize the type of leadership that a particular situation needs. Garrett did not focus nearly as much on leading up as Michael Fenn did; it was simply not neces-sary (or in one case, possible) in the situations in which Garrett worked. Both of the regions in which he worked had full-time chairs who were surrounded by part-time, indirectly elected councillors. In both cases, the chairs played a strong role in guiding council, and Garrett worked closely with them. In Toronto, the mayor and his staff played a key role in leading council, and Garrett faced obstacles, such as the size of coun-cil and the enormity of his administrative role, that prevented him from doing much leading up. He did use his abilities at key times, however, to have an impact on council.

In York, there was little ongoing, systemic conflict on council, other than between the "big three" southern municipalities and the other six that was sufficiently institutionalized that it had become routine. Specific issues, such as the big pipe, incited heavy discussion, but the chair was an experienced and well-respected politician who was able to manage council.

In Peel, the main conflict occurred sporadically around Mayor Mc-Callion. Council also consisted of indirectly elected councillors who spent little time on region business and a regional chair who had a good ability to manage issues. Therefore Garrett did not need to work closely with councillors on issues.

In Toronto, Garrett was working for a highly fractious fifty-seven-person council headed by a strong mayor in a situation where the mayor and Garrett had a great deal of difficulty establishing a positive rapport with each another. Even subtle attempts to lead up likely would have been seen as challenges to the mayor's authority. The mayor already had a large staff to assist him in political management. As well, during the early years of the amalgamated city, councillors seemed to be con-sumed more with the high politics on the council floor and managing their image with the large contingent of media that follows Toronto city hall than with administrative matters, except those councillors who wanted to interfere in hiring decisions. In any event, Garrett had a huge job creating the large new administrative structure for the amalgamated city, which left little time to attempt to lead up.

It is also possible that there were at least two aspects of Garrett's background that did not prepare him for the sort of leading up that needs to be done in a municipal government. First, in parliamentary systems, senior officials deal with one minister who is a member of a government that speaks with one voice (at least for public consumption). This is very different from the balancing act required in dealing with a municipal council. Second, his background at the conservation authorities and in parks made him a "good news guy" in terms of his relationship with politicians. Politicians always like new parks, and people with backgrounds in such services do not get much experience in delivering bad news or saying no to politicians. In municipal governments, it is the treasurer, CAO, or even commissioner of social services who frequently must bring bad news. Garrett had never had that experience.

All of the councillors interviewed spoke highly of Garrett, but most interviews began with statements like, "I didn't really know him very well, but ..." Fenn counsels against schmoozing with councillors or lobbying them in a heavy-handed manner. It was clear that Garrett approached his relationship with councillors in a reserved and professional manner. Councillors were satisfied that they were always kept informed of activities, confident about Garrett's abilities to handle difficult administrative situations, and comfortable about leaving him in charge, but they did not speak of having a close personal relationship with him.

Councillors appreciated the fact that Garrett approached issues in a rational way and always spoke to them in a straightforward manner. One councillor contrasted Garrett's style with that of another senior manager: "She was more of a power broker and a gamesman. She would negotiate with councillors: 'OK, if I keep you happy in your riding [sic], can I do all of these things for the administration.'"

Garrett emphasized to his staff that their role was to present to council their best professional, administrative advice. He has no sympathy for managers who tell councillors what they want to hear, and he is particularly critical of those who keep score of how many times their recommendations are accepted. "It's not our job to be politically successful. Our job is to give good technical advice. I ran afoul of certain politicians in that regard."

His views were well respected by council. Councillors clearly trusted his judgment and were willing to assign great weight to his advice. One manager described why he felt this occurred: "I think a part of it was history ... He had a track record of success, and of course success breeds success ... He spoke with authority. He spoke without hesitation. There was no doubt in his voice. This was the right way to go. He wasn't excitable ... He was very calm and reassuring."

Garrett's rational approach, communication skills, and the care he took in preparation were certainly important. Interviewees talked about how there was a certain tone in his voice that indicated quiet confidence. He was never strident or excited, but always just quietly presented the information he had taken great effort to gather and ensure was correct.

His reputation for professionalism and integrity also carried considerable weight:

> I've seen him in private moments where he had to be very firm with some of the council members. ... [O]n some issues you [had] to convince them that this was the right way to go. [I]t might not feel right at the right time, but "trust me, we have to do this." Even when there was pushback, he was very firm, and very convincing, compelling in his arguments, not disrespectful at all, of course, but more or less giving them a rationale as to why this needed to happen, and indicating that, at some point, he was prepared to draw that line in the sand and say "I'm not crossing it." ... He was very well regarded by council. You could see, whenever he engaged with them, when he spoke to them, ... [that] they listened intently. They respected his opinion.

One councillor, however, described how Garrett had the ability to get to know individual councillors on a personal basis and to work with them on specific issues: "I think Michael was good at figuring out what motivated everybody around the table, so that you know how to deal with them, because you can't deal with each person exactly the same way, you have to know what ... motivates each one, where they're coming from, where their soft spots are, and then you can deal with them."

Another councillor described how Garrett would sometimes strike up a seemingly casual conversation with a councillor that turned into something a bit more pointed: "Sometimes [he] would make you feel that ... your opinion on something was very important, when it probably really wasn't. I mean, let's be realistic [laughs], but he'd like you to think that it was, because then he floats his thing in and gets you thinking, maybe a little differently, or the way he'd like you to think. So I guess in a way he's opening your eyes to another idea. And I think he was good at picking out the people that would listen, that he could do that with."

Garrett seemed to have had a number of techniques for dealing with councillors. One observer suggested that he dealt with Mayor McCallion by trying to get issues off the floor of council so that she could not stir up other councillors. He would then meet with her later to politely brief her about the issue. When an issue is removed from the limelight, some councillors are not as interested in it. Another of his techniques was to defuse difficult situations with councillors by ensuring that the discussion always focused on issues, rather than becoming personalized; this also played to his strength, which was an emphasis on rationality.

He also knew how to use the political process to smooth the administrative process. One interviewee described how he greatly improved the budget process in Peel by using a council committee to assist in its preparation. When other councillors wanted to attack the budget, they ran up against a group of fellow councillors who had prepared the budget and therefore would defend it.

Garrett also was not shy about speaking frankly to council:

He was straight with politicians ... He told them the truth and the goods. I can remember a couple of presentations during budget time ... when ... he would tell them, "that decision that you made last week – have a look at the result that this is going to have as we move forward." ... And a couple of times, he scared the pants off them, which needed to be done, but I think they're not used to having someone tell them the straight goods like that. So that's why I think things started to sour. As a staff person, with him as my boss, I was just in awe. I thought that was gutsy beyond I don't know what, and I thought it was wonderful. That's a leader.

The comment at the end of this quotation about things starting to go sour refers to an occupational hazard for any good leader. Sometimes leaders have to tell people things they do not want to hear. The manager quoted above went on to say, "Quite frankly, I think that it's normal that, after a few years – by the end of year five or so in these situations – you're likely to have people that aren't happy campers with you because you didn't do what they wanted you to do for them."

Garrett was well thought of in both Peel and York, and even by many in Toronto, but he did discuss how his itchy feet and need for a new challenge caused him to move on. It might be that one of the important characteristics of a good leader is an understanding of when it is best to head on to the next challenge.

As mentioned at the beginning of this section, leadership is situational: the most important task of the leader is to read the situation and respond to it appropriately. Leaders must have some leadership skills in all three directions, but that does not mean that every leader will actually use all three skills equally at all times. In Peel and York, Garrett developed a rapport with the regional chairs that served him well. He also seemed to get along well enough with other councillors, but this was less important because they were part time and the chairs seemed to exercise a certain level of control. Garrett simply did not need to lead up as much as some of the other CAOs described in this book. In Toronto, the circumstances were such that he had little opportunity to do so, and any attempt to lead up on his part likely would have exacerbated his already difficult position with Mayor Lastman. In the two regions where Garrett worked, the chairs were quite capable of leading their councils. He worked closely with them, but also had a reasonable rapport with other councillors. Although Garrett was not as involved in leading up as some other CAOs, he seems to have carried out the responsibility well enough given his situation.

Leading out

Garrett claims that he did not spend a great deal of time leading out, but he clearly knew when he needed to become involved in issues in a strategic manner. He left much of the day-to-day contact to his senior managers, who were working with developers, community groups, and others on some particular issue. He was busy leading down, and there was simply little need for him to engage in leading out. He nevertheless seems to have pursued the same approach to leading out as he did to leading down. He recognized that his senior managers could handle most issues, but some issues had to be handled by the CAO.

Leading out can be particularly awkward in upper-tier governments such as Peel and York. The area municipalities want to develop a direct relationship with citizens, so upper-tier representatives risk getting into turf battles. In Toronto, the full-time councillors and their assistants were very involved in citizen engagement, and Garrett was busy with the internal organization of the city. In Peel he instituted meetings with the local board of trade to ensure that its members were properly informed of regional activities.

Because Garrett felt that the CAO was responsible for the overall budget in Peel, he also felt he was the proper person to deal with "budget watch" groups or "tax coalitions" there. His tactic for dealing with such groups was to involve them in an advisory committee, which seemed to mollify them. In Toronto, he was only somewhat involved in the budget consultation process, in part because it was a difficult process in a situation where his mandate from the mayor and council was clearly to reduce the budget, while groups appearing at budget consultations generally wanted more money.

In York, Garrett played a significant role in many of the administrative aspects of making VIVA work. Complex public-private partnerships such as VIVA have been hugely beneficial to municipalities, but they have also sometimes gone awry and caused serious problems – the MFP situation in Toronto is a sterling example. A significant part of Garrett's role in VIVA was to make sure that all of the contractual arrangements were in order so that the municipality's interests were protected. His concern for due diligence was criticized, however, for slowing down the process; it was suggested that his experience in Toronto had made him cautious. Nonetheless, the contractual arrangements around VIVA seem to work properly, and the region has not experienced any problems.

The other major project during Garrett's tenure in York was the big pipe. Because of some environmental issues early in the process, before Garrett arrived on the scene, the provincial Ministry of the Environment had imposed stringent safeguards on how the project was to be carried out; indeed, people in York felt they were labouring under some of the most stringent regulations for such a project ever imposed by the ministry. Some expressed the view that, had Garrett been there earlier, this would have been handled differently. For example, Garrett established a liaison committee of environmental leaders, which could have defused the situation if it had been in place earlier. It was felt that Garrett's strength in this situation was his ability to deal with the provincial government. He could not turn the clock back, but he ensured that York's relationship with the ministry did not worsen.

Garrett says that his major interest was the "foreign affairs desk," as he puts it: activities outside his municipality that had an impact on the municipality. He developed a reputation as a strong protector of Peel

Region in the face of proposals for significant changes in government in the Greater Toronto Area, such as those put forward in the Golden Report.[36] He also takes pride in the fact that he twice served as chair of the CAOs group of MARCO.

Garrett's approach to leading out was situational in the same way as was his approach to leading up. Regional governments do not have the same extensive involvement with community groups that area municipalities do, so it should not be surprising that he was not heavily involved with these types of groups. He did play a major role, however, in mediating relationships with stakeholders around such issues as the big pipe and VIVA, and in protecting his organization from outside attacks – important aspects of leading out.

Conclusion: Putting It All Together

What separates great leaders from adequate managers is the ability to lead down, lead up, and lead out all at the same time and to balance them properly. It is not enough to be good at just one of these. What lessons can be learned from Garrett's experiences as a CAO?

BALANCE TASK ORIENTATION AND PEOPLE ORIENTATION

The leadership literature puts great emphasis on the need for leaders to exhibit both task orientation and people orientation. The literature also suggests that, as leaders move up the ladder, task orientation becomes less important and people orientation more so. In this context, task orientation is generally defined as the knowledge and ability to undertake specific tasks such as building a bridge or preparing a financial statement. Garrett and those around him used the term in a more generalized manner, as in successfully completing the task at hand, whatever that task might be. He was quite good at not inserting himself into the details of a project; that territory belonged to the operating manager. But he had a real talent for making sure that particular projects stayed on track in terms of time and were completed in a careful and conscientious manner. This was clear in the way he handled the big pipe and VIVA projects in York Region.

This might indicate that task orientation (properly defined) is more important for a good leader than some of the literature suggests. Being people oriented does not get an organization far if it cannot meet its goals and deliver on major projects. Thus, one would not expect a senior leader to be involved in the details of constructing a bridge, but to drive the bridge construction in such a way that it is completed on time and within budget.

BUILD ON YOUR STRENGTHS; STRENGTHEN YOUR WEAKNESSES

One reason Garrett was so effective is that he recognized his strengths and weaknesses. He did not really try to restrain his task orientation; he knew it was an important aspect of getting his job done. He focused on tasks, and ensured that the kinds of things he was well known for – performance measurement, team building – happened as they should. Delivering on tasks is a major part of being a good leader.

Garrett says that people skills do not come as easily for him, yet virtually all interviewees commented positively on his skills in this area. He knew such skills were important, and he developed them in himself and tried to ensure that they were developed within the organizations for which he worked. He was recognized as instrumental in creating a strong learning environment at York. Several people talked about his instituting leadership development programs even though he was unsure about this kind of soft service.

DEVELOP SITUATIONAL LEADERSHIP

Garrett was an astute judge of the situations in which he found himself, and he built on these situations rather than fight against them. He worked in three municipalities with strong heads of council who were able to exercise significant influence over councillors. Recognizing this, he used it to focus on leading down. He could have insisted on having a major role in leading up. But such a challenge of the head of council would only have led to conflict and made him less effective in leading down.

The lesson here is that, although it is important to lead in three directions, not every situation calls for an equal emphasis on all three. The leader must be aware of her or his orientation in all three directions, but sometimes discretion suggests emphasizing certain directions over others. In the two places where Garrett was successful in leading up, he did it by working through the regional chairs and building some rapport with other councillors. In Toronto, he developed rapport with some councillors, but, for reasons beyond his control, he was not able to do so with the mayor, and this was a part of the reason for his problems there.

TRUST YOUR SUBORDINATES, BUT BE THERE FOR THEM
WHEN THEY NEED YOU

Staff felt strongly that Garrett placed a great deal of trust in them and did not attempt to micromanage their operations. They also understood that, through the performance measurement system and their periodic reviews, he was holding them accountable for doing their jobs properly. They were given the scope to do their jobs, but they were not free agents.

They also knew that he was there to support them in tough situations. Whether it was associating himself with their reports to council or writing a stern letter to a mayor about a councillor's behaviour, staff members were confident that Garrett would support them in their actions. They also understood that one way of supporting them was his being frank with them about when they had not measured up, and helping them make the best of the situation.

BE RESILIENT

Great leaders almost always suffer setbacks at some point. The only people who do not suffer setbacks are those who never attempt to do anything difficult. Garrett took on a tough job as the first CAO of the amalgamated City of Toronto; indeed. most observers suggest the job was likely impossible. Despite his efforts, he was caught up in a huge scandal and his appointment was "rescinded," to use the polite Toronto euphemism. He nevertheless emerged from this experience with his dignity and his integrity intact. He was welcomed into his next position by a group of people who felt it was a coup to be able to hire such a good leader. Garrett, in short, refused to quit, but made the best of a difficult situation.

Overall Assessment

How does Mike Garrett fare according to the definition of a leader developed in Chapter 1? Everywhere he worked, he clearly moved the municipality forward. In York, his fingerprints are on two major projects: the big pipe and VIVA. In Peel, he tore down silos and built a performance measurement system. Both innovations have had a lasting effect on the organizational culture in the two regions. Even in Toronto, he made great strides in building an organization from the ground up.

His success was based on his style of mutual influence, rather than authority. He had a reputation as a great communicator, which included being a good listener. The fact that he mentored many people who themselves have gone on to leadership roles says a great deal. He focused on building teams and on empowering them to make decisions, instead of handing down decisions from the CAO's office. He also ensured that council, external stakeholders, and organizational subordinates were all involved and on side in order to accomplish the big tasks.

A municipal CAO who is a good leader has the ability to move the municipality forward by interacting in a mutually influential way with and motivating council, external stakeholders, and organizational subordinates.

4 The Relationship-oriented Leader: Judy Rogers

My philosophy would be to bring around you the very best talented people you can. Make sure you have a framework of support and respect and trust that they can work within. Assist them when they need you. Know what they're doing and empower them to be the best they can be. And seek the support of colleagues. I think relationships are really important so if I don't trust you, you're not going to do your best job because you're always going to be second-guessing whether I trust you or not. So to develop the collegiality of an environment of empowerment is really what it's all about. So you hire people who are experts, who are passionate, who love public service, then you need their professional mindset to be able to do the work they do. That's what I looked for. That's the kind of team I worked to assemble.

– Judy Rogers, in an interview for this chapter

When I became a city manager, I knew enough about team, about creating a vibrancy, and interface among the people who work together. I brought around me the smartest people, the best team workers that I could in their various fields ... My job was to knit everyone together ... I tried to always stay at the strategic level, supported people as they had tough decisions to make and places to go.

– Judy Rogers, in an interview for this chapter

Judy Rogers first learned about the importance of personal relationships and working through teams on playing fields and in classrooms in Kimberley, British Columbia, where she grew up. She further developed that knowledge early in her career when she worked for the

YWCA in Vancouver. She carried these lessons with her throughout her working life, and they were a significant part of her management style.

The two previous case studies focused on professional managers who moved around and plied their trade in a number of municipalities and at other levels of government. This case study tells the story of a leader who spent virtually her entire adult life in one city and most of her working life in the employ of that city. It shows how a CAO can be attached to a city as much as being an employee of the city.

Judy Rogers started to work for the City of Vancouver in 1988, in the Equal Employment Opportunity Office, but she had worked for a number of social agencies in the city before that. She climbed the city hierarchy fairly quickly and became assistant city manager in 1994, deputy city manager in 1996, and city manager in 1999. She served in that position until 2008, when she was fired by a new council three days after it took office. The incoming mayor spoke highly of her service to the city, but indicated that the new council wanted to go in a different direction. Even after leaving public office, she is still a visible presence on the Vancouver scene in all sorts of volunteer activities.

Rogers has been the recipient of a number of personal rewards, and for several years she was recognized by the Women's Executive Network as one of the one hundred most powerful women in Canada,[1] and she eventually won permanent membership in the Network's Hall of Fame. She was the first recipient of the Alumni Award of the University of Victoria School of Public Administration.[2] In 1993 she won the Lieutenant Governor's Award of the Institute of Public Administration of Canada (IPAC) for being the outstanding public servant in British Columbia. The City of Vancouver also won a number of awards during Rogers's time as city manager,[3] and in 2007 the city was recognized as one of Canada's Top 100 Employers.[4] Rogers was instrumental in the development of the Vancouver Agreement, which won awards as an innovative intergovernmental program. She was also influential in establishing the award-winning Neighbourhood Integrated Service Teams program. By any standard, Rogers clearly had a distinguished career. She was recognized in her profession and in her city as a successful public servant.

The raw material for this chapter was drawn from two sources. The first strand of research was a detailed review of various background sources of information, including a number of books about this era of Vancouver politics. My research assistant also undertook an extensive review of the *Vancouver Sun* newspaper during Rogers's tenure in office, as well as wide-ranging Internet searches. The second strand was thirty personal interviews, with Rogers at the beginning and end of this project, the three mayors for whom she worked, four present or former councillors, twelve present or former staff members, and nine community members who were familiar with her.

The City of Vancouver

Vancouver is a unique city in many ways, and Rogers's career was intertwined with the city in ways quite unlike those of the more itinerant CAOs discussed in other chapters of this book.

The population of the City of Vancouver grew from 545,671 in 2001 (shortly after Rogers became city manager) to 578,041 in 2006 (shortly before she left), or about 28 per cent of the population of the Greater Vancouver Regional District, as the upper-tier regional government was then called.[5] Vancouver is blessed with the natural beauty of several interesting waterways and striking mountain views from almost anywhere in the city. The climate of the city and surrounding area is such that, on many days, the sports enthusiast can play golf or drive an hour north and go skiing. Its residents and civic leaders have made a number of important decisions over the years to keep the city and its neighbourhoods both beautiful and efficient.[6] Yet, in 2011, residents engaged in a great deal of soul searching because the *Economist* moved Vancouver's ranking as the most livable city in the world to third place, a ranking most cities would be happy to achieve.

Vancouver is not just beautiful; it is also a significant commercial centre as Canada's face in the direction of the growing Asia-Pacific market. It has attracted many Asian immigrants who provide a bridge for both commerce and tourism between Canada and their home countries. Its many modern office towers house the head offices of numerous companies and significant regional offices of many others.

The local political scene is unusual by Canadian standards in three ways. First, the city itself contains a relatively small and declining portion of the population of the metropolitan area,[7] which has had an impact on the city's influence in the urban region.

Second, it is the largest city in Canada with a system of at-large election of municipal councillors. This has been the subject of some debate and several plebiscites over the years, but it has never changed.[8] At-large election has produced the expected result in that the ten councillors tend to have a decided middle- to upper-class tinge and usually come disproportionately from certain small areas in the city, although the system has also produced some strong left-wing councillors such as Harry Rankin and Jim Green.

The third anomaly in Vancouver municipal politics is the presence of a long-established, but somewhat volatile, system of municipal political parties.[9] The oxymoronically titled Non-Partisan Association (NPA) is a business-based, somewhat right-wing party that has been around since the 1940s. The Coalition of Progressive Electors (COPE), founded in the late 1960s, is a left-wing party with ties to the union and environmental movements. Vision Vancouver is a more recent addition to the scene on the left with particular environmental concerns. The two left-wing parties have flirted with an alliance, but by the 2008 election the courtship had progressed only to the point where they decided not to compete with each other in the election by nominating complementary slates. One should be careful, however, about making too much of the left-right labels of these parties. As at the federal and provincial levels, the parties usually lean in their respective directions, but elections are fought with an understanding that most electors occupy the broad middle ground. The successful party generally is the one that captures the large middle range of voters without abandoning its distinctive position on the political spectrum.

The effect of the combination of at-large elections and a party system has been to produce pronounced swings in voting. One party generally has been dominant in holding the mayor's office and a significant majority of council seats, and for most of the time from the 1940s until the turn of the century that party was the NPA. In recent years, however, the NPA's hegemony has started to crumble. The COPE candidate won the mayor's chair in 2002 and brought a solid majority of COPE councillors with him. The Vision Vancouver-COPE slate won convincingly both the 2008 and 2011 elections.

During the time Rogers was city manager, from 1999 until 2008, she served three different mayors of two different political stripes. When she was appointed city manager in 1999, it was during the term of Philip Owen, who had been elected mayor under the NPA banner in 1993 after having served for seven years on council. He was the stereotypical NPA mayor, having been a successful businessman who came to politics late in his career. He claimed he had no aspiration to run for mayor, and that it had been thrust upon him when the obvious NPA candidate stepped aside.

From 2002 to 2005 Rogers served as city manager under Mayor Larry Campbell, a high-profile, somewhat iconic figure who had been a member of the Royal Canadian Mounted Police, then a crusading coroner on whom the popular TV series, *Da Vinci's Inquest*, was based. He ran under the COPE banner, but did not fit well with the party. His electoral future in the 2005 election would have been unclear, but this became moot when he was appointed to the Senate of Canada shortly before his term ended.

Rogers's third mayor was Sam Sullivan of the NPA, who served as mayor from 2005 to 2008 after having been on council since 1993. Sullivan, the son of a Vancouver businessman, became a quadriplegic at age nineteen as a result of a skiing accident. He was seen as a visionary leader with many new ideas for the city, but problems during his term of office soured his relationship with city residents generally and even with his own party.[10] The NPA accordingly chose not to support him in the 2008 election by a narrow margin, although Peter Ladner, the NPA's replacement candidate, was soundly defeated.

The new mayor, Gregor Robertson, was elected under the Vision Vancouver banner, and nine of the ten councillors were also elected from the Vision Vancouver-COPE slate. Vision Vancouver had set out to make some basic changes in the way the city operated, including making it the greenest city in North America.[11] Presumably there was a sense among a majority of councillors that Rogers did not fit into Vision Vancouver's plans, and council fired her three days after it formally took office.[12]

Career Path

Kimberley, British Columbia, in the east Kootenays, where Judy Rogers was born in 1949, is a relatively isolated community that had a population of about 6,000 when she was growing up. It was home to what was billed as the largest lead-zinc mine in the world, where her father worked; its second-largest export seems to have been athletes, particularly hockey players and skiers. Her mother was a teacher, but chose to stay home after she was married. Rogers speaks positively of her family, which she describes as "trusting, supportive, loving ... who gave me a lot of room to be who I was [so that] ... nothing was impossible." Her family did not particularly push her to succeed, but she remembers that it was just assumed she would obtain a solid education.

Rogers has fond memories of Kimberley. She feels she had many opportunities to shine and to be involved in community activities that
would not have been the case in a larger city: "That small community
just gave me huge opportunities to do anything I wanted ... Success is a
big influence. In a small community, you can do really well just because
you're in a small community. And you did everything. I mean, you
couldn't field a team, you couldn't have a debate, you couldn't do anything unless everybody did it together, because there weren't enough
of you otherwise." Years later, in 2010, Rogers would carry the Olympic
torch through Kimberley, a testament to her love of her hometown and
her attachment to the Olympic Games.

Rogers showed leadership both in the classroom and in athletics
from an early age. She was usually captain of the sports teams and
president of the student associations. Her particular interests were skiing and swimming, but she participated in many other sports. It seems
that, for her, sports were about the obvious physical activity, but they
were equally an avenue to make friends and connect with people in
the community.[13] Through such activities, the local recreation director
recognized her leadership potential by giving her considerable responsibilities when she was quite young, as well as a glowing recommendation to the community recreation program at the University of British
Columbia.

Rogers was attracted to the Bachelor of Physical Education program
at UBC in part because of her athletic prowess, but she also saw a major
attraction in the program's emphasis on community recreation and
working with people. As a foreshadowing of her later career, she notes
that "I was particularly interested in the value of play ... I was observing that people who played together, who had a sense of joy and spirit
about them, did really well. If I could engage people in the activity of
learning to play, then ... there were a whole bunch of things that would
change if people engaged in humour, play, teamwork." As we will see,
bringing people together was a hallmark of her career.

Vancouver was a big place for a young woman from a small town.
She recalls having her first taste of public transit when she arrived in
Vancouver, but she must have grown up fairly quickly. By her second
year at UBC she was married, and the couple's first child was born
while she was still a student. Even today, such a situation would be
a challenge; then, with no on-campus daycare facilities or other support mechanisms, it was particularly difficult – women were supposed

to stay home with their young children. It must have required a great deal of energy and organizational skill to balance her family life and her studies. She obviously did this well, however, as she received the Gold Medal as the top graduating student in her program. The energy and organizational skills she exhibited at UBC would stay with her throughout her career.

Her first job after completing her degree was in community development with the YWCA. She then left to teach high school in Kelowna for two years, but the big city drew her back, this time as a single mother of two young children. She returned to the YWCA, as director of the Social and Community Services Department, where she had an opportunity to employ the community engagement skills she would use throughout her career. She spent a total of eight years with the YWCA, was quite happy there, and would have been pleased to spend her career in the voluntary sector.

Not surprisingly, however, her career moved in a direction where she could put her skills at mediation and conflict resolution to work. After her time at the YWCA, Rogers moved on to a rather short stint in a contract position of the City of Vancouver as general manager of the Vancouver Indian Centre, with the task of resolving some operational problems there. As sometimes happens in these cases, she turned over some rocks and exposed things that some people preferred to remain hidden, resulting in physical threats to her and her family. Managers in the city knew she could not stay in this position, but as the contract was a multi-year one, they had to figure out what to do with this obviously talented woman.

She then came to the attention of Ken Dobell, who was the deputy city manager but soon would become city manager. Vancouver has had a succession of well-respected city managers cut from a particular mould. Dobell and his predecessor, Fritz Bowers, were both engineers by training who were regarded as exceptionally smart and capable managers. Dobell saw something in this bright young woman with superb people skills that complemented his more task-oriented, engineering approach. When asked specifically what he saw in her at that time, he said "Judy … is a woman who raised kids on her own, went to school … clearly a tough, strong character. I think people saw the strong character, I think they saw a whole lot of facilitation skills, social skills, working with people of very different backgrounds. She'd done quite a bit in the non-profit sector prior to that as well." This was the beginning of a strong mentoring relationship. Dobell took her under his wing, but he was the sort of no-nonsense guy who expected that she would develop on her own, not just ride on his coattails.

She was moved from the Indian Centre into the civic administration proper, to work in the Equal Employment Opportunities (EEO) Office. This new position fit her well. She had the interpersonal skills to make the case for equality, and she could be tough when that was warranted. This combination, which one interviewee described as a "velvet glove with an iron fist," is a trait that Rogers exhibited throughout her career.

It was a short step from the EEO Office to becoming the first executive director of the Hastings Institute, a wholly-owned corporation of the City of Vancouver that "offers training and consulting services to external organizations in the areas of equity, human rights and diversity."[14] The institute began as an offshoot of the EEO Office to provide training and related services within the city, but the reputation of Rogers and others in the organization was such that it soon started offering these services on a fee-for-service basis to a variety of other public and private sector organizations.

Her six years as head of the Hastings Institute showed that she had the combination of the interpersonal skills to deal with issues around equal employment opportunities and diversity, and the hard management skills needed to turn a fledgling internal training program into a financially sustainable organization selling its services on the open market in a very competitive environment. With Rogers at the helm, the institute developed an excellent reputation for good programs, and it is still recognized as a strong force in training and development in the areas of diversity and equity.

Her next step was to become assistant city manager in 1994; in 1996, when it was discovered that she was being courted by another municipality, her title was changed to deputy city manager. Her precise role in these positions was somewhat flexible. She worked closely with City Manager Ken Dobell and with councillors. The idea was that she and Dobell would function as a team in the city manager's office: Dobell, the engineer, would handle hard service issues, and Rogers, the mediator and conciliator, would handle issues around human services and those requiring her relationship-oriented skills.

She took on responsibilities for various kinds of project management, particularly those involving mediation and conciliation. For example, during this time, she won kudos for working out an agreement between conflicting factions around a planning issue in the fashionable Shaughnessy area.

Another part of her duties involved stepping in as a temporary department head when a position was vacant, or handling a particularly difficult slice of activity within a department. This broadened her municipal experience considerably.

She also used her status in the city manager's office to begin to undertake projects that would bear fruit over time. She developed the idea of Neighbourhood Integrated Service Teams, which would win awards for innovation in 1996, and she also began laying the groundwork for the Vancouver Agreement, which would be signed in 2000. Both of these innovations are discussed more fully later in this chapter.

Rogers was earning a reputation as someone who had well-developed interpersonal skills, but she could also be tough.[15] One interviewee who worked with her at this time suggested that "she [didn't] hesitate to bring out the heavy lumber" when necessary, but he was quick to make it clear that she never chastised anyone publicly. She knew how to combine her softer interpersonal skills with her iron fist in ways that accomplished her goals without embarrassing others.

During this time, she completed the Master of Public Administration program at the University of Victoria. It was obviously difficult to undertake the degree while working in a senior position and balancing a home life with two children, but she felt she needed to take courses in areas, such as finance and law, where she did not have a solid background to round out her recognized interpersonal skills.

She was appointed city manager in 1999, when her long-time mentor Ken Dobell left to be the founding chief executive officer of the Greater Vancouver Transportation Authority, now known as TransLink, a regional local government agency responsible for urban transportation in Greater Vancouver.

Rogers's time as city manager

Vancouver has long had a reputation as a progressive, well-managed city. A number of significant developments occurred during Rogers's time as city manager that supported that reputation.

THE VANCOUVER AGREEMENT AND THE DOWNTOWN EAST SIDE
The Vancouver Agreement[16] is an agreement signed in 2000 between the City of Vancouver, the province of British Columbia, and the government of Canada to coordinate the provision of services in Vancouver's

downtown east side. It was an innovative approach to a difficult issue that won many awards.

Downtown east side is a notorious area in an otherwise affluent city. Its problems are the usual ones facing poorer neighbourhoods – substandard housing, homelessness, drug addiction, HIV/AIDS, mental health issues, prostitution – but they have been recognized as much more severe in the downtown east side than in other areas. Rogers had become personally familiar with the area when she worked for the YWCA and the Vancouver Indian Centre. Its problems were not being solved, however, in part because each level of government was acting independently in the area, and the lack of coordination meant that their programs failed to achieve the maximum effect.

The Vancouver Agreement constituted a commitment on the part of the three governments to work together on any undertakings in the downtown east side. The strength of the agreement was the ongoing nature of its existence, and funding and programs could flow through the agreement as they started and stopped. Tripartite agreements tied to particular funding and programs are fragile because, if any one of the three governments terminates or changes its program, the agreement must be renegotiated. Framework agreements such as the Vancouver Agreement, however, allow a number of different programs and funding arrangements to operate within it.

The obvious weakness of framework agreements, however, is that programs and funding are not assured. The Vancouver Agreement also was not particularly effective in coordinating the ongoing activities of local police services, as indicated by reports of the Missing Women Commission of Inquiry into the actions of Robert Picton.[17] The ultimate weakness of such agreements is that with no ongoing programs embedded in them, it is easy for participants to allow them to die, which is exactly what happened to the Vancouver Agreement in 2010.

A complex agreement like this requires the cooperation of many people at many levels in many organizations to make it work. Of course, the political leaders always take the front positions on the podium, and public servants play a supportive role. But this makes it hard to identify precisely who has done most of the heavy lifting to get the project going. It is difficult to single out any one person who was responsible for the Vancouver Agreement, but Rogers's presence was one constant throughout its gestation period and most of its life while representatives of other governments came and went. A number of people involved with the agreement identified Rogers as a prime mover in developing it at the concept stage, and noted that she spent a great deal of time commuting between Vancouver and Ottawa to make sure everything stayed on track. She used her connections and her conciliation skills to keep the concept on everyone's agenda. There seems little doubt that Rogers was a key player, if not the most important player, in bringing the agreement to fruition.[18] She also played a significant role in implementing the agreement after it was signed and in developing many of its projects – a major triumph was the conversion of the grand old Woodward's department store, which had become an eyesore and a serious point of contention, into a mixed-use development.[19]

The highest-profile initiative in the area was the development of the first legal safe injection site in Canada. As with the Vancouver Agreement itself, the development of Insite, as the facility is called, involved many people,[20] but Rogers was a leader on this issue when others in the city did not want to become involved. Insite is still controversial despite some positive evidence about its value,[21] but it clearly was an important step toward improving the streetscape and life in general in the downtown east side.

The Vancouver Agreement was not entirely ground breaking – a similar agreement was already in place in Winnipeg – but it was sufficiently innovative to win a number of awards: the Institute of Public Administration of Canada's annual award for innovative management in 2004, one of eight winners of the United Nations Public Service Award in 2005 – the top prize for "[i]mproving transparency, accountability and responsiveness in the public service"[22] – and a Partnership Award from the Association of Professional Executives of the Public Service of Canada. The agreement clearly was an innovative approach to a difficult problem.

THE 2010 OLYMPICS

Another important event that occurred during Rogers's time as city manager was the awarding of the 2010 Winter Olympics to Vancouver. She had left the position by the time the Olympics were held, but she played a significant role in much of the organizational activity leading up to the Games. In fact, by the account of a number of people, Rogers was the only continuing city presence from the early stages of bid preparation. She provided valuable advice to the bid organizing committees, and she used her extensive network of contacts to locate office space for staff and to bring people on side at the right time.

It all came together at the end, with all three levels of government supporting Vancouver's bid, but throughout the development process, every government wavered at some point. The city even held a plebiscite to gauge the support of its citizens. Rogers, however, was the one constant who did not waver. One person from the private sector involved in the bid process described her role in this way: "[S]he was absolutely one of the four or five key people. She made things happen. She knew how to get things done. She had the ear of almost anybody in town that was important. She brought her council along very skilfully – totally above board and everything, but she knew how to manage contentious issues in the most effective way to get a result that was wanted. And she was absolutely no nonsense. She's a very attractive lady, but when push got to shove, she's tough as nails."

A fellow public servant who watched her work from a proximate location described her involvement in a more nuanced manner:

> She was instrumental in getting the Olympics to come for reasons that people may not appreciate ... One of her skills was that, because of her personality, her perspective, and her philosophy, she recognized that everyone was acting in the interests of the city of Vancouver ... regardless of their stripes and regardless of how long ago they served ... She was firstly able to bridge the old to the new and make them understand the importance, and then, as a companion to that, [she was] able to put in place a structure or a process that would actually support whoever was going to be the driving force. So while she certainly took the lead when it was necessary, it was my recollection she was attempting to be secondary to the elected parties whether they [were] provincial or municipal. But as she undertook that, when she understood there were gaps, she would leap in with enthusiasm and vigour and make sure that was something that she seized upon, and when the support came from the elected officials, she would then again withdraw to make sure they had all the tools necessary to succeed. Ultimately I think it was the supportive/collaborative role that was so instrumental in bringing the Olympics to Vancouver.

The ability to step in when necessary to move things forward and then to disappear into the shadows at the right time is a hallmark of the consummate public servant.

Rogers was also credited with some seemingly small, but possibly important, touches that could have had an impact on the acceptance of Vancouver's bid. It is a long-standing complaint about both the Summer and Winter Olympic Games – and all such major events, for that matter – that host cities put up a veneer of wealth and happiness that crowds out poor and marginalized people. For example, Vancouver's Expo 86 was criticized for pushing the poor out of low-cost accommodation to make way for wealthy tourists. Vancouver's Olympic bid, however, included an Inner City Inclusiveness Commitment that "programs and policies will be developed that support the goals and objectives in the Commitment Statement to create a strong foundation for sustainable socio-economic development in Vancouver's inner-city neighbourhoods, particularly in Downtown Eastside, Downtown South and Mount Pleasant ... Also during the implementation phase, steps will be taken to ensure incorporation of the interests of different groups, such as aboriginal people, women, youth, people with disabilities, people of colour, immigrants and other groups."[23] One never knows why a particular city's bid is successful, and it would be simplistic to say that this commitment, or any other one thing, swung the awarding committee's decision. The committee was fully aware, however, that the Olympics have a long history of complaints about mistreating and shunting aside vulnerable groups, and Vancouver's commitment to avoid such side-effects surely must have allayed some of the committee's concerns.

By almost any account, the Olympics were successful. They put Canada on a worldwide centre stage, and Canada looked very good. Tragic events such as the death of a Georgian luger were much overshadowed by Games that were well planned and that left a lasting legacy for the area.

Although Rogers had many successes during her tenure as city manager, one must mention two significant problems that occurred toward the end of her career.

THE 2007 CIVIC WORKERS' STRIKE

In 2007 there was a difficult strike of civic workers. Such strikes are not unusual in Vancouver; in fact, they happen fairly regularly. This strike, however, was particularly noteworthy for its length (the second-longest in Vancouver history) and the way in which the union personalized this as "Sam's strike," after Mayor Sam Sullivan. Some of the personalization of the strike seems to have rubbed off on the city manager as well.

The strike involved some significant issues related to compensation and working conditions, but there were undertones as well. Some described the Vancouver civic union as particularly political and as wanting to break the NPA and Sullivan, which it saw as bastions of conservatism. The union supposedly also wanted to break an agreement among Vancouver-area municipalities intended to prevent unions from whipsawing the various municipalities. Finally, Rogers was seen as taking a hard line on union issues, and the union wanted to send a message to, and about, her. The handling of labour negotiations is an area where municipalities are not required to operate in a public manner, so it is impossible to determine how much of the city's negotiating stance came from the political or administrative sides of the house. Various union leaders have suggested, however, that the length and ferocity of the strike was due in part to Rogers's bargaining stance.

THE OLYMPIC ATHLETES' VILLAGE

Another thorny issue was a major glitch in preparations for the Olympics that had to do with the construction of the athletes' village. The project started well: it was in a great location on the south shore of False Creek, and a new rapid transit line, the Canada Line, would bring people from the airport and take them downtown, and provided a convenient stop at the village (thanks to some hard lobbying by Vancouver). The plan was for the village to be built by a private developer who would then make money after the Olympics by selling most of the units at market prices and turn the rest over to the city for social housing.

The details of what went wrong are both contentious and complicated, and airing them out does not matter for this discussion anyway. Basically, the city thought it had a deal with a private developer to construct the village with limited financial involvement by the city. For a variety of reasons, the deal went bad, and the city ended up providing guarantees that could have put it on the hook for much more money than it had ever contemplated.[24]

Even in retrospect, it is a subject of endless debate how much of the problem stemmed from the city's lack of due diligence and how much was the result of events, such as the 2008 global financial crisis, that the city could not have reasonably anticipated. The point is that the city was placed in a difficult financial position, and there was even some fleeting concern that the village might not be completed on time.

The 2008 municipal election

The political dimension of the Olympic village issue was that it unfolded during the 2008 municipal election campaign. It is not clear that anyone in the city made serious mistakes, but there were questions about exactly what should have been done and when that made residents uneasy; the issue gave the opposition COPE-Vision Vancouver group an opening to attack the NPA and Mayor Sullivan.

In the November 2008 election, the sitting NPA council was soundly defeated. It is impossible to determine exactly why a particular party wins or loses an election. The NPA's decision not to support the incumbent mayor and the way in which this unfolded arguably did not help its chances. In any case, that was a purely political decision having nothing to do with Rogers. The civic workers' strike cut two ways, as such strikes generally do. The NPA did not win much union support, but it probably picked up support among businesspeople and non-unionized workers. The problems around the athletes' village did make the NPA look bad, rightly or wrongly.[25]

No administrator wants to feel that her or his actions had an impact on an election. In that way, administrators are like umpires at a baseball game; they know they have done their best work when no one notices their presence. It is difficult to determine the role senior administration played in the strike and athletes' village issues, but it is impossible for senior administration, including Rogers, to separate itself completely from the decisions that were made.

Replacing the NPA and Sullivan were Gregor Robertson of Vision Vancouver and nine councillors (out of ten) from the COPE-Vision Vancouver slate – a commanding position for the new group. Three days after the new administration took office, council voted to fire Rogers and hire Penny Ballem, a physician and former provincial senior public servant, as the new city manager. As usual in these situations, little background was offered about the reasons for the decision. Mayor Robertson thanked Rogers for her "remarkable" work for the city, but said that his council wanted to go in a "new direction." He affirmed that the issue around the athletes' village was not the reason for her dismissal.[26]

Media accounts of the firing generally praised Rogers for her service to the city.[27] Various people interviewed off the record for this chapter used words such as "disappointed" or "horrified" to refer to her dismissal, but no one, including Rogers herself, expressed a great deal of surprise at the turn of events. Commentators offered a number of reasons the new regime made the change. One of the most frequent was an acceptance at face value of council's statement about wanting to pursue a new direction, accompanied by the idea that Ballem was a known quantity who was willing to pursue that course. Another point sometimes expressed was that, during COPE's previous time in office from 2002 to 2005, Rogers might not have pursued the party's agenda sufficiently aggressively, leading to concern on the part of the new administration about her suitability this time. She also might have been seen as a small-c conservative who would not have felt comfortable with the kind of large-scale changes the new regime had in mind. Some interviewees suggested that the COPE-Vision Vancouver group wanted to send a message that they would be pursuing significant change during their time at city hall. This message was directed not just at Rogers, but at all senior managers, many of whom left within a year or two after Rogers was dismissed. Finally, many people commented that ten years in one place is actually a good, long run for a city manager, and she simply had "run out the string," as one person put it. Throughout this discussion, which played out on the civic scene for some time, no one questioned Rogers's competence. She accomplished a great deal in her ten years in office, and won a great deal of respect from politicians, city staff, and colleagues in other places.

In retirement (if that is the right word), Rogers remains attached to her adopted city. She lives a few blocks from the city hall where she worked for many years, and she is active in all sorts of volunteer causes and fundraising campaigns. She remains as well connected in her city as ever.

The Leadership Role of the CAO

In this section, I offer some general statements about Judy Rogers's personality and leadership style that will set the stage for an analysis of how, as city manager, she led up, down, and out.

General characteristics

PEOPLE ORIENTED

Virtually every interviewee referred to Rogers as being strongly people or relationship oriented. Indeed, this orientation comes across in one's first meeting with her. She has a ready smile and a charming and friendly personality. Moreover, this is not just a veneer; Rogers is a good listener. As one interviewee put it, "[t]here is nobody who meets with Judy and talks to her and comes away and says, 'She didn't hear me.' Judy pays attention." Another interviewee suggested that it says a great deal about Rogers that, whenever you had an interaction with her, you took something of value away from it: "Judy is one of those rare personalities ... [E]very time she made a connection in a relationship, the people that she was connecting to always felt a positive aspect of it so that ... even if they were on opposite sides of the issue, there was a respect and ... a furtherance of not only her objectives but of their objectives. ... I can't think of a single person that she came across that felt like they didn't have a positive relationship with her and therefore weren't prepared to work with her in future."

A number of interviewees suggested that her style was never to challenge someone else's views directly, but to register her reservations in a clear, but more positive way. A long-time friend said, "[e]ven if there's something she'll disagree with, she'll say, 'Oh, [name], I don't think so.' ... It's never aggressive ... Even if she doesn't agree with you, she'll still do it in a nice, respectful way."

Several interviewees referred to her emotional intelligence. As one commented, "I have never seen anyone who can read a person's motives better than Judy. You walk into a room – (laughs) I used to enjoy this actually. We'd have some discussion over some controversial matter, and the first thing I would always say to Judy after the door was closed was, 'OK, what did you think?' and we were fairly aligned. We were both fairly good at that, but Judy was brilliant. Judy could say, 'You know what's really going on here is some other agenda,' and she could always sense [that]. She was uncanny in her ability."

A significant aspect of her people orientation was that she was perceived as having no ego or need to get recognition for her accomplishments: "What I've been most impressed with [about] Judy is her lack of ego ... [S]he was always more concerned about what needed to get done, and less concerned about who got the accolades or recognition for it getting done."

One interviewee discussed how Rogers was not only bright but also sensitive, feeling that, although Rogers had thought something through and was three or four steps ahead of the person she was interacting with, she would allow the person to work her or his way through the various steps rather than jumping ahead.

A number of people who worked closely with her commented on her even temperament. No matter what was happening around her, she always kept her composure and rarely showed anger or frustration outwardly. She never had to raise her voice because she commanded respect without having to demand it in that way.

WELL CONNECTED IN THE CITY

Virtually every interviewee talked about Rogers's connections. Throughout her career, she met people in a variety of walks of life and maintained contact with them. Part of this ability to connect comes from the fact that Rogers is simply a warm, friendly, and outgoing person, but it goes beyond just having a friendly manner. Interviewees talked about her being free and open in providing advice. She knew so many people that she could easily make connections between disparate people who needed a particular contact. Her wealth of connections simply made her aware of many things. When the Olympic bid committee needed some cheap but strategically located office space, she just happened to know someone who had such space available. When a friend was going out on her own to start a business, Rogers was able to connect her with some clients.

A city manager has certain automatic kinds of connections by virtue of the position. Leaders in the business, labour, health care, and other sectors will always return the manager's calls promptly because they want to stay on that person's good side, but that is not the same as being really connected at a personal level. Rogers went far beyond this superficial type of connection.

Rogers's ties, however, were not just with the usual groups that need to connect with a city manager. She had broad and deep roots in the community. As one interviewee noted, "[s]he's got her finger on the pulse. I felt when she was in the manager's office that was one of her big advantages … You didn't pigeonhole her as being connected with this group or that group, but she just had this feel for things."

A FOCUS ON TEAM BUILDING

Given these basic skills, it should not be a surprise that Rogers was seen as a strong team builder. Building teams and coalitions requires an ability to understand the people you are dealing with, and Rogers's exceptional people skills came to the fore here. She could explain a proposal in a way that made sense to an individual and that got the person to agree. The earlier examples of how she worked on the Olympic bid and the Vancouver Agreement illustrate how she built coalitions to accomplish particular goals.

CHANGE ORIENTED

Rogers did not accept the status quo; she was always looking for ways to improve the situation. This started early in her career when she was instrumental in founding Crabtree Corner,[28] a family resource centre of the YWCA in the downtown east side, after a resident mentioned that she could not find appropriate local daycare. Her career was marked by so many examples of this kind of activity that it is difficult to choose the best one, but the way she tackled issues concerning the downtown east side illustrates her refusal to accept the status quo. She had a significant amount of experience in this area of the city, and she wanted to improve the situation of people who lived there. This led her to push for the Vancouver Agreement, the redevelopment of the Woodward's site, the development of the safe injection site, and other major changes.

She was viewed as instrumental in the development of the legacy plan for the Olympics. From an early stage, the Vancouver bid team focused beyond the Olympic Games themselves, and on the legacy they wanted to create in terms not only of facilities, but also of philanthropy and social change. Rogers is currently chair of the Board of Directors of the 2010 Legacy Foundation, which is making these things happen.

She did not readily accept the idea that her responsibility and influence stopped at jurisdictional boundaries. Even though the city had no direct control over the construction of the Canada Line, she formed a task force at city hall to consider how to protect the city's interest. One result was an additional station in a strategic location for Vancouver.

THE COURAGE OF HER CONVICTIONS

Rogers's orientation toward change was based on a strong belief in her convictions. When she knew what needed to be done, she was not shy about taking the lead. As one interviewee commented, "[s]he has the most important quality of all in leadership, which is the courage of her convictions. The woman is incredibly courageous. She does what she believes in and she is a quick learner, and had good instincts."

She was not reticent about taking a leadership role even with regard to her political masters. When one interviewee was asked about Rogers's unwavering push for the Olympics even when council was wavering, he responded, "[t]hat's Judy's nature. Once she decides that something is the right road to go down, there's no stopping her. She's respectful to council if they unanimously say no, but when she's got the bit in her teeth on something, she goes for it … She had periods where council needed somebody to gently prod them or keep them cohesive, or show them the way." Municipal managers frequently are cautioned not to get out in front of their councils, but Rogers seemed unconcerned about this. She used her emotional intelligence and political acumen to determine when she needed to take the lead.

INTEGRITY

One interviewee suggested that, throughout his career, he did not learn about ethical behaviour from books or in a classroom; rather, "it's in the air." His point was that Rogers and the people around her demonstrated ethical behaviour and integrity in ways that permeated the entire organization.

Vancouver is a big city with huge amounts of major development going on. In such situations, temptations can be great, yet scandal never touched Rogers personally or the civic administration during her tenure as city manager. One developer reportedly referred to her wryly as "integrity Jude." The Olympic athletes' village issue is sometimes called a scandal, but all the major decisions were made by council, and it is difficult to see who derived unjust benefits from the situation. The worst that could be said is that there might have been certain errors in judgment, and even that is arguable.

Rogers' integrity fit with the rest of her personality and led people to have a great deal of trust in their dealings with her. As one interviewee said, "[s]he had an immense integrity ... Her integrity regarding the city was inviolable; there [were] no deals made ... It gave her a remarkable power and made people very secure in dealing with her." She also exhibited integrity at the day-to-day, personal level. A number of interviewees commented on how they had great faith in anything Rogers said, regardless of the importance of the matter under consideration. This day-to-day integrity is often overlooked, but it is important in building trust among colleagues.

A ROLE MODEL FOR WOMEN

Rogers was a trailblazer, although she does not like to emphasize this aspect of her career. There are few hard data about the gender distribution of senior municipal management positions in a historical perspective, but a recent survey suggests that women are significantly underrepresented, especially in large municipalities.[29] When Rogers was appointed city manager, she was one of the first women to hold the position in a large city in Canada, and although good data are lacking, there seem to have been more women in senior administrative positions in Vancouver city hall during her tenure than one typically finds in city halls.

She claims she encountered no real gender-based obstacles during her ascent of the hierarchy. Her time in the Equal Employment Opportunities Office sensitized her to the difficulties many women face, but she says she was fortunate throughout her career to have had very good mentors and to have worked with highly ethical people who gave her opportunities when she was ready for them. This mentoring experience is probably the reason she is currently mentoring about a dozen women. That she was viewed as a competent manager with exceptionally good people skills would have made it difficult in any case for even the most avowedly sexist male to muster arguments against her.

Many of the women interviewed for this chapter, both those who worked in city hall and outside, indicated that they had learned a great deal from Rogers. Her leadership style clearly emphasized teamwork, and the remainder of this chapter focuses on how she used that foundation to lead in three directions.

Leading down

Rogers worked in the city in senior positions for a number of years before becoming city manager, so she well understood the organizational culture – indeed, she had a major role in creating the culture she inherited. Therefore, it should not be surprising that she did not make many immediate, high-profile changes at city hall when she became city manager. Numerous people commented, however, that, over time, her presence and the force of her personality introduced some significantly different aspects into the organizational culture at city hall. Previous managers were task-oriented engineers, well thought of by city staff, and clearly had a good way with people, but there was a strong sense that Rogers brought something different with her when she arrived. In the words of one staff member, "she de-engineered it." Another interviewee elaborated in more detail:

> Under the previous processes, it was a very well-run organization and it was probably very visionary and directed, meaning it wasn't always all that inclusive. There was a stronger approach in terms of, 'this is the way we're going; everyone needs to get on board.' I think Judy actually realized the pros and the cons of that and began to look at a more collaborative approach. Not that there wasn't direction – there certainly was direction – but to make sure there was a greater level of buy-in than one would have previously seen. She spent much more time in trying to get

the organization to buy in to the model, direction, or process that was being promoted, making sure there was going to be ... greater delivery, greater enthusiasm, greater efficiency. And that is what really characterized her ... [S]he actually took the organization and made it very much a living, breathing thing that was a major contributor to the governance and culture of Vancouver.

Rogers was also much more concerned about new ways of thinking in terms of things such as diversity, inclusion, and multiculturalism than were her predecessors. This reflected her time with the Hastings Institute. The general environment was changing, and Rogers had exactly the right kind of background and temperament to make sure that these concepts were not just words, but were integrated throughout city hall.

Given her relationship orientation, it should not be surprising that she saw one of her tasks as city manager as creating her own team of senior managers: "When I became a city manager, I knew enough about ... creating a vibrancy and interface among the people who work together. I brought around me the smartest people, the best team workers, that I could [find] in their various fields ... My job was to knit everyone together ... I tried to always stay at the strategic level, [to] support people as they had tough decisions to make and places to go."

She wanted to combine her staff into a real team that trust one another and shared broad goals about furthering the interests of the city, not just those of the organizational unit. As one interviewee noted, "[a]nother of Judy's characteristics is trust relationships ... She had to trust her team. We had to trust each other. She insisted on collegiality and professionalism, [and was] not keen on turf talk."

Several interviewees commented that other city managers did not see the city at the community level the way Rogers did. Senior managers are encouraged to take a broad view, but that perspective can miss what is happening at the street level and affecting residents' daily lives; instead, "[o]ne of the hallmarks of Judy's leadership [was to bring] various organizations together, at different levels, not just the senior levels, but at all levels, to start identifying and then taking action on the issues." Interviewees attributed this community focus to the time Rogers spent working in the community at the YWCA, the Indian Centre, and the Hastings Institute.

One innovation in which she was involved since her time as assistant city manager was the creation of Neighbourhood Integrated Service

Teams (NISTs).[30] As "teams" suggests, their purpose was to break down silos and deliver services on the basis of neighbourhood needs, not departmental structures. The NISTs involved representatives from city departments and other government agencies, such as public health and the liquor licensing agency. Besides improving service delivery, it was recognized as a staff development exercise because it gave staff the opportunity to develop a more comprehensive understanding of government services.

Again, in keeping with her experience with the Hastings Institute, there is a sense that Rogers focused more on training, particularly in-service training, than had previous senior managers. People felt they had opportunities for formal training and also that Rogers herself acted as an informal mentor for many people: "[A] number of us at the city ... would not be where we are currently without her, because she gave us opportunities that most people wouldn't."

She also contributed to the emphasis on training and development through her own interactions with senior managers. She continued the tradition of allowing managers to present their own reports to council. This is not particularly unusual, but Rogers spent time advising officials before they presented their reports. They were the functional experts, so she did not have much to tell them about their own specialties, but as an experienced city manager, she had a great deal to tell them about how their report fit into the overall city perspective and how councillors were likely to react to it.

The Vancouver situation was a bit unusual in that there was a tradition of allowing managers to deliver conflicting reports to council. The city manager would try to develop a consensus and ensure that conflicting reports were not based on minor disagreements that could be resolved at the implementation stage. When two (or more) departments had a basic disagreement, however, they would present their reports, making council aware of the conflict and permitting it to make its own decision. A typical example would be a conflict between planning and engineering about work that should be done in a neighbourhood. The planners sometimes wanted aesthetic enhancements while the engineering people knew that a low-cost option would deliver the same functionality. It was then up to council to decide whether the benefit was worth the extra cost.

This is not the usual practice among municipalities, and it requires a great deal of forbearance and confidence on the part of a city manager to allow disputes like this to be aired in public. It had been a part of the local scene in Vancouver long enough, however, that everyone seemed comfortable with it. Several councillors commented that it was useful to hear diverse approaches to an issue.

Rogers also had a reputation of being supportive of staff at the personal level in several ways. First, she was renowned for knowing staff members at all levels of the city administration, not just at the top tiers. Because she had worked for the city for some time, she had a network of contacts throughout the organization. And because members of this network knew she was interested, she was given information about the well-being of staff and that of their families. As one interviewee noted, "she treats people very well. She knows who they are as people, and deals with people as people. [She] takes an interest in the people that she works with."

She did not use her knowledge of people in the organization just for personal purposes; she was also an astute judge of people's abilities. She was not shy about reaching down into the hierarchy and leapfrogging a lower-ranking person over a higher one if she felt that the more senior person had reached the limits of her or his ability, or moving people across the organization in unconventional ways. She moved a librarian into a senior position in planning and a superintendent in engineering into a senior position in human resources.

Mostly what people felt about her, however, was that she was highly supportive of her staff: "Judy is pretty up front ... She deals very directly [with and is] very supportive of staff – [an] important consideration. There were no people in Vancouver hung out to dry, unless they were deserving of being hung out to dry, which is sometimes the case. She had a reasonable – not perfect – sense of where council's prerogatives were and what they decided and how staff should function ... [C]ouncil gets the advice, council does what they do, we implement what council says, but along the way we want to do our job professionally. That was clear. She was well supported by staff."

In return people felt motivated by her and were highly loyal to her: "She really was one of those rare people ... [Y]ou went to work each day thinking, I want to support Judy ... and ensure that she's a success because she's personally vested in me and my career ... Everyone who worked for her was phenomenally loyal to her."

People also felt empowered by her, but they always knew that she was there for them when they needed support: "As a manager, she's very empowering. I have always appreciated the fact that, when I worked with her, my philosophy was: I'll do as much as I can. [I'll] make as many decisions as I can … I'll try not to bother her. The city manager is very busy, so I don't need to go to her and bother her. But I know that whenever I need her to make a phone call or take a position … I can go to her, and she will always support me. And I also know I'm willing to take the risk, to take the decision to some extent because I know that if I make a mistake … she will always back me up. So that's a very comfortable position."

She had a reputation for supporting people even when they found themselves in trouble as a result of an honest mistake. In her words, "I let people make a lot of mistakes, because I gave them a lot of room." She could be quite firm, however, in response to unethical behaviour or attempts to take advantage of the system. As one interviewee noted, "don't screw her around though … Judy is a genuinely nice person … who's very supportive of her people and not very forgiving of people who would screw around. And that's part of the appeal. Nobody likes to be trying to play straight in a game where someone else isn't and see them get away with it."

Rogers was tremendously popular with the senior staff with whom she worked closely. Her relationship with unionized staff was more complicated. She liked to feel that her time working her way up through the hierarchy had made her many friends among rank-and-file staff, but she had a reputation as being fairly hard nosed about management-union relations. Reportedly, she would sometimes suggest that the city had given away too much in management rights, and some rights should be won back.

She became city manager at a somewhat difficult time for management-union relations. For many years, unionized staff in Vancouver had benefited from a "nine-day fortnight," whereby employees were allowed to work a bit extra for nine days in a two-week period and take one full day off. This was tremendously popular with staff, but it caused operational problems for the city. In one of his final acts, Ken Dobell, Rogers's immediate predecessor and mentor, succeeded in winning the cancellation of this provision. His intention seems to have been to wear it and take it with him when he left, but some of the resentment about this rubbed off on his protégée and hand-picked successor. So Rogers did not start her tenure as city manager on the best of terms with unionized staff. Yet, even in the middle of a highly contentious and sometimes highly personalized strike, Rogers was still concerned about the well-being of unionized staff. More than one interviewee recounted how

Rogers worked quietly behind the scenes to ensure that extraordinary needs of individual unionized employees were met.

In sum, Rogers exhibited an ability to move the organizational culture quite subtly from a rather top-down orientation when she arrived to one that was more collaborative and inclusive. She drew on her strengths in terms of people skills to motivate and empower people. Drawing on her work with the Hastings Institute, she built inclusion and diversity into the culture while maintaining a culture of excellence. One interviewee suggested that one of her major strengths was an ability to keep staff focused on their operational tasks while she managed the tricky waters of relations with council. The next section discusses how she maintained that relationship.

Leading up

Vancouver's civic administration has a long-established tradition of a separation between the political role of council and the administrative role of staff.[31] Of course, all cities pay lip service to this, but what is surprising in Vancouver's case is how frequently this came up unprompted in interviews and how even members of the broader community had a fairly sophisticated understanding of the concept and its importance in good governance.

This separation of politics and administration was firmly in place before Rogers arrived on the scene, and is something about which she feels strongly:

> I'm pretty unrelenting about the role of a public servant, so I refused to ever ... join a team. I wasn't an NPAer. I wasn't a COPEr. I was there to manage the public service. That's not to say that some of my staff didn't have leanings, but I always ensured that everything was neutral, that the best decisions were made, options were given to council. Whether it was politic or not, council always got the right facts, and the facts to make a decision ...
>
> I always knew that I was their employee. I knew that it was my job to give them the very best information that I could about any decision they were going to make, and that in my discussion with them it was absolutely inappropriate for me to give them political advice, but just simply provide them with the very best tools I could manage to bring to the forefront to enable them to make a decision ... I respected them [she first said trusted,

but thought better of it], honoured them for having run for politics. I was friendly, but I wasn't their friend, and I wasn't their enemy ... I just think there's real danger in getting too close to anybody ... I think of [names various mayors]. I know all of these people. You might in the future count them as your friends, but not while you're working because they have a different role, and I might not always agree with what they might be doing, but it doesn't matter. It's my job to give them the information. They have to be accountable to the public. While I [also] have to be accountable to the public, the decision rests with them.

She obviously conveyed these views to staff because interviews frequently revealed that she maintained a clear separation between the roles of council and staff: "Judy just never wavered from the role of the municipal bureaucrat and what it is the city as a bureaucracy can do and not do ... While she was politically incredibly canny and she was always aware of what was happening politically[,] ... she never crossed the line to do things that were the politicians' role to do. So we were kept as staff as a professional organization that provided professional advice in a neutral way."

One can interpret this firm separation between politics and administration in two ways. On the one hand, it provides for clearly separate roles, with the administration always subordinate to the political. On the other hand, it can be viewed as giving each solitude significant latitude for action within its own sphere. Although she clearly understood her position with regard to council, she also understood that there were occasions when she needed to take a leadership role on some issues, and she did not hesitate to do that.

For whom, then, does the city manager work – the elected council, or more broadly for the city or the residents of the city? The narrow, legal answer to the question is clear: city managers are appointed by council, take their marching orders from council, and can be disciplined and fired by council. But what should a conscientious city manager do when dealing with a short-sighted or misguided council? Is leadership simply a matter of carrying out the instructions of one's political masters regardless of the wisdom of those instructions? Or does leadership require a city manager to make her or his own decisions about some matters?

Rogers seems to have seen her role as working for her community and taking a leadership role with regard to council. A mayor who worked with her put it this way: "She saw herself very much [as] an employee of the people, of the citizens, and it was her job to make sure the city was run in the most efficient, cost-effective, and law-abiding manner that she could ... She had no allegiance to the council whatso- ever, from the point of view that councils come and councils go, and especially councillors come and councillors go, so the allegiance was to the city. It was to keep the city on a path. Now, the path can change, but you don't want it veering suddenly right or left."

This approach can be illustrated in particular in several areas. Rog- ers was a booster of the Olympics from the time the first attempt was made to win the Games for Vancouver, and she never wavered in that support throughout the process even though mayors and councillors sometimes did. During the city-run plebiscite on whether or not to hold the Games, she was outwardly neutral and insisted that staff take the same position. It was fairly difficult, however, to ignore the strong role she had played in supporting the Olympics on a variety of committees, and her name was on the document that committed Vancouver to host them. One interviewee described how she led the fight for the inclusiv- ity commitment in the Olympic bid document: "Judy led that charge ... politically and with the very senior bureaucrats ... I watched her time after time go into a meeting and remind everybody why they were there. They'd all want to do small things – you know, token things. Judy would ... bring them back on target – wait a minute, there's a larger issue here – and remind people of their role."

She adopted a similar position with regard to the constellation of issues involving the downtown east side. She felt strongly the city needed to address this major issue, and she took the lead in developing the Vancouver Agreement: "Judy had a clear sense of what needed to happen there if there was ever going to be any substantive change ... [and] the vision to see that if we didn't bring all the levels of govern- ment together and actually focus their minds on this, we were never going to get anywhere."

She also led the four-pillars approach to drug use, which included the controversial idea of having a safe injection site.[32] She played a role in converting the views of some of her political masters on this subject. One observer described how she moved Mayor Philip Owen and some council members on this issue:

The other thing that was absolutely remarkable, absolutely miraculous, was the work that she did with council ... [W]hen we first started meet- ing with Mayor Owen and that council, ... it was like "these people are criminals, these people are using drugs, drugs are illegal, what could be clearer than this?"

[But] ... you watch [Judy] walk around the room, and ... you don't really notice anything happening at the time. But when Judy leaves the room, everything is moved slightly ... She has this way of moving things, of moving people, of moving ideas, of moving things forward that is so beautifully subtle and so beautifully effective. [She] somehow turn[ed a mayor who was opposed to the project] into the biggest supporter of the four pillars drug strategy that Canada knew! ... [A]fter that, [he] was leading the way, he understood the issues, he got what was happening – that was Judy.

We have a progressive policy, not only towards drugs but towards the whole issue of what it takes for a city to deal with a community like the downtown east side, which is on a whole bunch of fronts – policing, housing, health, food, social services, all of that. We have that ... primarily because of Judy Rogers.

One reason administrators must take this kind of leadership role arises from the perspective that politicians have a time horizon that coincides with their electoral cycle, while administrators must take a longer-term view. "Things that are important to the long-term health and welfare of the city are not very important to politicians who are only here for three years." Another interviewee elaborated: "That's part of her perspective, and what I think is the right perspective – for a city manager to not react to every pronouncement or every sudden change in direction that comes along, but [to work] for the longer term for the city. The city supported the Olympic Games bid, and those decisions were made by city council, and until city council changes that direction, that is the policy of city council."

Another example of the long versus shorter perspective was in the area of borrowing and the municipality's credit rating. Councillors are strongly tempted to borrow, rather than to raise taxes, and to leave to future councils the obligation to repay the debt. Vancouver had always had a strong credit rating, which Rogers felt was her responsibility to maintain. Obviously, these decisions belong to council, but she made sure that councillors understood the consequences of their decisions.

Rogers's actions indicate that her idea of leadership involved representing the interests of the city and its residents to councillors. In this, it differed from the more traditional view of neutrality that administrators hold, whereby they have an obligation to ensure that council is fully informed of all aspects of an issue, and then to implement loyally the wishes of their political masters, no matter what their personal views might be. Rogers was loyal in implementing council decisions, but she was fairly proactive in placing new ideas before council.

Much of what she did in moving council on a particular issue was less miracle and more simple, day-by-day thoughtfulness and hard work. It was not Rogers's style to try to push people overtly into a particular policy, but to present information and let others make up their own minds. She would submit reports, invite expert speakers, and sometimes organize study tours, all geared to presenting solid evidence on an issue, not to direct people's thinking. Of course, because Rogers was usually three or four steps ahead of most other people, she had an idea where this information would lead.

This approach was aided by her dislike of turf talk, as noted earlier. One interviewee commented that "Judy's skill was really in keeping everybody's eyes on the target as much as possible," rather than spending time and effort arguing about who was responsible for hitting the target. Of course, this requires the delicate touch of knowing when to step to the rear and allow the mayor and councillor to take responsibility. "She never blew her own horn ... [She] would always stay just on the periphery and then come out and take care of it and then go back ... to the periphery." One interviewee described how she handled the four pillars drugs strategy: "In the very beginning, Judy took it and paved the way for it, but then she was smart enough to let the mayor, once he got the bit in his teeth, [to take] off with it."

A manager must have built up a great deal of credibility to be able to work with council the way Rogers evidently did. She had a great deal of experience working with councillors – some knew her from her days at the Hastings Institute, and all became aware of when she became assistant city manager in 1994. She had a reputation for being fair and even handed in her treatment of councillors. She also had a reputation for being courteous with them, but keeping them at arm's length and ensuring that there was never a perception that anyone received special treatment or private information. As a councillor described it, "[w]hen I would ask for information ... she would very gently, but very politely, remind me that ... all the information that I requested would go to all other councillors ... I didn't know that when I came in ... but it ... gave me a real [sense of] security because it let me know that, if somebody else is requesting information, I would know that ... [I]t also [produced] a government that can work together because you're all getting the same information."

One small item several people mentioned was that Rogers never rode in a private car with a councillor. Having a private meeting in your office is a business activity, but having a private conversation with someone could result in casual comments that might look bad to other councillors: "There were no private chats taking place with Judy Rogers. If you were in her office, you were there to deal with A, B, C, and D, which was the agenda you'd set out, which was then going to be sent out to everybody else, but there were no private chats in cars."

She had ways of discussing issues that helped to build her credibility and show her respect for councillors. One interviewee remembered her prefacing comments with phrases such as "with all due respect" or "I wonder if I might," in order to show appropriate deference. No one remembers her losing her temper or otherwise showing disrespect to councillors: "I never heard her raise her voice ... and she had a lot of provocation. I mean she had people yelling at her and screaming at her in council, and sometimes other councillors were vile and horribly rude, and she responded with grace and dignity and civility, and just rose above their appalling [behaviour]."

Sometimes the proper course of action is clear, but the way in which the manager deals with a request needs considerable care. Rogers gives the example of being approached by a councillor who wanted to "help" a constituent who had been unsuccessful in a tendering process at city hall. The ethical aspect of the matter was clear, but the specific response required some finesse. She discussed the nature of the tendering process with the inquiring councillor and why the bid had been unsuccessful. Without bending any ethical principles, this gave the councillor something to take back to the constituent to demonstrate due diligence, and even to offer the person advice for next time. From the manager's perspective, the key was to simply explain the process without being confrontational.

Some interviewees suggested that one of her tactics in discussions was always to focus on issues rather than on individuals or political parties. A policy was not "Smith's idea" or "an NPA policy," but simply a policy to be discussed on its merits. One interesting way to get both councillors and staff to focus on policies was to hold a series of informal meetings. Each year councillors met informally with each department head for an off-the-record, blue-sky kind of discussion of what they hoped to achieve. These were not opportunities to air specific grievances; they were meant to look to the future. They allowed councillors and staff to exchange ideas and to get to know one another informally.

All of the councillors and staff who were interviewed had great praise for Rogers's interaction with council. She seems to have been the consummate professional, politically neutral public servant. Yet, when a new party came to power in 2008, among its first actions was to fire her. Why?

Political neutrality is a relative easy concept to describe, but it is more difficult to operationalize and test because it is hard to measure in any meaningful manner. In the latter part of the twentieth century, federal public servants spoke a great deal about their ability to work with whichever party got elected. Of course, the fact that the Liberal Party was Canada's natural governing party through much of that period meant that this laudable idea was put to the test only occasionally. Rogers was in much the same position. She and her predecessors had spoken a great deal about neutrality, and no doubt they were committed to every word. But the NPA or some close facsimile had been the natural governing party in Vancouver since the 1940s, and her new political masters were understandably sceptical about such avowals of neutrality. True, Rogers had worked with COPE under Larry Campbell from 2002 to 2005, and the relationship had been described as generally satisfactory, although some COPE supporters felt that Rogers had been less than enthusiastic in implementing some of COPE's agenda. Moreover, Campbell's COPE credentials were not viewed as deeply ingrained anyway. If Rogers had dragged her feet for a lukewarm COPE Mayor Campbell, how was she likely to work with Robertson, who was intent on turning the city in a very different direction? The new broom wanted to sweep clean, and the party opted for a new manager who was certainly competent, but squarely in the Vision Vancouver camp.

Rogers was viewed as superb at leading up, but she seems to have interpreted her role rather differently from other CAOs discussed in this book. She was immersed in and attuned to the Vancouver community in ways that one would not expect from more itinerant managers, which is one reason she seemed inclined to lead council on some issues. As well, the separation of politics and administration had been an accepted part of the political culture in Vancouver for some time, which gave her scope for autonomy. These two factors allowed her to take a position considerably in front of council on the Olympics and on a variety of issues related to the downtown east side – where she seemed to see her role as being more responsive to the community than to council. This can be an uncomfortable position, but the question of whom you work for is one that every CAO must address at some point.

Leading out

Rogers was exceptionally strong at leading out. As mentioned, she had close connections with the community. Connecting with other people and with the broader community was deeply ingrained in her personality; it was not something she grudgingly did when she became city manager. As one interviewee noted, "Judy knitted herself into this community not only because she was city manager, but ... on many different fronts as Judy Rogers." Indeed, she has continued to be heavily involved in the community since leaving the city manager position, and is currently chair of the board of directors of 2010 Legacies Now. On the day she was interviewed for this chapter, she hosted a small luncheon to organize a fundraising program for a local hospice. Everyone who was interviewed had examples of how active she was and still is in the community.

Of course, it is a part of the job of a city manager to be connected with the community, and interviewees mentioned that previous city managers did that part of their job appropriately. They also suggested, however, that previous city managers had built their connections with business people or high-profile power brokers, rather than extensively throughout the community. Rogers, in contrast, lived in the city and worked her way up the hierarchy from street-level positions. She knew the inner workings of communities, and was connected more extensively and intensively than other city managers had been. This is probably one reason she was instrumental in the development of the Neighbourhood Integrated Service Teams, which involved city staff, but went significantly beyond just city involvement in recognizing the importance of listening to members of the community.

Her ability to lead out was also evident in the way she put together deals that, although they might have occurred anyway, went through smoothly because of her involvement. For the Vancouver Agreement, she had to bring together people from all three levels of government. The city's presence in the downtown east side involved a complex partnership of several government organizations, local developers, and many non-governmental organizations. The Olympic Games were an even more complicated partnership. Rogers never took complete credit for any of these events, but people involved in them credited her for facilitating certain aspects of each of them:

> She was very good about trying to integrate city hall into various aspects of the community ... I would see her at events with the who's who of the city ... She really took the government of the city out to different parts of the community. I think she was good at doing that. And [she] looked at different ways that the city could partner with, and not necessarily always take the lead in ... other entities out in the community in order to make it a stronger community.

She also had many significant dealings with the provincial government.

> Judy played a different role than I'd seen in city managers before in that she was much more connected into the province ... She was out there doing the intergovernmental work building relationships. She was phenomenally successful at that, finding money for the city, both federal, provincial, other things, building private-public sector coalitions to fund various initiatives. Rather than do the day-to-day management, although certainly she had a role in that, she played a slightly different role.

An important aspect of the community in Vancouver's case is working with the upper-tier municipality and other municipalities in what was called the Greater Vancouver Regional District, later Metro Vancouver. Within the area, there is also a regional committee of administrators called the Regional Administrative Advisory Committee (RAAC), composed of the city managers of all the municipalities. Vancouver, of course, is both the urban core and the largest city in the area. This poses problems for the Vancouver representative on the RAAC because, as the big kid on the block, it can be more powerful than other members. In dealing with colleagues, however, it is not advisable to wield that power in an overbearing fashion. One person described Rogers's style at a RAAC meeting: "My recollection of her ... [is] how well prepared she was, how thorough and professional she was, and how she could come into the room and maintain a presence, yet not be perceived as being overbearing or ... confrontational. She was very cautious, professional, ... but she appropriately expressed her opinion at the right time in a manner that made the entire room feel quite comfortable."

The interviewee also commented that she generally tried to present and be sympathetic to the regional view. He went on to lament that some changes at the political level over the years had made it difficult for both Metro and RAAC to continue to take that regional view.

Despite her highly visible presence in the community, Rogers was seldom seen in the media. Journalists who were approached to be interviewed for this work claimed not to know her very well, because she seldom spoke to them in an official capacity. Most references to her in the media were second-hand reports of her actions at a council meeting or similar gathering, rather than an interview or press conference. Rogers knew the role of the administrator was to stay in the background and allow the media access to the politicians.

Leading out was one of Roger's real strengths. It was a role she relished not just as the duty of a CAO, but as part of the fabric of who she is. She made a significant contribution to her community through this role, and she bridged the relationship between the city government and the city.

Conclusion: Putting It All Together

In her time as Vancouver's city manager, Judy Rogers clearly led successfully in all three directions. What lessons can we learn from her experience?

HAVE A PASSION FOR WHAT YOU DO

Almost every interviewee commented on Rogers's passion for her job. She loves her city, and she loves doing things that improve the lives of its residents. As one person noted, "[i]t was not only Judy's job to make the city of Vancouver a great place, it was Judy's life's mission to make Vancouver a better place."

Whether it was major undertakings such as redevelopment in the downtown east side or capturing the Olympics, or smaller things such as finding funding for a hospice, she clearly did these things because she had a passion for them, not because she was instructed by council to do them. This is important, because others can sense the difference between pursuing something passionately and going through the motions. She clearly motivated others to follow her and to believe that difficult things could be accomplished, because she was so passionate about what she was doing.

BUILD TEAMS

One aspect of Rogers's people skills was that she knew the importance of people in an organization and the importance of building teams. One of the first things she did when she became city manager was to develop a team around her. A mayor she worked with said "[h]er structure, while not rigid, rested on the fact that she had good people in senior positions, and if you needed something from them, that's where you went." He commented that, when you develop this kind of reputation, it becomes easier to recruit high-quality staff.

Her focus on teams did not stop at the city hall door. The Neighbourhood Integrated Service Teams combined people from city hall with people from other government agencies. The Vancouver Agreement is a good example of team building writ large. In this case she orchestrated a team stretching from Ottawa to Victoria to Vancouver's downtown east side. The Olympics bid required an even larger array of teams. She was not the leader of this exercise, but she was an important team player.

It seemed to be her natural reaction to a problem or a new issue to build a team to deal with it. It was something her school and athletic background conditioned her to do, but it was also a strength she developed throughout her career. She was always quick to give credit to the team, but teams need leaders, and Rogers deserves a great deal of credit for recognizing the importance of teamwork, bringing good teams together, and sustaining the work of those teams.

BUILD ON YOUR STRENGTHS; STRENGTHEN YOUR WEAKNESSES

From an early age, it was clear that Rogers's great strength was her people orientation. She has a pleasant manner and a winning way with people. Early in her career she worked for the YWCA in capacities that developed those people skills. Her work in the Indian Centre would have honed those skills considerably had her time there not been cut short by circumstances beyond her control. At the Hastings Institute, she enhanced her concern for equity, diversity, and inclusion, and also started to develop her managerial skills.

She was aware, however, that her emphasis on people skills would take her only so far. She knew that, to be a complete manager, she needed to develop other skills, so she chose to go to the University of Victoria to do a post-graduate degree in public administration. She deliberately threw herself into courses on law, finance, and accounting, and similar areas in which she had absolutely no background. This must have been uncomfortable, but it was important in making her a well-rounded manager.

BIG CITIES ARE BUILT FROM SMALL COMMUNITIES

Leaders are always told to be broad visionaries, to see the big picture and not allow themselves to be diverted by smaller issues. Rogers clearly is a visionary, big-picture thinker. A meek person would not have tackled the downtown east side issue. Visions do not get much larger than the Olympics. Her early experience, however, was in neighbourhoods doing things like helping single parents organize a local daycare facility, and she never forgot the lessons she learned there. She championed doing something about the downtown east side when others would have been happy just to contain the mess within a confined area. She pushed hard for an additional station on the Canada Line at the Olympic Games athletes' village because she knew it would be important for the future development of that neighbourhood. She understood that the biggest cities are only as strong as their smallest neighbourhoods.

RESPECT THE PROCESS

The shortest distance between two points is not always a straight line. This runs counter to what we all learned in geometry class, but it is good advice for anyone working in a complex government organization. There are many examples of situations where Rogers did not drive a conclusion home relentlessly or push people to do things against their will. She understood when a heavy-handed approach to an issue would have resulted in a quick defeat, which would have made it difficult to reintroduce the policy. Instead, she respected the process. Her political antenna was legendary. She knew when to move things forward, and when to take her time. She knew that various groups had to get on side before something would work, and that this could take time. It was not a matter of disrespecting councillors' wishes and manipulating them, but she was good at tactfully stimulating and motivating people at the right times.

WHO DO YOU WORK FOR?

At some point, virtually all public servants must decide whether they work directly for their political masters or for their community. At first glance, the answer seems obvious: the CAO is appointed by council, receives instructions from council, and can be fired by council. But what sort of obligation does a public servant owe to the broader community?

One sometimes hears that it is dangerous for a CAO to get too far out in front of council. Rogers did not seem to be worried about that. Her attachment was to her community, and she was committed to doing whatever she felt was necessary to make her community better. Of course, councillors also want to better their community, but what constitutes betterment can be defined differently by different groups.

Rogers's idea of bettering her community included working unstintingly to bring the Olympics to Vancouver despite sometimes lukewarm political support, or driving to improve living conditions in the downtown east side despite lack of political interest. She was always respectful of the clear wishes of council, but she was not shy about introducing new ideas to council when she felt that was necessary. She pushed fairly hard to get issues relating to the downtown east side on the agenda when it seemed that councillors had little appetite for them, but she did it in a respectful manner. She recognized that both council and the city manager are ultimately concerned about the welfare of the city. Working together to improve that welfare is important, but she recognized that sometimes she had to take the lead.

This proactive approach on her part might seem to have been at odds with Vancouver's emphasis on the separation of politics and administration. There is no question that Rogers treated both council and individual councillors with a great deal of respect, or that she was anything but loyal in implementing the wishes of council. There was also a sense, however, that she saw herself as working for the community, and in that role she wanted to ensure that council was aware of community issues and needs. In the downtown east side, she arranged for speakers and tours that helped make councillors aware of the situation. In the Olympics case, she continued to attend meetings but did not make any public commitments. She never lectured council on what it should do or made any pronouncements that would embarrass council, but she did try subtly to guide council in the interests of the community.

Overall Assessment

In sum, Judy Rogers was a successful city manager because she was good at leading up, down, and out. Her highly attuned people skills led her to emphasize inclusiveness and a focus on developing teams.

> A municipal CAO who
> is a good leader has
> the ability to move the
> municipality forward by
> interacting in a mutually
> influential way with
> and motivating council,
> external stakeholders,
> and organizational
> subordinates.

She was greatly attached to the city in which she has spent most of her adult life, and she was not shy about serving as an advocate for causes that were important in the community even when it might mean being a bit out in front of her council. She tied this all together with a highly developed political antenna and good judgment. It is not surprising that she was seen as such a good leader by those around her.

5 The Leader as Partnership Builder: Keith Robicheau

"He wrote the book," was how one councillor responded to a question about Keith Robicheau's involvement in partnerships. Unlike the previous three CAOs discussed in this book, Robicheau has worked exclusively in relatively small municipalities. Large municipalities generally have the resources to do what they want to do by themselves. Smaller municipalities must learn to cooperate with neighbouring municipalities to provide services to their residents. Everywhere Robicheau has gone, he has put turf protection aside when cooperation and partnerships better served the needs of residents. This focus on partnerships is one of the hallmarks of his career.

The three previous case studies focused on CAOs who spent their careers in medium or large cities. The next two will tell the stories of leaders whose careers have been in smaller places, although that has not made their jobs easier or their roles less important. As we will see, in some ways their jobs have been more difficult and more important because many duties that CAOs in large cities delegate to others become the direct responsibility of the CAO in smaller places.

Keith Robicheau has been a CAO in four municipalities to this point in his career. He started as town manager in his hometown of St Andrews, New Brunswick, in 1983 at the ripe old age of twenty-four. He served there until 1990, when he joined the New Brunswick provincial government. He found he was still interested in local government, however, so he became CAO of Annapolis County, Nova Scotia, from 1994 to 2008. He then moved to the nearby Town of Kentville, Nova Scotia, as CAO from 2008 to 2011. He is currently the county manager of the Municipality of Norfolk County, Ontario. Since he took this position shortly before this research began, it is not considered in this chapter.

Throughout his career Robicheau has been recognized as an outstanding CAO. In 2000 he received the Lieutenant Governor's Medal
of Excellence presented annually by the Nova Scotia Regional Group
of the Institute of Public Administration of Canada for exemplary service in the field of public administration. In 2006 he received the Award
of Excellence from the Association of Municipal Administrators, Nova
Scotia (AMANS), which "recognizes a member of AMANS who currently provides an exceptional level of professionalism, leadership and
innovation in their job, community service at a tireless level, and exemplifies the ethics and responsibility that a community desires to consider them a positive role model."[1]

Robicheau also has been in demand to serve on various provincial
advisory bodies looking at issues ranging from highway signage to
property tax assessment to fair and equitable funding for municipalities. He is tapped for these important, but time-consuming, committee
assignments because he is seen as knowledgeable, but also well connected throughout the municipal system. He is also sufficiently community spirited that he is always willing to take on this extra work.
Robicheau's outstanding career shows no signs of slowing down.

The raw material for this chapter was drawn from two sources. The
first strand of research was a review of various background sources of
information. My research assistant and I attempted to do the same kind
of background research in newspapers and similar media that we did
for the other case studies. That proved difficult for smaller towns, but
we were able to find some background material on the Internet and
in published sources. We were also forced to rely more on what we
heard from the people we interviewed than was the case for the CAOs
examined in earlier chapters, and that was the second strand of our research. We conducted twenty-six personal interviews: with Robicheau
at the beginning and end of the project, and with councillors, staff, and
community members from the three municipalities in which Robicheau
worked before going to Norfolk County, Ontario, as shown in Table 5.1.

Career Path

Keith Robicheau was born in 1959, and grew up in the picturesque town
of St Andrews (also known colloquially as St Andrews By-the-Sea),
New Brunswick. He came by his interest in public service naturally
because both his grandfather and father were involved in their communities. His grandfather was a businessman and a charter member of

Table 5.1. Interviews about Keith Robicheau

	St Andrews, NB	Annapolis County, NS	Town of Kentville, NS	Other	Total
Councillors	2	5	3		10
Staff		4	3		7
Others		2	2	3	7
Total	2	11	8	3	24

Note: "Other" represents people who have known Robicheau throughout his career or in several capacities, and did not fall neatly into any one municipality.

the local Lions Club. His father was a technician at the biological re-search station of the federal Department of Fisheries and Oceans and also served on the town council in the 1970s – well before his son was appointed CAO. His mother was a hair stylist who sometimes worked in real estate sales. He also talks fondly about how he was influenced by a parish priest who emphasized community-mindedness and ser-vice. Robicheau's description of Father Gillis seems similar to how many interviewees described Robicheau himself: "Father Gillis ... was probably my ideal of someone who had strong principles, very much a person who encouraged solving problems by resorting to logic and rea-son, but also a very caring and compassionate person ... [W]hat I really admired was someone who really made it a point to listen to people, understand issues, ask good questions, ... [H]is vocation was some-thing that he lived and breathed."

That Robicheau's parents strongly pushed the value of education is reflected in the fact that he and all his siblings have at least one univer-sity degree. He went to Mount Allison University in Sackville, New Brunswick, where he obtained a Bachelor of Commerce with a double major in accounting and management. He was on the Dean's List for four years and, foreshadowing his future career, he was involved in service activities such as the Commerce Society and the Campus Police, rising to be assistant chief.

He then embarked on a career with a major accounting firm, and was well on his way to becoming a chartered accountant when he decided that the amount of travel involved in this line of work did not mesh with his view of the family life he wanted. This led him to take his first municipal job as town manager of his hometown of St Andrews.

St Andrews, NB (1983–90)

It seems like a real stretch for a young man of twenty-four to become a town manager, even in a town with only 2,020 permanent residents.[2] Robicheau recalls that he was probably the youngest employee of the town save for the summer students who passed through every year. He does not remember being particularly intimidated, however; he had grown up in the town, and knew many of the politicians and staff personally. He saw the position as simply an opportunity to apply the management education he had received at Mount Allison.

Councillors who were involved in the hiring process did not recall the choice of Robicheau as being a particularly difficult decision. He was well known as a serious, mature, and knowledgeable young man – one person used the word "steady" several times to describe him. In fact, they were so impressed with him that they were well aware that he would outgrow this small-town appointment and leave, but they were confident that he would move the town forward in the meantime.

Interviewees remembered councils of the time as composed of high-quality councillors who recognized the dividing line between policy and administration and did not intrude on the town manager's sphere. The previous manager had served for many years, and seems to have left the place in good shape. Nevertheless, Robicheau did not allow his being young to intimidate him. He saw St Andrews as full of undeveloped possibilities. It was home to the venerable tourist magnet of the Algonquin Hotel and its famous golf course, but the town itself – particularly its waterfront – had other tourist opportunities that were not being exploited.

One of Robicheau's first tasks was to establish a town manager system. The previous clerk-administrator[3] had been a long-serving and well-respected municipal employee, but council wanted to move to the next level, and it knew this required installing a real town manager, with all the duties the name implied. Robicheau seemed to have little difficulty moving the town's administration in this direction with the help of a supportive council. A councillor involved in the hiring process described it this way:

> The interview really sold us on his ability to analyse what the job required and where it needed to go ... He took it from the town clerk level to the administrative officer level, and he did it admirably ... We seemed to grasp during the interview that he was the guy that was capable of doing that.

He sold himself to us admirably ... We just had the feeling that Keith was the guy that could finesse the changes that needed to take place in that office with the relationship with council and with ... the town. He had an air about him that was non-confrontational ... a good negotiator ... Upon hiring Keith we were never disappointed.

Robicheau championed the formation of a business improvement corporation, now called Waterfront St Andrews, and the development of a downtown/waterfront plan to attract more tourism businesses to the area. This was supplemented by changes in the official plan that emphasized infilling (using the existing land base more intensively rather than spreading out), upscale bed and breakfast inns, and more home-based businesses. In other words, it aimed to attract more tourists without radically changing the area's distinctive heritage character.

The town had a problem with developers locating new housing just outside the town's boundaries so that new residents could draw on town services without paying town taxes. To combat this, St Andrews decided to develop a subdivision of its own on land it owned. This is not something a municipality would normally do, but in the circumstances the town felt it was necessary to stabilize its population. The process seems to have worked well, and to have had its desired effect.

Robicheau showed his rationalist bent by developing the town's first five-year capital plan. Prior to his arrival, the town's attitude to infrastructure had been to "put off as much as you can for as long as you can." He brought in a proactive approach that involved a capital works budget, an assessment of infrastructure, video inspection of sanitary sewers, and other innovations.

How did a young man of twenty-four accomplish so much? He is quick to admit that he had plenty of help, and he was not afraid to ask for advice. The father of a boyhood friend had become New Brunswick's deputy minister of municipal affairs, so Robicheau went right to the top. He also drew on the advice of John Robison, then city manager of Fredericton, who would become a mentor to many people in the municipal field. Some people are wary of asking for advice because it could indicate weakness on their part, but Robicheau was not shy about drawing on many people to help him. In his words, "I learned so much from so many people and from developing relationships with people."

Robicheau remained town manager at St Andrews for seven years and accomplished a great deal, but he wanted to move to a bigger playing field. New Brunswick had elected a dynamic young premier, Frank McKenna, in 1987, and Robicheau wanted to be a part of what McKenna was doing. When he saw a job advertisement for a position as an internal management consultant with the province's Treasury Board, he responded.

A short detour (1990–94)

One of the significant roles of a provincial treasury board is to serve as the cabinet committee on administrative management. In other words, it is responsible for establishing government-wide policies on administrative issues in such a way as to promote efficiency and effectiveness, and also to keep the government out of political trouble by ensuring prudence and probity in all government administrative activities.

One of Robicheau's first tasks was to review the government-wide travel policy. This might seem mundane, but governments spend large amounts on travel, and it is important that that money is spent wisely. Extravagant travel expenses are not only wasteful; they can cause huge political damage to a government. It is an administrative issue, but one with the capacity to be a political minefield. The task is far from easy, however, as it requires balancing the interests of public servants and their unions, government's need to restrain expenditures, and travel agents' desire for a piece of the action.

Treasury boards also look at issues that do not fit neatly into any one department. This is how Robicheau became involved in a study of provincial liquor policy – another task that required a great deal of stakeholder consultation. He was also involved in the development of Service New Brunswick, one of the first examples of one-stop government services for residents and a model that has been emulated by the federal government and most provinces.

Another of his roles was going into provincial government departments to serve as a strategic planning facilitator. This helped him further develop his skills in consultation and mediation, skills that he would use frequently and well in the municipal governments in which he would work later.

Although Robicheau might not have realized it at the time, his last position in the provincial government would be his stepping stone back into the municipal sector. In the 1990s, many provincial governments, including New Brunswick's, were addressing the related issues of regional development and the amalgamation of municipalities. He was seconded to the Department of Municipalities, Culture and Housing to serve on the secretariat that was responsible for restructuring the province's seven largest regions, and became deeply involved in restructuring in the Miramichi region.

At this point, several factors came together to stimulate his interest in returning to local government. He found himself travelling more than he wanted, which was the reason he had left the accounting firm a number of years previously. He also found the provincial government less dynamic than working directly with stakeholders in local government. Seeing an advertisement for the job of CAO in Annapolis County, Nova Scotia, he ignored the advice he received that its council was dysfunctional and at war with staff, and applied for the position. He felt he could get along with people, and he knew people in other municipalities on whom he could rely for advice, and decided he could handle the Annapolis County situation. So, at the still relatively young age of thirty-four, he embarked on his second posting as a municipal CAO.

Annapolis County, NS (1994–2008)

Annapolis County, in western Nova Scotia on the Bay of Fundy and on the main highway between Halifax and Yarmouth, is a physically beautiful but somewhat economically stressed area of 23,641 residents.[4] Its operating expenditures in fiscal year 2007/08 were $13.1 million.[5] One gets the impression that not too much has changed in the area from the hardscrabble existence depicted by Ernest Buckler in his 1952 classic novel, *The Mountain and the Valley*.

In Nova Scotia, counties are single-tier governments responsible for the delivery of all local services to residents in predominantly rural areas. The towns of Annapolis Royal, Bridgetown, and Middleton are located within the boundaries of Annapolis County, but are politically and legally separate entities. Geography dictates that the county and the towns will have some connections, but the nature of the relationship between the urban and rural areas depends heavily on the personalities of key people in the different organizations. Sometimes they work well together; sometimes they are at war.

When Robicheau arrived in 1994, the county was frankly in a difficult state. The advice he received about problems on council and between councillors and staff only scratched the surface. One councillor summarized the depth of the situation by saying that staff members were not happy, residents were not happy, and many councillors were new because some previous councillors had been thrown out due to their poor handling of a planning issue. It could also be added that the county was virtually at war with the provincial government, and was not on great terms with nearby municipalities. Robicheau had some things working for him, however, in the person of two individuals who arrived on the scene at about the same time he did: Peter Terauds at the political level and Laurie Emms at the administrative level.

Terauds, the proud offspring of Latvian immigrants, was transplanted into "the Valley" from Quebec's Eastern Townships, and elected warden[6] of the county in 1994. He describes himself as a farmer, but a better term would be entrepreneur. When he was interviewed for this work, he was leasing his farmland to another farmer, and was in the process of selling a restaurant that he and his wife had built up over the previous five years.

Terauds is clearly intelligent and does not suffer from uncertainty about his goals; he is also impatient and a bit abrasive with people who do not see things as clearly as he does. In the community, he is respected as someone who got things done, but ultimately his impatient, abrasive side was his undoing; after he had served three terms, his fellow councillors rebelled and did not select him as warden in 2004.

The arrival of two strong people like Terauds and Robicheau in top positions at the same time could have been a recipe for a scene out of an old gunslinger movie – as in "this town ain't big enough for the both of us" – but the opposite occurred. The impatient, stormy Terauds and the patient, professional Robicheau found they could work together in a complementary fashion to effect some real changes.

Robicheau also speaks positively of Marilyn Wilkins, who served as deputy warden and played an important role in making changes. Indeed, the presence of Terauds and Wilkins was a bit of luck for Robicheau, but another person who came on the scene was the product of good judgment on Robicheau's part. Laurie Emms had had a successful career as a consulting engineer with a large international firm, but grew tired of the pressure and travel involved, and decided to move to the public sector. Rural Annapolis County suited him fine, even though he would have to take a cut in pay.

Robicheau and Emms have very different personalities. Emms is a bit crusty and readily admits that he does not like people much. In his retirement, he enjoys playing golf – by himself. He is also incredibly bright, and not only understands the traditional, technical side of engineering, but also has experience in value engineering and in negotiating major projects. Despite their differences, complementarity is what made the relationship between Robicheau and Emms click. As one councillor put it, "[they] were a team. They were joined at the hip."

Robicheau hired Emms as county engineer in 1996, but rather quickly moved him to deputy CAO, with responsibility for all service delivery and operational aspects of the municipality, while Robicheau maintained responsibility for the policy and corporate services functions, particularly finance. Given the serious problems facing the new CAO, it was extremely fortuitous that Robicheau could clear the decks of these operational responsibilities and focus on problem solving.

ESTABLISHING THE CAO SYSTEM

Annapolis County needed to undergo an administrative modernization that many other local governments had pursued a bit earlier, and decided to move from the council-committee system to a CAO system. Robicheau actually was the second CAO who had been appointed to effect this change. No one interviewed said much about the first CAO except that he was in the position for only a few months before moving on. Effectively, it was Robicheau who really focused on implementing all aspects of the CAO system.

At the political-structural level, the council-committee system is known for inviting close contact between councillors and rank-and-file staff. In particular, a close relationship usually develops between the chairs of council committees and the heads of departments such that the two groups almost jointly run services to the exclusion of full council. Individual councillors may become heavily involved in administrative activities, but the system does little to promote the position of full council as a policy-making body. One person remembered the public works committee reviewing and approving every invoice before it was paid.

Moving to a CAO system means breaking this close personal relationship between councillors and staff and convincing councillors that they should be making policy and leave administration to administrators. The CAO must also establish herself or himself as the head of the administration and convince department heads that they should no longer have a direct relationship with individual councillors.

The fact that a majority of councillors had voted in favour of establishing a CAO system did not mean that they necessarily understood completely what they were voting for, and Robicheau and some councillors were quite honest in saying that he had to train them to perform their duties as councillors. The idea of a nominal subordinate training his superiors how to carry out their duties stands the usual relationship between councillors and staff on its head, but some councillors seemed to understand that the previous arrangement was dysfunctional and they needed some assistance to get themselves out of their problem. As is discussed in greater detail later, Robicheau had a particular approach to this training function that made it palatable.

He talked to councillors about how their role would change and what his role should be. He also brought in Gordon McIntosh, an experienced municipal trainer and facilitator from Victoria, British Columbia, to talk to councillors. Robicheau's general approach was to take things slowly and move councillors in the desired direction without pushing them so hard that they became uncomfortable and pushed back: "I'm not sure I had a definitive plan. I just realized that I had this organization that had very little policy structure, [and] was in serious want of processes ... It was very much a one-minute-manager approach. If you have the opportunity, take [it] ... It's not any one thing. I think it's just looking for your opportunities, taking them, recognizing when something wasn't working and saying, 'somebody may be upset by what they're seeing here, but, folks, let's keep emotion out of it. If we haven't done it right, let's step back from it, and see how we can do it right.'"

For example, Robicheau did not begin by suggesting that committees had to be abolished, even though he knew that was where council needed to go in the long run. Instead, he gradually moved responsibilities away from committees either to the full council if they involved policy or to staff if they involved administration. This maintained councillors' comfort levels, while moving toward the desired goal.

Robicheau also faced some challenges at the administrative level. The staff members he inherited, many of whom are still there more than twenty years later, were described as competent and self-directed, but accustomed to working without much leadership or team spirit. They were good bureaucrats in the neutral meaning of the term, in that they were given certain narrow, prescribed duties, which they were quite capable of carrying out, but they were never encouraged to look beyond those duties and be innovative or to gain a broader understanding of what a municipality is or how it works.

Previous managers were also described in that same bureaucratic mould. They were competent to supervise staff in normal situations, but when difficult situations arose, several interviewees said that managers had a tendency to go to their office and close the door. It is uncertain whether this was meant literally or figuratively, but the prevailing culture was clear.

The county had few proper written rules and procedures. In particular, staff members were demoralized by the absence of a job classification system, and they appear to have cut individual deals with their bosses, with all the anomalies and inequities that this entails. One of Robicheau's early projects was to establish such a system, which did much for morale and set the tone for his professional style of management.

To break down silos and develop team spirit, Robicheau instituted regular meetings with senior staff, something that had not been done before. Staff felt that no one had asked for their advice before; under Robicheau, they began to feel part of a team, which also improved their morale and efficiency.

The totality of these changes created a situation in which council, staff, and county government in general were much more respected in the community. Prior to Robicheau's arrival, council was seen as a dysfunctional group leading a government that was not particularly competent. One councillor talked about how she had spent a great deal of her time putting out fires because there was inadequate funding to do things that were obviously needed or because a staff member had done something foolish. After Robicheau arrived, it seemed that "[w]e started doing everything right for the right reasons," and the nature of her job changed. Council received more respect in the community because the county was now operating in a more functional manner.

THE COUNTY'S FINANCIAL POSITION

When Robicheau arrived, the county had a reserve of less than $50,000.[7] For a municipality with an annual budget of approximately $12 million, this is a dangerous situation. At the end of fiscal year 2007/08, when he left, the reserve was $3.3 million.[8] The standard method of building a reserve would be to increase revenue or decrease expenditures and begin a systematic pattern of setting aside a certain amount of the surplus generated each year to add to the reserve. For a municipality in a relatively economically distressed area of the province, either of these alternatives was politically difficult.

Robicheau introduced a more professional system of accounting and budgeting, which helped council understand its financial position and make some of these difficult decisions. Reportedly, before Robicheau arrived, senior staff did not allow councillors to examine the municipality's books, and information was presented in a way that made it difficult for them to understand the county's current financial situation and to appreciate the consequences of the decisions they were being asked to make. As part of making council a policy-making body, Robicheau presented the budget in a more transparent manner that showed council the consequences of its decisions. In this way, he wanted council to take a broad view of planning and to separate desirable projects from those that were essential. As one councillor put it, "he was always very good at laying out in the budget the difference between the needs and the wants." This then provided some breathing room in the budget.

Robicheau and Emms found a number of other ways to strengthen the reserve. For example, they began funding capital projects out of operating funds, thus not touching reserves. The main way they built up the reserve, however, was by finding lump sums of money either by changing operating practices or by seeking funds from other levels of governments. The next two sections provide examples of how they did this in particular cases.

CONTRACTING OUT PUBLIC WORKS

When Robicheau arrived, Annapolis County had a fully equipped public works department despite the fact that it had fairly limited responsibility for public works. As a rural area, it had only limited water and wastewater systems, and most roads were the responsibility of the province. Emms recalls that he and Robicheau were in agreement that governments should be arrangers of services, not necessarily direct providers of services. When Emms arrived, the county "had all kinds of construction equipment ... It got used once a year, and normally when somebody went to use it, it didn't work." Emms wondered why the county needed to own so much equipment when "there's a backhoe in every other backyard in Annapolis County. Why do we own a backhoe? I mean, I can get one in five minutes with a phone call."

Therefore, Robicheau and Emms decided to contract out public works activities, which would reduce the cost of providing the public works function. It also allowed them to sell off the equipment to make some money which went into the reserve. Not surprisingly, there was some resistance to the concept of contracting out and the related reduction of staff, but Robicheau presented a convincing case that won over council fairly easily.

CFB CORNWALLIS

In February 1994 (shortly before Robicheau arrived), the federal government announced that Canadian Forces Base (CFB) Cornwallis, located in the northwest corner of Annapolis County, would be closed. The decision was part of the then Liberal government's cutbacks in military spending, and Cornwallis was listed with CFB Chatham in New Brunswick as the bases with the highest per person costs.[9]

This was a devastating two-fisted blow to the county. First, the county would no longer receive payments in lieu of taxes related to the base from the federal government; second, the staff employed on the base would no longer be spending money in local businesses. This was very bad news for an area that was already economically distressed.[10] The federal government's original plan was to spend about $10 million to level the base and return the area to its natural state. At this point, the team of Terauds, Robicheau, and Emms sprang into action. Terauds, in particular, was influential in encouraging the federal government to leave the base intact and work with local governments to redevelop it. The federal government eventually agreed to provide $13.5 million of redevelopment funds through the Atlantic Canada Opportunities Agency and the Department of National Defence, although this attracted a great deal of criticism because of delays and allegations of wasted funds.

Robicheau then began working with neighbouring Digby County to create the Annapolis-Digby Economic Development Corporation. Throughout his career, Robicheau has developed a number of partnerships. This one made a great deal of sense because both counties would be significantly affected by the base closure and they shared a number of other interests in the area of economic development.

By July 1997 the federal government was beginning to make moves, first by offering 246 former military homes for sale at very low prices (ranging from $30,000 to $50,000); many of the new owners renovated their homes, resulting in about $2 million in spending at local stores. The vacant buildings at the base were then renovated for industrial purposes, and incentives were provided for businesses to maintain certain jobs quotas. Through the joint efforts of Terauds and Robicheau, a number of businesses were attracted to the industrial park. Terauds was instrumental in attracting a wood-processing operation that sold its product to IKEA, while Robicheau is credited with attracting a call centre. A number of other businesses also located in the area. By 2003 the *Globe and Mail* was reporting that the former military base had a "new lease on life," and was employing more people than the military base ever did. It was "widely seen as one of the most successful redevelopments of a military facility in Canada."[11]

One of the federal government's final acts was to turn over the base's municipal infrastructure (water and wastewater systems, streets, and sidewalks) to the county, although it had significant deficiencies that the county eventually would have to correct. Emms drew on his bargaining skills to maximize the amount of the settlement the county received. This money then went into the county's reserves in recognition of the future need to make major improvements to the infrastructure.

The entire project brought significant economic benefits to the county in the form of jobs and increased property assessment. But just as important as these tangible benefits were, the county also accrued important intangible benefits. A local government that had been seen as chaotic and unprofessional now had a significant "win" under its belt. Of course, federal involvement and money helped, but much of the direction of the undertaking had come from the county. These kinds of success stories are always the product of many people working together, but Robicheau's initiative clearly was a strong driving force in making it happen.

INTERMUNICIPAL PARTNERSHIPS: VALLEY WASTE MANAGEMENT, KINGS TRANSIT

One thing that has characterized Robicheau's career wherever he has gone is an emphasis on partnerships. He has done a good job of protecting the interests of his own municipality, but he also recognizes that taxpayers frequently benefit from shared initiatives rather than having the municipality go it alone.

By the late 1990s it was becoming clear that environmentally sound solid waste management required significant improvements in methods of handling waste. To accomplish this, Nova Scotia created seven waste management districts that were basically forced marriages of counties throughout the province to handle solid waste.[12] Forced marriages are not usually happy marriages, and these arrangements created considerable tension in some areas of the province. It seems to have worked easily in the Valley, however. Part of this was luck. Kings County's landfill was now full, and Annapolis County had been using two incinerators that the province ordered closed. Therefore, neither county was bringing anything to the table – except a dire need to find a new way of handling its solid waste.

Robicheau took a strong lead in making the partnership work. One councillor said flatly, "[i]t wouldn't have happened if it hadn't been for Keith." This is probably an overstatement because the province had mandated that these cooperative arrangements must occur, but Robicheau almost certainly made it happen more smoothly than was the case in other places. Cooperation between county governments and the separate governments of the towns within the counties is difficult because there is a prevailing view that the counties get a sweet financial deal from the province, while the towns are required to deliver more services. Robicheau, however, managed to pull it off. Even though he had been in Annapolis for just four years at that time, he was already well known and well respected throughout the area. This allowed him to bring the representatives of the member municipalities together. He is given credit for personally drafting the agreement that defined the governance and financing of the joint authority, eventually titled Valley Waste Resource Management (VWRM). One interviewee commented that Robicheau was always the best-prepared person around the table and the one who was always willing to take the initiative, so that the other people at the table were willing to leave it to him.

It speaks volumes that, after more than a decade, VWRM is still using the basic agreement prepared by Robicheau, whose fingerprints are on it in at least two significant ways. First, reminiscent of the way he handled public works in the county, VWRM contracts out virtually all of its operations, from collection to disposal. The only major assets it owns are its new administration building and two transfer stations. Second, Robicheau suggested that the debt incurred be financed over ten years instead of the allowable twenty. This provided the authority the financial room to build its new administration building after paying off its initial capital cost.

Having successfully tackled solid waste, Robicheau moved on to transit. Councillors and others in the community began to feel that it was important for Annapolis County (and three towns within the county) to have a public transit system to encourage job creation and promote a feeling of unity in the area. The problem was that for a large, rural jurisdiction to develop its own transit system, the cost would have been prohibitive. Somewhat more urban Kings County already operated a transit system, however, that ran to the border of Annapolis

County. So Robicheau put his partnership development skills to work and negotiated an agreement between Kings Transit and the county and towns in Annapolis County to extend its service. This was an awkward balancing act for Robicheau because it required some work to get all three towns to make a contribution, but he felt that the unified show of support was an important principle. With relatively limited cost to the county and towns, the public transit system now provides a tremendous benefit to small, rural areas by allowing people to shop and take up employment outside their own communities. It also helps to unite a large rural county that does not have much else to tie it together.

THE LIFEPLEX CENTRE

Robicheau's final major activity in Annapolis County was advising on the county's involvement in the development of what came to be known as the Lifeplex Centre. One of the amenities that the federal government left behind as a part of the military base was a well-equipped fitness centre, a real attraction for the people buying the base houses. Unfortunately, the building housing the centre was destroyed by fire. This prompted a local group to organize to raise money to build a new fitness complex dubbed the Lifeplex Centre. The group was better at good intentions than at organizing and financial skills, however. It was able to raise some funds to begin to convert the existing base exchange building to a fitness centre, but eventually the fundraising stalled and the group came to the county for funds.

This was a difficult decision for the county. The group needed a significant amount of money by county standards – about $2.5 million – to complete the renovation. As well, the facility was located in the extreme northwest end of the county and so would benefit only a limited number of county residents. And finally, the group did not have a convincing plan for the sustainable operation of the facility after completion – indeed, they apparently had already been turned down for bank financing for this reason.

Because of Robicheau's prudent development of the reserve, the county could come up with the funds, but was it wise public policy? How would taxpayers in other parts of the county react? What would happen if the group was not able to operate the facility in a sustainable manner and had to return to the county annually for operating funds? Robicheau did not make a recommendation to council one way or the other. He felt this was probably the most politically charged decision this council ever had to make, so his report provided only an assessment of the various options, and asked for guidance from council about how to proceed. He was uncomfortable going beyond offering his neutral, professional advice.

After great soul searching and considerable pressure from the group, the council decided to provide the necessary funding. Over time, however, this has become a roller-coaster story. The facility opened as planned, but the group was not able to cover its operating costs after all, and the facility closed. At the time of writing, the county is working with the YMCA to reopen the facility using YMCA expertise and some county funding.

TIME TO MOVE ON

After fourteen years in Annapolis County, Robicheau felt it was time to move on. He had had a positive relationship with Peter Terauds as warden. They saw eye-to-eye on many things and were keen on moving the county forward. Robicheau has nothing negative to say about other wardens, but it seems he was unable to duplicate the extremely positive relationship he had with Terauds.

All good CAOs are philosophical about giving advice to council, and recognize that their advice sometimes will be rejected. The CAO who does not accept that simply will not be a CAO for long. But that does not make the CAO immune from sometimes feeling uncomfortable about the direction council is taking, and wondering if it might not be time to move on. Robicheau never speaks critically of anyone or any council, but there is a sense in talking to him that he was troubled, not by the decision that council made with regard to the Lifeplex Centre, but by the fact that "the dissenting views didn't go away afterwards ... It was very disappointing to see some of the very negative and festering after-effects of that." He had suggested to council that, if it approved funding for the centre, everyone would have to support the initiative or it would fail. He seemed bothered by the fact that "the dissenting views didn't go away."

Robicheau is the sort of person who takes his work seriously, which is a good thing, but he recognized the danger of becoming too tied up with a job and of identifying too much with an organization. In his words, "[t]he municipality is a body corporate. It's not a family member; it's not your wife; and ... you shouldn't care at the level that I was caring" – a perceptive comment that is discussed in more detail later in this chapter. It was probably in neither his interest nor that of Annapolis County to stay there for the rest of his career. After fourteen years he had both family and professional reasons for wanting to move on. As well, the county had seen a number of changes at the council level, and he felt that the new people should have the opportunity to choose a CAO reflective of their views.

He emphasizes that no one big reason encouraged him to leave; instead, a succession of smaller things made him feel it was time to go. It happened that the Town of Kentville, in adjoining Kings County, was looking for a new CAO. Some of its councillors were already quite familiar with Robicheau – indeed, by 2008, he was recognized throughout Nova Scotia as an excellent administrator – and they asked their recruiter to approach him.

Town of Kentville, NS (2008–11)

Compared to the difficult situation he encountered in Annapolis County, Robicheau found the Town of Kentville to be much more settled. Kentville's population is approximately 6,000, although it punches a bit above its weight because it functions as the regional centre for Kings County and, to a certain extent, for the entire Annapolis Valley. Its consolidated expenditure in fiscal year 2010/11 was $10.7 million.[13] Upon Robicheau's arrival, he found a council that was a competent, reasonably unified group quite experienced working with a CAO system. The staff was also competent, and the town had no immediate disconcerting issues such as the closure of a major military base hanging over it.

His predecessor, Bill Boyd, was a well-respected, thirty-three-year town employee who had spent the previous fourteen years as CAO[14] and, by all accounts, left Kentville in great shape. In an unusual quirk, however, Boyd had run successfully for council shortly after retiring, so that the recently retired CAO was in the position of supervising the new CAO, although the odd situation seems to have created no problems.

Robicheau did not need to train Kentville's councillors as he had in Annapolis County, but he did make a significant contribution to the operation of council by helping to develop two strategic planning sessions, making use of his considerable experience as a facilitator that he had developed while with the New Brunswick government. Many people say that, regardless of the facilitator's skills, it is difficult to be a facilitator in your own organization – which is why most organizations bring in an outsider to help develop a strategic plan – but virtually everyone interviewed praised Robicheau for the quality and results of his work as a facilitator.

Robicheau stayed in Kentville for only three years and in a much more settled situation than he had faced in Annapolis County, so his impact was not as great as it had been in the county. Nevertheless, he did play a role in a number of important accomplishments.

EDUCATION LEVY

Probably the most serious issue that Robicheau dealt with during his time in Kentville was a proposal by Kings County to change the method of funding the local board of education.[15] In Nova Scotia, boards of education are funded by levies on the counties and towns within the board's geographic area, allocated by the number of students from each jurisdiction or based on a uniform property assessment for taxation purposes. Most areas opt for uniform property assessment, but Kings County and its adjacent municipalities had always used a per student calculation to determine their contributions to the Annapolis Valley Regional School Board. The county decided that it could save a considerable amount of money by switching to a uniform assessment basis, but such a move would have a devastating effect on many towns in the county, since previous levies had been built into their budgets, and increasing the amount significantly would put an impossible strain on them. Some informal discussions were held to try to resolve the issue, but when it became clear that it would go to court, Robicheau worked with other local CAOs to develop a unified position among the affected towns, and to hire and manage their legal defence. Ultimately, the towns won their case, and the system was not changed.

Such successes are the product of a number of people working together, but interviewees gave Robicheau a great deal of credit for guiding the towns' opposition to the proposed change, for holding them together, and for exercising good judgment throughout the process.

KINGS COUNTY ACADEMY AND THE PROPANE DISTRIBUTION CENTRE

Robicheau inherited another difficult education-related issue. Kentville's grade school was situated in a seventy-five-year-old building that was in bad shape. The provincial Department of Education planned to renovate it and continue to use it, but Kentville's residents wanted a new building to house the school. Robicheau is given credit for working with the department to get a brand new building, rather than settling for renovating the old one.[16] Selecting the site for the new school involved the town's identifying three or four locations and submitting them to the department for a final decision. Kentville particularly wanted a certain location that was close to residential and recreational areas, and Mark Phillips, the director of parks and recreation, took the lead, with Robicheau's support, in urging the department to choose it. There was a fly in the ointment, however: the location was close to a propane sales location with a large storage tank, which made both the department and local parents nervous. Robicheau eventually helped to persuade the propane company to relocate, which successfully opened the way for the new school to be built where the town wanted it.[17] Robicheau was not as involved in this issue as he had been with the education funding issue – indeed, he left before the final decision about the propane relocation was made – but he is credited with moving it toward a resolution that the municipality desired.

PARTNERSHIPS AND REGIONALIZATION

Another aspect of his career that Robicheau continued to carry forward in Kentville was his interest in partnerships and regionalization. In Kentville, he was still involved in the Valley Waste and Kings Transit partnerships, just wearing a different hat. He also worked with the volunteer fire department, which is an independent body with a contractual agreement with Kings County and Kentville.[18] Some in the fire service felt it was time to hire a full-time chief. This had both financial and organizational ramifications. Robicheau was acknowledged for demonstrating the requirements, benefits, and implications of moving to a full-time chief and for working the department through the difficult issues of revising its organizational structure and actually hiring its first full-time chief.

MOVING ON AGAIN

Virtually everyone in Kentville knew that hiring someone of Robicheau's stature was a mixed blessing. They were glad to have him ply his trade for them, but they also understood that he likely would move on to a larger place and a higher-profile posting. They hoped he would stay for five years, but at the three-year mark a number of things happened. He was happy in Kentville, but he was disappointed with how Nova Scotia's municipal system was evolving. He had served on a number of advisory bodies over the years that had offered recommendations in this area, and was disappointed that the province had rejected some key advice that he felt would have improved the development of the municipal system. At the same time, his children had finished their schooling and left Nova Scotia, and he and his wife wanted to move closer to them.

His next stop would be Norfolk County, in Ontario, a position he took just a few months before this research was undertaken, and so it is too soon to discuss his work there.

The Leadership Role of the CAO

With Robicheau's biographical sketch as background, this section discusses his general leadership qualities before examining how he has led in each of the three directions – down, out, and up.

General characteristics

CHANGE ORIENTED

Like many of the other CAOs in this book, Robicheau has never been happy with the status quo when he has arrived in a new place. In St Andrews, he was instrumental in developing the downtown and waterfront areas. In Annapolis County, he made many organizational changes and developed important partnerships in economic development, waste management, and transit. In the short time that he was in Kentville, he helped the volunteer fire department hire its first full-time chief. But his change orientation has not been confined to such high-profile issues – he has also made some important changes that have flown below the radar. In Annapolis County, he improved the budgeting system so that council could make more-informed decisions. He also fostered training and development to enable staff members to broaden their contributions to the county and feel better about themselves.

RESPECTFUL OF THE LOCAL CULTURE

Robicheau has always approached the process of change in a particular way. Some leaders pride themselves on the gunslinger approach: quickly imposing changes from the top down and blowing away the opposition. Robicheau, in contrast, has always taken the slow and steady approach. He knows that people accept change more readily if they are comfortable with it. He is also aware that rapid change imposed on an organization that is not ready for it makes people defensive. Accordingly, he takes his time and develops a good understanding of where he wants to go, and is willing to get there in slow, but steady steps. He also takes the time to assess the organization and the people in it. He then uses this information to design his change strategy. As a part of that process, he patiently explains the reasons for particular changes at every step of the process.

A RATIONAL THINKER

Robicheau's slow, steady approach to change is accompanied by rational thinking about change and about management in general. His university degree and his early work experiences were in accounting, and wherever he has gone he is seen as a "numbers" man. He not only understands the numbers himself, but, considerably rarer still, he is able to explain the numbers to others in a way that brings sceptics around to his way of looking at things. Initially, councillors in Annapolis County were not keen on contracting out major aspects of the public works function, but when he presented the rational, numeric arguments, he was able to win them over.

KNOWLEDGEABLE

Robicheau's rationality is supported by his being extremely knowledgeable. Many interviewees commented in particular about his extensive knowledge of the Nova Scotia Municipal Government Act. Since he had spent the early part of his career in New Brunswick, it required a certain effort on his part to familiarize himself with the Nova Scotia legislation. Interestingly, no one in Annapolis County (his first position in Nova Scotia) suggested that he had any difficulty adapting to his new province.

WELL PREPARED

One reason Robicheau has always appeared to be so knowledgeable is that he prepares himself thoroughly for any meeting or new situation. In addition to his knowledge of the Municipal Government Act, he is always well prepared on financial issues. As one interviewee noted, "believe me, if you wanted to discuss finances with Keith, you wanted to be well prepared, because he had them all right here [in his head] ... You're not going to bluff Keith Robicheau when it comes to finances." People commented that any report he took to council was exceptionally well prepared and that he had considered all the alternatives, which obviously inspired a great deal of confidence among councillors. One said, "[h]e was good at research and background. Any report that he brought to our council was thoroughly researched ... He'd bring examples from other parts of the world." Another suggested that, if anything, Robicheau had a tendency to overdo it: "You can't fault him for being capable, but sometimes you say, 'OK, that's good enough, Keith. We don't need any more.'"

GOOD RELATIONSHIP SKILLS

Robicheau is seen as a keen judge of people – a number of interviewees referred to his emotional intelligence. He has a reputation for taking the time to get to know the people around him, and he treats everyone from the mayor to the janitor, with a great deal of respect. In Annapolis County, the councillors he worked with varied significantly in terms of their formal education. He had to interact with different councillors in a very different manner – a good example of his emotional intelligence. He had the patience to spend a great deal of time with some councillors to ensure that they understood fully the issues before council.

But he also has humility in that he does not feel he is better than anyone else, although he probably is smarter than most. As one interviewee put it, "he respected every person he talked to, and if he didn't respect them he certainly put on one hell of a good show ... You would be talking to Keith and you would feel that your conversation ... was the most important thing that he had to do during the day, that you were the most important person that he was talking to, your issue/question/problem was the most important thing that had to be dealt with, and I think everybody felt that way."

But he does not just read people passively – he works hard at maintaining relationships. Wherever he has gone, he has been seen as a leader among his peers. This made sense in Annapolis County, where, as a county official, he worked with all the towns, but he played the same role when he moved to Kentville. One CAO recalled Robicheau's phoning him and inviting him for lunch shortly after the CAO was appointed. Another government official said that Robicheau would call him once in a while and suggest that they go to lunch, and they would chat about things that were in no way related to work. These are the small things that build trust and relationships.

HARD WORKING

Many people commented on how hard Robicheau works. A number recalled his being the first in the office in the morning and the last to leave at night, and seeing his car at the municipal building on week-ends. Some councillors even said they worried that he was working too hard, although none seem to have suggested that they spend money to get him some help, and he seems to have been reluctant to request it. Some interviewees noted that the municipal clerk might have been able to help, although the clerk's full-time job – as clerk – likely precluded the possibility. Of course, all CAOs work hard – no one sees this as a nine-to-five job – and possibly this drive just stands out more in a smaller place. When he left Kentville, Robicheau was moving toward availing himself of a provincial government program that assisted municipalities in hiring an intern. This would have been an improvement, but there is still only so much that someone in her or his first municipal position can do.

PROFESSIONAL

A number of interviewees referred to Robicheau's professionalism. This covers everything from his style of dress to his personal demeanour to his expectations of others. It seemed odd to hear so many people referring to professionalism, as though this would not be a normal expectation of a CAO, but Robicheau has found himself in situations, particularly in Annapolis County, where the lack of professionalism among those around him when he arrived was a problem, and his possession of it thereby stood out. In these cases, he not only displayed it himself; he also had to instil it in others. One person described how, before Robicheau's arrival, it was common for staff in Annapolis County to gossip about one another or even about councillors, behaviour that ceased during Robicheau's tenure. He knew he had to extend the professionalism beyond himself, and he encouraged others to avail themselves of training and development opportunities. He not only arranged for financial assistance programs, but he also met with people taking courses and discussed the course content with them.

CORE VALUES

Robicheau developed a set of core values quite early in his career. He attributes his interest in the idea of core values to some research he heard about that suggested that well-performing organizations likely are based on a set of core values shared by all in the organization. Others refer to this as developing an organizational culture.

Of course, most leaders say they have a set of core values that motivates them. What is different about Robicheau is that he has committed these values to paper (see below), which he carries with him in his agenda wherever he goes at work. When he comes to a new place, he shares these values with councillors and staff, and asks all those around to hold him to these values and to tell him if they feel that he has deviated from them. He emphasizes that these values are what he lives by; they are not just for show:

> I hope when the going gets tough that people don't see me setting aside my values. In fact, they would see me changing my methods, my approaches, but not my values ... It's not something that's there as a matter of convenience. I really do believe these things, [in] good times or bad ... I'm not professing anything here that is novel or unique; [they] just happen to be things that help me keep grounded and they provide a foundation. As much as I would like to think that I would grow [and be] accepting of new ideas, that I'm looking to mature, change, grow intellectually, emotionally, and increase my abilities over time, I'd like to think that [these values] are a constant.

CORE VALUES AND OPERATING PRINCIPLES

- I value the people the municipality serves and I am committed to quality service and continuous improvement on their behalf.
  - ○ Citizens are served equitably, respectfully, and in a caring manner.
  - ○ I am accessible to communicate, provide information about our services, and listen to the municipality's citizens.
  - ○ I respect and honour the trust and confidence placed in me by the council and citizens of the municipality.

- I value the municipality's employees. I believe they should be empowered to do their jobs, and high performance is a result of people who care about what they do.
  - ○ Staff are challenged, encouraged, and developed.
  - ○ Staff are delegated appropriate authority and responsibility to act and use their judgment to tackle challenges that confront them.

- I value creativity, innovation, and achievement. I am accepting of innovative ideas, work styles, and methods.
  - Staff are encouraged to be self-reliant and self-starting and not to rely solely on supervisory direction, guidance, and control.
  - I incorporate challenge and a results orientation into programs and services and require consideration of cost/benefit and risk/return.
  - I foster a climate of good will and recognize achievement.

- I value a mindset that seeks optimum performance and adaptability in the face of change.
  - I strive for excellence and to be strategic in plans and actions.
  - I maintain methods of monitoring performance and seek feedback.
  - I seek improvement in individual and organizational performance.
  - When conditions change, I adjust my methods, not my values.

- I value teamwork and participative decision-making.
  - My leadership style is participative whenever possible.
  - Purpose and goals are developed in a participative setting as much as possible, to foster understanding and commitment.
  - Although formal levels exist for administrative purposes, they do not inhibit collaboration in achieving results.
  - I build supportive relationships by cultivating formal and informal communications.

Robicheau is well respected as a leader and well liked on a personal level everywhere he has gone. He seems to have a good balance of relationship skills and task orientation. He knows what he wants to do, and he has the people skills to accomplish his goals. He has the ability to transform organizations, as evidenced by his twice introducing the CAO system to municipalities in which he has worked. Moreover, he made change in a deliberate fashion that respected the people in the organization and helped them embrace the change. Through his professionalism he has been a role model even in organizations that did not exhibit a good dose of professionalism before he arrived. He clearly has the personal skills to be a good leader. How has he gone about using those skills in the three directions?

Leading down

Robicheau is viewed as excellent at leading down wherever he has gone. He is a personable man and a keen judge of people, and he has used this skill in all his positions. Some words kept recurring in interviews of former staff members: respect, fairness, equity, transparency. People also talked about his level of knowledge, especially of finance and the Nova Scotia Municipal Government Act – interestingly, knowledge of provincial legislation on municipalities was never mentioned in any of the interviews related to CAOs in the larger jurisdictions.

The initial impression of him is one of formality. One person described him as a shy, retiring, and private person. Another suggested he would never be regarded as the life of the party. At work he is always dressed in a suit and tie, as befitting a CAO, even though many others in the small-town environments in which he has worked did not dress so formally. He has a way of signalling that he really cares about people at the personal level. He takes a real interest in employee social functions – rolling up his sleeves and cooking burgers at staff picnics – but he keeps himself aloof from gossip and office politics. Several people commented how he treats everyone in the office in the same way, friendly with both the senior management team and the janitors.

Staff commented on how he supported them in all sorts of ways. In Annapolis County, as mentioned, he established a job classification system; he also personally dealt with angry citizens who delivered their garbage to the front counter when the county could not pick it up because its incinerator had been condemned. This paints a picture of an ambivalent personality who can be both formal and a bit standoffish, but also deeply involved when the situation calls for it. It is not surprising that many people mentioned his ability to instil passion and enthusiasm in them.

He was also praised for the way he acts as a buffer between councillors and staff. In Annapolis County, in particular, the political process sometimes became difficult. He was able to absorb those shocks and insist the staff do their best professional administrative work while he handled relationships with council.

He encourages staff to bring forward new ideas, as long as they are supported by solid arguments. Many people referred to his door as always open if anyone wanted to discuss any issues that were important to them.

He is an astute judge of people, a skill he uses to develop people in cases where others might not see their potential. One interviewee noted that "he looked for people's strengths and tried to give opportunities to build on those strengths to use those to the advantage of the organization. I think sometimes he recognized talents in people that they themselves didn't recognize or didn't have the confidence to pursue." Another interviewee told the story of a person who worked at the Annapolis incinerator mentioned earlier. Instead of being let go when the incinerator closed, he was encouraged by Emms and Robicheau to take some additional training; the individual is now a valued employee working in the wastewater plant.

Indeed, Robicheau has always emphasized the importance of training and development. He ensured that there was money in the budget to help staff undertake training, and he encouraged them to pursue a variety of courses. One person talked about how he loaned her books and pointed her in the direction of interesting readings. Since he was interested in and familiar with the topic of the course, they also had periodic discussions about the course content. She maintained that this had been helpful to her in the course, and had signalled his interest in training and development. Robicheau describes his perspective on training and development as follows: "My purpose in ... being a promoter of life-long learning and education [is] actually to encourage [staff members] to broaden their contributions to the organization ... I saw a lot of talent and a lot of potential there, and certainly when you see people with a tremendous willingness and inherent motivation and what they're lacking is just some *capability* in terms of training and education, boy, what a combination in terms of what they can contribute when they are both willing and able" (emphasis in original).

Robicheau lets people manage and make their own decisions. He does not micromanage, but there is a sense that he is always there to support his staff if they are in a difficult position. He manages by setting reasonable goals for people and allowing them to decide how to work toward those goals. In his own words: "I've always been very clear with councils that my preferred style is not to be looking over people's shoulder all the time ... My motivational approach is very much goal-setting. It's making sure that we're doing work planning and review. I don't need to know everything you're doing as a department head and every part of the organization. I need to know what are the top two, three, or four things that you've got to be doing among everything else, and balancing with your other priorities in order for this organization to be successful to be doing those things over the next three months, six months, whatever our check-in period's going to be." This is reflected in the view that staff members had of how he dealt with them. As one commented, "it's comforting to know that, if you did have a question, he was always there to answer it, and he would give you his take on things, his feedback, but he wouldn't make the decision for you … He would let you grow as an individual."

One way Robicheau has demonstrated his emotional intelligence and management skill is by taking a very different management approach in different places. As discussed above, he faced some fairly difficult issues when he arrived in Annapolis County, but a much more settled situation in Kentville. He was obviously guided in both places by the core values he always carries with him, but he clearly was astute enough to adapt his specific actions to the circumstances.

When he arrived in Annapolis County, he inherited a staff that was quite competent at the individual level – almost twenty years later, many of them are still there – but no one had helped them to work as a team or had demonstrated professionalism. It was like a sports team whose players know how to play their own position, but that lacks a coach to help them work together. He thus needed to build a team, and set out to do this by first removing some irritants, then working proactively to teach staff what it meant to work as a team. As discussed above, he developed a job classification system that improved equity and transparency. He then complemented this by introducing a performance evaluation system to ensure that staff received feedback on their work.

Robicheau also introduced an aura of professionalism in some small, but important, ways. According to one interviewee, when Robicheau arrived in Annapolis County in 1994, there was one computer in the building; gradually he brought in more. As well, the building had been allowed to deteriorate, a condition that Robicheau reversed. Such small things sent a signal to staff that they were valued.

Robicheau also instituted meetings of senior staff – something which apparently had not been done before – which created a management team and gave staff an opportunity to have input into decisions. It also gradually moved decisions to lower levels in the organization, rather than having every decision go to council. He promoted the idea that decisions should be made at the lowest level that was reasonably possible.

Kentville was very different. There, he had the much easier task of maintaining the system already in place, but even system maintenance requires some effort. Robicheau was the first "outside" CAO that most staff remembered, so he had to win their confidence. He worked with staff to ensure that a number of issues were moved forward at the appropriate speed. He also mentored a bright, young department head who eventually succeeded him as CAO. Indeed, many interviewees, including some who did not work for him, spoke of Robicheau as a mentor. Among his staff, several interviewees admitted they would not be in their current positions if Robicheau had not mentored them at crucial stages in their career.

It was not always a matter of formal mentoring. Several interviewees commented how, at various meetings, he would describe not only what action he was taking, but also why he had chosen this particular route. Staff really appreciated these insights. Both councillors and staff commented that, although Robicheau did not become overly familiar with staff, he was always available to discuss any work-related issues they might have.

Whether by coincidence or design, women seem to have particularly prospered under Robicheau's guidance. Today, there are a number of women in senior positions in Annapolis County – including one who started as an administrative assistant in 1999 and is now the acting deputy CAO – and those interviewed spoke highly of the mentoring they received. For his part, Robicheau is proud to name the women who have won outstanding student awards in various programs.

Unlike the other CAOs examined in this book, Robicheau has retained a fairly direct involvement in the finance function of the small municipalities for which he has worked. All CAOs make the point that the final budget belongs to them, but Robicheau has been much more deeply involved in the preparation of the budget than other CAOs have been. He feels comfortable doing this because of his background in accounting, but it has also given him an in-depth understanding of the various organizations that would have been difficult to obtain otherwise. Indeed, his involvement in the financial function seems to have gone beyond budget time to include other areas of finance as well. This could have been seen as intrusive or micromanaging, but somehow he did it in a way that staff regarded as a beneficial form of mentoring.

Robicheau's staff clearly respected him. He cared about their well-being and their future development, and they appreciated him for that. They seem to have been highly motivated to work for him, but how has he fared working with council?

Leading up

Being a CAO in a small municipality is qualitatively different from being a CAO in a larger place. This difference comes through strongly when one examines the CAO's role in leading up. Working in small municipalities, Robicheau has been more proactive in leading up than have been any of the previous CAOs discussed in this book, although his style did change somewhat between Annapolis County and Kentville.

Annapolis County is a rural area with a broad range of educational levels among its population and, not surprisingly, among its council members as well: some councillors are relatively sophisticated professional people, while others lack a strong formal education. On top of this, Robicheau had to move the council from a council-committee system to a CAO system. Several people commented that councillors had been accustomed to supervising works crews virtually directly, while in the new structure their role was to make policy; if they had any administrative concerns, they were to take them to the CAO. In these circumstances, both councillors and staff were fairly frank in seeing Robicheau's role partly as "educating" councillors. As one noted, "Keith led. I wouldn't call it taking orders from councillors ... He had that educational approach." This stood the normal council-staff relationship on its head, but everyone seemed to recognize that it was necessary. In the words of one experienced councillor, "[h]e was always prepared to educate us. He wanted us to be a successful council and successful as councillors, so he was always prepared, never was in a rush not to talk with us, and in that I always felt that I was being educated on how to be a better councillor ... in a very relaxed manner. He's not a pushy fellow – personable, but not personal." Another councillor admitted that process was not his strength, so he relied on Robicheau for advice, "and I considered Keith my teacher."

One councillor described how he wanted to obtain funding for a particular capital work in his ward. He recounted how Robicheau explained to him both the formal process to get the project into the five-year plan and the informal process that he should follow to help move it toward approval. "That's why I remember Keith so well ... he was able to teach me how the system really works and how it was designed to work."

In addition to the personal touch, Robicheau organized orientation sessions and strategic planning sessions that had an educational component involving outside experts, so that local councillors could develop an understanding of how things were done in other places.

This educational role could have put Robicheau in a difficult position, but he seems to have carried it out with a sensitivity and delicacy that made everything work out well. An important part of educating is establishing a relationship of trust. This could have been particularly difficult in Annapolis County, where he was making significant changes. He describes how he went about developing that relationship:

> Communicate, communicate, communicate. Listen, listen, listen. Recognize and value difference ... It's not terribly profound. [It's] making sure people understand where you're coming from, what your values are ... but it's also getting people to take the strategic approach to things ... It's the typical leadership toolbox that I've described here, you know, shared vision and mission, values and operating principles, a results orientation with clear goals ... Very much into ... clarifying results expectations, try[ing] to make goals clear, ... try[ing] to make sure that you get people to buy in. Make sure that you're checking in, you're measuring things, getting feedback, and that people share knowledge and results ... – being action oriented, having action plans.

Several people commented on Robicheau's ability to explain relatively complex issues in a clear and straightforward manner. Without obviously talking down to councillors who were not familiar with a particular issue, he could present the issue so that all councillors could understand it. "Any issue that Keith would bring forward to council, he would explain it and do it well. If it needed a yes, he'd probably get it, because we [had] high respect for him and we knew that he was right."

Several interviewees noted Robicheau's extreme patience in dealing with issues, commenting that he had more patience than they would have had under the circumstances. Robicheau demonstrated that patience by recognizing that every councillor was different, and he seemed to have a remarkable ability to read each councillor and determine the kind of support the councillor needed. He saw a certain councillor struggling to understand something at a meeting, so he phoned the councillor the next day just to chat and to see if there was anything the councillor wanted to discuss. This led to an opportunity to discuss the issue in more detail, which then made the councillor more comfortable.

In Kentville, in contrast, Robicheau was dealing with a fairly experienced council that had been operating with a CAO system for a number of years. He seems to have adopted an approach completely different from that employed in Annapolis County, but with the same result in that councillors there developed a great deal of confidence in him and spoke highly of him. Indeed, some of the terms used to describe him were common to interviewees from both municipalities, such as "courteous," "diplomatic," and "polite." No one ever remembers his showing anger or losing his composure in a public setting.

He had a reputation for always being available and willing to explain or discuss an issue with a councillor. At the same time, he was careful not to be directive in his discussions with councillors, preferring to use phrases such as "have you thought about this?" "I was talking to somebody about that, and ..." and "what do you think about looking at it like this?" He sometimes used his facilitation skills to advantage not just in the strategic planning exercise, but also in stepping into the council arena to help councillors arrive at a decision. He tried to keep council away from the knee-jerk style of decision making that can occur. He was "always trying to lead them to the strategic rather than the simplistic decision making processes." He would use his facilitation skills "to bridge the gap [between people and to] ask questions in such a way as to help develop consensus. He would often start with the thing he knew they could all agree on and develop from there."

He also became involved in council discussions in ways that were somewhat minor, but still helpful. Several people recall his suggesting ways to reword motions to make them clearer. One councillor remembered making a statement in debate that would have looked bad in the media. Robicheau was regarded as having good media sense, so when he interjected to suggest that she had intended to say something a bit different, she immediately agreed and was grateful for his helping her avoid a potentially serious misunderstanding.

A significant part of Robicheau's strength is that he is recognized as knowledgeable. Councillors also clearly respected his financial acumen. In Annapolis County he served as the chief financial officer in the early years because the county had serious financial issues and he knew he had to get a good handle on these. In both Annapolis County and Kentville, he was known for ensuring that councillors were familiar with the financial implications of any decision they made. In general, councillors talked about Robicheau's being well prepared and relying on strong rational arguments supported by financial information or legislative requirements. Councillors did not seem to begrudge the fact that he had a great deal of influence on their decisions because they had a great deal of confidence in his abilities.

Robicheau's relationship with the provincial government was also helpful in his dealings with councillors. One councillor praised him for helping them to put their best case to the province and avoid antagonizing people there: "One of the things that he was good at doing as our CAO was making sure that we didn't put our foot in it, at any time. If there was an issue going on that we had to deal with, he made sure that our approach was good, we got our facts straight, very factual, and what we were asking for, that was laid out too, very clear."

At the personal level, Robicheau seems to be able to establish the distance that needs to be maintained between council and staff. Councillors interviewed used phrases such as "very personable, but not familiar"; "He didn't want to be my best buddy"; and "He wanted me to be successful, but he didn't call up to talk about the weather." One councillor focused on the idea of fairness and equality: "The main thing that I would say that strikes me about Keith [is that] everyone is treated the same with Keith whether you're a brand new rookie on council really just trying to ramp up the learning curve, or you're a twenty-year member that should [have been] retired ten years ago. He treat[s] everyone the same, gives everyone the same opportunity to give input."

One senses, however, that things are a bit different for a CAO in a smaller place, where the likelihood of crossing paths with councillors in social situations is higher than is the case in larger municipalities. Robicheau is an avid curler and golfer, which brought him into frequent contact with some councillors. One councillor said that they kept a certain distance at first, but that they eventually did end up being 'buddies.' Another interviewee noted that "[Robicheau] had a chameleon-like ability to shift his decorum" in that he interacted with councillors one way on the golf course, but in a much more formal way in the council chamber.

Robicheau clearly is able to engage in a leadership role with regard to council. This has meant something a bit different for each of his councils, but it always involves councillors giving him a great deal of respect and deference because of his knowledge and judgment.

Leading out

Everywhere Robicheau has been, he has worked on building partnerships with other organizations. Some people suggested that his experience in the restructuring of Miramichi gave him a good understanding of the importance of seeing things on a regional basis and appreciating that, particularly in rural areas and small towns, the best solutions might be regional ones.

He is keenly focused on both good service delivery and delivering that service at a reasonable cost. But he recognizes that the smaller municipalities where he has worked find it difficult to do this on their own. In St Andrews, he wanted to see the waterfront redeveloped, and the town had the planning and regulatory tools to allow it to happen, but that was not enough to effect change. He had to work with local entrepreneurs and others to make it happen.

Robicheau's ability to develop partnerships is an outgrowth of his well-regarded ability to build relationships. But partnerships have to be built on more than good intentions, and they will not last unless they are beneficial to all the partners. Robicheau is able to open the door to commence discussion about partnerships, but what sets him apart from other well-meaning proponents of partnerships is that he is sufficiently skilled in the areas of governance and finance to write agreements that meet the needs of all the partners. He demonstrated this when he wrote the agreement for Valley Waste Resource Management, which has lasted thirteen years without major changes and has resulted in a reasonably satisfactory relationship among all participants. The same could be said of the Kings Transit situation and a number of smaller agreements. He is good at hammering out these agreements because he is willing to take the initiative and do the work, and because he understands the benefits each party needs to derive from the agreement and is able to put those into words using his knowledge of financial and governance issues.

He has also been able to guide these kinds of agreements in a more subtle way by cultivating relationships with his fellow CAOs. One CAO from the Annapolis Valley recalled how, when he was new on the job, Robicheau phoned to invite him to lunch. Other CAOs talked about his mentoring them in their positions when they came in. It seems that, in a diverse and sometimes fractious group of Valley municipalities, Robicheau was one degree of separation from everyone. That placed him in a strategic position.

It is not just friendship, however, that helps him get agreements; he also falls back on his rational approach to policy to bring people on side: "He was able to get the team players to be on the same page not through browbeating them, but through taking them through and really showing them the benefits, the cost-benefit analysis ... of coming along ... He wasn't always successful ... but I think the process he takes, showing everyone an equal amount of consideration[,] ... was rewarding for the municipalities involved."

Robicheau was instrumental in developing the Kings County Warden and Mayors Committee. As suggested earlier, there is a natural division of interests between counties and towns. One person described this process as getting a partnership between a cat and a dog. There can still be divisions of interest, as indicated by the education levy fight, but many people suggested that the county and towns are now working together better than they have for the past twenty years.

One technique Robicheau uses to deal with arguments generally is to get people talking about the things they have agreed on, rather than focusing on their disagreements. In the education levy case, he pushed hard for the idea that education should be a provincial responsibility, and should not fall on any local government. As one interviewee noted, "[t]hat led to the idea that it's not just education; it's everything the towns are being burdened with. We need to take our case on a province-wide basis to the higher powers and so they're studying that right now, and I would credit Keith with having the wherewithal and the vision to step outside Kentville and see the threat that was there and realize that this is across the province of Nova Scotia. Kudos to him for that. I hope something good comes of it."

Robicheau was frequently tapped to play a role in various provincial advisory bodies. His knowledge of taxation and financial issues got him involved in committees on property assessment and fair and equitable funding, which indicates the level of confidence provincial officials had in him. These appointments are provincial, but the province takes care to ensure that appointees have the respect of their peers at the municipal level. His involvement also shows his willingness to give of himself in these endeavours. This kind of activity surely lengthened his already long work day, and he sometimes took some criticism for being away from his municipality, but one person said that Robicheau "loved getting involved in these to make things work."

He was also heavily involved in professional associations outside the municipality, including the Union of Nova Scotia Municipalities and the Association of Municipal Administrators of Nova Scotia, and in negotiating his employment contract he made sure funds would be provided to allow him to attend various municipal conferences.

The CAO of a small community is, along with the mayor, highly visible, and personifies the municipality in ways that the CAO of a larger place does not. Robicheau sees his role as a two-way conduit between the municipality and the community, and particularly as helping council by gathering information in the community. As he explains,

> [w]hen you live in a rural area, you're never off the clock. I mean, you don't talk about municipal affairs and municipal politics until tears come out of people's eyes, ... but you [have to] use every opportunity you can to get information and find out what people are thinking ... Part of building ... trust with council [is finding out what's going on in the community.] You don't want to become more visible than the mayor or the warden. I'm talking about being out there subtly in the community talking to people, flying below the radar, just finding out what everyday life is like out there, and ... what's going on.

Robicheau and his wife are active in their community. In Nova Scotia he was a member of Rotary, and virtually everyone commented on his interest in curling and golf. He seems to have been not just an occasional player, but someone who took an active role in the local clubs and made friends there. Always the CAO, at golf tournaments he was frequently there early to ensure that everything was set up properly.

Some commented that, in the community as in the workplace, he is not an elitist; he makes friends easily with people at all levels of the community. One person suggested that "it was difficult for him to go grocery shopping. He was a person who was very accessible to the community. People wouldn't hesitate to bend his ear." A local businessman said, "One of the things I found about Keith was that he was always looking out for somebody else's interests ... If he could anticipate that you might need something ... he'd be there offering before you would have to ask for it." One person summed it up well: "In the local community he was really outstanding. When we had special events, he [and his wife were] always there ... Whatever was going on, ... Harvestfest or whatever, Keith was always there front and centre and supported the initiatives ... He was really cognizant of being involved in the local community. He got a membership in the local curling club ... He took pride [in] ... work[ing] and liv[ing] in Kentville."

Robicheau is good at leading out. He makes contacts in the community easily, and he works on maintaining them. He knows that an important aspect of developing a lasting partnership is making sure that everyone involved benefits from it, and he has the sensitivity to understand what others need in a partnership. He is also willing to give of himself to the community. Becoming involved in various provincial advisory committees is demanding, but he gave of himself unstintingly in that regard.

Conclusion: Putting It All Together

BIG IS DIFFERENT FROM LITTLE

One major conclusion to be drawn from the case of Keith Robicheau, a CAO who has worked in smaller places, is that there is a real qualitative difference in the role of the CAO in places of different sizes.

The successful CAO must be able to lead in three directions: down, up, and out. In truth, however, CAOs of larger places cannot give equal emphasis to all three directions all the time; they are forced to focus on one or two at once, and to shift that attention over time. In smaller places, where the CAO's role is much more personalized, this changing of focus is more difficult. In larger cities, it is understood that much interaction goes on by having "my people" meet with "your people." In smaller places, residents expect to be able to talk to the top person personally, and not to be sloughed off to a subordinate.

CAOs in larger places frequently comment that CAOs in smaller places have a more intensive knowledge of how a municipality really works. Many people commented on Robicheau's encyclopedic knowledge of the Nova Scotia Municipal Government Act. Of course, CAOs in large places are expected to have a general knowledge of the main sections of the relevant municipal legislation, but they would have to refer detailed questions to the legal department. Robicheau *was* the legal department.

Many people also mentioned that Robicheau is a good writer. It was known that he personally wrote many reports to council, whereas in larger places these come through a long and winding road that makes claims to authorship unclear. He was recognized as even having the ability to draft by-laws and legal agreements, work that is done in the bowels of a large legal department elsewhere. In a smaller place, in the absence of much specialized assistance, all these things end up on the CAO's desk.

PEOPLE SKILLS ARE IMPORTANT

Although Robicheau clearly is able to lead in all three directions, one skill that crosses all three is his exceptional emotional intelligence. Everyone described him as personable and able to connect with everyone from senior executives to janitors. This skill comes partly from frequently mentioned qualities: respect, fairness, equity, transparency. He seems to enjoy getting involved. He has been a member of a number of professional, service, and recreational clubs. He works at staff social events. He is always there. Yet he manages to keep his distance in a proper and professional manner. He is there when people need him, but becoming a personal friend of councillors or staff amounts to crossing a line.

BE AN AGENT OF CHANGE

Robicheau is able to be a change agent, but he also knows when to turn this on and off. He installed the CAO system in both St Andrews and Annapolis County. In the former, the council was ready for the change; in the latter, it required considerably more work. He changed the official plan in St Andrews to encourage more waterfront tourist attractions. He helped develop the former CFB Cornwallis into a viable industrial park. He never accepts the status quo, but makes changes where they are needed, while exhibiting the good judgment not to force changes when they are not necessary.

CHANGE NEEDS TO HAPPEN CAREFULLY

Robicheau is successful in implementing change when he really wants to, but he seems to know how to do so in ways the affected people can accept. He does not push change by brute force; he surveys the situation and takes the slow but steady approach. He builds trust with the councillors and staff whose support is needed, and he uses rational arguments to sell the need for change to them.

BUILD PARTNERSHIPS

One of the ways Robicheau initiates change is through the development of partnerships. He has done this from waterfront development in St Andrews to solid waste management, economic development, and public transit in Annapolis County, to town and county cooperation in Kentville. His credibility means he is trusted by potential partners when he approaches them, and he knows how to develop partnerships in such a manner that there is something in it for everyone. This ensures that the partnership will last after the initial enthusiasm wanes. He has written agreements with appropriate attention to financial and governance arrangements that future incumbents could live with.

GOVERNMENTS ARRANGE FOR SERVICES; THEY DO
NOT NECESSARILY PROVIDE SERVICES

Wherever Robicheau has gone, he has been concerned about providing taxpayers good value for their money. He recognizes this means that governments sometimes should act as catalyst or facilitator, rather than as direct service provider. In St Andrews, he helped stimulate tourist activity by initiating changes in regulations to make it easier for small businesses to operate there. In Annapolis County, he saved money by contracting out many of the public works functions.

BUILD TEAMS THROUGH COMPLEMENTARITY, NOT SIMILARITY

In Annapolis County, Robicheau was successful in initiating many changes because he worked with Warden Peter Terauds and his deputy CAO, Laurie Emms. Terauds was the brash, impatient politician who contributed energy, wanted everything done right away, and did not have much time for people who did not agree with him. Emms was the task-oriented engineer who did not like people very much, but knew how to get things done. Robicheau was the reserved professional who was good at developing relationships and working with people. The three could not have been more different, but working together they accomplished a great deal.

"[Y]OU SHOULDN'T CARE AT THE LEVEL THAT I WAS CARING"

In explaining why he moved on from Annapolis County, Robicheau offers some insightful advice: "The municipality is a body corporate. It's not a family member; it's not your wife; and … you shouldn't care at the level that I was caring." This is not a prescription to take one's job lightly; no one would ever accuse Robicheau of that. It is a reminder not to allow yourself to become so invested in a job with a "body corporate" that you identify yourself too much with every decision the body makes. You need to be able to separate yourself from your job in some ways. The job of the CAO is to provide the best professional administrative advice; the job of councillors is to listen to that advice and make the best political decision that will get them re-elected. Both should have the best interest of residents at heart, but the two could have different perspectives on how to achieve it. A CAO cannot become so invested in her or his view of the municipality that it becomes impossible to implement council's decisions that do not align with the CAO's perspective. A CAO needs to be committed and passionate about the advice he or she is giving, but a good CAO needs a certain level of clinical detachment as well. When you can no longer muster up that detachment, it might be time to move on. In Robicheau's words:

> I'm just glad I woke up one day and said, "I've been here long enough," because I think there may have been a point … where I did lose perspective about where the distinction between Keith Robicheau and the County of Annapolis [was] … I'm not the County of Annapolis. I shouldn't be personally identifying myself with every issue.

> If we as managers, particularly as CAOs, ... do not try to build our own little checks and balances, procedural safeguards, safety nets, whatever you want to call them, distant early warning systems ... we can really set ourselves up for failure because I think there is a real danger in investing ourselves too much in [the job and the advice we provide council].

Overall Assessment

Keith Robicheau is clearly a successful leader. He is people oriented, which he uses well to help him lead in all three directions. He is excellent as a change agent, but he knows when to turn that on and, equally important, when to slow it down or turn it off. He clearly moved St Andrews and Annapolis County forward by installing the CAO system in both places and by making other changes such as the waterfront plan in St Andrews and the development of the former Canadian Forces base and the partnerships in transit and waste management in Annapolis County. He also made positive changes in Kentville, but he had the judgment to understand that the environment there did not require the major changes he instituted in his previous stops. One of his major accomplishments in Kentville was mentoring a young successor who has taken over quite ably. He clearly moved these municipalities forward by using his people skills to lead in all three directions.

> A municipal CAO who is a good leader has the ability to move the municipality forward by interacting in a mutually influential way with and motivating council, external stakeholders, and organizational subordinates.

6 "I think I'm a better employee when I love the community I'm living in": Robert Earl

Has your municipal ever organized a festival to celebrate the fact that your main street would be torn up for several months during the local merchants' busiest season? If you live in Banff, Alberta, where Robert Earl is the town manager, then you saw this happen in 2007. By everyone's account, the strategy did not exactly keep everything normal, but it did make the best of a difficult situation, and everyone describes it as memorable. The town won a number of awards for how it handled the communications around the situation.

This is the second case study that focuses on a manager who has made his career in smaller communities. Robert Earl has been a CAO in three municipalities. His municipal career began pretty much by accident in Port Edward, British Columbia, in 1993. In 1998 he moved to Invermere, British Columbia, where he stayed until he moved to Banff, Alberta, in 2004. He is still in Banff, where he is quite content.

During his time in Banff, the town has collected a huge number of awards that reflect on many people, but are emblematic of Earl's leadership. In 2006 the town won two Heritage Tourism awards – one for its promotion of a local golf tournament and another for its use of interpretive panels and trailhead kiosks to convey information about local history. In 2007 Banff and nearby Canmore shared a Government of Alberta Municipal Excellence Award for their busing program. In 2009 *Maclean's Magazine* named Banff one of Canada's thirty greenest cities. Finally, in 2012, it won a Tereo Award for an asset management system that assists council in prioritizing capital spending.

In addition to his regular job, Earl has made significant contributions to his profession. He has sat on the boards of the Local Government Management Association of BC, Civic Info BC, and Columbia Valley

Table 6.1. Interviews about Robert Earl

	Port Edward, BC	Invermere, BC	Banff, AB	Other	Total
Councillors		2	7		9
Staff	1	2	7		10
Others			7	1	8
Total	1	4	21	1	27

Note: "Other" represents someone who has known Earl throughout his career, and does not fall neatly into any one municipality.

Greenways. He has also worked with the Local Government Leadership Institute to assist in the delivery of regional workshops. He is currently spearheading a project to develop performance measurement and benchmarking in municipalities in Alberta. In the international sphere, he has spent time in the Philippines and Malawi as part of a Canadian International Development Agency (CIDA) local government leadership program. Robert Earl clearly is midway through an exemplary career as a municipal manager.

The raw material for this chapter was drawn from two sources. The first strand of research was a review of various background sources of information. As mentioned in the previous chapter, it is more difficult to obtain information about smaller communities than about larger ones, but my research assistant and I were able to find some background material on the Internet and in published sources. We were forced to rely more on what we heard from respondents in this chapter than in previous chapters. The second strand was twenty-nine personal interviews. Earl was interviewed at the beginning and end of this project. Between those bookends, my research assistant and I interviewed nine councillors, ten staff members, and eight community members from all three municipalities where he worked, as shown in Table 6.1.

Career Path

Robert Earl was born in 1964 in Edmonton, but he moved around quite a bit as the family followed his father's job as a chemical engineer. His mother began her career as a nurse, but studied accounting while the children were growing, and eventually became a chartered accountant, pursuing this second career as the children became older. Earl remembers that, with two professionals as parents, it was always understood that he would go to university and have a professional career, but it took him a while to decide what that career would be.

He remembers his parents as working hard in their careers, and he was heavily influenced by that work ethic, but their work habits also influenced him in a more subtle way. He makes it clear that, although they were not absent parents in any way, they were heavily involved in their careers to the exclusion of other activities. He recognized the need for a better work-life balance than theirs, and although he developed a reputation as a hard worker, he was also drawn to recreational activities. He and his wife enjoyed mountain climbing, but moved to the comparatively safer sports of mountain biking, hiking, and skiing after taking on family responsibilities. Earl is currently one of the prime movers in the Bow Valley Mountain Bike Alliance, which works with Parks Canada to clear and maintain trails.

Although the family moved around quite a bit, Earl feels that he grew up in Winnipeg, where he obtained a BA in Economics from the University of Winnipeg in 1988. His major interest was economics because he saw himself going into a private sector career in finance, but he was also interested in philosophy and the philosophical underpinnings of what he was studying. He was still uncertain of what he wanted to do when he graduated, however, so he spent a year in Taiwan working for the British Columbia Trade Development Corporation and studying what an emerging capitalist country looks like. When he returned to Canada, he continued his journey of discovery by going to northern British Columbia to study fly fishing.

As accidents happen, he learned about fly fishing from Rick Trayling, who would have an influence on him throughout his life. During his fishing trips, he also met a local who mentioned that the Port Edward Historical Society needed someone who was comfortable with numbers to serve as its business manager. The society was actually an adjunct to the District of Port Edward, so it was a short jump from his position as the society's business manager to becoming the accountant for the local government in 1993. As he put it, "I wouldn't say I was attracted to local government. I fell into it more than anything else."

As a young, single man in a fairly quiet town, there was not much to do except work, so he learned his craft well and impressed his employers with his work ethic. Therefore, it was not surprising that, eighteen months later, when the position of chief administrative officer became vacant, he was tapped for the position even though he was still quite young.

He really enjoyed working for the district, married a local woman, and was in no particular hurry to leave, but he and his wife found it difficult to indulge in their love of mountain climbing near Port Edward. So, when an opportunity in Invermere, situated between the Purcell and Rocky mountain ranges, came up in 1998, it was really a lifestyle decision to switch jobs.

When he was being interviewed for the job in Invermere, the hiring committee was concerned that a highly competent, young person like Earl would use it just as a stepping stone and move on quickly. He assured them, however, that he was committed to Invermere, and would leave only if a similar position came up in either Banff or Whistler, as these were his two dream jobs.

He settled into the job in Invermere well, and became well respected in the community. In 2004, however, the job of town manager of Banff came open, and he made good on his earlier wish and applied for the job. He talks easily about how much he enjoys Banff, and those around him spoke of how well he fits into the local community, not only as town manager, but also as a leader in the outdoors and mountain biking community.

From Taiwan to fly fishing in northern British Columbia, Earl became a municipal manager by accident, but he has warmed nicely to the position in a number of different venues.

District of Port Edward, BC (1995–98)

Port Edward is in a relatively isolated region on the north coast of British Columbia. It is a small community – its population was just 700 in 1996 when Earl was there[1] and is in steady decline. It draws many of its commercial, educational, and health services from Prince Rupert, about fifteen kilometres away. Its relationship with Prince Rupert is such that the two communities share an economic development agency.[2] As one might surmise from its name, Port Edward has a small port, and at one time it had a pulp mill and a salmon cannery, but now most of its population works in Prince Rupert.

Although a small community, Port Edward gave a hard-working young man like Earl an excellent opportunity to embark on his first professional position as an accountant when it hired him in 1993. The district was ripe for modernization in a number of ways. Earl inherited a paper-based accounting system, which he converted to a computerized system, adding a job-costing component. He also overhauled the recordkeeping system, which had been quite inadequate. He made similar improvements in the method of maintaining council minutes. He clearly had an impact in moving the municipality to modern administrative methods.

Earl proved himself to be a competent young professional, so it was no surprise when he was appointed CAO in 1995, even though he was just thirty. Councillors were so confident about him that the position was not even advertised. And the staff was "pleased as punch," in the words of one person who was there. He continued the process of modernization and professionalization that he had started as the accountant. His predecessor actually had been called a clerk-administrator, but Earl moved the district to a real CAO system. The administrative style already had moved some distance toward that of a professional manager, but council was still involved in a number of administrative decisions, so Earl worked on a greater separation of councillors and administration.

The district also undertook a large public works project while Earl was there, involving the reconstruction of a dam on a nearby lake, combined with a new sewage treatment facility. The first potential obstacle was when the tenders came in. Earl was set to recommend against construction because he considered that the district did not have enough funds. The public works superintendent, however, who was experienced in the local construction industry, felt strongly that he could make it work. Earl, showing confidence in his staff, changed his mind. The project was completed within budget, but there was a significant glitch along the way. During construction, one of the contractor's trucks went over an embankment, and its ruptured gas tank sent diesel fuel into the district's water supply. This set off a complicated train of events involving federal and provincial authorities. It was eventually worked out, but it was a good learning experience for a young CAO.

At this time, the federal government was divesting itself of local harbours such as the one in Port Edward. The district therefore had to determine how it was going to manage the facility itself – another learning and maturing opportunity for Earl.

All of these issues paled compared to concerns about the long-term future of the town, whose population declined from 739 in 1991 to 544 in 2011.[3] The pulp mill, a major employer, closed while Earl was there, and has never reopened. In the face of these difficulties, Earl encouraged council to engage in more strategic thinking, and he introduced a strategic planning process for council.

By 1998, Earl had worked for the District of Port Edward for five years, three as CAO. He had accomplished a great deal and was well liked. As one person summed it up, "[h]e created a way better culture here ... Robert ... created a workforce that's a healthy unit to this day." Earl says that he was in no hurry to leave Port Edward, but as an avid outdoorsman and mountain climber, he jumped at the chance to move to Invermere, British Columbia, a larger community surrounded by rugged mountains.

District of Invermere, BC (1998–2004)

The District of Invermere is a picturesque community situated between the Purcell and Rocky mountain ranges, so far east in British Columbia that it is actually oriented more to neighbouring Alberta. It is a classic four seasons resort community: it is the service town for the Panorama Ski Resort, a major destination resort attracting skiers from across the world, and it is situated on the shores of Lake Windermere, which has a beautiful beach and is large enough for all sorts of boating. There is actually some local dispute about whether this body of water should be called a lake, since it is really a widening of the Columbia River, which originates just a few kilometres south in Canal Flats. By whatever name, the lake and the surrounding area offer excellent opportunities for kayaking, whitewater rafting, casual boating, and swimming. There are also great venues for mountain biking, hiking, and mountain climbing. The number of golf courses in the area is growing. The airport offers opportunities for scenic helicopter rides and fixed-wing aircraft flights as well as gliding. The area is also part of a scenic drive through the Rockies that brings bus and car tourists in the summer to soak in both the scenery and the famous Radium Hot Springs, about twenty minutes up the road. In short, Invermere is a beautiful community that offers virtually every kind of recreational opportunity that could be imagined.

All of this natural beauty only a three-hour drive from Calgary is a recipe for rapid development. According to the 2001 census, the population was 2,858 permanent residents,[4] but the district Web site says there are 20,000–30,000 "shadow" residents in the summer.[5] Whether permanent or shadow, residents live in pleasant, well-maintained older homes and medium-rise condominium developments through which deer are known to wander.

The area's economy has changed over the past fifty years. In the 1960s the economic drivers were somewhat diversified, with employment in farming, especially of Christmas trees, mining, and a lumber mill. When booming Calgary discovered this idyllic community only three hours away, however, everything changed. The traditional industries were dying a natural death, but Invermere began to transform itself into a tourist economy catering to the "second-home" industry, as it is called: selling land, developing and constructing subdivisions and condos, and employment at resorts, restaurants, and golf courses catering to second-home owners.

As noted, Earl moved to Invermere because its mountain environment fit the lifestyle he and his wife wanted. As he put it in an interview, "I think I'm a better employee when I love the community I'm living in. So, for me, it was important to choose the community, and then find a job there."

Invermere's council was described as reasonably congenial in style, but it also reflected a deep divide in the community. No one could live long in such a community without having a healthy respect for the preservation of the natural environment, but some people did not want any development at all, while others felt that the environment could be preserved if development was confined to certain areas. To Earl, this kind of split on council tests the mettle of senior administrators in a positive way. They know that every report they prepare for council will be carefully scrutinized by people on all sides of the issue, so that reports must cover all the angles while being scrupulously neutral. As Earl puts it, "because most reports were put through that crucible, it made for better reports. The reality was that we, as staff, had to provide better information because we knew that the decision was going to be principle based, and as such you needed to get it right."

One idea he brought with him from Port Edward was the need for a strategic plan. Unlike Port Edward, Invermere was growing fairly rapidly and needed such a plan to support future development. It had taken a run at a strategic planning exercise before, but the results had not been particularly satisfactory. Earl brought in the same facilitator whom Robicheau had used in Nova Scotia – Gordon McIntosh – and this time people were much more pleased with the outcome. Of course, councillors were concerned that their pet projects would not make the list, but, over time, they appreciated the usefulness of working with a defined list of priorities. The process also helped to meld council into a team.

Earl was always looking for better ways of doing things, and if that involved some risk, he was not averse to that. He accepted a certain level of risk when he climbed mountains; he did the same thing in the confines of his office. One of the interesting things that he did was produce a novel and informative official community plan. These plans typically are filled with precise, but dull legalese about the number of metres of setback permitted in particular areas of the community, and so forth. Earl and his director of planning and development services, Chris Prosser, produced a document with aerial photos and informative pictures of the kind of development that could occur in the community. The visual presentation made it easier for residents to understand and comment on the plan. The small amount of accompanying text was deliberately written at the grade 8 level to make it understandable.

He and his staff understood that significant change such as this required a strategy to be sold. When it was time to present the document to council, he and Prosser did not drop the entire document on councillors' desks; instead, they worked through the plan one chapter at a time, spending about a month on each, and giving councillors and the public time to understand the lengthy document.

Earl also modified the district's budgeting system. Assessment was growing fairly rapidly in Invermere at this time, and some felt that the budget system then in place did not identify the revenue impact of the growth adequately, allowing the administration simply to scoop up all the additional revenue without giving council a chance to decide what to do with it. Earl's revisions showed the revenue flowing from assessment growth separately so that council could make its own decisions.

Earl also had to handle some staffing issues when he arrived. Some senior staff members left around the same time – possibly because they had been passed over for the position – so he was able to hire a director of operations and a director of planning and development to go along with the director of corporate services who had been with the district for some time. This created an excellent team at the top.

There were also some problems at the middle and lower levels among the approximately twenty-five staff members. In the words of one observer, "[t]here was not a group identity as you would hope in the organization. And Robert did try to work on that, but he ... didn't jump in and try to tell everybody what to do. He walked a good line between ... respecting the union itself and the people who represented it and the people here. I found him just straightforward." The observation reflects Earl's style in a number of situations in dealing with staff. He was not shy about handling difficult situations, but he was also careful and deliberate so as not to make the situation worse. One interviewee said that, although Earl was not pushy, he persisted in turning around certain staff attitudes, and brought order to what had been described as a chaotic and difficult situation before he arrived. As one interviewee commented, "[i]t became first class; it became professional. It wasn't so much that when we first started."

The interviewees in Invermere all spoke positively of Earl. They felt that he had made a real difference there, and they were sorry to see him leave, but they all understood that he had been honest with them about wanting to go if one of his dream jobs opened up.

Banff, AB (2004–present)

Idyllic, postcard-beautiful Banff exemplifies the Rocky Mountain image of Canada that foreign visitors come to see. The town is located in the mountains just over an hour's drive west of Calgary. The fairly small townsite is relatively flat, with the Bow River flowing through it, and the main street, Banff Avenue, is bracketed with views of jagged Mount Rundle at one end and the equally majestic Mount Cascade at the other.

Banff is a tourist town. It is surrounded by numerous destination ski resorts that, because of their location high in the Rockies, operate for well over half the year. In summer, the beautiful mountain views and picturesque main street attract weekend visitors from Calgary and nearby, as well as bus tours that bring large numbers of Asian and European tourists. Banff's residents understand why their community is so appealing to others and are conscious of the need for environmental protection of natural areas and to maintain the charm of the main street. Great attention is paid to Banff Avenue's streetscape, and although there are a few chain restaurants and stores, local stores are favoured to give visitors a unique Banff experience.

Development in Banff has a fairly long history, at least by western Canadian standards. The original Banff Springs Hotel was constructed in 1886,[6] at about the same time that the railway was being built. Development occurred around the hotel, but through most of its existence the town has been under the direct control of national parks officials. The town was officially incorporated and granted self-government only in 1990, so the pioneers of self-government are still around.

In 2011 the town's consolidated expenditures were \$31.1 million[7] and its population was 7,584.[8] Because of the large number of tourists, however, municipal officials measure infrastructure needs by the number of beds or the number of toilets. By these measures, the municipal infrastructure needs to handle a peak load of about 40,000 people.[9] Unlike in Invermere, there is no pressure for "second homes" in Banff because Parks Canada's rules stipulate that only those people who are employed there or are retirees who worked in the town for at least five years before they retired may live there. You cannot even be buried in Banff unless you have had significant ties there.

Because the town is located entirely within Banff National Park, all planning and development decisions are closely controlled by Parks Canada and the minister responsible for Parks Canada. The boundaries of the townsite are fixed by agreement with Parks Canada, which also controls the number of square metres of commercial development within the town. Some locals feel that the limit on the extent of commercial development is a way of limiting population. In Alberta, when a municipality's population exceeds 10,000, it can apply to become a city. Having a *town* within park boundaries sounds quaint; no one wants to see a *city* located within a national park.

The limit on growth poses certain problems. In 2012 the average house price was \$641,474,[10] making the town unattractive for young families. The young people who work at the ski resorts and in the hospitality industry usually live in accommodation supplied by their employers, which increases the cost of doing business. The controls also limit the ability of the town to make its own decisions. For example, the town is currently revising its land use bylaw. In addition to the normal approval process that any municipality would have to follow, Banff's plan must also be approved by the minister responsible for Parks Canada in Ottawa. The level of control can be quite detailed: Parks Canada and the town currently are locked in a dispute over the location of a lawyer's office that likely will go to the courts.[11]

The controls can be frustrating, but the limitations also mean that Banff is not confronted with some of the difficult decisions that other municipalities must make. Economic diversification and expansion is not an issue – Banff likely will reach its maximum allowable commercial development in about five years, after which no further development will be allowed. Banff's only industry is, and will continue to be, tourism. It is a strong industry, and the mountains that fuel it are not going anywhere. Of course, there are services for residents, such as grocery stores and accountants' and lawyers' offices, but even these are specialized – the local lawyers advertise that they are knowledgeable about national park law.

Banff's council is similar in some respects to that in Invermere. No one can live in Banff without having a commitment to maintaining the beauty and environmental integrity of the place; many residents express the idea that Banff is a special place that they are holding in trust for all Canadians. Within that overarching focus, however, gradients range from staunch conservationists who want no development of any kind to others who feel there is a place for business and a need to support the commercial sector within environmental constraints.

The council that was elected shortly after Earl arrived was described as congenial and mutually respectful, but also reflective of the division within the broader community. The atmosphere was not so positive at the staff level. Earl's predecessor was the first manager of the newly incorporated town, whom interviewees generally described as fairly by-the-book and conservative. Management of staff might have been a bit lax, which led to some distrust between council and the administration. A number of senior staff left around the time of Earl's appointment, reportedly not always on the best of terms. This gave Earl the ability to develop his own team, which he proceeded to do.

Earl was hired in part because of his financial skills, but also because councillors wanted someone who was forward thinking. One person involved in the hiring process remembers being very impressed with Earl: "He had a pretty solid approach on how we could address the financial challenges we had here. He had done his homework immaculately, because he knew our circumstances. He knew the hot buttons that were going on in Banff. And that's one of the things that resonate with me quite strongly."

Earl's innovative management style sat well with the council that was elected shortly after he was appointed, a council that interviewees described as a relatively cohesive group that understood the respective roles of council and staff fairly well and was willing to give Earl considerable scope for action.

A number of important initiatives have occurred in Banff since Earl became town manager. In any complex public organization, it is always difficult to assign credit or blame to any one individual; almost all decisions are group decisions in some way. Certainly Earl himself is reluctant to take full credit for any of these initiatives. Interviewees did indicate, however, that Earl played a significant role in all of them.

In some cases, it was providing information and exhibiting the confidence that the town could undertake what others wanted to pursue; in other cases, it was creating a positive risk-taking environment or acting as a facilitator to ensure that others developed a positive course of action. It is probably correct to say that, although Earl was not the prime mover on any of these initiatives, they would not have moved forward as quickly or as smoothly if he had not played a significant role. This is what the team leadership style is all about.

BANFF REFRESHING

Banff Refreshing, as it came to be called, was a project that had been on the books since at least the early 1990s. Banff Avenue is the main street and lifeblood of the town. In the downtown section, it contains all the restaurants, bars, souvenir shops, candy stores, art galleries, and hotels that fuel the tourist draw. Anything that affects the two blocks of downtown Banff Avenue has an impact on the entire town.

Banff Avenue's hidden problem was that its underground services (water and wastewater pipes) were about a hundred years old and in danger of failing. This would be problematic anywhere, but Banff's residents' keen awareness of their stewardship role made them acutely concerned that a break in the sewer line could discharge raw sewage into the Bow River in the centre of Banff National Park. The cost of remediation, however, was high for a small town, and exacerbated by construction issues. The construction season coincides with the heaviest tourist season: the two-month period when the downtown stores make a huge portion of their entire annual profit, and the cheapest way to do the work would involve tearing up Banff Avenue during the busiest part of the tourist season.

Initially, the town had considered the less intrusive alternative of working around the tourist season by doing some work in the spring and finishing in the fall. After serious consideration, however, this option was deemed unattractive – it certainly would have increased the cost, and one construction company did not even want to bid on the job because of liability issues.[12] But by 2006 it was obvious that the work could not be put off any longer. Mayor John Stutz and his council, working with town staff, decided to have the work done during the 2007 tourist season, even though it would cause problems for local businesses. Fortunately, much of the cost would be covered by federal and provincial funding.

The implementation part of the project had several aspects, some of which were more complicated than others. The engineering aspect was a fairly large project from Banff's perspective, but not particularly challenging for construction companies that do this kind of work on a regular basis. The more complicated aspect of the project had to do with communication. One face of the communication project was directed to tourists – assisting them in navigating the construction terrain and making certain that they felt comfortable enough to stay in Banff for a few days and visit the restaurants and shops. The other face was more behind-the-scenes – communicating with local businesses to ensure that they understood what was happening and when, and also to ensure that they could provide feedback to the town, which could then adjust aspects of the construction work as needed.

The town's innovative approach to communicating with visitors was to treat the project as a festive event. The street would be torn up so that it could not be used by cars – nothing could be done about that – but the sidewalks would be protected so that tourists could still do their shopping unimpeded. Bridges were built over the underground construction work to allow people to cross the street at several locations. The hoardings were constructed with opaque material to allow people to watch the construction taking place. The squirrel was made the official mascot of the project. Squirrel-themed signs were used for way-finding, and people who had "survived" the experience were given squirrel pins. The festival atmosphere was extended by having informal entertainment at various places around the work.

The other aspect of communication was working with local businesses. Each block had a designated block captain, and the town appointed a visitor experience coordinator whose major responsibility was to meet with the captains on a regular basis to take the temperature of the situation and determine what needed to be done to minimize the disruption.

The additional communication effort was estimated to cost about $1 million, none of which would be covered by grants from any other government.[13] This was a hefty sum for a small town, and there was a real risk if it did not produce the desired results. Although the federal and provincial governments picked up most of the tab, some of the project's total cost of $24 million required Banff reluctantly to go into debt,[14] which drew criticism from some during the next election campaign.[15] Mayor Stutz had led the charge to incur the debt, but Earl, working behind the scenes, organized the financing, pushed for innovation and risk taking, and generally gave everyone the confidence that the project could be done.

At the end of the process, Banff had completely reconstructed its underground infrastructure to the appropriate standard. It also now has wider and much more attractive sidewalks, with benches, trees, and other aesthetic amenities. The result is both functional and attractive. Business owners who went through the Refreshing generally regard it as making the best of a difficult situation. They recognize that the work needed to be done, and they respect the fact that the town did its best to minimize disruption.

The town also drew a great deal of positive outside recognition in the form of rewards for its communication strategy. It won *Alberta Construction Magazine*'s 2007 award for top civil project of the year,[16] and in 2008 it won two awards from the International Association of Business Communicators, one of which was for the way the town addressed multiple audiences by communicating with tourists, local business, and the general public.

A number of interviewees suggested that Banff Refreshing changed the tone of the town's communications process in a number of ways. The town and the community, especially the business community, had worked together to bring a difficult situation to a successful conclusion, and one reason for the success was a good program of consultation and communication. This was a valuable lesson for everyone involved in the process, and Earl suggests that it has had a continuing effect on how the town relates to the business community:

> Through that project, I would argue that we've *improved* our dialogue with the business community, opened up new channels. Not only were we able to move forward a project that we needed to have happen, but ... in a way that did not have [a] negative impact economically. But the legacy of that, notwithstanding the beauty of Banff Avenue, is this new relationship with [these businesses] ... They know we're not just city hall [and] we're going to do what we want. No, we're here to listen, [we] recognize you are the lifeblood of our economy and that for us to survive, you need to survive, and you are us.

Although it was clearly Mayor Stutz and council who made the decision to move ahead with this long-delayed project, those interviewed credited Earl with playing a number of key roles, including putting the finances together in such a way that the council was confident about undertaking the project. As one councillor put it, "[c]learly, council directs administration, but I think when our chief administrator says, 'I think we can do this,' I think council pays attention."

Earl was also instrumental in developing the communications strategy and festival atmosphere around Banff Refreshing. It was not his original idea – credit for that generally goes to the owner of the local Petro-Canada gas station – but he seems to have been the one who took the idea and ran with it. As one businessperson put it, "[a]ny engineer could have replaced the pipes; it was the things around it that were handled very well."

THE ROAM TRANSIT SYSTEM

The next major initiative was the creation of the Roam bus service in 2008. Banff had had a local public transit service for several years, but then it was contracted out, and concerns grew about the quality of customer service, reliability, and equipment. Councillors and staff had seen how other resort communities, such as Aspen, Vail, and Whistler, had developed much better transit systems, and it was felt that Banff's needed to improve. Interest in enhancing the public transit system also arose from environmental concerns. Parking is a big problem in high season in Banff, and a good transit system would allow people to leave their car at their hotel, thus relieving traffic congestion and reducing pollution.

Consultations were held with Banff Lake Louise Tourism and other interested parties on how to create a first-rate transit system for a relatively small community. The idea was to make it not only environmentally friendly to ride a bus, but also a fun and educational experience. The buses then in use were old and not particularly attractive; the new ones would be modern, reliable, and comfortable. But Banff went beyond that: through a partnership with Parks Canada, each vehicle would be wrapped with different artwork produced by a world-renowned photographer and illustrating animals found in the park. Inside the vehicle would be educational information provided by Parks Canada.

Environmental concerns were also reflected in the decision to purchase hybrid buses. Town officials like to boast that they spent an extra $970,000 for hybrid vehicles for their entire fleet[17] – the joke being that the fleet consists of just four buses – but that is a lot of money for a small town. As a town in a national park with a commitment to environmental issues, however, it was important to send a signal by obtaining the hybrids.

Another feature of Roam draws on Banff's techno-savvy outlook. Shortly after the service started, a system called nextbus was established that uses the GPS system to provide real-time information about when the next bus would be coming on illuminated signs at selected stops. This has now been supplemented by an application that provides nextbus information on a rider's mobile device.

The Roam system generates over 70 per cent of its revenue from the farebox,[18] an exceptionally high proportion for any transit system, but particularly for one in a small town. The main reason for this is that a number of local businesses, particularly hotels, have agreed to provide monthly flat payments that allow them to give free passes to their employees and guests – a positive win-win situation.

The Banff system has been so successful that, in 2012, it was expanded into the Bow Valley Regional Transit Services Commission, which serves the area from Canmore to Lake Louise.[19] Its success is also marked by the number of awards it has won. In 2007 Mayor Stutz won an award from the Canadian Urban Transit Association for his work in bringing hybrid busses to Banff. The town won an award for sustainable tourism from Alberta Tourism in 2008[20] and a sustainable communities award from the Federation of Canadian Municipalities in 2009, and was a runner-up for an Alberta Emerald Award for environmental initiatives in 2010.

As with Banff Refreshing, the idea for Roam coalesced as a result of the efforts of a number of people; Earl does not take credit for the initial idea or even for being a driving force, but again he played an important behind-the-scenes role in putting together the financing, developing the idea of using hybrid busses, and generally pushing staff to innovate and take risks in implementing the project.

THE FENLANDS RECREATION CENTRE

Good recreation facilities are important for Banff, because they help attract young people to work in the tourism industry. When the town was incorporated, it inherited from Parks Canada a serviceable recreation centre called Fenlands, containing a hockey rink and a curling rink. By 2009, however, the centre needed to be replaced or substantially renovated.

Ultimately, the decision was made not just to renovate the facility, but to enlarge it substantially and to design it in such a way that it would be a showplace for the community. An additional skating surface was added, along with new rooms for fitness equipment, office space, and so forth. The idea was to make the facility attractive for tournaments or even pre-season training for a National Hockey League team. The curling rink was redesigned to use visually striking arch features known as glulams recycled from the original building in the form of a half-arch that supports a glass wall looking out on the fenlands and beyond that to the mountains. The building was transformed from a nice, functional facility to an attractive building with a curling rink that has a definite "wow!" factor. As well, reflecting Banff's concern about environmental issues, the renovated building meets the LEED (Leadership in Energy and Environmental Design) silver standard.

As with Banff Refreshing, the Fenlands renovation required the town to borrow funds. The total cost was $30 million, of which the town had set aside about $14 million. The remainder came from a combination of grants and loans to be repaid by 2019.[21] Because of how the grants work, the money was borrowed at effectively no interest.

Again, although Earl was only one player in the ensemble putting the package together, one participant described his role this way: "He was able to provide all of the detail [so] that we could bring those projects – all three of them (Banff Refreshing, the transit system, and the rec centre) – [forward] … [so that] at the council table … people would say, 'oh, we can do this.'" As with the other projects, Earl was able to create an environment that made others comfortable taking risks.

THE COMPETITIVENESS INITIATIVE

Economic competitiveness is as important to Banff as it is to any other community, but it has a somewhat different meaning in a town where tourism drives everything, either directly or indirectly. And although the picturesque nature of the town and the surrounding area is not going to change, the town and the tourism industry do not want to become complacent – they need to ensure that they remain competitive with other comparable tourist areas. Therefore, in early 2011, the town, Banff National Park, and Banff Lake Louise Tourism initiated a consultation process called the Competitiveness Initiative, geared to ensuring that everyone was working together to provide visitors with the best possible experience. The task was to "determine how we were going to proactively evolve as a consumer relevant, economically sustainable tourism destination that embraces and respects our iconic, protected and extraordinary place as Canada's first National Park."[22]

The process was co-chaired by Earl, representing the town, Pam Vei-notte, the superintendent of the park, and Julie Canning, the president and chief executive officer of Banff Lake Louise Tourism. It was time-consuming for the three lead partners, who met about twice a month with a working group of local businesspeople and other stakeholders. The process resulted in a report[23] that identified certain initiatives that needed to be carried out, and assigned them to one of the three partners in the project. Not only was this an incredibly important and worth-while project on its own; it is an excellent example of a partnership among the three major players in Banff that produced a major benefit for the community.

TECHNOLOGICAL INNOVATION

Banff is technologically innovative, as illustrated by much of what goes on around the town. The town's Web site is more sophisticated than that of most municipalities, and is attractive and easy to navigate. It contains a great deal of information, including useful links such as an "Action Request" that allows the user to report a problem relating to road repair, streetlighting, garbage, and so forth, and to request a re-sponse from the town. It even includes all the information one needs to know about getting married in Banff, which is useful because, ac-cording to the town's Web site, Banff has the highest marriage rate in the country. Other examples of the town's technological innovativeness include its work on developing a three-dimensional model of the com-mercial district, which will assist development decisions and help visi-tors find their way around; the nextbus system and related mobile app, mentioned above; and the development of a mobile app to inform mo-torists about available parking spots.[24] As well, both the mayor and Earl have Twitter accounts; Earl uses his only sporadically, but the mayor sends several tweets a day extolling the virtues of life in Banff – inviting people to come to Banff for Father's Day, recognizing a loyal fifty-year employee of the Banff Springs Hotel, and the like.

Banff's desire to be technologically innovative is not difficult to un-derstand: the town likes to see itself as a youthful, leading-edge com-munity, so technology fits nicely with that ethos. Many interviewees felt that Earl played a role in the early adoption of new ideas in the civic administration. Earl describes his approach this way: "I like to support the team in taking risk. I think there is risk in the front end of tech, but it's often a great way to save money ... I challenge each team member to be leading edge in their thinking and often that involves technology."

Earl's role in this regard is much like his role in other activities: he is not out front and visible, but he pushes staff to think about new ideas. As one interviewee noted, "Robert definitely pushes our tech buttons; he sees the benefit in that." He also is known to keep a keen eye out for innovations occurring in other jurisdictions to look for ways to adapt them to Banff. he clearly has created an environment in which innovation and risk taking can flourish.

STRATEGIC PLANNING

Earl had had success with strategic planning exercises at his two previous stops, so it should not be surprising that he established the process in Banff as well. Banff's previous planning exercises had not been entirely satisfactory – one person described them as products of the latest fad, rather than real strategic planning exercises – and they had produced a large number of priorities, which is difficult to work with. Earl, however, pushed council to settle on just three to five priorities every year. There seems to be a pattern in the process now. Earl brings in Gordon McIntosh after each election to help the new council organize itself for the next three years. Then he leads a smaller planning exercise each year to assess progress on each priority. Sometimes council and staff meet together to talk about priorities, and sometimes they first meet separately and then get together to mesh their ideas.

It can be difficult for an "insider" to lead a strategic planning exercise. The major argument for bringing in a consultant is that an outsider has no vested interest in the outcome. Participants need to have a great deal of confidence in an "insider" to trust that person to lead the exercise. A councillor described how Earl's role in this process is viewed: "He's a very tactful and diplomatic man. He had the capacity to bring those issues that should be right on the gunsights of council, to bring them forward, and then massage us to be able to come up with strategies by which we can deal with them, and also have it be council-led. It was always perceived to be council-led." Another councillor discussed how Earl avoids being too directive in his approach, while still keeping council on track: "He keeps us focused and reminds us where we've come from. Moving forward, he has almost zero opinion. However, he's the guy that says, 'six years ago we tried that and this was [the] obstacle. We can go after it again, but I think that obstacle's still there.' Or he will say, 'I see this complementing this, so we can bundle those together.'"

SERVICE LEVEL REVIEW

A standard criticism of strategic plans is that, once completed, they are often put safely on a shelf and never implemented. Under Earl's guidance, however, Banff's strategic plan is integrated with an annual service level review, a document given to council each year and also made available to the general public[25] that provides detailed information on approximately eighty-five town services. For each service, the document shows what the service provides; what councillors would like to see the service provide; a discussion of "what works well" and "areas of attention"; quantitative information about how well the service is operating compared with benchmarks set by outside organizations such as the Ontario Municipal Benchmarking Initiative; and an indication of whether the service should be increased, maintained at the current level, or decreased. A sample of the section related to public transit is shown in Figure 6.1.

This process began in 2009 in the wake of concerns that all governments were having about their financial situation. As Earl describes its genesis, "the ... economic crunch forced government at all levels to look inward and to really think about all the programs and services that we provide and [to] try to establish [if] we [are] providing the services that we need ... and ... at the right level ... It became clear to me that the budget process that we had at ... Banff wasn't enough. There wasn't a systemic way in which council every year looked at all that we did as a community and determined [what was appropriate] ... And so I saw a gap."

The nature of the service level review and the process associated with it are heavily influenced by Earl's association with what he describes as the town's strong communications department: "This document needs to be easily consumable ... and at different levels. If you're looking for detail, we need to be able to link you through to that detail, but first and foremost the reader needs to be able to easily look at it and understand what council wants from a service ... Also from my standpoint as an administrator, it's an important part of connective tissue that ties together the budget and administration so that the administration clearly understands how to create a budget for a particular program and services based on council's expectations."

The document is particularly helpful to new councillors because it provides an easy overview of all of the town's programs and activities, written in a way that allows them to understand council's influence on them. The entire document is relatively imposing at 122 pages, but it

Figure 6.1. Banff Annual Service Level Review: Public Transit

Department: Engineering – Transit

Service Area: Transit

- Operation & management of ROAM transit system
- Route planning & enhancements
- Public & media relations
- ROAM partner contract management

COUNCILLORS' EXPECTATIONS

- Ridership at capacity
- Frequent service
- Local riders
- Maintain current operating cost recovery percentage
- Seamless integration transportation
- Constant monitoring and communication of the system

ASSESSMENT

What Works Well
- Environmentally friendly buses
- Clean buses/great drivers
- Partnerships
- Unique service (change receipts)
- Use of fleet for special events
- Route enhancement

Areas for Attention
- Real time information expanded
- Continue communication, including stats with tax payers
- Expanding coverage
- Bus shelters

Performance Benchmarks

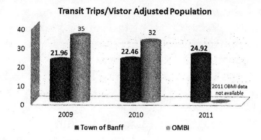

Transit Trips/Vistor Adjusted Population

- 2009: Town of Banff 21.96, OMBI 35
- 2010: Town of Banff 22.46, OMBI 32
- 2011: Town of Banff 24.92, 2011 OBMI data not available

■ Town of Banff   ▩ OMBI

covers each service in a maximum of three pages. The information, presented in point form and simple graphs, is useful, succinct, and easy to understand. It is one of the best documents of this sort that I have ever seen in its balance of useful information and economy of presentation.

Figure 6.1. (Continued)

Cost/Passenger Trip

Percentage of Total Cost Recovered through Revenue

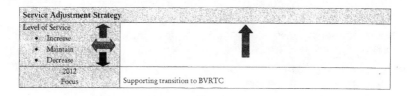

Service Adjustment Strategy	
Level of Service • Increase • Maintain • Decrease	
2012 Focus	Supporting transition to BVRTC

One councillor gave Earl a great deal of credit for tying all the various pieces of the strategic plan and reporting together: "We're seeing the priorities be delivered on … [H]e's just brought so much in terms of the structure of how you set goals, … budgets, … the information that you develop to help form the budget, of sharing that information with the community. [The service level review] really improved it, and I think we're leaders in the province in terms of our service review and how that all feeds right into budgeting."

As of this writing, Earl continues to serve Banff, and he seems quite happy in his "dream job." He fits well in the position of town manager, and he and his family fit well into the fabric of the town. There seems to be a great deal of satisfaction about how the town is operating.

The Leadership Role of the CAO

Robert Earl is clearly a successful leader, as he has demonstrated in three places. This section examines the various aspects of his leadership style to see why he is so highly regarded. The section begins with an overview of some of his general personality characteristics, then proceeds to examine his style in leading down, up, and out.

General characteristics

QUIET, BUT A GOOD LISTENER

A large number of interviewees described their first impression of Earl as quiet and reserved, and not particularly animated. Then they talked about how, on getting to know him, they realized he was thoughtful and an exceptionally good listener. His apparent reserve comes from his being quite aware that he will learn more if he does not try to dominate the conversation. As one community member praised his listening skills, "[p]robably his most incredible quality is what an incredible listener he is. He will listen actively to what you've got to say, until you're done saying it, without interrupting you. And then he'll … put it together with his own thoughts and feelings … and … come back to you with a question, and then another question, and then another question … He's tremendously curious. And … he really, really does care. He may or may not agree with the person he is talking to, but he has time to listen to what they've got to say, and he will take their perspective into account."

Earl's reserve – more than one person described him as stoic – seems to be a cultivated part of his personality. He would rather listen carefully and understand the situation around him than weigh in too quickly with an ill-founded opinion. A councillor suggested that his quiet style has two dimensions. On the one hand, "he said what had to be said; there wasn't a whole lot of extraneous information tacked onto it." However, because he speaks relatively seldom, people know that when he does speak, he has something significant to say: "Robert always struck me as the type of person that, when he spoke, other people listened."

A staff member told a story of his job interview with Earl and two other people. The others peppered him with the standard interview questions, while Earl sat a bit back from the table, and the candidate was not certain that Earl was listening. Then, as if on cue, Earl leaned forward and asked, "[i]f you were a tree, what kind of tree would you be?" The candidate described how the off-the-wall question led to an interesting and enlightening discussion of creativity. Other people told of similar experiences of not being certain that Earl was listening, only to have him quote them back almost verbatim and follow it with an incredibly insightful question.

INNOVATIVE, RISK TAKING, CHALLENGING

Earl prides himself on taking risks and always challenging the people around him. He talks about how he used to like mountain climbing, but since taking on the responsibilities of parenthood, he has switched to what he regards as the less risky sport of mountain biking in the Rockies. He applies the same idea of risk taking to his work environment: "I ... like to be bold. I like to break the mould. I don't subscribe to the philosophy, if it's not broken, don't fix [it]. I think, let's constantly fix it. I worry that governments are often painted with the brush of being too complacent, so I don't want to be that government. I want to be the government that's out front, that's got a great relationship with the business community ... So I like to take risk. I like my employees to work in an environment to take risk and to push decisions as far into the organization as possible ... I want individuals to help collectively govern, administer this community."

His staff talked about how they were always being challenged to think about innovations and new ideas. One councillor put it quite strongly: "One of the reasons why Robert is so successful ... is [that] I don't think he's ever satisfied ... He's always challenging himself [and] ... the people around him ... He always wants to make the town better ... From what I've seen with his managers, he always challenges them ... to look five or ten years down the road." One interviewee referred to this trait of Earl's as entrepreneurship, in the sense that Earl is a very determined person who would go "around, under or through any obstacle" he encountered.

One example of Earl's innovation and risk taking is the way he has handled the location of his and others' offices over the years. He has moved his own office a number of times, even moving out of the town hall to locate temporarily in the fire hall and the utilities building. In doing so, he wanted to get a sense of how each department that reports to him works. He is also aware that the location of your office is a prime determinant of whom you are likely to meet in the hallway and engage in casual conversation. As he puts it, he "thought it would cause different patterns of conversation to occur." He once went even further and scrambled everyone's offices in the town hall so that people in different departments were located next to one another. No one liked the new arrangement, and he relented in about six months, but it shows the way that he likes to innovate.

FOCUSED ON PLANNING AND DELIVERING

Earl's penchant for innovation fits with his focus on planning. Everywhere he has gone, including tiny Port Edward, he has encouraged councillors to engage in planning, which makes sense from an administrator's perspective. It is much easier to work in an environment in which council has clearly identified a small number of priorities than one in which every council meeting sends staff off in a new direction. What separates Earl from many other planning-oriented managers, however, is that he is equally focused on closing the circle: measuring how well the town is doing on delivering on the plan. Banff's well-developed service level review is a good example of this emphasis. As one staff member described it, "[g]oals and strategies and sticking to them – it sounds really trivial, but a lot of people get sidetracked, because ... there's a lot of things going on and you have that vision, but few people can actually say that they accomplished it or they executed it. But he's one person that is very focused and very goal-oriented, and will keep at it and ... influence the people around him so that we're all going in the same direction ... [G]etting people excited about one big idea and working together in that direction ... [is] part of his success in Banff."

INCLUSIVE AND COLLABORATIVE

Earl's management style is open and collaborative. At Banff, he convened managers' meetings early in his tenure, something that had not been done before, and encouraged managers to discuss their department's goals and objectives so that all knew what other managers were doing. He clearly wanted to break down silos, and he was not shy about bending convention at these meetings. He sometimes invited middle- or junior-level staff to attend if they had something important to say or if they needed to be involved.

He signalled his emphasis on collaboration to staff in a variety of ways. All staff reports to council were circulated among departments in their draft state, and department heads were expected to work out any differences among themselves. His practice of moving his office around and trying, though unsuccessfully, to get others to do so was also an attempt to encourage people from different departments to work together.

PASSIONATE ABOUT THE COMMUNITY

Banff is a small place, and in Earl's tenure there he has become well known throughout the community. One observer said "he seems to be everywhere." For Earl, as noted, Banff is a "dream job," but he also loves the town itself and the outdoors activities in which it allows him to indulge. He emphasizes work-life balance to his staff, and he practises what he preaches. He is a hard worker who is well known for arriving at the office very early in the morning, but, as noted, he also makes time to be a prime mover in the Bow Valley Mountain Bike Alliance.

Because of his passion for the community, Earl does not see any tension between working hard and enjoying life in the community. In fact, he sees a passion for one's community as contributing to a positive work environment: "People who love to live in the community they're in [are] better at everything they do. They're better at their relationships, they're better in their jobs because they've got this background happiness ... Folks who work in the Town of Banff have a higher capacity to be happy ... If you're doing what you love, you produce so much more when you come to work."

To drive home the work-life balance principle to staff members, Earl instituted what he calls the gear purchase plan, whereby the town provides an interest-free loan to new employees to purchase a complete set of the gear they need for whatever sport they are interested in. Apparently, there has been some concern about whether the town should be doing this, but Earl points out that the cost is minimal because the loans are always repaid, and he feels strongly that it is a way of helping new people fit into the community quickly.

Interviewees obviously were pleased that Earl is not just an employee of the town, but a part of the community.

Leading down

The previous section discussed how Earl is concerned about tying planning and performance together, and how he always challenges himself to come up with new ways of doing things. Clearly, these qualities also have an impact on how he leads down.

He supports his staff members and is loyal to them, but he also expects solid performance from them. The service level review document is an excellent example of his sense of fairness in dealing with staff by making it clear exactly what is expected of them for the next year, and by holding them accountable if expectations are not met.

He challenges his staff, but he is not afraid to face challenging situations, either. In both Invermere and Banff, he inherited difficult staff issues that had been allowed to fester for some time, and garnered praise for taking a firm, but careful and judicious approach to solving them with minimum disruption to the organization. The changes he made also gave him an opportunity to develop a team around him. In Invermere, he kept one long-serving employee and brought in two new ones, forming a management team of four (including Earl himself). Banff's situation was larger and more complex, but he gradually developed a team whose members are comfortable with his performance-based, innovative, risk-taking approach to management.

Earl claims he took no special measures when he arrived to change the existing culture, but just did what he would normally do: listen carefully to the views of the people around him and make sure he understood the situation before attempting changes. His prime concern was that the people around him should be comfortable with what he was doing. One way he did this was by working with the management team to develop, in his words, "a set of guiding competencies, principles that define who we are, what we're about" (see the accompanying box). This was not only a significant product; it also served as an important team-building exercise.

He also talks about the way in which he introduced empowerment in an organization that had been more accustomed to top-down management: "It was listening to people ... giving people the latitude to make decisions. I think, when I came, there was a reticence on the part of folks to feel that they had the authority to make decisions, and I continued to push decision making not just to the team that I work directly with, but for them to push decision making into their teams as far as possible. The people who are out on the front line know best, and if we can learn from them and learn what they need, the rest just falls into place."

HOW YOU DELIVER TO MAKE A DIFFERENCE (CORE COMPETENCIES)

With passion and energy ... your excitement about work, love of learning and thrill of witnessing others succeed is genuine. You set a high standard and are driven [by] a sense of purpose in the larger mission.

With edge ... no one would ever describe you as predictable. By taking calculated risks and taking tough, principled positions regardless of popular opinion, you devise original solutions.

With instinct and intuition ... political savvy and emotional intelligence make you an astute judge of situations and the players.

By inspiring and being inspired ... imagining the unimaginable, thriving on action and relishing change make your own activities, and others', engaging. You support and encourage ambition and achievement.

By being authentic ... you approach your work with self-confidence and self-assurance, you are known as much for your convictions as for your sense of humour and perspective on your own abilities and limitations.

By balancing work and play ... you know there are options for arranging work effectively and organizing work intelligently. You know this because you do it, and love your work as much as your play.

By being clear ... you understand who you serve and how best to serve them. Within the mandate of your organization, you realize your ability to serve is limited by the resources available to you, but you do not make promises you cannot keep.

One staff member compared the organization before and after Earl's arrival: "[W]e're working more as a team to take on challenges and face issues. I think that was one of the big things that Robert has done since he's been here ... I think he's done a really good job of focusing the team and getting everyone on the same page."

Part of developing a good team is for the manager to have confidence in those around him so that he can empower them. It is clear that this is what Earl has done. He talks about pushing people to innovate and take risks: "As a CAO most of what you do is through others and empowering others to be great at what they do. I try to listen to what they say. I have to believe that they are way more expert in the field [than I am]. [I] trust that expertise. I'd like to try to encourage people to constantly question the status quo, to take risks. I like to push the boundaries. I don't think in local government we should just do what was done before. I think we need to constantly evaluate what it is we're trying to achieve for the community and figure out [if there's] a better way."

In turn, staff members who were interviewed said that they felt empowered: "I think the biggest thing he does as far as leadership [is concerned] is he empowers people ... He pushes people to take chances, ... take calculated risks. It gets people thinking ... People rise to occasions and challenges, and I think he tries to create that environment ... He challenges you to go to the next step ... What else are you going to do?"

One of the difficulties with empowerment is ensuring that employees do not exercise too much latitude and become complete free agents. Some businesspeople interviewed suggested that some staff were a little too free-ranging. It requires balance on the part of the leader to ensure that people are aware of their goals and limits. One staff member pointed out how Earl handled this balance: "He gave perspective, but he never tried to make the decision for you ... He lets people run. We're like a group of internal companies within a larger framework ... He has enough confidence and we have enough feedback from him that we know what we need to do and know to see him when the wheels come off ... We have a very strong working relationship with him at that managerial level."

Several people told a story that provides an excellent example of empowerment. Earl was involved with a project sponsored by CIDA in Africa. On the afternoon of 8 March 2006, the day he left to be away for several weeks, the entire town of Banff was hit with a boil water order because some remedial work to the water system had introduced some turbidity into the system. A boil water order is a severe problem in any community, but for an internationally recognized tourist-driven town like Banff, it could have been both a public health and a public relations disaster.

People who described the situation were impressed that, in the absence of the town manager, the acting manager and an entire group of city employees swung into action very quickly to arrange for water trucks for local residents and for large quantities of bottled water to be delivered to hotels. This involved a significant unbudgeted expenditure, but staff seemed to be instinctively aware that the first goal in such a situation is to provide the proper service, and the money will fall into place later. A councillor praised Earl saying, "his team clicked in, took control of that situation, and managed it unbelievably well. The fallout from that was minimal, and it was still one of Banff's finest moments." Even the local newspaper wrote a laudatory editorial: "In a town where we sometimes want to collectively hide problems rather than address them because of the fear – real or justified – of potential bad publicity and economic loss, the organized effort to communicate the boil water warning and put it in perspective was worthy of a little admiration. Even more worthy of praise was the town's positive response to the need of restaurants and householders for water."[26]

Staff members interviewed are loyal to Earl, and felt that he is supportive of and loyal to them. One person also mentioned that Earl's loyalty is tempered with honesty: "The first year I worked here was one of the smoothest of my career and partially it was because he gave you unrelenting support. You needed money – he found you the money and the finances to get things done. That was the nice thing, knowing that you always had that support there. And at the end of the day, too, if you did something really well, he wasn't afraid to tell you. If you did something that was questionable, he'd come in and he'd find a way to communicate it."

Earl clearly has acted as a mentor for many people. He seems to have a talent for understanding people's abilities, and can pick out people who need to be pushed a bit. One staff member talked about how he had been quite happy working in his specialization until Earl suggested that he had the ability to become a CAO. The staff member then began consciously modelling himself after Earl and talking with him about furthering his career. He remembered that he had always had difficulty taking criticism, but Earl gave him some tips on how to handle it. This person later became a CAO, and he credits Earl for pointing him in that direction. The current CAOs in Port Edward and Invermere both worked for Earl in those municipalities. It would be difficult to think of a better example of superior mentorship.

In sum, Earl has done an excellent job of leading down. He built a strong team around him in both Invermere and Banff. He not only empowered the team members, but he aggressively challenged them to take risks and do new things. This is why Banff was innovative in the way it handled Banff Refreshing and the development of its transit system, and why it sees technological innovation as important. Earl has not undertaken all of these things personally, but he has created an atmosphere where innovators and risk takers thrive.

Leading up

Earl clearly is highly respected by the councils he has worked with. He has built this respect in a number of ways. He has a reputation for being unbiased and highly rational in his recommendations. His general demeanour with council is proper and helpful, but also a bit aloof at the personal level so that he is not drawn into any camp. This is further assisted by his general style of being quiet and offering advice when it is requested, but not attempting to insert himself when he is not asked to do so.

He faced a conscientious but divided council in Invermere, and learned that his reports would face serious scrutiny regardless of what he recommended. Thus, the only viable course of action was to focus on arguing from a position of rationality and logic. He faced much the same type of council at Banff upon his arrival. He impressed upon staff members that their recommendations needed to be firmly grounded in logic. As one noted, "I would say one of Robert's greatest strengths in how he dealt with council was an ability to be unbiased. You'd be very hard pressed to find out, if he had a personal opinion on something, what it was, which I find very valuable … He'll raise a flag if council's going down a road that it shouldn't."

In Banff everyone emphasized that anything that goes to council is rational and well supported. Not only is the report rational, but if Earl is called on speak about it, he is seen as intelligent, as having a good memory, and as well prepared. This does a tremendous amount to stop acrimonious debates before they start: "Robert has an amazing memory, so he is able to pull out facts and figures to an extraordinary degree to support particular arguments or to answer questions that council has. And I find that most of the time he's quite accurate … to an impressive degree … He has the ability … to think big picture and to think about details. If you can't do both, I don't think you can be a CAO." He is never directive in his advice to council, but he has a way of conveying important information when necessary. As one councillor put it, "Robert has never [told] me what to do. What Robert does do extremely well is tell you implications of decisions."

When he arrived in Banff, there was no uniform template for reports going to council and no prescribed process for moving them through the management side of the house. He established a template that made it easier for staff to prepare reports and easier for council to review them. He also established a procedure of first passing a report to all affected departments so that administrative issues could be worked out before the report went to council. Staff members were also helpful in sharing information with one another to help anticipate council concerns and further refine the report.

Earl's attitude in council was described as respectful of the councillors. He responds to questions, but he never tries to get "bossy," as one councillor described. He also never seems to get upset or show emotion outwardly at a meeting. However, he was described as politically savvy enough to warn councillors if they are approaching a contentious issue. Some councillors admitted that his intuition about these things is even better than theirs: "Council is seven people, but you don't think of everything. And without feeding his ego too much, he thinks of everything, and that's his job."

He showed his political savvy in Banff when the 2007 election returned a council with a somewhat different character than that of the 2004 council. He seems to have adjusted his approach without serious problems. Some people also suggested that his persona shifts between public and private meetings. In public meetings he is conscious of deferring to council and not wanting to be in the limelight; in private, he is more likely to speak out in a respectful, but informative manner.

Several councillors commented that he is careful to work with council as a whole, rather than be seen to be too close to any individual councillor. One councillor from Invermere talked about how, at conferences, when he was invited to go for drinks with councillors, he always seemed to have "the sniffles." After he moved on to Banff, however, when the Invermere councillors invited him for a drink, his health had improved. As one staff person summed it up, "Robert has actually built a real culture of ... professionalism." He has done an excellent job of guiding council when it has needed professional assistance, as on projects such as Banff Refreshing and the Fenlands renovation, without overstepping his role as a loyal public servant.

Leading out

Leading out required quite different approaches in the various municipalities, but Earl has done a good job of adjusting to the different environments he has faced.

Leading out in Banff is less complex than in more conventional towns in some ways, but more complex in others. Because Banff is a relatively small, one-industry town in a somewhat isolated location, the number of actors who must be considered in leading out is fairly small. However, the complexity comes from the fact that the importance of each of them is magnified. The town's well-being depends on a single industry, and almost every action the town takes must be approved by Parks Canada, so a bad relationship can make things very strained. By all accounts, Earl has handled the leading out part of his job exceptionally well, and has been able to maintain a good relationship with all the local actors.

His relationship with the business community has changed over time. When he arrived, businesspeople sometimes found that his professional reserve as a public servant clashed with their extroverted boosterism. Earl, however, is aware that his role is to serve as a two-way conduit between the council and the community, and not to allow his own feelings to enter into discussions. In the eyes of the business community, this makes him difficult to read.

Over time, however, businesspeople have come to understand him better, to see that he understands their concerns and is helpful and accommodating: "He's always accessible to sit down for a period of time, give you some background as to what the topic is, and why it's on their table ... [H]e certainly is also able to say, OK, if you want to further your cause, here are the avenues you have to go down to try and communicate it, here's your opportunities to communicate it, here's some of the evidence you have to consider in that process ... [I]n an unbiased way he'll give you advice as a business to be able to provide input in the proper fashion to council."

He maintains a good relationship with the major industry association, Banff Lake Louise Tourism (BLLT). In a one-industry town, BLLT functions as the chamber of commerce and economic development office. It is seen as doing its job well, and wins international awards for the quality of its publicity. The Competitiveness Initiative discussed earlier provides a good example of Earl's work with BLLT and Parks Canada. A major part of his success with Parks Canada is that he works at it intensively. The park superintendent, the mayor, and Earl have fairly formal scheduled meetings four times per year, but this is the tip of the iceberg. The superintendent has less formal breakfast meetings with the community several times through the year, and Earl is a regular attendee. He also ensures that the relationship runs deeper than this.

Staff members at multiple levels from both organizations meet regularly. Parks Canada officials are invited to serve on some town committees or at least to attend meetings, so that there are no surprises when matters are sent to Parks Canada for approval.

Many interviewees suggested that part of the reason the relationship works so well is that Earl is perceived as someone who is a real member of the community: "[H]e lives in the community [where] he works, and I mean that in every sense of the word ... so he knows the community. We are such a tight-knit community and we are all about living our lives and living it big in the outdoors, and for someone like Robert I think it would be really difficult ... to find that level of satisfaction, that concept of work-life balance, anywhere else." Indeed, his lifestyle fits well in Banff. He loves the outdoors, and everyone is aware of his interest in mountain biking. He is not just another biker; as noted, he has taken a leadership role in the Bow Valley Mountain Bike Alliance. He probably even saved the life of another biker, a town employee, who was being mauled by a bear when Earl came along and interrupted the attack.[27]

There is nothing magical about how Earl has developed such a positive relationship with the local community. His open and collaborative style was mentioned many times; as one businessman put it, "he's approachable, for a man of his stature and power." His style of working with BLLT, Parks Canada, and the broader business community is to develop intensive contacts and relationships, which make him proficient at leading out.

In his previous posting in British Columbia, he was involved with various provincial associations of administrators. He has not done that so much in Alberta, but he recently took on an interesting initiative. As mentioned earlier, he had been using the Ontario Municipal Benchmarking Initiative and various other benchmarks as a part of Banff's service level review, but there are problems of comparability with some of these benchmarks. As a result, Earl has developed an Alberta equivalent of OMBI, which has involved extensive touring around the province. So far, fourteen other Alberta municipalities have banded together to apply for a grant from the provincial government to start the new benchmarking process. This consumes a great deal of Earl's time, but it will provide the Alberta municipal system a significant benefit when it is up and running.

Earl approaches leading out the same way he approaches his other leadership tasks. He does not accept the status quo, but is always looking for ways to improve things. He then approaches the change with equal measures of energy and judgment. He seems to have as much success leading out as he does leading in the other directions.

Conclusion: Putting It All Together

BIG IS DIFFERENT FROM LITTLE

The idea that being a CAO in a small place is qualitatively different from the same position in a larger municipality was explored in the chapter about Keith Robicheau. This chapter provides further evidence of the nature of that difference.

Earl clearly is deeply involved in leading in all three directions, whereas his counterparts in larger places would delegate some kinds of relationships to others. In Banff the mayor is the most recognizable figure, but Earl's stature is close behind. As one councillor put it, "you can't hide in Banff ... He's always the fall guy." Another former councillor provided more detail: "Robert is out there in the community, and it's easier in a smaller community ... [H]e becomes more valuable because of his community involvement ... [H]e's got kids in the schools, he's active in the sports and activities that are embraced in this area, and that community involvement makes you a much stronger town manager. Also ... he can't help but absorb the issues that are in town and the general pulse of the town if you're in those environments." Managers in smaller communities clearly must know more of the details about running their municipality than people in larger places, who can manage by exception. As well, Banff's close, intense interaction with Parks Canada requires Earl to be familiar with every aspect of his municipality.

BE INNOVATIVE, TAKE RISKS, AND CHALLENGE
YOURSELF AND THOSE AROUND YOU

Earl clearly has delivered on his list of core competencies introduced earlier in this chapter. In terms of taking calculated risks, for example, when Banff's main street had to be torn up for the summer, Earl turned it from something people might have spent months grumbling about to a spectacle that seemed to satisfy everyone. Although the town had always found it unacceptable to borrow money for infrastructure projects, Earl was able to assemble a package for the Banff Refreshing and Fenlands Recreation Centre projects that allowed council to be comfortable taking the risk. When it came time to upgrade the public transit system, Earl took the innovative step of getting the town to acquire a fleet of hybrid buses and having them decorated to become tourist attractions in their own right whose revenues, moreover, cover 70 per cent of their costs.

Earl also pushes his staff to share his dissatisfaction with the status quo, and challenges them to do something new and different. For example, not content with allowing riders to guess when the next bus would be coming, they decided to provide next bus information on both a mobile app and fixed signs at some bus stops. They are also developing an app to help visitors locate available parking places. These might not have been Earl's ideas, but they are the product of the environment he has created in which people are comfortable innovating and taking risks.

BE PASSIONATE

The top core competency on Earl's list is "passion and energy." Earl loves his community, and he wants it to be the best tourist experience that any visitor can have. Everyone in the organization knows how passionate he is. They know he is excited about his work, and that he is passionate about mountain biking and the outdoors experience generally. Those kinds of things are infectious. Earl is considered loyal to his staff, and staff members in turn are loyal to him. They reflect the passion he instils in the organization.

PLAN IT, THEN DO IT

In many organizations, planning is considered a needless frill; sometimes managers even consider it a threat. In all three municipalities where Earl has worked, he has developed a good system of strategic planning, and has ensured that it became institutionalized so that everyone is solidly committed to it.

One of the main criticisms of strategic planning is that it is time wasted if the plan only sits on a shelf. In Banff, Earl developed a system of integrating planning with the service level reviews so that the two processes complement each another. That these processes are used as devices to communicate priorities to staff and to hold them accountable means that virtually everyone in the organization is familiar with the priorities set by council and everyone works toward accomplishing them. If you just plan it, it probably will just sit on the shelf. If you approach it as Earl has done and make the plan an integral part of operations, it will get done.

COMMUNICATE AND COLLABORATE

Communication is important, and there are many ways to accomplish it. Earl is a good communicator because he talks only when he has something to say, which ensures that people will listen to him. It also allows him to sit back and listen and to understand what is going on around him. That insightfulness is an important part of communication.

Collaboration goes with communication. In an environment such as a one-industry town, where the CAO's actions could be constrained by outside actors over whom the CAO has no control, collaboration is important – not just at formal meetings, but as an everyday activity that affects people throughout the organization.

Earl is seen as a good collaborator because he has the emotional intelligence espoused in his statement of core competencies. He understands that collaboration requires good communication and that communication must be both intensive and extensive. It involves respect for other people, to ensure they are never caught unawares by some action on the CAO's part.

Overall Assessment

Robert Earl has been a successful leader because he has done a good job of leading in all three directions. He inspires loyalty in his staff because he has created a competent, empowered team. He is well respected by councillors because he is seen as good at helping them establish priorities, but also because he ensures that the priorities are met. Finally, he is good at leading out because he is an excellent communicator and collaborator, and he has an infectious passion for his community and his organization. He has developed a guiding statement of "how you deliver to make a difference." That he lives by that statement has a tremendous impact on his leadership style.

> A municipal CAO who is a good leader has the ability to move the municipality forward by interacting in a mutually influential way with and motivating council, external stakeholders, and organizational subordinates.

Earl has done much to move Banff forward by facilitating much-needed infrastructure improvements through Banff Refreshing. He was instrumental in the new and improved Fenlands Recreation Centre. His greatest achievement, however, is to introduce a new organizational culture of empowerment and risk taking.

7 Conclusion

The study of leadership has attracted a great deal of attention from both academics and practitioners over the years. This has generated a rich literature, and several people have written excellent summaries of how the field has developed.[1] I prepared myself for writing this book by reading widely in that literature, but I deliberately avoided staking out an opinion about how my five cases would fit the literature until after they were complete. In retrospect, this was probably a good strategy because in truth the case studies did not fit any of the theories precisely, but spoke to many of them in some way.

Since my approach was to identify five exemplary individuals and report on their achievements, it was foreordained that my findings would fit into the earliest school of leadership studies: the great man approach. They were all great individual leaders; that is why they were selected for inclusion in this book. In truth, however, none of them fit the exact mould of Carlyle's "hero as king," whose role is "to *command* over us, to furnish us with constant practical teaching, to tell us for the day and hour what we are to *do*."[2]

In fact, modern times have not produced many great individual leaders in Carlyle's mould. Two characteristics of these times have changed our expectations of leaders. One is that diplomacy and war are no longer individual efforts, as they were earlier. The scale and scope of contemporary governing have become so large and complex that single individuals can no longer stand astride events in the way they did in Carlyle's time. The second characteristic that marks contemporary times is that followers are not as passive as they used to be, but now will trade their followership for some involvement in the actions of the leader. Therefore, the mark of a great contemporary leader is no longer the ability "to command over us," but the ability to motivate undecided followers and to assemble a good team of people who will help the leader achieve goals.

We should not discard the idea of the great individual leader too easily, however, even in modern times. The chief administrative officers (CAOs) in this book were selected not because they are "great men" in Carlyle's mould or because of one major achievement, but because success seems to have followed them throughout their careers. All five seem to have left their organizations in considerably better shape than they found them – no mean feat in an increasingly complex world. As they would be the first to acknowledge, whatever they accomplished, they did as part of a group, but they had a significant role in assembling and enervating that group. Judy Rogers was a member of the group that was instrumental in bringing the Olympics to Vancouver. It would be too dramatic to say that it would not have happened without her involvement, but if she and a handful of other like-minded people had not come forward at key times, the Olympics certainly could have gone elsewhere. In that sense, she made a difference. Keith Robicheau managed the shift from a council-committee form of government to a CAO system in two municipalities. His work in Annapolis County in particular had a huge impact on professionalizing and improving the quality of management, and his actions improved the lives and living conditions of thousands of people in that area. That made him a hero for them. Mike Garrett pioneered and championed the idea of performance measurement, which is now commonplace in virtually all governments. Of course, this likely would have occurred at some point anyway, but probably not in the same way and at the same speed.

Another way that all of the CAOs in this book have left their mark is through their mentorship of a group of young professionals. It is difficult to quantify the immediate benefits of mentorship, but in the long run it clearly creates the next generation of professionals, who in turn will mentor the next generation, and so on, to significant long-term effect.

In considering the accomplishments of these five leaders, one needs to discuss what Barbara Kellerman and others have called the leader attribution problem: the fallacy of attributing all the good (or bad) things that happen on a particular leader's watch to that leader.[3] How do we know that events can be attributed to the presence of a specific leader? Would the events have happened anyway regardless of who was leader? The honest answer is that we will never know. This is not like a chemistry experiment where a reaction can be tested a number of times – with and without the presence of a catalyst labelled CAO – and the varying results tallied.

The weight of the evidence presented in these chapters, however, allows one to make some strong inferences. When Robicheau arrived, Annapolis County was in some disarray, both financially and organizationally. When he left, it was on a solid footing. Similarly, Robert Earl inherited administrations in both Invermere and Banff with some organizational problems that have now been turned around. Garrett was hired by an organization in Toronto that did not yet legally exist, and he had to create a new one. The other CAOs in this book did not inherit organizations with quite the same kinds of problems, but some major accomplishments occurred on their watches.

Were these leaders single-handedly responsible for all the improvements in their organizations? They would be the first to say that they certainly were not. The major responsibility of a contemporary CAO is to assemble a strong team and to create an environment in which the team can excel. This does not happen by accident. Robicheau was able to identify Laurie Emms as the kind of person he needed at Annapolis County, and then to attract him to join the team. Rogers plucked people out of middle-management positions and moved them to unconventional positions, where they thrived, to the benefit of the organization. Michael Fenn identified a strong group that he wanted around him, and was able to convince them to play a role. This is what the contemporary CAO does.

It might be that people who focus on the leader attribution problem expect too much. There are seldom direct links from the leader's office to some great accomplishment – that is not the way contemporary leadership works. What we can attribute to good contemporary leaders is the team of people they assemble around them. Not only are they able to identify the talent they need, but there is something about leaders that causes good people to gravitate toward them.

Earlier I criticized the leadership literature as too generic in suggesting that all leaders can or should possess the same qualities. Accordingly, I intended this book to contribute to the literature by identifying the specific traits, skills, and behaviours found in senior municipal managers in Canada, and to serve as a road map for mid-career public servants who aspire to become senior managers.

In this chapter, I provide an analysis of the traits, skills, and behaviours of exemplary managers, but I also focus on a number of related tasks. In the first section, I identify exactly what CAOs do and what they do not do. In the next section, I elaborate on a point discovered in a number of ways throughout the research – namely, that the role of the CAO is clearly influenced by the size of the municipality, or, as Graham White puts it, "big is different from little."[4] In the third section, I analyse the traits, skills, and behaviours of CAOs. This is logically followed by a discussion of whether leadership can be taught or is something with which a few people are born. After that, I discuss the extent to which the CAO has become a true profession. Finally, I offer a few words of advice to mayors and councillors about the hiring and care of CAOs.

What the CAO Does

There are a number of ways of describing what a CAO does. For example, one could examine the job descriptions of city managers. The description from the City of Vancouver's Web site is fairly typical:

> The City Manager's Office oversees the overall conduct of the City administration in pursuing the City's purpose, and serving City Council. The City Manager's Office:
>
> - Reviews departmental programs, budgets, and policy initiatives
> - Makes recommendations to City Council
> - Ensures that Council's directives are carried out (in consultation with Council and departments)
> - Establishes standards and priorities for the civic administration
> - Motivates and monitors performance to ensure that standards are met, priorities are pursued, and high-quality City services are consistently delivered
> - Manages a continuing organizational development program to ensure good communication between departments and coordinates efforts to address City priorities.[5]

Such job descriptions are useful in terms of defining the totality of the CAO's responsibilities, but everyone knows that a job description seldom tells us much about what really fills the CAO's days. Studies analyse how senior municipal managers allocate their time,[6] but these approach the issue at too micro a level, and do not tell us much about the overall influence the CAO has on the organization.

The most significant finding in this book is that each person analysed viewed the job a bit differently. Leaders are sometimes described as either relationship oriented or task oriented. Rogers was the ultimate relationship- or team-oriented leader, but she built those relationships and teams with a goal in mind. She accomplished a great number of tasks while she was city manager: landing the Olympics, establishing a safe injection site, making a difference in Vancouver's downtown east side. Garrett, in contrast, was the self-described ultimate task-oriented leader, but he used his focus on tasks to motivate people around him and to build teams and relationships to accomplish a great deal: the big pipe, performance measurement systems, VIVA transit. Although it seems that Rogers and Garrett approached their roles from completely opposite directions, in the final analysis their success looks remarkably similar: they both accomplished important tasks by motivating people.

The lesson here is that there is a variety of ways of accomplishing the same objective, and that perhaps the classic textbook distinction between people orientation and task orientation is not as useful as it seems. Leaders must be aware of both orientations, but it is more important for them to build on their strengths – relationships in the case of Rogers, tasks for Garrett – than to try to be something they are not.

Every position and every incumbent is a bit different. No single job definition exists, but one can get a sense of the position by how a number of successful incumbents saw it. Indeed, many of the factors I discuss below about what a CAO does are not so much unitary guides to action as they are thoughts about decisions that a CAO must make about her or his position in the organization.

It might be best to begin with a short discussion of some things that the CAO does not do.

WHAT THE CAO DOES NOT DO

The CAO is perched atop the administrative organization chart, so it looks as though the person in that position has a great deal of power, but there are practical limits on what the CAO can do. Several CAOs made the point quite strongly that they had a minimal role in the day-to-day management of their organizations. Garrett saw the role of the CAO in a large municipality as equivalent to being the manager of a holding company: "The works commissioner did most of the work [on a particular project] … He was lead[,] … the key guy, not me, but you're involved as the CAO, with the money, and so is the treasurer … I can't honestly say I was the lead dog. I was the supporting cast member. When you go to the CAO's job in a big place … you've got many different businesses you're overseeing. Whether you like it or not, you're the manager of a holding company." This view reflects Gordon McIntosh's finding that, for some CAOs, shifting from a project focus to a broader strategic focus "was the biggest mindset adjustment they faced. They could no longer be directly involved in projects."[7]

Some CAOs seemed a bit lonely and frustrated because they were separated from the service provision function, and suggested that they were a bit jealous of the relationship that department heads had with councillors. CAOs frankly admitted that they knew little about some services, and even when they did know about a particular service, they understood that they would be undercutting their manager's authority if they intervened too heavily. From the CAO's perspective, department heads have the enviable task of bringing good news to councillors: a new park in your ward, a satisfactory compromise about that new development in your ward. CAOs often have to bring a different kind of news: there's no more money left for a new park unless you increase taxes.

CAOs have the broad overview of the entire municipality, which means that their direct involvement in any particular project is limited. There is a great sense of accomplishment with building a new park or finally sorting out a persistent problem at a difficult intersection, but these are the accomplishments of department heads; the CAO is at one remove.

W. George R. Vance discusses a CAO who said that one of his greatest achievements was developing a training system for staff; another referred to a salary review for senior staff and a new process for council reports.[8] These are important achievements that go a long way toward setting the tone for the municipality and setting up future results, but in terms of catching the public eye, they pale compared to the accomplishment of a recreation director who opens a new arena or a public works director who builds a new bridge.

This separation from the action is something the aspiring CAO needs to consider: you might sit atop the administrative hierarchy and have your fingers in everything, but you will have little direct day-to-day involvement in anything. Some people will like that higher perch; others will feel isolated.

Another thing CAOs tend not to do often is actually to use the authority vested in them from their position atop the hierarchy. Power is generally viewed as composed of two components: formal power – the power to discipline, fire subordinates, and so forth – and influence – the ability to persuade people to do certain things through expertise, peer pressure, and so forth.

Most of the CAOs in this book suggested that they relied more on influence than on authority; one even suggested that too great a reliance on authority would indicate problems within the organization. They saw themselves as part of a team consisting of department heads who were all knowledgeable in their respective fields, and their role was to ensure that the broad corporate view was reflected in all decisions made across all departments. They also were aware that interfering too much in decisions made within departments brings certain perils with it.

In several cases, CAOs wanted to accomplish certain things, but backed off when they realized they did not have the support of their team. Influence alone was not enough, and they could have exercised control to accomplish their objectives, but they chose not to, which says a great deal about how the CAO viewed the team. Often, maintaining the support and solidarity of the team will be more important than accomplishing some particular objective. Choosing between personal objectives and the needs of the team is a continual balancing act for any CAO.

Having set the range of some things that CAO choose not to do, what are the activities they do engage in?

DECIDE WHO YOU WORK FOR

The first thing that, as a CAO, you must decide is: who do you work for? This might sound obvious. Council hires the CAO, provides instructions, and ultimately can discipline or fire the CAO. Surely, the CAO works for council. This recalls the distinction discussed in Chapter 1 between Robert Putnam's classical bureaucrats, who follow the rules as set down, and political bureaucrats, who are more oriented to the public interest and take proactive steps to help achieve it even if that means sidestepping the traditional rules.[9]

To what extent do you also have some obligation to the residents of the community? Should you ever look over the heads of councillors and have a greater obligation to the community as a whole?[10] The easy case would be if council were to ask you to do something illegal or unethical, but there are many more subtle cases. In commenting on the Irish system of local government, Neil Collins suggests that politicians can become captive of narrow interests, whereas administrators' professionalism gives them a broader perspective.[11] The issue of whom the public servant works for is the conundrum that Larry Terry addresses in his idea of public servant as conservator: sometimes, public servants must rise above the concerns of their political masters to conserve constitutional principles or to protect the broader public interest.[12] This, however, is a difficult ethical issue. Claiming to know the public will can be slippery: "In a liberal democracy, [entrepreneurial leadership] is morally suspect. There is no small amount of arrogance in claiming to know the public good. Lurking behind such claims may be nothing more than greed, or ambition, or odd and untested ideas of public value or the public interest."[13]

Traditional approaches to accountability suggest that public servants owe their direct and only accountability to their political masters. This seems to be the view of the Institute of Public Administration of Canada, as expressed in its Statement of Principles Regarding the Conduct of Public Employees, which does not seem to have been revised since 1987: "Public employees are accountable on a day-to-day basis to their superiors for their own actions and the actions of their subordinates. They owe their primary duty, however, to their political superiors. They are indirectly accountable to the legislature or council and to the public through their political superiors. Public servants also have a responsibility to report any violation of the law to the appropriate authorities."[14] This view, however, focuses purely on accountability to political superiors, with mention of a broader responsibility to the general public only through "their political superiors."

Other organizations' codes are more ambivalent. The Statement of Values of the Canadian Association of Municipal Administrators covers both sides in stating that "the chief function of a municipal manager at all times is service to his/her employer and the public,"[15] but it does not provide much advice about what to do when the two perspectives conflict.

The American Society for Public Administration seems to lean more toward accountability to community. Part I of its Code of Ethics is titled "Serve the Public," and contains prescriptions such as "[e]xercise discretionary authority to promote the public interest," and "[a]ssist citizens in their dealings with government." Part II is titled "Respect the Constitution and the Law," but it does not say much about accountability to political superiors. Instead, it encourages public servants to "[w]ork to improve and change laws and policies that are counterproductive or obsolete," and "[e]ncourage and facilitate legitimate dissent activities in government."[16]

Rogers knew a great deal about Vancouver's downtown east side because she had worked there early in her career. The city, having an at-large electoral system, generally had no representation on council from the downtown east side, an area with a unique set of difficult problems. Rogers seems to have taken the lead on issues such as the redevelopment of the downtown east side and the initiation of a safe injection site when none of her political masters wanted to touch these hot potatoes. As a good administrator, she knew when to step forward and offer guidance to her political masters and when to step aside and let her political masters take the credit, but there is little doubt that she played a significant leadership role.

When Robicheau came to Annapolis County, he knew that it was in the best interests of its residents to have a proper CAO system and accompanying level of professionalization. Council had voted in favour of the change before he arrived, but some councillors recanted their decision and others did not understand quite what they had voted for. In that environment, he took it upon himself to educate his political masters about what a CAO system was and why it was superior to the system then in place.

In both cases, the CAO made the interests of the community paramount, and took a risk by getting out in front of council. Subsequent events vindicated the CAO and showed the contribution the CAO made to the community by taking a proactive stance. This is why it is so important for you to decide whom you work for.

DECIDE ON THE POLITICS-ADMINISTRATION BALANCE

Related to the question of whom you work for is the need to determine the extent to which you see yourself as a part of the political team or as an independent advisor to council. Textbooks frequently raise the concept of the politics-administration dichotomy, mainly for the purpose of making the point that no such dichotomy exists: in practice, there is a great deal of overlap between politics and administration. There is still some value, however, in recognizing the distinction between political and administrative issues.

Poul Erik Mouritzen and James Svara identify four different types of council-staff interactions.[17] They reject the one they describe as "separate roles": a complete separation of politics and administration such that the CAO refuses to take any role in policy making. They also are not sympathetic to the idea of the "responsive administrator," where the distinction between politics and administration becomes blurred, and the CAO becomes a political agent of council. The problem here is that the administrator loses the ability to provide independent advice to council. McIntosh describes the problem in this manner: "If the CAO is just a servant of political aspirations they [sic] may renege on public management values to serve the public interest or protect staff from political interference."[18] In both of these cases, Mouritzen and Svara suggest that the skills of the administrator are not being used fully – in the first case because the CAO opts out of the policy-making process; in the second because the CAO becomes completely captured by council. Their preferred arrangement is what they call "overlapping roles," where council and the CAO have complementary roles in the policy-making process, and the outcome of a policy decision is determined by the interaction of these two differing perspectives based on mutual accommodation and respect.

Decide where you are going to stand with respect to the politics-administration divide. Some CAOs – Mouritzen and Svara's responsive administrators – are derisively called "political bag-carriers" because they become so closely aligned with councillors. The opposite extreme is the "autonomous administrator," who runs her or his own administrative show without much reference to council. None of our successful CAOs fits either of these extremes; instead, we see shadings between the responsive administrator and a more independent stance.

Fenn seems to have spent a significant amount of time with individual councillors in order to understand what they wanted to accomplish and what put "raspberry seeds under their dentures," in his picturesque phrase. He had a strong administrative bent, and seems to have used his knowledge of councillors' likes and dislikes to accomplish some of his goals, such as program budgeting and strategic planning. He was probably somewhat on the political end of the spectrum, but he was close enough to councillors that he could be seen as having some elements of a responsive administrator.

Garrett, by his own admission, did not feel that comfortable with councillors, and did not develop a strong rapport with most of them. In Toronto, this was really not possible anyway, for reasons described in that chapter. His provincial experience had not prepared him for the type of intensive interaction that occurs at the municipal level. Garrett had a strong sense of the separation of the political and the administrative. In Toronto, he clashed with politicians over the protection of the merit principle in hiring. In York Region, he delivered a stern speech to council about the impact of its decisions on the future of the budget. These are justified and important stances that administrators must take at the appropriate times. Garrett clearly was an independent administrator providing advice to council.

The only easy advice that one can give is avoid the extremes. Specific situations require situational responses. A challenge to the merit principle needs to be met with a polite, but firm rebuke; this is an example of the assertion of administrative independence. Overcoming councillors' concerns about strategic planning needs a softer touch; Fenn accomplished his goal by getting closer to politicians than would been comfortable for Garrett. Understand the logic of the situation and adjust your position on the politics-administration balance accordingly.

An emerging nuance of this issue arises with the increasing prevalence of mayors and councillors in larger cities to have their own political staff. This could be useful in the sense that, if these staff members are providing political advice, then the CAO is less likely be asked for it. But political staff members who do not understand their role properly can erect an inappropriate buffer between councillors and administrative staff. Fenn saw this as a problem: "It makes the kind of relationship building I did in Burlington and Hamilton exceeding more complicated and difficult. Young political staffers with short-term, media-obsessed perspectives are the antithesis of the typical CAO's orientation towards institutional sustainability and strategic objectives ... [T]hey also effectively undermine the chain of command, enlisting staff well down in the organization in their research, program-delivery and policy-development objectives."

HAVE A PARTICULAR TYPE OF VISION

Vision is a problematic concept to apply to a municipal CAO – or to any public sector manager for that matter. The private sector literature paints a picture of a relatively hands-off board of directors that hires a CEO who has a vision of where he or she wants to take the organization. The board then checks in once in a while to see how things are progressing.

Vision is more complex in municipal government, because it is clearly the role of council to engage in it – some councils do it better than others, but most want to retain a hands-on approach to it. All the CAOs in this book had vision, but their style was governed to a large extent by whether they felt they worked for council or the broader community.

In most cases, their vision was limited to the administrative aspects of the organization, and did not extend to the broader vision of the municipality – that view belongs to council.

Fenn frankly stated that his vision was to have the best administrative machinery he could, and he pushed hard against resistance to the introduction of program budgeting and strategic planning in Burlington. It is not clear that Robicheau had a definite vision of where Annapolis County should go, but he did see clearly that the successful installation of a properly functioning CAO system would improve the ability of council to realize its own vision of where it wanted the county to go. Garrett was concerned with performance measurement wherever he went; like Robicheau, his emphasis was on providing a tool to help council get where it wanted to go.

CAOs sometimes also exhibited a broader perspective, however, so that they had a foot in both the political and the administrative. Robicheau shepherded through a downtown and waterfront plan in St Andrews, but shifted to improving the administration when he moved to Annapolis County. Rogers was probably the most politically visionary: she pushed for Vancouver to host the Olympics even when council was wavering, and she never let council forget about issues in the downtown east side even when it was not interested.

ESTABLISH THE ORGANIZATIONAL CULTURE

In Chapter 1, I discussed the importance of organizational culture, and the significant role the leader of the organization must play in establishing that culture. Many interviewees commented on the way their new CAOs changed the organizational culture of their municipalities. Robicheau, for example, having installed the CAO system in two municipalities, clearly intended to do more than just tinker with structure. In Annapolis County, in particular, he changed the structure from one in which councillors were heavily involved in administration to one in which there was an appropriate division between policy and administration. In Burlington, Fenn took over from a manager who had been the municipality's first CAO and had been seen as somewhat rigid. Fenn was hired with the explicit purpose of introducing a more collaborative and consensual style of management. Rogers inherited a city that had been run by engineers for many years, and she was credited with changing the tone to a more open, consultative approach. Earl has changed the tone of the administration in Banff from a top-down approach to one based on empowerment and risk taking.

MOTIVATE THROUGH INFLUENCE; USE AUTHORITY SPARINGLY

Many CAOs probably underestimate their ability to influence their organizations simply through modelling appropriate behaviour and setting the tone for those around them. When Robicheau treated everyone from department heads to janitors in the same way, he was sending a powerful signal about the value he attached to every person in the organization. When one senior staff person said that he learned about ethical behaviour from Rogers because "[i]t's in the air," he was providing an example of this form of role modelling leadership.

The CAOs in this book were not flamboyant John Wayne–style leaders but quietly charismatic, in the sense that they had an understated way of drawing people to them. People wanted to follow them. A number of interviewees talked about striving to do their best because "[t]hey didn't want to let [the CAO] down." This is the ultimate in motivation by charisma. Really good CAOs seldom need to resort to the stick of authority because those around them understand from behaviour modelling what is expected of them.

MONITOR PERFORMANCE, BUT DO NOT MICROMANAGE

Monitoring performance is an important part of a CAO's duties. Earl has moved around and located himself in a number of different offices to get an understanding of what happens in each department. Fenn knew how to ask probing questions, and developed contacts in the community to give him insights into how service delivery was perceived. At first, Garrett developed a performance measurement system to defend Peel Region from attacks on its efficiency, but he soon discovered that he could use benchmarking to compare the performance of his managers to that of managers in comparable jurisdictions.

Good CAOs discover how to balance their monitoring of their municipality's activities. A CAO who is too intrusive and engages in micromanagement signals a lack of confidence in her or his department heads. A CAO who is too distant signals disinterest, and is likely to lose control. The key is to obtain the necessary information in respectful ways, and to use that information to monitor and motivate performance.

MANAGE FINANCIAL AND HUMAN RESOURCES

Although the CAOs in this book made a point of not managing most aspects of service delivery, they deliberately kept other functions close to them. It is frequently suggested that an organization's two most important resources are people and money, and our five CAOs retained a significant involvement in the management of these essential resources in their municipalities.[19] The financial backgrounds of both Earl and Robicheau made this a natural decision for them. Earl put together project funding in such a way that his council was comfortable borrowing money – something that had never been done before in Banff. Robicheau moved Annapolis County from a dangerously small reserve fund to a more comfortable situation. Rogers, in contrast, was involved more on the people side. She knew the abilities of certain people throughout her organization, and she was not shy about broadening their experience by moving them into unexpected positions. All the CAOs talked about remaining on top of collective bargaining negotiations.

"Big Is Different from Little"

Graham White has argued persuasively that there is a significant qualitative difference between large and small governments.[20] He focuses particularly on comparing the federal government with provincial governments of various sizes, but McIntosh finds that this distinction carries through to the municipal level in that CAOs in small and large municipalities view their jobs differently. As he notes, "CAOs from larger organizations, with more managerial personnel, indicated they spent more time in the strategic directions than service delivery sphere," while those in smaller places had limited time to devote to organizational issues.[21] David Morgan and Sheilagh Watson also find a variety of differences between small and large municipalities.[22]

One difference is that large places have full-time councillors, sometimes with their own staff, while smaller places have part-time councillors who sometimes visit town hall only once a week to attend meetings. One result of this is that CAOs clearly must lead up differently depending on whether their municipality is large or small. Fenn discussed the way in which councillors' staff can pose a challenge to the role of the CAO as intermediary between council and administrative staff. Garrett discussed the way in which full-time councillors in Toronto played to the media, unlike his experience with the part-time councillors in Peel Region, whom he sometimes had difficulty getting involved in decisions except those that touched directly on their local municipality. CAOs, such as Fenn and Robicheau, who worked with part-time councillors developed a direct relationship with them; Robicheau sometimes even had to mentor them in their roles. Full-time councillors, particularly those with staff assistance, did not really need or want to deal so much with the CAO.

Size also affects how a CAO leads down. Garrett suggested he did not manage directly very much in his organization; he described himself as the head of a holding company, implying that it was the heads of the "subsidiary companies" who really ran the place. At the opposite end of the spectrum, Robicheau was renowned for having an encyclopedic knowledge of the Municipal Government Act – something that would be delegated to the legal department in a larger municipality.

The jealousy of CAOs toward department heads who are directly involved in service delivery is maximized in larger places, whereas CAOs in smaller places feel much more connected to service delivery. One interviewee who is a CAO in a small municipality rhapsodized about his daily inspection of some major improvement work being done downtown:

> In my situation here, you have to understand every inch that you're working on. You have to understand water flushing, sewer jet rodding. We're doing this major capital project ... I'm out there every other day ... looking at curb lines. You have to understand all that. When you're in a larger centre, you may not ever touch on what is a 450 mm curb pan versus a 400 mm curb pan in the greater scheme of things ... In a small community, that's where some of the best CAOs are being created. They get this breadth of experience. They get their fingers in engineering, in finance, planning, administration, union issues ... You don't have teams to delegate things off to.

CAOs in larger places sometimes expressed envy of their counterparts in smaller places because the latter really know how their municipality operates. One CAO gave the example of dealing with a development application. In a smaller place, the CAO would know every step and potential problem in the process. A CAO in a larger place is captive of her or his staff and would hear about slices of problems with large applications, but would never be able to take the time to understand all the complexities of the system.

Earlier in this chapter, I argued that CAOs do not engage in much hands-on management. This is probably a better description in larger places than in smaller ones. In Annapolis County, Robicheau functioned as the treasurer, partly because he had the skills to do it, partly as a way of training staff, and partly because there were significant financial problems when he arrived. During a garbage crisis, Robicheau spent time dealing with irate residents who were bringing bags of garbage to the front counter of the county building. He also developed great skill at drafting partnership agreements and other legal documents that would have been done deep in the bowels of the legal department in a larger municipality, except that, for Annapolis County, he was the legal department.

The job is different in a smaller place because the entire structure of the organization is different. Large municipalities operate like classical bureaucracies: positions are boxes on an organization chart. Interactions among different large organizations of this type are frequently handled as in the old joke about "my people will call your people." In smaller municipalities, the bureaucracy is more relaxed, and the main actors do not have "people" – they interact directly with one another. In Banff, Earl personally spends quite of time working with the superintendent of the national park and the president of Banff Lake Louise Tourism. These are two of the town's most important partners, and the relationship with them could not be delegated to someone else.

The differences also extend to relationships in the community. No one expects to see the president of Canadian Tire when you go there to buy a light bulb, but I know the owner of my local hardware store, and I would be a bit miffed if he failed to take a moment to chat with me when I went in. According to White, a similar thing happens in government organizations: people who would be satisfied talking to a director general or lower official in the federal government would expect to deal with a deputy minister in a small provincial government.[23]

In larger places, being the CAO is a job; you are an important block in the organization chart, but still a block. In smaller places, the CAO is conscious of being the familiar face of the municipality to large numbers of residents. Robicheau was well known in his small community for his love of curling and golf; Earl in his for being an avid mountain biker. The other CAOs were active in their communities as well, but the places they worked were so much larger that they did not stand out in the same way.

Traits, Skills, and Behaviours

The entire motivation of this book was to identify the traits, skills, and behaviours of successful leaders in the hope that succeeding generations of municipal leaders would emulate those characteristics. What have we learned from our five case studies about the traits, skills, and behaviours needed to be a successful CAO? There is remarkable diversity among the five CAOs in factors such as career paths, orientation (task versus people), and so forth, but also a great deal of similarity among them in certain characteristics. Before I describe and discuss those shared characteristics, recall a caveat I raised in Chapter 1 – namely, that it is possible to develop a clear conceptual distinction between the role of a leader and that of a manager. In practice, the same person frequently fulfils both roles and does not make a clear distinction between the two. A good senior administrator does what is necessary in the circumstances without bothering to think much about classification. Thus, the characteristics of the leaders profiled in this book probably cross some lines between leadership and management. Here, I focus more on the practicalities of being of good CAO than on placing characteristics in the proper pigeonholes. Many CAOs probably fall unclearly along the boundary between leadership and management.

Some writers make clear distinctions between traits, skills, and behaviours. For example, Montgomery Van Wart defines traits as "relatively innate or long-term dispositions," skills as "broadly applied, learned characteristics of leader performance," and behaviours as "concrete actions that are taken in performing work." Having made these distinctions, he then goes on to minimize the difference between them, which, he says, "is largely one of degree"[24] – for example, characteristics such as self-confidence or energy could be seen as all three. This section follows Van Wart's lead in distinguishing between them, while recognizing that, in fact, the lines between them can get somewhat blurry.

Some of the advice I provide here will seem contradictory – for example, show your passion while being cool as a cucumber; adapt to your environment while being change oriented. These doublets likely will remind some readers of Herbert Simon's "proverbs of administration," and his lament that these contradictory principles are not really guides to action at all. My only defence is that all forms of management are to a large extent more art than science, and this applies particularly in the local sector. As mentioned in Chapter 1, Robert Denhardt and Janet Denhardt argue that "the dance of leadership" requires considerations of space, time, and energy, as well as an ability to be creative and improvisational.[25] Being a good leader requires judgment and intuition as much as the application of cold facts.

Simon concludes that, in fact, these contradictory statements should be seen not as firm guides to action, but rather as "criteria for describing and diagnosing administrative situations."[26] A good leader needs to be able to judge which of the possibly contradictory characteristics to emphasize in a particular situation. The wise leader will have the judgment to determine when he or she needs to ride with the existing environment for a while until the time is right to make a change. Judgment and timing thus are key.

Lead in all three directions, but with varying intensity

A major thrust of this book is that good CAOs must learn to lead in three directions: up, down, and out. This is meant as advice about the skills that aspiring CAOs must develop, but also as a checklist for working CAOs on how to approach issues.

When approaching a particular problem, it is good practice to think: what do I need to do in terms of leading up, leading out, and leading down? You likely will get different answers to each of these questions, but you must ensure that your actions reflect the answers you receive.

When I was working on this book, I taught a class of mid-career public servants that included an experienced CAO. She commented that using the three-direction checklist would have been useful to her in a situation in which she had experienced some difficulty. Her community had suffered a fairly severe natural disaster. She got the works crews out immediately to deal with the damage, and that part went fine. Council wanted to be kept informed, and she did that well. But she realized in retrospect that, in the pressure of leading down and up, she completely forgot about the importance of leading out. She did not work with the community in the way she should have, which had an impact on how her efforts were perceived.

The lesson is that, in any situation, use the checklist to ensure that you are leading in the appropriate manner in all three directions. Also, use the checklist to prioritize the three directions, since you will not likely be able to give the same attention to all three. In a natural disaster, your first priority needs to be repairing the damage and getting services back in place. Then, you need to keep councillors informed about what is happening. Finally, you need to ensure that the general public is aware of what is happening. In the above example, the CAO certainly had her priorities in the proper order, but she did not give enough emphasis to the third.

Also, be aware that the order of the three priorities might change. In developing Banff Refreshing and the Competitiveness Initiative, Earl focused on leading out, as he needed to ensure that the business community was on side. Then, with the business community on side, he could be fairly certain that council and staff would accept what was decided. When Robicheau was developing partnerships in transit and waste management, he needed to do a great deal of leading up because his council had to be sold on the idea that these initiatives would be cost effective and that his suggested governance approach would work properly. Every issue does not require an equal emphasis on the three directions, but every issue should invoke a thought process along the lines of: what impact will this have in terms of leading up, down, and out, and what are the priorities?

Traits

INTEGRITY

Integrity is one of the prime characteristics any leader needs. It came up prominently in discussions about all five CAOs in this book, not surprisingly, because it comes up in virtually all the literature on leaders. In McIntosh's surveys of a large number of Canadian CAOs, "is credible" and "builds trust" are the top two leadership competencies.[27] James Kuzes and Barry Posner have surveyed thousands of people over many years in many countries about the characteristics they most admire in a leader, and honesty consistently holds top place. Their explanation is worth quoting at length:

> We want our leaders to be honest because their honesty is a reflection upon our own honesty. Of all the qualities that people look for and admire in a leader, honesty is by far the most personal. More than likely this also is why it consistently ranks number one. It's the quality that can most enhance or damage our own reputations. If we follow someone who's universally viewed as being of impeccable character and strong integrity, then we're likely to be viewed the same. But if we willingly follow someone who's considered dishonest, our own images are tarnished. And there's perhaps another, more subtle, reason why honesty is at the top. When we follow someone we believe to be dishonest, we come to realize that we've compromised our own integrity. Over time, we not only lose respect for the leader, we lose respect for ourselves.[28]

In addition to the high ethics of integrity, a lack of integrity in a leader poses certain practical problems for those around the leader. In a contentious purchasing situation, it is much easier to explain how the decision was made following certain transparent, ethical principles than to bob and weave trying to fabricate an explanation of why the contract was awarded to the CAO's good buddy. Integrity is desirable not only in terms of high ethics; it also makes day-to-day management much easier.

In our interviews, integrity was discussed at two levels: external integrity and internal integrity. With respect to external integrity, no one can be a good leader if her or his focus on furthering the positive goals of the organization is blighted by a desire to put personal interests ahead of those of the organization by accepting bribes, employing favouritism, or other inappropriate types of behaviour. Not only does this discredit the organization; it sends out a terrible signal to others in the organization.

None of our five CAOs was personally touched by scandal. The MFP computer-purchase scandal occurred in Toronto during Garrett's watch, but the inquiry into the scandal exonerated him of any involvement in it – in fact, his stature was considerably enhanced by the approach he took to it. In Vancouver, the Olympic athletes' village situation that occurred on Rogers's watch is sometimes referred to as a scandal, but of a peculiar type from which no one derived any illicit benefit and all actions were approved in an open and transparent manner by council. It might be called a mistake in judgment, but even that is questionable given that many of the events that led to the problem, including the global financial crisis, were largely unforeseeable. Our five CAOs were insulated from scandal because they projected an aura of integrity. MFP's representatives seem to have found everyone's vulnerable point – golf, cash, hockey tickets, hanging around with relatives of minor celebrities – but there is no evidence that they even approached Garrett. In Vancouver, a developer wryly referred to Rogers as "integrity Jude."

With respect to internal integrity, staff frequently praised these CAOs for always standing behind their word in somewhat smaller, but still important, internal matters such as budgetary allocations or the approval of new programs. It is a natural tendency not to want to disappoint staff, so some managers will "promise" that, say, a unit will get a new position, only to discover later that they cannot keep the promise. While this sort of thing pales in comparison to genuine scandal, it is disruptive for the organization. Subordinates need to know that they can rely on commitments a leader makes.

RESPECT

Along with integrity goes respect. Democracy is a wonderful institution. It produces all types of elected representatives. Some are highly responsible, sophisticated, productive representatives of their community; others can be a bit rough around the edges. Some take the job seriously, and make solid contributions to their communities; others are there to attract attention to themselves and cause trouble. To be blunt: not all elected people are deserving of the same level of respect. But all our successful CAOs treated all officeholders with the high level of respect that is owed to the office. They never showed their frustration with councillors even when everyone could see that the CAO was not receiving the level of respect that he or she deserved. Interviewees described numerous incidents in which the CAO was the victim of an unfair attack, but the CAO did not respond in kind.

Respect does not stop at the council chamber door. Interviewees frequently commented on how CAOs were respectful to everyone they dealt with, from senior administrators to cleaning staff. In turn, they were well respected by councillors, staff, and everyone else around them. A prime way of earning respect seems to be to respect others.

ENERGY

All the CAOs in this book were described by those around them as having a great deal of energy, and it is clear from their daily schedules that they worked long hours and still had time for a healthy personal life. Earl is known for being one of the first people in the office every morning, and he spends several evenings a week mountain biking. People who worked with Fenn were not sure when he slept, given the odd hours at which they received e-mail from him, but he still had time to pursue his artistic endeavours.

Obviously, the day-to-day requirements of the CAO are such that one needs a great of energy to stay on top of them. Beyond energy, however, a leader also must project a particular image. The CAO is a role model, so if you project an image of being overwhelmed, tired, and just generally unable to cope, that image will spread throughout the organization. Conversely, if you project an image of being in control and ready to tackle whatever challenges come along, that is the image that will spread through the organization. The CAO who strides quickly and confidently down the hall to take on the next challenge is likely to be as tired and uncertain as anyone else, but the successful leader learns not to show it outwardly.

RESILIENCE

If you try to accomplish major changes and improvements, you are virtually guaranteed to experience failure at some point in your career. As Shirley Hufstedler, the first US secretary of education, told Warren Bennis, "[i]f you haven't failed, you haven't tried very hard."[29] This could be a relatively minor event, such as failing to get approval of a particular project you feel is important, or it could be more significant, such as getting fired, as happened to 40 per cent of the people in this book devoted to highly successful CAOs. The failure could be your fault if you have overreached or been guilty of a mistake in judgment, or it could be related to something over which you had no control. When a new party came to power at Vancouver city hall, an easy way to demonstrate its commitment to change was to fire the long-time, well-respected city manager. Garrett was in an impossible position as the first CAO of megacity Toronto, and he ultimately was fired because of his inability to get along with an eccentric mayor.

Failure thus should be seen as just another stop along the road. Franklin Roosevelt is regarded as one of the greatest US presidents, and is mentioned prominently in many books on leadership, yet Roosevelt suffered a number of failures during his political career. His biographers document these failures, and generally go on to say that his approach seems to have been that failure simply means that he had to find a different way to achieve his goal.[30] As Roosevelt himself put it, "[t]he country needs and, unless I mistake its temper, the country demands bold, persistent experimentation. It is common sense to take a method and try it: If it fails, admit it frankly and try another. But above all, try something."[31] Warren Bennis and Burt Nanus, in their seminal book on leadership, devote an entire section to how the great leaders they profile dealt with failure.[32] Like Roosevelt, these leaders generally embraced failure as a way of learning and an opportunity to move forward. Bennis and Nanus conclude that it is important to strive for success, but, paradoxically, a focus on avoiding failure seems likely to cause failure.

Having council reject an important initiative is obviously a humbling experience for a CAO, whose normal, first reaction is to feel a deep sense of personal rejection: "Those misguided people rejected my initiative." Instead, pause and consider why the experience occurred. Perhaps a series of circumstances came together to scuttle the initiative this time. Rather than see the rejection as a sign of personal failure, determine what you can learn from the unfortunate event, and decide how to do it better next time.

A much more serious setback is to be fired. Garrett took some time to regroup, and went on to become CAO in another jurisdiction, where staff felt they had scored a major coup by getting such a highly respected leader. Rogers was at a different stage in her career when she was fired, and had no interest in leaving Vancouver, but she continues to have a high profile in many community organizations.

Getting fired is clearly a traumatic event. It is devastating for the individual, and the fact that it frequently happens in public and sometimes in an acrimonious fashion takes a toll on the person's family as well. But being a CAO is not a high-security career, and many CAOs get fired at some point. The only solace that one can take in such circumstances is that very few CAOs are fired for legitimate cause, and that there is little stigma associated with being fired. Most firings are a matter of lack of fit between council and the CAO. If you are fired, use the difficult experience to take stock of why it happened, and remember that most CAOs who are fired find another job in the municipal sector fairly quickly. It is important to get over the inevitable anger and bitterness, and take a positive outlook to the next job. The tragedy is not in getting fired, but in letting it affect you in such a way that it destroys your career.

Roosevelt demonstrated that failure is an important learning process. Be resilient. Pause and learn from failure – like Roosevelt, recognize that failure simply means that you need to find another way to accomplish your goal.

PASSION

As a public servant, you are supposed to be personally reserved and outwardly politically neutral. This does not mean that you should never show passion for your community, your organization, or your job. People like working for someone who is passionate about what they are doing. Elizabeth Thach and Karen Thompson argue that what they call being inspirational is particularly important in the public sector because of the social purpose of public organizations and the fact that "performance-based incentives are minimal or non-existent."[33]

Passion is something that just emanates from certain people and motivates those around them. Rogers and Earl love their respective communities, every action they took reinforced that passion, and everyone around them felt it. Fenn, Garrett, and Robicheau did not evince the same passion for a particular place; instead, they were passionate about professionalism and excelled in their jobs wherever they were.

Bennis describes the importance of passion this way: "The second basic ingredient of leadership is *passion* – the underlying passion for the promises of life, combined with a very particular passion for a vocation, a profession, a course of action. Tolstoy said that hopes are the dreams of the waking man. Without hope, we cannot survive, much less progress. The leader who communicates passion gives hope and inspiration to other people."[34]

When you work for someone with passion, you are conscious that not excelling in your job is not just a minor flaw that could be punished by a weak performance appraisal or a negative letter in your file. When those around you are passionate about their jobs, your penalty for malfeasance is that you have let the side down, which is a much more serious offence than some administrative penalty. About Fenn, one person mentioned how bad it would be to "let Michael down."

HUMILITY RATHER THAN CHARISMA

Although it is important to be passionate about your work and your organization, passion is not the same as charisma. Collins argues that good leaders frequently are seen as not being particularly charismatic in the traditional sense, because they prefer attention to focus on their organization rather than on themselves. Good leaders can still be ambitious, but they minimize their personal ambition and emphasize ambition for their organization: "The moment a leader allows himself to become the primary reality people worry about, rather than reality being the primary reality, you have a recipe for mediocrity, or worse. This is one of the key reasons why less charismatic leaders often produce better long-term results than their more charismatic counterparts."[35]

This is particularly important in public sector organizations where politicians, rather than administrators, enjoy the spotlight. All the leaders in this book were described as humble by some interviewees, frequently in the context of wanting to share the spotlight with others who were involved in a project, rather than taking too much credit themselves. Collins also makes this point about sharing the spotlight: "In contrast to the *I*-centric style of the comparison leaders, we were struck by how the good-to-great leaders *didn't* talk about themselves. During interviews with the good-to-great leaders they'd talk about the company and the contributions of other executives as long as we'd like but deflect discussion about their own contributions."[36] In the preparation of this book, several CAOs asked that sections of their cases be rewritten to minimize their own role in a particular event and to ensure that the credit was spread among a team.

Skills

EMOTIONAL INTELLIGENCE

All five CAOs studied in this book exhibited high degrees of emotional intelligence. In fact, they could have been models of the five-part definition devised by Daniel Goleman, presented in Chapter 1: they were self-aware, they controlled their emotions, they were highly motivated, they were able to recognize emotions in others, and they consciously managed relations with others.

Fenn did not use the phrase "emotional intelligence," but his idea of talking with each councillor and finding out what motivated the person both positively and negatively is the essence of emotional intelligence. Garrett claimed not to be people oriented, but those around him begged to differ with him. They felt that he was keenly attuned to others, and that this was a significant part of his vaunted communication skills. Rogers developed a large network of people both in and out of government.

As I have pointed out in several places, CAOs tend to use influence more than control to motivate people. Emotional intelligence is an absolute prerequisite to being able to use influence with those around you. You must understand the other person's emotions, and what buttons to push to influence that person.

POLITICALLY SENSITIVE, BUT NOT POLITICIZED

Being politically sensitive, but not politicized, is one of the most delicate balancing acts that the CAO must perform. Mouritzen and Svara's distinction between the politics of governing society and the politics of securing office is useful here.[37] As a CAO, you must remain strongly separate from the politics of securing office, but you have an important role to play in the politics of governing society – in others words, in the politics of policy making. In McIntosh's survey, being "politically astute" was regarded as the most important leadership attribute that could lead to the "success or demise of the CAO."[38] You need to have a good sense of the political tenor of council and the broader community, which will give you a feel for what you can put forward now, and what you need to put on the back burner until the time is right. At the same time, respect the fact that councillors are the political experts and that you cannot usurp their role. A good CAO can walk this delicate line. In writing about the Irish system of local government, Collins argues that "[t]he manager ... must be a better politician than the mayor because his leadership must always be unobtrusive."[39]

In Vancouver, Rogers was politically astute in the subtle way in which she kept the downtown east side issue before council and brought in outside experts to discuss it. Then, as the nature of the issue changed, she turned it over to the mayor and some councillors. A councillor in Banff suggested that Earl was actually better than councillors at detecting when an issue might become problematic in the community, and praised Earl for warning councillors. Fenn was aware of what was happening in each area of the city, so he knew how a proposal would affect each councillor's prime constituency and how each councillor likely would react to a proposal.

CONFIDENCE GROUNDED IN HARD WORK
AND PREPARATION, NOT IN HUBRIS

Discussion of confidence presents a paradox. Many interviewees described the CAOs in our sample as humble or self-effacing. Our CAOs did not exhibit that boisterous kind of confidence seen in overbearing glad-handers. None seemed to be touched by hubris – the hollow kind of exaggerated confidence that frequently comes before a fall. Van Wart suggests that leaders might lack confidence early in their careers, but develop it as they mature. Senior managers indicated to him that "lack of self-confidence was not entirely negative; it aided them to be more inclusive and thoughtful before acting, and ultimately encouraged them to be more flexible."[40]

All of these CAOs, however, were aware of their abilities and strengths. Indeed, you cannot take on a role like that of a CAO, which invites so many detractors, unless you are confident in your own skin. But such confidence deserves detailed comment. Our five CAOs stayed on top of all the major issues affecting them. They worked hard to prepare themselves for major presentations and key meetings. Garrett was recognized as excellent at making clear and concise presentations on even the most difficult topics, but people around him talked about how hard he (and they) worked to prepare for these presentations. Although all five CAOs exhibited high levels of confidence in their abilities, it was a form of confidence grounded in a great deal of preparation. That is how they protected themselves from hubris.

DON'T MICROMANAGE, BUT SUPPORT YOUR STAFF

I have mentioned in several places that our successful CAOs seldom actually used the control mechanisms that were available to them. They tended to opt for the lighter touch implicit in the word "influence." A good CAO must have confidence in her or his senior staff, otherwise a change needs to be made, and a good CAO will not shrink from that task.

Having surrounded yourself with a strong management team, you then must have confidence that the members of that team will make the right decisions. In some cases, CAOs admitted that they did not know enough about certain services to inject themselves too much into their delivery. Of course, there will be cases when you must show support for a team member even when you have some doubts. In Port Edward, Earl was concerned about whether a major works project could be completed within budget, but when his public works superintendent expressed confidence that he could deliver on the project, Earl went along with him – and everything worked out fine. Garrett dealt with a similar situation when some staff members made some overly optimistic promises around the big pipe. He could have left them to cope on their own, but instead he earned great credit among staff for standing behind them and finding a way to help them solve the problem they had created.

The prescription not to micromanage, but to support staff, can put you in a difficult position. Some managers might feel that, if they cannot control what their staff does, why should they be expected to stand behind staff members when they make bad decisions. The way out of that conundrum is to select staff carefully and mentor them wisely, then be confident that they will make the right decisions. This approach is epitomized by Fenn's management style, described earlier: Be sure that the right person is in the right place, then "don't dig in the weeds," as one of Fenn's former subordinates described it.

GOOD COMMUNICATION SKILLS, INCLUDING LISTENING

Leaders need to be able to get their ideas across, and clearly all five of our CAOs did that well. Fenn was praised for writing skills and for his ability to understand the position of the reader and to communicate at the level of the reader's understanding without being patronizing. Several people commented that Garrett's verbal presentations demonstrated his ability to make complicated issues clear to an uninitiated audience.

Good communication, however, is not just about talking and writing – listening is important, too, to discover what is important to others. Mats Alvesson and Stefan Sveningsson have found that what some might describe as mundane activities such as chatting and listening could have an important beneficial impact on the work environment in terms of team building, establishing trust, and making people feel more involved and less anonymous.[41]

The CAOs in this sample did not generally dominate the conversation – in fact, several of them were described as quiet or aloof. Interviewees frequently qualified their descriptions, however, by noting that the CAOs were careful listeners who, while they seemed detached, could interject a perceptive comment that indicated not only that were they listening carefully to the conversation, but that they were also several steps ahead of everyone else.

"COOL AS A CUCUMBER"

Passion is an important virtue at times, but at other times it is better to be more stoic and restrained. Senior administrators are subject to all sorts of both praise and criticism – some of it is highly justified, some not so much. The wise administrator takes both praise and criticism in a calm and reserved manner.

A municipal council chamber is no place for the squeamish. In the midst of intense debates, nasty insults are hurled indiscriminately, and sometimes fall on innocent bystanders as well as on the intended targets. Of course, it is inappropriate for a number of reasons for councillors to attack staff publicly,[42] but these niceties frequently are lost in the heat of the moment.

One's first impulse when attacked is to respond in kind. This is the sort of primal response that helped our ancient ancestors defend their caves from marauding animals, and saving face when attacked is still important in modern civilized society. There are times, however, when retaliation is not the best response. Responding in kind simply reduces the responder to the level of the attacker. In any case, duelling personal insults does not contribute to resolving the problem.

The CAOs in this book developed a reputation for not responding in kind when they were the victims of harsh attacks. Instead, they always tried to reduce the intensity of the debate. Several commented that their approach was to move the discussion away from personalities, and to talk about the issue under discussion. Another approach is to focus on the future and how to correct the problem, rather than spending time on fixing blame. Several people praised Robicheau for using his skills as a facilitator to get people to talk about their areas of agreement first before tackling parts of the issue on which they disagreed.

BUILD ON YOUR STRENGTHS; STRENGTHEN YOUR WEAKNESSES

Obviously, our leaders had some significant strengths or they would not have attained the positions they did, but none was perfect – all had weaknesses. Our CAOs seemed to be aware of their strengths and built on them. They were also aware of their weaknesses and compensated for or strengthened them. They did not attempt to be something they were not. This coincides with the advice of Bill George, who suggests that to be an authentic leader requires "being your own person, ... developing your unique leadership style, ... [and] being aware of your weaknesses."[43]

Fenn knew it would be tough for someone like him with a generalist background to get a job as a CAO. Therefore, he consciously managed his career by taking a job as deputy-administrator in a small town in northern Ontario (an area many would find unattractive) in order to gain valuable experience.

From a young age, Rogers was a team player. She developed this further when she studied physical education and community development in university, and she really honed this skill while developing an excellent team around her when she became city manager. She emanated a warm and friendly personality that just naturally attracted people to her and motivated them to work with her. She used that skill to accomplish some difficult and important tasks. In mid-career, she realized she needed to know more about finance and law, so she earned a master's degree in public administration. She never studied engineering, but she surrounded herself with good engineers. She did not try to be something she was not; instead, she recognized her weaknesses and compensated for them in a variety of ways.

Garrett knew he was not a warm and fuzzy people person, openly describing himself as a task-oriented engineer. Those around him said he had more people skills than he let on, but they all ultimately agreed that he was driven more by the task at hand than by concern for people. He used the feeling of accomplishment in a tough task well done to motivate the people around him, rather than pretend that he had great people skills.

Rogers and Garrett were about 180 degrees apart in personality, but they were equally successful. They just approached their tasks in different ways.

Behaviours

ADAPT TO YOUR ENVIRONMENT

Every organization has its own history and culture. When a new employee comes into an existing organization, it is up to her or him – regardless of how senior he or she might be – to adapt to the existing environment. The CAOs in this book did that quite well.

Fenn shifted gears quite radically when he moved from the quiet, genteel environment of Burlington to the rougher, more politically charged environment in Hamilton. Similarly, Robicheau had to shift gears when he went from Annapolis County, where he had to make major changes in installing a CAO system, to Kentville, where it was much more a matter of system maintenance in an environment that was already working well.

I discussed this kind of adaptation in Chapter 1 as the contingency or situational theory of leadership. As McIntosh points out, "a CAO selects different leadership styles for different strategic contexts."[44] Throughout his dissertation, he emphasizes how important it is for CAOs to read the situation carefully and adjust their leadership style accordingly: "Their success is dependent on their situational leadership alignment with the expectations of council."[45]

Of course, one cannot be expected to change one's basic personality, so consider the culture in a new organization before you accept a position, and determine if you can be comfortable there. In some cases, it might be wise to decline an offer if the environment is not a good fit with your personality. Once you have accepted the offer, however, it is incumbent on you to adjust your outlook to fit the new organization. At the same time, understanding and being sensitive to the new culture does not mean that you should never attempt to make any changes.

BE CHANGE ORIENTED

When you take on a new position, it is easy and safe just to carry on with the status quo that you have inherited, but Bennis argues that a leader must be innovative: "Two more basic ingredients of leadership are *curiosity* and *daring*. The leader wonders about everything, wants to learn as much as he can, is willing to take risks, experiment, try new things. He does not worry about failure, but embraces errors, knowing he will learn from them."[46]

The successful CAOs in this book were all change oriented. Sometimes administrative changes, rather than high-profile public changes, were important. Robicheau installed CAO systems in two places; Fenn won a great deal of support from staff because he found a way to avoid reducing their pay during "Rae days"; Garrett established performance measurement systems wherever he went. Sometimes the changes were more public. Earl developed a pictorial official community plan in Invermere that was more understandable to the residents. In Banff, he convinced the council to issue debt for the first time and to spend additional funds on a communications strategy around a major works project that was already costing a great deal of money. Earl openly encourages his staff to take risks, which is not the kind of language one typically hears in a public service environment.

It seems that good CAOs are not content with tinkering with the status quo to make it work better. Instead, they take the broader view and ask themselves what changes they could make that would have a significant positive impact on the operation of their organizations. They have a good eye for what changes are needed, but they also recognize that effecting change involves getting the right people on side.

There is ample evidence that change, even beneficial change, does not just happen. As Kouzes and Posner put it, "[l]eaders venture out. None of the individuals in our study sat idly by waiting for fate to smile upon them."[47] All of the changes our five CAOs instituted had risk associated with them, and they all required a certain finesse to get enough of the right people on side. Making change thus requires a careful balancing act. Successful CAOs know how to attain that balance.

MAKE CHANGES CAREFULLY; RESPECT LOCAL CUSTOMS

Some leaders enjoy telling how they came into an organization and immediately shook it to its foundations, causing great consternation on the part of its existing members.[48] There are probably cases where that kind of action is necessary and produces a desirable result. None of our five CAOs chose to act in that manner. Some did not need to make significant changes. Those who did took the time to learn the local culture and to show existing members of the organization that they respected that culture. The new CAOs felt they needed to understand where the organization was before they could decide how to take it someplace else. Several mentioned the importance of not setting off people's defence mechanisms. It is easier to get people to move voluntarily than to force them to move against their will. It is also important to judge the proper timing to make change. As Mark Moore notes, good leaders "know that the pace and sequence of their actions matter. If they go too quickly, their organizations will rebel. If they go too slowly, they may lose the momentum they need to execute a large organizational change."[49]

Fenn pointedly spent about a year observing the organization in Burlington before he got the group of senior managers together to make a collective decision about reorganizing the civic administration. Robicheau was hired in both St Andrews and Annapolis County explicitly to make significant changes, but even then he proceeded slowly, making sure that everyone understood the nature of the changes and did not become defensive. He knew it would be difficult to accomplish much otherwise.

COUNCILLORS ARE IN CHARGE, BUT SOMETIMES THEY NEED PROFESSIONAL ASSISTANCE

An important area requiring a significant balancing skill is the CAO's relationship with council – in particular, the extent to which the CAO gets "out in front of council" – frequently a warning about the danger of making council uncomfortable by leading it rather than following it.

All of our CAOs were respectful of their councils. They spent a considerable amount of time and effort understanding the issues in which council was interested and the general direction in which council wanted to take the community. Fenn talked about getting to know each councillor individually and identifying the positive and negative things that motivated them. Our CAOs first got to know the ethos of their council, then developed a sense of the kind of innovative ideas it would accept. With that information as background, none of them was afraid to offer suggestions to council about new ideas. In fact, they all felt this was an important part of their role. Councillors are experts in what local residents want, but staff members are professionals with knowledge of trends in the broader environment and of innovations and developments in substantive policy fields. Councillors can be good at identifying areas of dissatisfaction in the community and areas that need improvement, but it usually falls to staff to determine the alternatives to the status quo.

Rogers led her councillors in a consideration of issues on the downtown east side at a time when most would have been happy to ignore the area. While others wavered, she was a constant force in support of the bid to land the Olympics. Earl assembled funding and made his council comfortable about going into debt so that the town could undertake Banff Refreshing and the renovation of the Fenlands Recreation Centre. Robicheau took a leadership role in converting a former military base to an industrial and residential site, rather than letting the federal government demolish the buildings.

These were all good ideas, but the way the idea is sold to council is perhaps even more important than the quality of the idea. Rogers worked slowly on the downtown east side issue, and brought in outside experts to convince council there was a problem it could solve. She took the lead not by being obviously out in the front, but by orchestrating a number of activities that gradually influenced council's framing of the issue.

Good CAOs also understand the importance of timing. Several CAOs talked privately about having had good ideas that they knew council was not ready to accept and that they might dust off and present when the time was right.

Not getting out in front of council can be good advice, but it can also be a recipe for inertia. It is important to exercise balance here. Moving away from the status quo will require you to develop a good sense of where your council would be comfortable going before you attempt to lead there. Fenn offered an astute comment on this issue of attaining the proper balance:

> There's also a temporal element to this balancing role. The CAO often has more community profile and credibility than she or he realizes. That is both a concern to council members and underappreciated by the CAO. Used selectively and infrequently, it can be both influential in advancing those few things about which the CAO feels strongly or wants to achieve ... independent of the agenda of his council or peers, and in demonstrating to council that the CAO has an independent base of community support that they ignore at their peril if they act unreasonably with the civic administration. But, as with formal authority, if it used often or used to frustrate council's priorities, the CAO better dust off his or her resumé.

ALWAYS BE GROUNDED IN RATIONALITY

Leading council is always a tricky business. It works only if the CAO always operates and argues from a position of rationality. Expediency always plays a role in the political process. In fact, as long as we force politicians to seek re-election, it is unreasonable to criticize them for being expedient and engaging in activities to maximize their votes. It is the job of politicians to be politicians and to inject the view of voters into the system.

It is equally the job of administrators to inject a high degree of rationality into the system. The system breaks down when administrators lose their way and try to act like politicians. All the successful CAOs in this book were praised for sticking with the rational approach even when they knew it would be unpopular.

In Annapolis County, Robicheau felt it would be beneficial financially to contract out most of the public works function. This met with a great deal of opposition from some councillors and staff. He persisted, however, and presented the hard data that showed the extent of the benefit to the county, at which point it became virtually impossible for sustained opposition to continue. Fenn knew that Burlington would benefit from strategic planning, but he also knew that some councillors had reservations. He spent time explaining the benefits to the reluctant ones, and eventually he was able to develop a majority in support of it.

BUILD TEAMS

Historians frequently personalize the leadership of such formidable leaders as Napoleon, de Gaulle, or Roosevelt. Our CAOs were certainly formidable people, but they generally worked through teams, or what has been called distributed leadership. This is a hallmark of organizations in the twenty-first century. The size, scope, and complexity of modern organizations are such that it is simply impossible for one person to dominate in the classical leadership style. In contemporary organizations, the role of the leader is to assemble a good team and to work with that team to accomplish important goals. As Kouzes and Posner put it, "exemplary leaders know that 'you can't do it alone' and they act accordingly. They lack the pride and pretense displayed by many leaders who succeed in the short term but leave behind a weak organization that fails to remain strong after their departure. Instead, with self-effacing humor and generous and sincere credit to others they get higher and higher levels of performance; they get extra ordinary things done."[50]

Rogers saw her main role as a team builder. Fenn and Earl also assembled teams around them with which they felt comfortable. Garrett's situation is illustrative in that he developed good teams around him in Peel and York regions. For reasons beyond his control, he was not able to develop such a team in Toronto, and this was his one unsuccessful stop on the circuit. Robicheau operated in a smaller venue, but he worked with Peter Terauds and recruited Laurie Emms to complement his personal style, and the three of them seemed to work well as a team.

SURROUND YOURSELF WITH GREAT PEOPLE; IF YOU DO NOT HAVE THEM, DEVELOP THEM

Teams are only as good as their members. Jim Collins, in writing about his "good to great" businesses, argues that the first priority of the successful leaders he studied was to surround themselves with good people; only then did they begin to decide where they wanted to go.[51]

The people around our five leaders commented that these CAOs were excellent judges of people's skills and abilities. In most cases, changes in senior personnel took place shortly after the new CAO arrived. When Earl was appointed in Invermere, some senior people left, possibly because they did not get the position. This gave him scope to appoint new people, who are still there almost twenty years later. When Fenn came to Burlington, he wanted to establish a new budget system. As the treasurer was not comfortable with this, Fenn worked with the deputy treasurer, and the treasurer left shortly thereafter. Rogers knew people throughout her organization and developed a reputation for moving people between units in somewhat unconventional ways, but they usually seemed to work out.

All these CAOs were conscious of their responsibility to mentor people. A fairly large group of Garrett's former staffers serve as CAOs in York Region and beyond. The current CAO in Invermere said he never really thought about moving beyond the planning department until Earl encouraged him and helped him develop his skills. Rogers developed some people within the Vancouver civic organization, but she is also actively mentoring a network of women across the city. Many interviewees spoke fondly and positively about the great impact their CAO had on their career development.

Collins argues that the difference between sustainable and nonsustainable companies is that the leaders of the former are able to develop a cadre of successors.[52] Robert Greenleaf argues that the essence of being a servant leader is: "Do those served grow as persons? Do they, *while being served*, become healthier, wiser, freer, more autonomous, more likely themselves to become servants?"[53] The CAOs in this book certainly fulfilled this obligation in that they were excellent mentors for the next generation of leaders.

PROMOTE TRAINING AND DEVELOPMENT OPPORTUNITIES

In addition to the personal involvement related to mentorship, the successful CAOs were all champions of training and development throughout their organization. In the larger organizations such as York Region, this involved developing a thick book of training opportunities for staff. In a smaller place such as Annapolis County, Robicheau did not have this same opportunity, but one staff member spoke about how he lent her material for a distance course she was taking, and then they had several discussions that she found useful in furthering her studies. She made it clear that these discussions not only helped her in this specific course, but they also signalled how much Robicheau valued training and development.

Training and development can be a tough sell in the municipal sector. In an environment marked by heavy pressures on the budget, it is frequently difficult to identify the immediate return on training and development. In fact, some short-sighted councillors will express concern that staff members will use training and development as a way to move to another employment opportunity. In that environment, training and development needs a high-level champion to rise above the budget pressure and the short sightedness. Our five successful CAOs were committed to doing that.

TEAR DOWN SILOS; AVOID TURF TALK

All of our successful CAOs talked about the need to create a team, which meant tearing down silos. Garrett created horizontal teams to manage issues such as growth that cut across all departments. Rogers did something similar with Neighbourhood Integrated Service Teams. She also had a reputation for not allowing "turf talk" at meetings of senior managers. She insisted that discussion focus on the need to solve problems for the entire city, not on how a decision would affect a particular department. Earl moved his office around and sat in a variety of departments. He also scrambled the location of other people's offices in an attempt to get them to think across departmental boundaries. He had to back off from this radical idea, but his attempt sent a message.

Obviously, integration of service is absolutely essential in a modern organization. The entire rationale of moving from a council-committee system to a CAO system is to have someone in place who can accomplish that integration. To put it bluntly, if the CAO does not integrate the separate organizational units, why even have a CAO? If integration is not important, the municipality might as well carry on with each department head running her or his own show.

YOU ARE NOT THE MUNICIPALITY; YOU ARE THE TEMPORARY HIRED HELP

Municipalities are corporate bodies with a perpetual existence. In most cases, they were around long before the current CAO came on the scene, and they will be around long after he or she has departed. Be dedicated to furthering the interests of your municipality, but retain a level of clinical detachment. Robicheau said it well: "The municipality is a body corporate. It's not a family member; it's not your wife; and ... you shouldn't care at the level that I was caring ... I'm just glad I woke up one day and said, 'I've been here long enough,' because I think [I] may have [reached] a point ... where I did lose perspective about where the distinction between Keith Robicheau and the County of Annapolis [was] ... I'm not the County of Annapolis. I shouldn't be personally identifying myself with every issue."

This clearly was not a plea to take the job lightly and adopt an apathetic attitude, but it is a reminder that there are dangers for the CAO who identifies too personally with the municipality. The wise CAO maintains a certain distance so as not to lose perspective. In the medical field, this is called clinical detachment. Some level of detachment is necessary because you must provide your best professional advice to council, and you need to understand that sometimes council will reject your advice. In those circumstances, make sure council understands the consequences of rejecting the advice, but, in the final analysis, it is council's decision, and you must implement it with proper respect and enthusiasm. It is important that council have confidence that you will execute its orders loyally even when it has rejected your advice.

If you lose that clinical detachment and imagine that only you understand what is best for the municipality, you will not be a good CAO because you will have lost the real meaning of the position. Surgeons do not operate on family members because their personal feelings can cloud their clinic judgment. Following Robicheau's imagery, the CAO who begins to see the employing municipality as though it were a family member will no longer be a good administrator.

As with many other points made in this section, a balance is required here. Take the job seriously and be dedicated to furthering the interests of the municipality, but know where to draw the line.

THERE'S LIFE OUTSIDE YOUR OWN MUNICIPALITY

Obviously, as CAO, your main job is to administer your own municipality, but it is no accident that all of our successful CAOs were heavily involved in activities beyond their municipality. Rogers was strongly committed to the Institute of Public Administration of Canada (IPAC), ultimately becoming president. Fenn was also involved in IPAC and in the Ontario Municipal Administrators' Association. He is an inveterate traveller, but as CAO he travelled with a purpose. He deliberately met key people wherever he went, and he was always on the lookout for new ideas to apply back home. Earl undertook work on a Canadian International Development Agency project in Africa. All played some role in provincial-municipal advisory groups.

This kind of involvement is important not only as a source of new ideas, but also in building a network of peers who can share ideas and provide advice. As a number of people pointed out, being a CAO is a lonely occupation – there are certain things you cannot share with anyone in your own organization, but other CAOs might have faced a similar problem.

RESPECT THE WORK-LIFE BALANCE

Being a CAO can be an all-consuming endeavour if you let it. A huge amount of work ends up deposited on your desk for information or decision. Garrett lamented that he talked to others about the importance of work-life balance, but did not apply it to himself. He found time, however, for family vacations to go hiking or skiing in the Rockies. Rogers was a competitive athlete when she was younger, and she still participates in charity runs. Mountain biking is the standard pastime for many people who live in Banff, including Earl. Robicheau has always been involved in golf and curling; he has both winter and summer covered. Some people might be surprised to see a creative, artsy side to someone in the city management profession, but Fenn is an accomplished artist.

This is not just a matter of personal health and well-being. As Earl argued, "[p]eople who love to live in the community they're in [are] better at everything they do. They're better at their relationships, they're better in their jobs because they've got this background happiness ... Folks who work in the Town of Banff have a higher capacity to be happy ... If you're doing what you love, you produce so much more when you come to work." Kellerman makes the point more broadly: "*Stay balanced.* More than a few leaders named in [my] book were famous workaholics, far more dedicated to their jobs than they were to family and friends. This is a danger. As Bill George, former chairman and CAO of Medtronic, points out, 'Balanced leaders develop healthier organizations.' They make more thoughtful decisions and lead more effectively."[54]

The point is that even these highly respected leaders at the pin-nacle of their field were able to balance work and family and other commitments.

How durable are these characteristics?

To what extent will this list of traits, skills, and behaviours remain rel-evant into the future as leaders deal with succeeding generations of followers who perhaps have different attitudes and as environments change? Local governments seem caught in a continuing cycle of fund-ing constraints and other environmental pressures. Will the character-istics that worked in one part of the cycle work equally well in other parts?

The answer is that, to some extent, these characteristics have already endured over time. The period covered in the five case studies ranges from 1987 to the present, and the geography covered most sections of Canada. Yet certain characteristics seem to have endured over time and space. Furthermore, the nature of these characteristics is broad and encompassing enough that they should span many situations. Advice such as demonstrate integrity, show respect, and focus on communica-tion is timeless and placeless; surely, these basic values will suit any environment and any group of followers.

Table 7.1 summarizes the traits, skills, and behaviours discussed ear-lier in this section.

Are Leaders Born, or Can Leadership Be Taught?

In earlier times, when the traits approach to leadership was dominant, there was a belief in the idea of the born leader. Obviously, traits such as height, weight, or age cannot be taught, but when one examines the traits, skills, and behaviours identified in this chapter, it is difficult to see which cannot be developed consciously by virtually anyone. Of course, no one has all these characteristics in equal measure, and some people have certain skills naturally while others have to work at them. In fact one of the characteristics of our good leaders is an ability to use their strengths and strengthen their weaknesses.

After an extensive review of many leaders, Kouzes and Posner make this point about learning to be a leader: "It's just pure myth that only a lucky few can ever understand the intricacies of leadership. Leader-ship is not a place, it's not a gene, and it's not a secret code that can't

Table 7.1. Characteristics of the Successful CAO

Traits
Integrity
Respect
Energy
Resilience
Passion
Humility rather than charisma

Skills
Emotional intelligence
Politically sensitive, but not politicized
Confidence grounded in hard work and preparation, not in hubris
Don't micromanage, but support your staff
Good communication skills, including listening
"Cool as a cucumber"
Build on your strengths; strengthen your weaknesses

Behaviours
Adapt to your environment
Be change oriented
Make changes carefully; respect local customs
Councillors are in charge, but sometimes they need professional assistance
Always be grounded in rationality
Build teams
Surround yourself with great people; if you do not have them, develop them
Promote training and development opportunities
Tear down silos; avoid turf talk
You are not the municipality; you are the temporary hired help
There's life outside your own municipality
Respect the work-life balance

be deciphered by ordinary people. The truth is that leadership is an observable set of skills and abilities that are useful whether one is in the executive suite or on the front line, on Wall Street or Main Street, in any campus, community, or corporation. And any skill can be strengthened, honed, and enhanced, given the motivation and desire, the practice and feedback, and the role models and coaching."[55]

Kellerman is critical of the leadership industry because she sees organizations collectively spending more than $50 billion annually teaching leadership with virtually no metric to determine if the programs are successful.[56] Of course, the programs use the standard measure of whether people exiting them feel good about them, but that hardly determines if they provide any long-run benefit. Her prescription is that organizations generally should become less leader-centric and focus more on training followers, because followers are becoming more important and they have a significant role in supporting the actions of good leaders and restraining the actions of bad leaders.[57]

As Kouzes and Posner put it, there is no secret code involved in becoming a leader. The traits, skills, and behaviours demonstrated by the current generation of leaders are likely to be needed by the next generation. Even if one does not aspire to the top leadership position, or tries to attain it and falls short, all of the characteristics listed above would be useful for any individual to develop. Nothing on the list is tantamount to learning an obscure language spoken by a tribe of five hundred people living in an isolated mountain pass. Everything on the list is something any of us – whether leader or follower – can usefully develop.

Kellerman is also critical of those in the leadership industry who "make it short – they imply that leadership can be learned in little more than the time it takes to read this. In general they make it simple – they imply that leadership can be learned by mastering the material immediately at hand."[58] She certainly has a valid point: a two-day course never converted a klutz to a leader. But if the course and some other background learning help the prospective leader change her or his perspective and adopt a different attitude in the workplace, they will have served a valuable purpose. In this book, I have tried to help by identifying the skills and behaviours that aspiring municipal senior managers should master. I hope I have not made it appear easy. Many skills – communication, interacting with people – require a lifetime to master.

Denhardt and Denhardt liken learning how to be a leader to learning how to be a ballet dancer or mastering a sport. You need "studio experience" to be a dancer; to develop skill in a sport, you need to spend a great deal of time practising and perfecting technique. They argue that, to become a leader, you first need a good psychological and moral grounding, but then you must practise: "For most leaders, this practice is called *experience* and it involves basically a trial-and-error approach in which you try one thing and if it doesn't work you try something else."[59]

One impediment facing municipal staff members who want to become leaders is that municipal governments generally do a poor job of developing staff by moving them through a number of different functional areas. Usually, staff are hired into a department because they possess some functional skill (accounting, engineering, planning), and move up the silo within that department. Rogers was unusual in taking the risk of moving people between silos; this would not be seen as so remarkable in other types of organizations.

The lack of a breadth of experience makes it difficult to develop leaders who understand the entire organization. This is especially problematic in municipal governments because of the broad scope of services they provide. As Van Wart explains, "[t]hose trained in a 'silo' of experience and who have never worked in different areas of the organization will have difficulty understanding the language, norms, and mindset of many parts of the organization. The leader who has never been anything other than a financial analyst or accountant will find it exceedingly difficult to appreciate and communicate with operational divisions. Similarly, the leader who has always been involved in line operations may make very poor use of staff divisions."[60]

As an aspiring leader, you need to take responsibility for managing your career, and in some cases that will mean taking lateral transfers to gain experience or pushing employers to take unconventional actions like moving people between silos. Instead of setting your sights on becoming a CAO next week, it might be helpful to rate yourself on some of the traits, skills, and behaviours discussed earlier in this chapter, then focus on developing those characteristics in which you are weak. Whether or not you ever become a CAO, this will make you a better manager and leader.

The Emerging Profession of City Management in Canada

A sample of five people does not provide much scope for a discussion of the state of the profession of city management in Canada, but it does provide some insights. One problem with commenting on the state of the profession, however, is that "profession" is used in a variety of rather different ways.

"Professional" is often used to refer to a person who takes her or his job seriously and does it well, as in the house painter who did a really professional job on my house. Following this meaning of the term, all five of our selected managers are consummate professionals, and it is safe to say that Canadian local governments are well served by a solid core of competent, professional city managers who take their jobs seriously. "Professional," however, is also given a more precise definition grounded in sociology and other academic fields.[61] A typical list of the traits of a true profession includes

- a grounding in an educationally communicable body of knowledge generally agreed upon by members of the profession;
- practical application of that knowledge (insightful philosophers can be useful to the profession, but do not count as professionals);
- the presence of a code of ethics that emphasizes an altruistic motivation preventing the professional from using this expert knowledge to take advantage of the uninitiated;
- self-organization and self-regulation that allow existing professionals to control entry to the profession; and
- a monopoly on the application of the prescribed knowledge and techniques to prevent the uninitiated from doing damage by misapplying techniques reserved to the professional.

Within city management, the idea of the established and agreed-upon body of academic knowledge is clearly developing. Educational institutions and professional associations have developed a number of courses geared to moving mid-career people with a variety of backgrounds to the top tier of municipal administration. The professional associations have codes of conduct to govern their members, although enforcement mechanisms are generally lacking.

The weakness of the profession of city management lies in the fact that the profession is not self-regulating in the same manner as accounting, law, or medicine, and there is no monopoly of practice associated with city managers' professional bodies. These characteristics are not likely to develop. Councils as employers will want to retain the ability to appoint any person who satisfies their needs. It might be unwise for a council to appoint an individual without certain qualifications, but giving an elected council the right to make mistakes is part of the cost of democracy.

Saying that a particular occupation is not a full-fledged profession as defined above is not a criticism. Some kinds of occupations simply lend themselves more than others to self-regulation and monopoly. We entrust physicians with our lives, and laypeople have little ability to evaluate physicians, so full professional status is important. Municipal managers operate in a much more open environment where many people have some ability to evaluate the manager's performance.

Instead of pushing for full legal status as a self-regulating profession with monopoly status, it might be a better course of action for municipal managers to make the education and training component so strong and the professional associations so robust that they develop a de facto monopoly on the CAO position. In Ontario, it is difficult for someone to become a clerk (especially in small and medium-sized municipalities) unless he or she is a member of the Association of Municipal Managers, Clerks and Treasurers of Ontario (AMCTO). CAOs could strive for a similar status for their national and provincial associations. This would first require some education-based qualification for membership, similar to what AMCTO currently has. One way to build this credibility is by bolstering the existing educational programs and developing new ones. This brings us to a related but slightly different topic.

Another consequence of the strengthening of the professional status of the CAO would be to enhance the status of the position among the general public. Currently, the public's general lack of knowledge about the position and the position's lack of professional status make it relatively easy for the media or political elites to attack CAOs on the grounds of restoring power to the people's representatives that they regard as now in the hands of self-satisfied bureaucrats. Professional associations need to be vigilant and engage in an education campaign when that sort of attack occurs.

Implicit in the characteristics of a profession is that current professionals have an obligation to develop the next generation of professionals. The enhanced educational programs mentioned above require the appropriate raw material in the form of academic papers, case studies, and so forth. I hope that this book will make a modest contribution to that literature, but more senior managers need to make their own contributions. Of course, many are already conscientious in fulfilling that role through their involvement in educational activities and mentoring, but they could contribute more by sharing their wealth of experience and knowledge by adding to the existing literature.

I understand that it is difficult to expect public servants who have made a career of standing in the shadows while their political masters take credit for their successes to step forward and brag about themselves, but the truth is that these people have a great deal to brag about. There are some excellent examples of memoirs from US public servants. Louis Brownlow wrote about his experiences as a city manager in a 500-page volume entitled *A Passion for Anonymity*.[62] One wonders how long the book would have been had Brownlow not been so passionate about anonymity. LeRoy Harlow wrote a lighter collection of folksy, but highly instructive, anecdotes about his time as a city manager.[63] There are also examples of works about exemplary municipal public servants written by others.[64] There is a substantial body of work written by former Canadian federal government officials both as academic works on history or management[65] and as interesting memoirs.[66] It is virtually impossible to find anything similar at the municipal level in Canada. Thomas Plunkett wrote extensively during his academic career after a short stint as a municipal manager and a bit longer as a consultant. Kenneth Crawford had an extensive municipal career before he wrote his compendium on municipal government.[67] I have been unable to locate similar works of contemporary municipal administrators.

I hope this book does justice to the work of municipal managers, but this kind of work would be much better done by participants rather than trusting an outside observer to understand what would be second nature to an experienced practitioner. This is the challenge I toss out to municipal managers: You have an interesting and important story to tell. Please share it with us.

A Word to Mayors and Councillors

Most of this book has been directed at municipal managers, suggesting how they could improve their own status or the status of their profession. It occurs to me that another group could benefit from this book as well: those who work most closely with CAOs.

Appointing a CAO is the most important decision a council makes. A good CAO will have a tremendous impact on the functioning of a municipality. As Edward Glaeser has argued, "[m]uch of the world suffers under awful governments, and that provides an edge for those cities that are administered well."[68] Of course, councils need to make all sorts of good decisions on all manner of policy issues, but it makes little difference how good a council is at deciding on policy if its superb policy decisions are not implemented properly. In the introduction to this book, I made an important point about these leaders in the shadows that bears repeating here. Although usually invisible, municipal CAOs are important cogs in the machinery of government. They can make a mayor and council look exceptionally good (or not). They can be a source of great pride and motivation among the staff of the municipality (or not). They can be an important conduit in the two-way flow of information between community organizations and the municipality (or not). A tremendous amount hinges on how well a CAO carries out her or his responsibilities. Councillors can make superb decisions, but they still must depend on the CAO and the senior administration to make them look good every day of the week.

Let me say a word about a trend that I find somewhat alarming. One sometimes hears of a mayor who has decided that he or she can also function as the CAO. This might have come from a previous bad experience with a CAO or from a desire to save money by not filling a position. Some mayors are experienced and competent managers, and are well equipped to carry out senior management functions, but the roles of mayor and CAO are incompatible and so cannot be held by one person. A major thrust of this book is that both the mayor and the CAO have important roles and make important complementary contributions to a well-functioning municipality, but these roles are different. The mayor and councillors contribute an in-depth feel for the pulse of the community; the CAO contributes knowledge and experience about management of the substantive issues. The municipality will benefit when there are healthy tensions between those two views. One person trying to play both roles will not give the municipality the benefit of those two different perspectives.

Council needs to exercise care in choosing a CAO. It is important that a municipality have a professional CAO with appropriate training and experience. A local person who is a nice guy and beloved by all might seem attractive in the short run, but hiring someone without appropriate experience can produce problematic consequences. Having said that, as this book makes clear, CAOs follow no established career path.[69] Judy Rogers was promoted within her own municipality after spending several years working her way up the hierarchy; that was a low-risk appointment. Mike Garrett had substantial managerial experience, none of which was in the municipal sector; this was a slightly riskier appointment. Robert Earl and Keith Robicheau were both hired in their first CAO position at a young age with no managerial experience; these were high-risk appointments, but in small municipalities. It seems as though none of the CAOs in this book fits the same mould.

In hiring a CAO, the mayor and councillors should balance considerations of the long term and the municipality's immediate needs. Contingency theory argues that there is no one best leader who fits every situation. Councillors should begin by looking seriously at their own municipality and determining what kind of CAO it needs at this time. In this chapter, I have identified a list of traits, skills, and behaviours that the ideal CAO will possess. No one person could possess all of those characteristics. What are the specific needs of your municipality right now? Finding the best CAO in some absolute sense might not be the right decision if that person's experience and profile do not fit the current needs of your municipality. For example, Plunkett writes particularly about the qualifications of a person hired to install a CAO system in a municipality which had not had one previously.[70] McIntosh draws on his extensive consulting experience to provide this astute advice:

> The CAO leadership profile could also be further developed for council use in recruiting a CAO. All too often [I] observed that councils hire very competent line managers as CAOs. Political discussions about expectations beyond professional qualifications would enable council to articulate what kind of CAO would fit with its expectations and the prevailing strategic context. Council agreement on CAO expectations would enhance role clarity. A subsequent good fit candidate may lead to a foundation for positive council/staff relations and opportunities for CAO success in a leadership role that is deemed "appropriate."[71]

Robicheau was quite proficient at installing CAO systems because he did it in two different municipalities. Garrett was hired in Peel Region because he had significant managerial experience, but he also provided the municipality with a link to the provincial government that it wanted at that point. Michael Fenn was hired in Hamilton-Wentworth because restructuring was a high priority with the regional chair at the time, and Fenn had experience in that area with the provincial government. These people were all good managers in an absolute sense, but they also fit the needs of that particular municipality at that particular time.

Council should not be consumed, however, by short-run considerations. The CAO should also be a visionary who is not afraid to think about the long term. Rogers was willing to tackle issues such as Vancouver's downtown east side that clearly would not be solved in her tenure. Earl was building for the long term when he tackled the Banff Refreshing project, which had sat on the shelf for a number of years, and the renovation of the Fenlands Recreation Centre. Too much focus on filling immediate needs could short change the municipality in the long run.

Conclusion

Local government touches all of us intimately every day of our lives: the water we drink, the transit system that takes us to work, the emergency workers who keep our cities safe. Those services are only as good as the people who deliver them, and the quality of the people at the working level is determined by the quality of leadership they receive.

The role of the chief administrative officer is a difficult one. Municipal government delivers a broad range of services ranging from animal control to zoning. The CAO is in an important position in delivering those services because he or she sits at the pinchpoint of the hourglass between council, which makes policies, and the public servants who deliver them. The CAO must be able to lead in three directions at the same time, and each direction requires a different skill set.

As I set out in the introduction, this book had three purposes. The first was to identify the leadership qualities needed in a municipal CAO. The second was to demystify the concept of leadership and to help aspiring leaders understand the qualities they need to be a leader and how to develop them. The third was to tell the story of exemplary leaders as a way of illustrating the high quality of municipal management with which Canada is blessed.

In Chapter 1, I established a definition of leadership as it pertains to a municipal CAO: A municipal CAO who is a good leader has the ability to move the municipality forward by interacting in a mutually influential way with and motivating council, external stakeholders, and organizational subordinates. I went on to discuss the careers of five practitioners who met this definition. They all moved their municipalities forward in some way. Sometimes these were hard services; in other cases, it was forcing councillors to come to grips with an issue they rather would have ignored. All five CAOs did this in a mutually influential way by working in three directions. Significant change inevitably requires having council, external stakeholders, and organizational subordinates aligned in support of the change. And obtaining commitment from all three entities usually must be done through persuasion and influence, which requires much more skill and a much more sensitive touch than relying on the brute force of authority.

How does a successful CAO accomplish this alignment using only influence? The five case studies helped to identify a number of traits, skills, and behaviours that these practitioners possessed and that they used to move their municipalities forward in a mutually influential way.

One major lesson from these case studies is that there is no one best way of leading. One leader was highly task oriented; another was equally highly people oriented. One focused on developing partnerships; another thrived on taking risks. They were all highly successful.

There are many routes to the same end; CAOs must use their judgment to apply the right tools in the right situations.

The second purpose of the book was to demystify the concept of leadership and provide some advice to mid-career and younger people who aspire to become CAOs, and to the people who currently manage them, the professional associations who support them, and the academics who teach them. There is nothing mystical about leadership. Anyone can develop the traits, skills, and behaviours of successful CAOs I have identified, but that does not mean it is easy. Aspiring managers must manage their careers consciously to garner the needed experience and develop those characteristics, and the academics who teach these young (and some mature) students must ensure that they attain the knowledge and the confidence necessary to develop them. Professional associations need to play a strong role in developing the next generation of leaders. And those who manage these young public servants must ensure that they have the opportunity to develop these characteristics.

The third purpose was to begin to develop a narrative literature that tells the story of some heroes. We hear a great deal in the media about the relatively small number of scandals that afflict government organizations; we hear much less about the huge number of people who do their jobs well day in, day out to make life better for all Canadians. I hope my example will encourage more people to tell these kinds of stories.

We are well served in Canada by an excellent cadre of senior municipal managers. In truth, this has happened more by chance than by design. As I have indicated throughout this book, the CAO's job is both important and difficult, yet there is no established career path for CAOs and no formal required program of training and development. The current group of managers, academics, and professional associations needs to work together to develop the next cadre of managers. I hope this book makes a modest contribution to that enterprise.

Notes

Introduction

1 The chief administrative officer is defined for the purposes of this book as the highest-ranking appointed public servant who has responsibility for all public servants in the municipality and who reports directly to council. In practice, a variety of titles is employed for this position, such as city (town, village, township) manager, directeur général, and clerk-administrator. Each position is different in that it is governed by its own by-law or employment contract, but the problems the people in these positions face are sufficiently similar that I discussed them together under the general term CAO.

2 See Kurt Klaudi Klausen and Annick Magnier, "The Anonymous Leader," in *The Anonymous Leader: Appointed CEOs in Western Local Government*, ed. Kurt Klaudi Klausen and Annick Magnier (Odense, Denmark: Odense University Press, 1998), 25.

3 Barbara Kellerman, *The End of Leadership* (New York: HarperCollins, 2012), 154, 168. Some exceptions to the generic approach look at specific services or professions; see, for example, Stecie G. Goffin and Valora Washington, *Ready or Not: Leadership Choices in Early Care and Education* (New York: Teachers College Press, 2007).

4 Jacques Bourgault and Christopher Dunn, eds., *Deputy Ministers in Canada: Comparative and Jurisdictional Perspectives* (Toronto: University of Toronto Press, 2014).

5 The origins of the system are described well in John Nalbandian, *Professionalism in Local Government: Transformations in Roles, Responsibilities, and Values of City Managers* (San Francisco: Jossey-Bass, 1991), chap. 1; Clarence E. Ridley and Orin F. Nolting, *The City-Manager Profession* (Chicago:

University of Chicago Press, 1934), chap. 1; and Richard J. Stillman II, *The Rise of the City Manager: A Public Professional in Local Government* (Albuquerque: University of New Mexico Press, 1974).

6 Stillman, *Rise of the City Manager*, 14.

7 Horace L. Brittain, *Local Government in Canada* (Toronto: Ryerson Press, 1951), 65–8.

8 Kenneth Grant Crawford, *Canadian Municipal Government* (Toronto: University of Toronto Press, 1954), 169–72.

9 Ibid., 163.

10 Thomas J. Plunkett, *Urban Canada and Its Government: A Study of Municipal Government* (Toronto: Macmillan of Canada, 1968), 37–50. In a later book, Plunkett provided a good description of the genesis of the council manager system in the United States and its spread to Canada; see Thomas J. Plunkett, *City Management in Canada: The Role of the Chief Administrative Officer* (Toronto: Institute of Public Administration of Canada, 1992), chaps. 2, 3.

11 Paul Hickey, *Decision-Making Processes in Ontario's Local Government; with a Summary of 9 Systems of Local Decision-making in Other Canadian Provinces, the United States and England* (Toronto: Ministry of Treasury, Economics and Intergovernmental Affairs, 1973), 119.

12 Ibid., 133.

13 Ibid., 9.

14 Some cities in the United States have also used a commissioner system, but the system of elected commissioners there is quite different from the Canadian system.

15 The system is described in Crawford, *Canadian Municipal Government*, 174–6; Hickey, *Decision-Making Processes*, 33; Donald J.H. Higgins, *Local and Urban Politics in Canada* (Toronto: Gage Educational, 1986), 154–7; idem, *Urban Canada: Its Government and Politics* (Toronto: Macmillan of Canada, 1977), 112–15; and James Lightbody, "Edmonton," in *City Politics in Canada*, ed. Warren Magnusson and Andrew Sancton (Toronto: University of Toronto Press, 1983), 274–5.

16 Donald C. Rowat, "Do We Need the Manager Plan?" *Canadian Public Administration* 3, no. 1 (1960): 42–50; see also idem, *Your Local Government* (Toronto: Macmillan of Canada, 1965), 78–9.

17 W. George R. Vance, "The Managerial Approaches of Chief Administrative Officers" (PhD diss., University of Western Ontario, 1985), 262–3; Trevor Price, "Council-Administration Relations in City Governments," in *Canadian Metropolitics: Governing Our Cities*, ed. James Lightbody (Mississauga, ON: Copp Clark, 1995), 193–214; Plunkett, *City Management in Canada*.

18 Gordon A. McIntosh, "Defining Situational Leadership for the Local Government Chief Administrative Officer" (PhD diss., University of Victoria, 2009).

19 Patrick Eamon O'Flynn, "The Evolving Role of the Municipal Chief Administrative Officer in Canada, 1985–2010" (MA thesis, University of Guelph, 2011).

20 Plunkett, *City Management in Canada*, 21.

21 This gradual approach seems to have been the case in other countries as well. See Michael Goldsmith and Jon Tonge, "Local Authority Chief Executives: The British Case," in Klausen and Magnier, *Anonymous Leader*, 49–63; Maurizio Gamberucci and Annick Magnier, "Italian Local Democracy in Search of a New Administrative Leadership," in Klausen and Magnier, *Anonymous Leader*, 204–19.

22 Poul Erik Mouritzen and James H. Svara, *Leadership at the Apex: Politicians and Administrators in Western Local Governments* (Pittsburgh: University of Pittsburgh Press, 2002); James H. Svara, *Dichotomy and Duality: The Relationship between Policy and Administration in Council-Manager Cities* (Armonk, NY: M.E. Sharpe, 2003); idem, *The Facilitative Leader in City Hall: Reexamining the Scope and Contributions* (Abingdon, UK: Taylor & Francis, 2008); idem, *Official Leadership in the City: Patterns of Conflict and Cooperation* (New York: Oxford University Press, 1989); and James H. Svara and James R. Brunet, "Finding and Refining Complementarity in Recent Conceptual Models of Politics and Administration," in *Retracing Public Administration*, ed. Mark R. Rutgers (Amsterdam: JAI, 1989), 185–208.

23 Peter Dahler-Larsen, ed., *Social Bonds to City Hall: How Appointed Managers Enter, Experience, and Leave Their Jobs in Western Local Government* (Odense, Denmark: Odense University Press, 2002); Klaussen and Magnier, *Anonymous Leader*; Mouritzen and Svara, *Leadership at the Apex*.

24 Sandford Borins, *Governing Fables: Learning from Public Sector Narratives* (Charlotte, NC: Information Age Publishing, 2011), chap. 1; see also Mieke Bal, *Narratology: Introduction to the Theory of Narrative* (Toronto: University of Toronto Press, 1985).

25 Sonia M. Ospina and Jennifer Dodge, "It's About Time: Catching Method Up to Meaning – The Usefulness of Narrative Inquiry in Public Administration Research," *Public Administration Review* 65, no. 2 (2005): 145.

26 Boas Shamir, Hava Dayan-Horesh, and Dalya Adler, "Leading by Biography: Towards a Life-story Approach to the Study of Leadership," *Leadership* 1, no. 1 (2005): 13.

27 Ospina and Dodge, "It's About Time," 152.

28 Ralph P. Hummel, "Stories Managers Tell: Why They Are as Valid as Science," *Public Administration Review* 51, no. 1 (1991): 33.
29 Steven Maynard-Moody and Michael Musheno, *Cops, Teachers, Counselors: Stories from the Front Lines of Public Service* (Ann Arbor: University of Michigan Press, 2003), 30.
30 Shamir, Dayan-Horesh, and Adler, "Leading by Biography," 13–29.
31 Eugene Lewis, *Public Entrepreneurship: Toward a Theory of Bureaucratic Political Power* (Bloomington: Indiana University Press, 1980).
32 Jameson W. Doig and Erwin C. Hargrove, eds., *Leadership and Innovation: Entrepreneurs in Government* (Baltimore: Johns Hopkins University Press, 1990).
33 Mark H. Moore, *Creating Public Value: Strategic Management in Government* (Cambridge, MA: Harvard University Press, 1995); idem, *Recognizing Public Value* (Cambridge, MA: Harvard University Press, 2013).
34 Michael S. Dukakis and John Portz, *Leader-Managers in the Public Sector: Managing for Results* (Armonk, NY: M.E. Sharpe, 2010).
35 James MacGregor Burns, *Leadership* (New York: Perennial, 1978).
36 Melvin Holli, *The American Mayor: The Best and Worst Big-City Leaders* (State College: Pennsylvania State University, 1999).
37 Leonard D. White, *The City Manager* (New York: Greenwood Press, 1927).
38 Harold A. Stone, Don K. Price, and Kathryn H. Stone, *City Manager Government in the United States* (Chicago: Public Administration Service, 1940); see also Frederick C. Mosher et al., *City Manager Government in Seven Cities* (Chicago: Public Administration Service, 1940).
39 Barbara Kellerman, *Bad Leadership: What It Is, How It Happens, Why It Matters* (Boston: Harvard Business School Press, 2004).
40 A good discussion of the observational approach can be found in Robert S. Bussom, Lars L. Larson, and William M. Vicars, "Unstructured, Nonparticipant Observation and the Study of Leaders' Interpersonal Contacts," in *Leadership: Beyond Establishment Views*, ed. James G. Hunt, Uma Sekaran, and Chester A. Schriesheim (Carbondale: Southern Illinois University Press, 1982), 32.
41 Henry Mintzberg, *The Nature of Managerial Work* (New York: Harper & Row, 1973). He continues this style of generalization from specific cases in his later works; see, for, example, Henry Mintzberg and Jacques Bourgault, *Managing Publicly* (Toronto: Institute of Public Administration of Canada, 2000).
42 Tony J. Watson, *In Search of Management: Culture, Chaos & Control in Managerial Work* (London: Routledge, 1994).
43 Melville Dalton, *Men Who Manage: Fusions of Feeling and Theory in Administration* (New York: John Wiley & Sons, 1959).

44 Jay D. White, *Taking Language Seriously: The Narrative Foundations of Public Administration Research* (Washington, DC: Georgetown University Press, 2007), 48.

45 Borins, *Governing Fables*, 244.

46 August A. De Bard, Jr., "Council-Manager Government in Halifax," *Canadian Public Administration* 3, no. 1 (1960): 76–81.

47 Burns, *Leadership*; Terry L. Cooper and Thomas A. Bryer, "William Robertson: Exemplar of Politics and Public Management Rightly Understood," *Public Administration Review* 67, no. 5 (2007): 816–23; Lewis, *Public Entrepreneurship*. Each edition of the magazine *The Business of Government*, produced by the IBM Center for the Business of Government, contains a number of profiles of leaders and conversations with government leaders, although they are not particularly in-depth.

48 McIntosh, "Defining Situational Leadership."

49 O'Flynn, "Evolving Role of the Municipal Chief Administrative Officer"; Vance, "Managerial Approaches of Chief Administrative Officers."

50 Alexander L. George and Andrew Bennett, *Case Studies and Theory Development in the Social Sciences* (Cambridge, MA: MIT Press, 2005).

51 Gary King, Robert D. Keohane, and Sidney Verba, *Designing Social Inquiry: Scientific Inference in Qualitative Research* (Princeton, NJ: Princeton University Press, 1994).

52 George and Bennett, *Case Studies*.

53 Ibid.

54 Holli, *American Mayor*.

55 Kellerman, *Bad Leadership*, 32ff.

56 Eamon O'Flynn, "A Position in Flux: Municipal CAOs in Canada," *Municipal Monitor* (Spring 2012), 16.

57 David Siegel, "The Leadership Role of the Municipal Chief Administrative Officer," *Canadian Public Administration* 53, no. 2 (2010): 139–61.

58 Henry Mintzberg, "If You're Not Serving Bill and Barbara, Then You're Not Serving Leadership," in Hunt, Sekaran, and Schriesheim, *Leadership*, 239–59.

59 Direct quotations presented throughout this book without attribution come from the interviews.

1. The Leadership Role of the Municipal Chief Administrative Officer

1 Some good summaries of the huge volume of material can be found in Bernard Bass, *Bass and Stogdill's Handbook of Leadership: Theory, Research, and Managerial Applications* (New York: Free Press, 1990); Ralph M. Stogdill, *Handbook of Leadership: A Survey of Theory and Research* (New York: Free

Press, 1974); and Montgomery Van Wart, *Dynamics of Leadership in Public Service: Theory and Practice* (Armonk, NY: M.E. Sharpe, 2005).

2 Very good descriptions of the CAO's position and its evolution in Canada can be found in Plunkett, *City Management in Canada*; and Price, "Council-Administration Relations in City Governments," 193–214.

3 This is really the best comparison because both positions normally function as the head of the public service in their governments, and both have responsibility for a broad range of operating units rather than just one department. For a discussion of the role of the secretary to cabinet, see Jacques Bourgault, "Les facteurs contributifs au leadership du greffier dans la fonction publique du Canada," *Canadian Public Administration* 50, no. 4 (2007): 541–72; Patrice Dutil, ed., *Searching for Leadership: Secretaries to Cabinet in Canada* (Toronto: University of Toronto Press, 2008); and S.L. Sutherland, "The Role of the Clerk of the Privy Council," in *Commission of Inquiry into the Sponsorship Program and Advertising Activities, Phase 2, Restoring Accountability, Research Studies*, vol. 3 (Ottawa: Government of Canada, 2006).

4 Sancton is writing about the mayor, but he discusses many of these differences in "Mayors as Political Leaders," in *Leaders and Leadership in Canada*, ed. Maureen Mancuso, Richard G. Price, and Ronald Wagenberg (Toronto: Oxford University Press, 1994), 174–89.

5 Mouritzen and Svara, *Leadership at the Apex*, 10ff.

6 Sancton, "Mayors as Political Leaders."

7 Donald J. Savoie, *Breaking the Bargain: Public Servants, Ministers, and Parliament* (Toronto: University of Toronto Press, 2003).

8 Ibid., 181, 185.

9 Some very limited exceptions exist to the rule of providing information in public; these vary by province, but are generally related to legal advice, personnel matters, acquisition and disposal of property, and related matters.

10 Henry David Gray, ed., *Thomas Carlyle's On Heroes, Hero-Worship, and the Heroic in History* (New York: Longmans, Green, 1905), 1–2.

11 Van Wart, *Dynamics of Leadership in Public Service*, 78, emphasis in original.

12 Bass, *Bass and Stogdill's Handbook of Leadership*, 75; Ralph M. Stogdill, "Personal Factors Associated with the Study of Leadership: A Survey of the Literature," *Journal of Psychology* 25 (January 1948): 350–71.

13 Joseph C. Rost, *Leadership for the Twenty-First Century* (Westport, CT: Praeger, 1993), 82.

14 Stogdill, "Personal Factors," 39.

15 Thomas J. Peters and Robert H. Waterman, Jr., *In Search of Excellence: Lessons from America's Best-Run Companies* (New York: Harper & Row, 1982).

16 David Collinson, "The Dialectics of Leadership," *Human Relations* 58, no. 11 (2005): 1419–42; idem, "Rethinking Followership: A Post-structuralist Analysis of Follower Identities," *Leadership Quarterly* 17 (April 2006): 179–89; Barbara Kellerman, *Followership: How Followers Are Creating Change and Changing Leaders* (Boston: Harvard Business Press, 2008).

17 Jim Collins, *Good to Great: Why Some Companies Make the Leap … and Others Don't* (New York: Harper Business, 2001), 21, emphasis in original.

18 Ibid., 41.

19 Ibid., 42.

20 David V. Day, Peter Gronn, and Eduardo Salas, "Leadership in Team-based Organizations: On the Threshold of a New Era," *Leadership Quarterly* 17, no. 3 (2006): 211–16.

21 Van Wart, *Dynamics of Leadership in Public Service*.

22 Collinson, "Dialectics of Leadership," 1420.

23 Joyce K. Fletcher and Katrin Käufer, "Shared Leadership: Reframing the Hows and Whys of Leadership," in *Shared Leadership: Reframing the Hows and Whys of Leadership*, ed. Craig L. Pearce and Jay A. Conger (Thousand Oaks, CA: Sage Publications, 2003), 23.

24 Craig L. Pearce and Jay A. Conger, "All Those Years Ago: The Historical Underpinnings of Shared Leadership," in Pearce and Conger, *Shared Leadership*, 2.

25 Larry D. Terry, *Leadership of Public Bureaucracies: The Administrator as Conservator*, 2nd ed. (Armonk, NY: M.E. Sharpe, 2003), 107–32.

26 Pearce and Conger, "All Those Years Ago," 1, reference omitted.

27 Peter Gronn, "Distributed Leadership as a Unit of Analysis," *Leadership Quarterly* 13, no. 4 (2002): 428ff.

28 C. Shawn Burke, Stephen M. Fiore, and Eduardo Salas, "The Role of Shared Cognition in Enabling Shared Leadership and Team Adaptability," in Pearce and Conger, *Shared Leadership*, 103–22.

29 Jeffery D. Houghton, Christopher P. Neck, and Charles C. Manz, "Self-Leadership and Superleadership," in Pearce and Conger, *Shared Leadership*, 125.

30 Charles C. Manz and Henry P. Sims, Jr., *The New Superleadership: Leading Others to Lead Themselves* (San Francisco: Berrett-Koehler, 2001), 228.

31 Charles C. Manz and Henry P. Sims, Jr., "Superleadership: Beyond the Myth of Heroic Leadership," *Organizational Dynamics* 19, no. 4 (1991): 18–35.

32 Burns, *Leadership*, 18, emphasis in original.
33 Robert K. Greenleaf, *Servant Leadership: A Journey into the Nature of Legitimate Power and Greatness* (New York: Paulist Press, 1977), 10, emphasis in original.
34 Ibid., 13–14, emphasis in original.
35 Ibid., 21.
36 Kellerman, *Bad Leadership*, xiv.
37 Kellerman, *End of Leadership*, 1.
38 Kellerman, *Followership*.
39 Joann Keyton, *Communication & Organizational Culture: A Key to Understanding Work Experiences* (Thousand Oaks, CA: Sage Publications, 2005), 17–34.
40 Mats Alvesson, "Organizational Culture: Meaning, Discourse, and Identity," in *The Handbook of Organizational Culture and Climate*, 2nd ed., ed. Neal M. Ashkanasy, Celeste P.M. Wilderom, and Mark F. Peterson (Thousand Oaks, CA: Sage Publications, 2011), 11–28.
41 Edgar H. Schein, *Organizational Culture and Leadership*, 3rd ed. (San Francisco: Jossey-Bass, 2004), 17, emphasis in original.
42 Herbert Kaufman, *The Administrative Behavior of Federal Bureau Chiefs* (Washington, DC: Brookings Institution, 1981), 140.
43 John P. Kotter and James L. Heskett, *Corporate Culture and Performance* (New York: Free Press, 1992), 4.
44 Ibid., 146.
45 Ibid., 11–12 and passim.
46 Sonja M. Sackmann, "Culture and Performance," in Ashkanasy, Wilderom, and Peterson, *Handbook of Organizational Culture and Climate*, 188–224.
47 Schein, *Organizational Culture and Leadership*, 11.
48 Thomas W. Kent, "Leading and Managing: It Takes Two to Tango", *Management Decision* 43, no. 7/8 (2005): 1012.
49 John P. Kotter, "What Leaders Really Do," *Harvard Business Review* 68, no. 3 (1990): 103–4.
50 D. Katz and R.L. Kahn, *The Social Psychology of Organizations*, 2nd ed. (New York: John Wiley, 1978), 528, emphasis in original.
51 Howard Gardner, *Multiple Intelligences* (New York: Basic Books, 2006).
52 John C. Dagley and Shannon K. Salter, "Practice and Research in Career Counseling and Development – 2003," *Career Development Quarterly* 53, no. 2 (2004): 98–157; R.J. Sternberg, *Successful Intelligence: How Practical and Creative Intelligence Determines Success in Life* (New York: Simon & Schuster, 1996).
53 Peter Salovey and John D. Mayer, "Emotional Intelligence," *Imagination, Cognition and Personality* 9, no. 3 (1989–90): 189, emphasis in original.

54 Ibid., 200.
55 Daniel Goleman, *Emotional Intelligence* (New York: Bantam Books, 1995), 43.
56 Ibid., 148.
57 Ibid., 149.
58 Daniel Goleman, "Emotional Intelligence," in *Integrative Learning and Action: A Call to Wholeness*, ed. Susan M. Awbrey, Diane Dana, Vachel W. Miller, Phyllis Robinson, Merle M. Ryan, and David K. Scott (New York: Peter Lang, 2006), 144.
59 Goleman, *Emotional Intelligence*, 56–77.
60 Daniel Goleman, Richard Boyatzis, and Annie McKee, *Primal Leadership: Unleashing the Power of Emotional Intelligence* (Boston: Harvard Business Press, 2013).
61 Ibid., 8.
62 Martina Kotzé and Ian Venter, "Differences in Emotional Intelligence between Effective and Ineffective Leaders in the Public Service: An Empirical Study," *International Review of Administrative Sciences* 77, no. 2 (2011): 397–427.
63 Robert B. Denhardt and Janet V. Denhardt. *The Dance of Leadership: The Art of Leading in Business, Government, and Society* (Armonk, NY: M.E. Sharpe, 2006), 8.
64 Ibid., 10.
65 Fred E. Fiedler and Martin M. Chemers, *Leadership and Effective Management* (Glenview, IL: Scott, Foresman and Company, 1974); Fred E. Fiedler and Joseph E. Garcia, *New Approaches to Effective Leadership* (New York: John Wiley & Sons, 1987); Gary Yukl, *Leadership in Organizations*, 6th ed. (Upper Saddle River, NJ: Pearson Prentice Hall, 2006), chap. 8.
66 McIntosh, "Defining Situational Leadership."
67 Fiedler and Chemers, *Leadership and Effective Management*, 80.
68 Terry, *Leadership of Public Bureaucracies*, 24, emphasis in original.
69 Ibid., 23.
70 Mintzberg, "If You're Not Serving Bill and Barbara," 252–7.
71 Rost, *Leadership for the Twenty-First Century*, 7 and passim.
72 Ibid., 91–5.
73 Ibid., 102–3, emphasis in original.
74 Kotter and Heskett, *Corporate Culture and Performance*, 145–6.
75 Tracey Trottier, Montgomery Van Wart, and XiaoHu Wang, "Examining the Nature and Significance of Leadership in Government Organizations," *Public Administration Review* 68, no. 2 (2008): 319–23.
76 Henry Mintzberg, "Managing on the Edges," in Mintzberg and Bourgault, *Managing Publicly*, 29–51.

77 Kenneth Kernaghan, Brian Marson, and Sandford Borins, *The New Public Organization* (Toronto: Institute of Public Administration of Canada, 2000), 95 and chap. 11; Savoie, *Breaking the Bargain*, 214–15.

78 Mohamed Charih and Lucie Rouillard, "The New Public Management," in *New Public Management and Public Administration in Canada*, ed. Mohamed Charih and Arthur Daniels (Toronto: Institute of Public Administration of Canada, 1997), 27–45.

79 Janet V. Denhardt and Robert B. Denhardt, *The New Public Service: Serving, Not Steering*, expanded ed. (Armonk, NY: M.E. Sharpe, 2007).

80 James Lightbody, *City Politics, Canada* (Peterborough, ON: Broadview Press, 2006), 83.

81 Keith Culver and Paul Howe, "Calling All Citizens: The Challenges of Public Consultation," *Canadian Public Administration* 47, no. 1 (2004): 52–76; Katherine A. Graham and Susan D. Philips, eds., *Citizen Engagement: Lessons in Participation from Local Government* (Toronto: Institute of Public Administration of Canada, 1998), 13, 235–6, and passim; Matt Leighninger, *The Next Form of Democracy* (Nashville, TN: Vanderbilt University Press, 2008).

82 Denhardt and Denhardt, *New Public Service.*

83 Nalbandian, *Professionalism in Local Government*, 54.

84 Laurence Rutter, *The Essential Community: Local Government in the Year 2000* (Washington, DC: International City Management Association, 1980), 133.

85 Mouritzen and Svara, *Leadership at the Apex*, 140.

86 Karl A. Bosworth, "The Manager *Is* a Politician," *Public Administration Review* 18, no. 3 (1958): 219–20.

87 James H. Svara, "Dichotomy and Duality: Reconceptualizing the Relationship between Policy and Administration in Council-Manager Cities," in *Ideal & Practice in Council-Manager Government*, ed. H. George Frederickson (Washington, DC: International City/County Management Association, 1989), 56–7. See also Frank Marini, ed., *Toward a New Public Administration: The Minnowbrook Perspective* (New York: Chandler, 1971).

88 As quoted in Nalbandian, *Professionalism in Local Government*, 91.

89 There seems to be convincing evidence that many municipal councils are not representative; see, for example, Caroline Andrew, John Biles, Myer Siemiatycki, and Erin Tolley, eds., *Electing A Diverse Canada* (Vancouver: UBC Press, 2008).

90 Nalbandian, *Professionalism in Local Government*, 74–5, 90–1.

91 Robert D. Behn, "What Right Do Public Managers Have to Lead?" *Public Administration Review* 58, no. 3 (1998), 212.

92 Terry, *Leadership of Public Bureaucracies.*

93 Michael Useem, *Leading Up: How to Lead Your Boss So You Both Win* (New York: Crown Business, 2001).

94 Denhardt and Denhardt, *New Public Service*, chap. 4.

95 Jack Masson, *Alberta's Local Governments: Politics and Democracy*, with Edward C. LeSage Jr. (Edmonton: University of Alberta Press, 1994), 229–30.

96 Quoted in Mouritzen and Svara, *Leadership at the Apex*, 114.

97 Lightbody, *City Politics*, 149.

98 Mouritzen and Svara, *Leadership at the Apex*, 10.

99 Masson, *Alberta's Local Governments*, 221–2.

100 Ibid., 233–4.

101 Peter Self, *Administrative Theories and Politics*, 2nd ed. (London: George Allen & Unwin, 1972), 150–1, emphasis in original.

102 Robert D. Putnam, "The Political Attitudes of Senior Civil Servants in Britain, Germany, and Italy," in *The Mandarins of Western Europe: The Political Role of Top Civil Servants*, ed. Mattei Dogan (New York: John Wiley & Sons, 1975). Klausen and Magnier have applied these concepts of the local level; see "Anonymous Leader," 23.

103 Putnam, "Political Attitudes," 90.

104 Ibid.

105 Quotation from interview with a US city manager in Mouritzen and Svara, *Leadership at the Apex*, 110.

106 Self, *Administrative Theories and Politics*, 151.

107 Mouritzen and Svara, *Leadership at the Apex*, 108.

108 Mintzberg, "Managing on the Edges," 49.

109 Available online at http://www.camacam.ca/about_sov.asp, accessed 8 September 2012.

110 Gordon Robertson, "The Changing Role of the Privy Council Office," *Canadian Public Administration* 14, no. 4 (1971): 506.

2. The Leader-Generalist: Michael Fenn

1 The *Hamilton Spectator* also covers news in Burlington. In the early years of the period reviewed, there was a separate newspaper called the *Burlington Spectator*, which included much of the same content as the *Hamilton Spectator*, but with several pages of Burlington news. In later years the two separate papers were folded into the *Hamilton Spectator*, which included several pages devoted to Burlington news.

2 Donald R. Keating, *The Power to Make It Happen* (Toronto: Green Tree Publishing, 1975), 84, 89, and 106.

3 Michael Fenn, "Building Effective Council-Staff Relations," *Municipal World* 113, no. 4 (2003): 17–22; idem, "Emerging Trends in Urban Affairs – A Municipal Manager's View," in *Urban Affairs: Back on the Policy Agenda*, ed. Caroline Andrew, Katherine A. Graham, and Susan D. Phillips (Montreal; Kingston, ON: McGill-Queen's University Press, 2003), 289–302; idem, "Future Focus: Burlington's Strategic Planning Success," *Canadian Public Administration* 32, no. 2 (1988): 304–10; idem, "Reinvigorating Publicly Funded Medicare in Ontario: New Policy and Public Administration Techniques," *Canadian Public Administration* 49, no. 4 (2006): 527–47.
4 Available online at http://estat.statcan.gc.ca/cgi-win/cnsmcgi. pgm?Lang=E&ESTATFile=ESTAT/ENGLISH/SC_RR-eng.htm, accessed 16 May 2013.
5 An "edge city" sits on the edge of another larger city, but is in the process of moving from a bedroom community to a full-fledged city in its own right. See Joel Garreau, *Edge City: Life on the New Frontier* (New York: Doubleday, 1991).
6 When Fenn was appointed, the title of the position was chief administrative officer; it was later changed to city manager. For purposes of simplicity, I use CAO throughout this chapter.
7 Dan Nolan, "HECFI readies itself for new superboss," *Hamilton Spectator*, 22 July 1989; Eric McGuiness, "Superboss hunt process derailed by committee," *Hamilton Spectator*, 25 July 1989; "Macaluso is superboss after 11-6 vote," *Hamilton Spectator*, 26 July 1989.
8 Ken Peters, "Death knell for region?" *Hamilton Spectator*, 2 October 1996; Ted McMeekin, "Scrap the region," *Hamilton Spectator*, 3 October 1996.
9 Jim Poling, "Cooke calls for one-tier government," *Hamilton Spectator*, 30 September 1994; Editorial, "Terry Cooke offers energy and vision," *Hamilton Spectator*, 5 November 1994; Jim Poling, "Policing, reform are top priorities, Cooke vows," *Hamilton Spectator*, 15 November 1994.
10 Available online at http://estat.statcan.gc.ca/cgi-win/cnsmcgi.pgm?Lang= E&ESTATFile=ESTAT/ENGLISH/SC_RR-eng.htm, accessed 17 May 2013.
11 David Osborne and Ted Gaebler, *Reinventing Government: How the Entrepreneurial Spirit Is Transforming the Public Sector* (New York: Plume, 1992).
12 Fenn, "Future Focus," 304–10.

3. The Task-oriented Leader: Mike Garrett

1 Richard Yerema, "Top 100," *Maclean's*, 15 October 2007.
2 Available online at http://estat.statcan.gc.ca/cgi-win/cnsmcgi.pgm?Lang= E&ESTATFile=ESTAT/ENGLISH/SC_RR-eng.htm, accessed 17 May 2013.

3 See Garreau, *Edge City*.
4 This era is chronicled well in Tom Urbaniak, *Her Worship: Hazel McCallion and the Development of Mississauga* (Toronto: University of Toronto Press, 2009).
5 David Lewis Stein, "GTA roads crumble while Tories dodge responsibility," *Toronto Star*, 24 July 1996, A21.
6 John Barber, "Toronto suburban commando megacity mandarin," *Globe and Mail*, 16 October 1997, A12; Mike Funston and Brian Dexter, "Golden under attack over 'errors' on taxes," *Toronto Star*, 23 February 1996, A6.
7 Mike Funston, "Tax freeze likely for ratepayers: Lack of debt helps Peel absorb provincial cuts," *Toronto Star*, 25 January 1996, BR1.
8 Urbaniak, *Her Worship*.
9 http://estat.statcan.gc.ca/cgi-win/cnsmcgi.pgm?Lang=E&ESTATFile= ESTAT/ENGLISH/SC_RR-eng.htm, accessed 17 May 2013.
10 The earliest year available on the provincial Web site that captures this information is 2002; see http://csconramp.mah.gov.on.ca/fir/ViewFIR2002. htm#1999, accessed 19 May 2013.
11 The acrimony around this decision has been captured in a number of venues. See, for example, Julie-Ann Boudreau, *The Megacity Saga* (Montreal: Black Rose Books, 2000); and Martin Horak, "The Power of Local Identity: C4LD and the Anti-amalgamation Mobilization in Toronto," Research Paper 195 (Toronto: University of Toronto, Centre for Urban and Community Studies, 1998).
12 The contentious nature of the amalgamation decision and the precarious status of the transition team are well described in Boudreau, *Megacity Saga*.
13 Michael Grange, "Hold the hiring, Toronto councillors urge: Group tells Lastman, transition team to let new council decide bureaucratic structure," *Globe and Mail*, 28 November 1997, A9.
14 Don Wanagas, "Personnel management, Mel-style: Nothing is as it appears at City Hall," *National Post,* 30 June 2001.
15 Toronto Computer Leasing Inquiry: Toronto External Contracts Inquiry, *Report*, vol. 1, *Facts and Findings*, Hon. Madam Justice Denise E. Bellamy, Commissioner (Toronto, 2005), 43.
16 James Rusk, "Lastman had little patience for duties of office, former civil servant testifies," *Globe and Mail*, 6 December 2002, A29.
17 Toronto Computer Leasing Inquiry, 271.
18 Kim Honey, "1,600 could lose jobs, Lastman says: Mayor seeks consultant to assist with layoffs necessary to make tax-freeze promise possible," *Globe and Mail*, 20 January 1998, S8; John Spears, "City plans to hire consultants," *Toronto Star*, 20 January 1998, D3.

19 Toronto Computer Leasing Inquiry, 45.
20 James Rusk, "Treasurer resigns; move called 'serious blow' for city," *Globe and Mail*, 8 May 2001, A20.
21 Toronto Computer Leasing Inquiry, 78, 81, 93.
22 Don Wanagas, "Council sacked the wrong guy: Mayor Lastman, not chief accountant, deserved axe for MFP," *National Post*, 6 December 2002, A18.
23 Royson James, "Bad timing leads to lost money, lost confidence," *Toronto Star*, 27 June 2001, B01; James Rusk, "Motion to fire city official awaits vote," *Globe and Mail*, 27 June 2001, A14.
24 Don Wanagas, "Decision-making mocked, angry councillors say: Politicians told of sacking before council held debatè," *National Post*, 28 June 2001, A20.
25 Royson James, "Next to Garrett, mayor, council look spineless," *Toronto Star*, 4 June 2001, B01; Paul Moloney, "Council makes CAO's firing official," *Toronto Star*, 28 June 2001, B03.
26 James Rusk, "Toronto tax freeze means cut in services: Budget plan would end twice-weekly garbage pickup in North York," *Globe and Mail*, 23 February 1999, A1; "City budget ritual off to good start," *Toronto Star*, 27 February 1999, 1; "The new Toronto: making it work," *Toronto Star*, 2 August 1999, 1.
27 Paul Moloney, "Council makes CAO's firing official," *Toronto Star*, 28 June 2001, B03.
28 Wanagas, "Personnel management, Mel-style"; Royson James, "City administrator joins the exodus," *Toronto Star*, 26 June 2001, B01; Moloney, "Council makes CAO's firing official."
29 Toronto Computer Leasing Inquiry, 58.
30 Mike Garrett, testimony before the Toronto Computer Leasing Inquiry, 2 December 2002, 8–9; available online at http://mail.tscript.com/trans/toronto/dec_05_02/index.htm, accessed 16 March 2011.
31 Available online at http://estat.statcan.gc.ca/cgi-win/cnsmcgi.pgm?Lang=E&ESTATFile=ESTAT/ENGLISH/SC_RR-eng.htm, accessed 17 May 2013.
32 Ontario, Ministry of Municipal affairs and Housing, "Financial Information Return 2007 Data – by Municipality"; available online at http://cscon ramp.mah.gov.on.ca/fir/ViewFIR2007.htm, accessed 19 May 2013.
33 Toronto Computer Leasing Inquiry, 270.
34 Ibid., 175, 182, 272, 277, 358, 375.
35 Ibid., 271.
36 Greater Toronto Area Task Force, *Greater Toronto: Report of the GTA Task Force*, Anne Golden, chair (Toronto: Queen's Printer, 1996).

4. The Relationship-oriented Leader: Judy Rogers

1 See Women's Executive Network, "Canada's Most Powerful Women: Top 100 – Overview"; available online at http://www.top100women.ca/?w= winners, accessed 11 August 2011.
2 "Kudos," *Vancouver Sun*, 3 December 2007.
3 Emmanuel Brunet-Jailly, "Vancouver: The Sustainable City," *Journal of Urban Affairs* 30, no. 4 (2008): 385.
4 See Canada's Top 100 Employers; available online at http://www.canada stop100.com/national/, accessed 7 September 2011.
5 Available online at http://estat.statcan.gc.ca/cgi-win/cnsmcgi.pgm?Lang= E&ESTATFile=ESTAT/ENGLISH/SC_RR-eng.htm, accessed 17 May 2013.
6 Mike Harcourt and Ken Cameron, *City Making in Paradise: Nine Decisions that Saved Vancouver*, with Sean Rossiter (Vancouver: Douglas & McIntyre, 2007); John Punter, *The Vancouver Achievement: Urban Planning and Design* (Vancouver: UBC Press, 2003).
7 Vancouver's proportion of the total in 2011 was 26.1 per cent, down from 27.5 per cent in 2001; see http://www.metrovancouver.org/about/publi cations/Publications/Census2011PopulationGrowthTrends.pdf, accessed 4 May 2012.
8 Brunet-Jailly, "Vancouver," 379.
9 Donald Gutstein, "Vancouver," in Magnusson and Sancton, *City Politics in Canada*, 189–221; Kennedy Stewart, *Think Democracy: Options for Local Democratic Reform in Vancouver* (Vancouver: Simon Fraser University, Institute of Governance Studies, n.d.); Paul Tennant, "Vancouver Politics and the Civic Party System," in *Problems of Change in Urban Government*, ed. M.O. Dickerson, S. Drabek, and J.T. Woods (Waterloo, ON: Wilfrid Laurier University Press, 1980), 13–37; and Donna Vogel, *Challenging Politics: COPE, Electoral Politics and Social Movements* (Halifax, NS: Fernwood Publishing, 2003).
10 Frances Bula, "The anatomy of Sam Sullivan's downfall; 'In all my political years, I've never seen anyone fall from grace like that,' a former NPA councillor says," *Vancouver Sun*, 14 June 2008, A6; Alex Tsakumis, "Where's the Sam we voted for? Ten months ago, an energized and lucid Sam Sullivan took control of this city by storm. Since then, hopes for him and his vision have just trickled away," editorial, *Vancouver Sun*, 26 September 2006, A19.
11 Vision Vancouver, "A Vision for Vancouver: Bringing Leadership and Action to City Hall" (Vancouver, n.d.), 11; available online at http://www. votevision.ca/sites/all/files/vision_platform_web.pdf, accessed 15 August 2011.

12 Jeff Lee, "Dismissed city manager fears more jobs in peril; Mayor Robertson says he wanted to send signal, not clean house," *Vancouver Sun*, 13 December 2008, A.6.

13 Frances Bula, "One Tough Broad," *Vancouver Magazine*, 1 October 2008.

14 Available online at http://vancouver.ca/hastingsinstitute/index.htm, accessed 4 August 2011.

15 Bula, "One Tough Broad."

16 Vancouver Agreement, available online at http://www.vancouveragree
ment.ca/the-agreement/, accessed 4 August 2011; Michael Mason, "Collaborative Partnerships for Urban Development: A Study of the Vancouver
Agreement," Research Papers in Environmental and Spatial Analysis 208
(London: London School of Economics, 2006), available online at http://
www.lse.ac.uk/geographyAndEnvironment/research/Researchpapers/
108%20Mason.pdf, accessed 5 August 2011; "The Vancouver Agreement,"
in *Inclusion, Collaboration and Urban Governance: Brazilian and Canadian
Experiences*, org. Hugh Kellas (Vancouver: University of British Columbia,
Centre for Human Settlements, 2010), 99–110, available online at http://
www.chs.ubc.ca/consortia/outputs3/NPCBook-Brazilian_and_Canadian_
Experiences.pdf, accessed 4 August 2011.

17 Missing Women Commission of Inquiry, "Issues Related to the Structure and Organization of Policing Arising from the Missing Women
Investigation" (Vancouver, April 2012), available online at http://www.
missingwomeninquiry.ca/wp-content/uploads/2010/10/Issues-related-
to-the-structure-and-organization-of-policing-arising-from-the-missing-
women-investigations.pdf, accessed 4 May 2012.

18 Andrew Graham, "Case Study: The Vancouver Agreement," available
online at http://post.queensu.ca/~grahama/case_studies/VANAGREE
MENTCASE-1.pdf, accessed 5 August 2011.

19 Robert Enright, ed., *Body Heat: The Story of the Woodward's Redevelopment*
(Vancouver: Blueimprint, 2010); Craig McInnes, "City buys Woodward's
site," *Vancouver Sun*, 30 January 2003, A4.

20 Larry Campbell, Neil Boyd, and Lori Culbert, *A Thousand Dreams: Vancouver's Downtown Eastside and the Fight for Its Future* (Vancouver: Grey Stone
Books, 2009).

21 Carmen Chai, "Proof of Insite's value in the numbers," *Vancouver Sun*,
18 April 2011, B1; Peter McKnight, "Will dramatic drop in overdose deaths
be enough to save Insite?" *Vancouver Sun*, 18 April 2011, A3; Chris Johnson,
"Injection saving lives, says official," *Vancouver Sun*, 21 September 2004, B1.

22 Vancouver Agreement, "Vancouver Agreement wins United Nations
award," media advisory, 6 May 2005, available online at http://www.

vancouveragreement.ca/wp-content/uploads/050506_ADVISORYUN
Award.pdf, accessed 4 August 2011.

23 City of Vancouver, available online at http://vancouver.ca/commsvcs/
housing/sra/pdf/statement.pdf, accessed 9 August 2011.

24 Miro Cernetig and Derrick Penner, "Olympic village shock; taxpayers
could be on the hook for hundreds of millions to guarantee loan," *Vancouver Sun*, 9 January 2009, A1; KPMG, "Summary Report to the City of Vancouver, Southeast False Creek Development" (Vancouver, 19 January 2009),
available online at http://vancouver.ca/ctyclerk/cclerk/20091006/docu
ments/RR1KPMGreport.pdf, accessed 9 August 2011; Jeff Lee and Derrick
Penner, "An athletes' village project primer," *Vancouver Sun*, 8 November
2008, A5; Katie Mercer, "Olympic Village way over budget; athletes' housing already faces extra expenses of $60m to $65m," *Province*, 7 October
2008, A3.

25 Jeff Lee, "City officials stay silent on reported loan; municipal finance manager rumoured to have resigned over concerns about athletes' village,"
Vancouver Sun, 7 November 2008, A9; Christina Montgomery and Damian
Inwood, "Make secret deal public, council told," *Province*, 7 November
2008, A3.

26 Stuart Hunter, "Rogers out, Ballem in as city manager; auditor KPMG to
undertake review of Olympic village development," *Province*, 14 December 2008, A32; Jeff Lee, "Dismissed city manager fears more jobs in peril;
Mayor Robertson says he wanted to send signal, not clean house," *Vancouver Sun*, 13 December 2008, A6.

27 "Soundoffs; Vancouversun.com readers weigh in on Gregor Robertson's
decision to replace city manager Judy Rogers," *Vancouver Sun*, 13 December 2008, A7.

28 YWCA Metro Vancouver, "Crabtree Corner," available online at http://
www.ywcavan.org/content/Crabtree_Corner/258, accessed 14 August
2011.

29 O'Flynn, "Evolving Role of the Municipal Chief Administrative Officer," 59.

30 Brunet-Jailly, "Vancouver," 384.

31 Kenneth Kernaghan, "Politics, Policy, and Public Servants: Political Neutrality Revisited," *Canadian Public Administration* 19, no. 3 (1976): 432–56;
David Siegel, "Politics, Politicians, and Public Servants in Non-Partisan
Local Government," *Canadian Public Administration* 37, no. 1 (1994): 17–30.

32 Campbell, Boyd, and Culbert, *Thousand Dreams*. The four pillars of the
Vancouver drug strategy are prevention, treatment, harm reduction, and
enforcement. For more information, see: http://vancouver.ca/people-
programs/four-pillars-drug-strategy.aspx, accessed 23 July 2014.

5. The Leader as Partnership Builder: Keith Robicheau

1 Association of Municipal Administrators, Nova Scotia, "Keith Robicheau wins AMANS Award of Excellence," available online at http://www. amans.ca/index.php?/membership/2006-recipient.html, accessed 23 November 2011.

2 Statistics Canada, *1981 Census of Canada: Population, Occupied Private Dwellings, Private Households, Census Families in Private Households: Volume 2*, Cat. 93-916 (Ottawa: Statistics Canada), 2-1.

3 Interviewees were not certain of the exact title. The previous incumbent might have held the title of town manager by the end of his tenure, but there was an understanding that he did not fill this role in reality.

4 Statistics Canada, *Population and Dwelling Counts – Census Divisions and Census Subdivisions*, Cat. 93-304 (Ottawa: Statistics Canada), 22.

5 Nova Scotia, *Annual Report of Municipal Statistics for the fiscal year April 1, 2007–March 31, 2008* (Halifax: Service Nova Scotia and Municipal Relations, 2008), available online at http://www.novascotia.ca/dma/pdf/mun-2008-annual-report-of-municipal-statistics.pdf, accessed 12 May 2013.

6 The warden is the head of a county council. The position differs from a mayor in that the warden is selected by county council members from among their number, but in terms of roles and responsibilities it is otherwise equivalent.

7 Carolyn Sloan, "Setting the bar," *Spectator* (Annapolis County), 22 July 2008. The precise figures for this year could not be obtained and recollections of the exact amounts differed, but interviewees remembered that the county's reserve was then worrisomely low.

8 Available online at http://www.gov.ns.ca/snsmr/muns/info/pdf/NS_Report_2008.pdf, accessed 30 November 2011.

9 "Forces closed efficient bases," *Toronto Star*, 9 January 1995, A9.

10 Kevin Cox, "Prayer, rumours abound as town hangs in limbo," *Globe and Mail*, 2 January 1993.

11 Kevin Cox, "Defunct CFB Cornwallis gets new lease on life; community once dependent upon military base now boasts diversified business," *Globe and Mail*, 16 September 2003, B11.

12 Nova Scotia, Environment, "Solid Waste-Resource Management Strategy" (Halifax), available online at http://www.gov.ns.ca/nse/waste/swrmstrategy.asp, accessed 26 November 2011.

13 Town of Kentville, "Consolidated Financial Statements, December 31, 2011," available online at http://kentville.ca/wp-content/uploads/2012/12/financialstatements2011.pdf, accessed 12 May 2013.

14 Kirk Starratt, "Friends, colleagues bid fond farewell to retiring Kentville CAO," *Kings County Advertiser*, 11 July 2008.

15 Jennifer Hoegg, "Kentville frustrated with county tactics in education case," *Kings County Advertiser*, 20 January 2010.

16 "Mayor, MLA excited over new Kentville school announcement," *Kings County Advertiser*, 12 February 2009.

17 Jennifer Hoegg, "KCA concerns mount as move-in day nears," *Kings County Advertiser*, 8 February 2011.

18 Kirk Starratt, "Paid Kentville fire chief back on county agenda," *Kings County Advertiser*, 26 October 2009.

6. "I think I'm a better employee when I love the community I'm living in": Robert Earl

1 Population from the 1996 census, available online at http://www12.stat can.ca/english/census96/data/profiles/Rp-eng.cfm?TABID=1&LANG= E&APATH=3&DETAIL=0&DIM=0&FL=A&FREE=0&GC=0&GK=0&GRP= 1&PID=35782&PRID=0&PTYPE=3&S=0&SHOWALL=0&SUB=0&Tempo ral=1996&THEME=34&VID=0&VNAMEE=&VNAMEF=, accessed 12 June 2012.

2 City of Prince Rupert, "Prince Rupert and Port Edward, British Columbia, Canada: Investment-Ready Community Profile," available online at http:// investnorthwestbc.ca/uploads/Prince%20Rupert%20and%20Port%20 Edward%20-%20Investment%20Ready%20Community%20Profile%20 Draft.pdf, accessed 12 June 2012.

3 Statistics Canada, "Census Profile: Port Edward, British Columbia," available online at http://www12.statcan.ca/census-recensement/2011/dp-pd/ prof/details/page.cfm?Lang=E&Geo1=CSD&Code1=5947007&Geo2=CD& Code2=5947&Data=Count&SearchText=port%20edward&SearchType=Beg ins&SearchPR=59&B1=All&Custom=&TABID=1, accessed 12 June 2012.

4 Statistics Canada, "Census Profile: Invermere, British Columbia," available online at http://www12.statcan.ca/english/profil01/CP01/Details/Page. cfm?Lang=E&Geo1=CSD&Code1=5901039&Geo2=PR&Code2=59&Data= Count&SearchText=invermere&SearchType=Begins&SearchPR=59&B1= All&Custom=, accessed 12 June 2012.

5 Available online at http://www.invermere.net/about/invermere.htm, accessed 12 June 2012.

6 Available online at http://www.fairmont.com/bsh/hotelhistory, accessed 13 June 2012.

7 Town of Banff, "Consolidated Financial Statements of the Town of Banff, December 31, 2011," available online at http://www.banff.ca/Document Center/View/170, accessed 12 May 2013.

8 Statistics Canada, "Census Profile: Banff, Alberta," available online at http://www12.statcan.ca/census-recensement/2011/dp-pd/prof/details/page.cfm?Lang=E&Geo1=CSD&Code1=4815035&Geo2=CD&Code2=4815&Data=Count&SearchText=banff&SearchType=Begins&SearchPR=48&B1=All&Custom=&TABID=1, accessed 12 June 2012.

9 Grady Semmens, "Rising park fees raising temperatures: Banff desperately needs to find more sources of money," *Calgary Herald*, 10 April 2005.

10 Correspondence from Robert Earl, 2 August 2012.

11 Cathy Ellis, "Parks files appeal on law office," *Rocky Mountain Outlook* (Banff), 10 May 2012.

12 "Town to chase options for Banff Refreshing," *Crag and Canyon* (Banff), 14 February 2006; "Summer construction must be considered," *Crag and Canyon*, 12 September 2006.

13 "Advice giver happy with higher spending," *Crag and Canyon*, 16 January 2007; "Marketing plan set to lure in tourists," *Crag and Canyon*, 20 March 2007.

14 "To borrow or not to borrow," *Rocky Mountain Outlook*, 23 November 2006.

15 "Stutz wins by acclamation," *Crag and Canyon*, 18 September 2007.

16 Available online at http://www.albertaconstructionmagazine.com/topprojects.aspx?page=RULES, accessed 19 June 2012.

17 Town of Banff, media release, 28 May 2008, available online at http://www.banff.ca/news-room/media-releases/2008-archive/roam-banff.htm, accessed 19 June 2012.

18 Town of Banff, *2011 Town of Banff Service Review* (Banff, AB), 52, available online at https://www.banff.ca/DocumentCenter/View/650, accessed 26 June 2012.

19 Available online at http://www.banff.ca/Assets/PDFs/Locals+PDF/bvta-business-plan-100330.pdf, accessed 13 June 2012.

20 Available online at http://industry.travelalberta.com/Events/Alto%20Awards.aspx, accessed 19 June 2012.

21 Cathy Ellis, "Banff paying off debt," *Rocky Mountain Outlook*, 10 May 2012.

22 "2011 Competitiveness Initiative: Final Report," 29 August 2011, 3; available online https://dl.dropbox.com/u/36433245/Competitive%20Initiative%20Report/Final%20Report%20August%2029%2C%202011.pdf, accessed 12 July 2012.

23 Ibid.

24 Larissa Barlow, "Banff getting app for parking," *Crag and Canyon* 16 May 2012.

25 Town of Banff, "Town of Banff Service Review 2011."
26 "Water warning well done in Banff," *Crag and Canyon*, 14 March 2006, 18.
27 Dave Husdal, "Bikers recall finding bike and hearing injured victim," *Crag and Canyon*, 16 May 2006.

Conclusion

1 Bass, *Bass and Stogdill's Handbook of Leadership*; Stogdill, *Handbook of Leadership*; Van Wart, *Dynamics of Leadership in Public Service*.
2 Gray, *Thomas Carlyle's On Heroes*, 189; emphasis in original.
3 Kellerman, *Followership*, 11–12.
4 Graham White, "Big Is Different from Little: On Taking Size Seriously in the Analysis of Canadian Governmental Institutions," *Canadian Public Administration* 33, no. 4 (1990): 526–50.
5 City of Vancouver, "Organization Chart," available online at http://van couver.ca/citymanager/, accessed 23 March 2012.
6 David N. Ammons and Charldean Newell, *City Executives: Leadership Roles, Work Characteristics, and Time Management* (Albany: State University of New York Press, 1989).
7 McIntosh, "Defining Situational Leadership," 301.
8 Vance, "Managerial Approaches of Chief Administrative Officers," 262–3.
9 Putnam, "Political Attitudes," 87–127.
10 Mark H. Moore provides a very extensive and insightful treatment of this issue in *Creating Public Value*, 297–309 and passim.
11 Neil Collins, *Local Government Managers at Work* (Dublin: Institute of Public Administration, 1987).
12 Terry, *Leadership of Public Bureaucracies*.
13 Moore, *Creating Public Value*, 148.
14 Institute of Public Administration of Canada, "The IPAC Statement of Principles Regarding the Conduct of Public Employees (1987)" (Toronto: IPAC, 1987), available online at http://www.ipac.ca/OurPrinciples, accessed 8 September 2012.
15 Available online at http://www.camacam.ca/about_sov.asp, accessed 8 September 2012.
16 American Society for Public Administration, "ASPA Code of Ethics" (Washington, DC: ASPA, 2012), available online at http://www.aspanet. org/public/ASPA/Resources/Code_of_Ethics/ASPA/Resources/Code_ of_Ethics/Code_of_Ethics1.aspx?hkey=acd40318-a945-4ffc-ba7b-18e037b1 a858, accessed 10 September 2012.
17 Mouritzen and Svara, *Leadership at the Apex*.
18 McIntosh, "Defining Situational Leadership," 330.

19 O'Flynn finds a similar tendency in his survey of CAOs; see "Evolving Role of the Municipal Chief Administrative Officer," 87.
20 White, "Big Is Different from Little."
21 McIntosh, "Defining Situational Leadership," 296; for other differences, see 300, 303–5, 308.
22 David R. Morgan and Sheilah S. Watson, "Policy Leadership in Council-Manager Cities: Comparing Mayor and Manager," *Public Administration Review* 52, no. 5 (1992): 438–46.
23 White, "Big Is Different from Little," 546.
24 Van Wart, *Dynamics of Leadership in Public Service*, 292.
25 Denhardt and Denhardt, *Dance of Leadership*.
26 Herbert A. Simon, *Administrative Behavior: A Study of Decision-Making Processes in Administrative Organizations*, 3rd ed. (New York: Free Press, 1976), 36.
27 McIntosh, "Defining Situational Leadership," 233–4.
28 James M. Kouzes and Barry Z. Posner, *The Leadership Challenge*, 3rd ed. (San Francisco: Jossey-Bass, 2002), 27–8. Other studies have produced similar findings; see, for example, Elizabeth Thach and Karen J. Thompson, "Trading Places: Examining leadership competencies between For-profit vs. Public and Non-profit Leaders," *Leadership & Organization Development Journal* 28, no. 4 (2007): 363.
29 Warren Bennis, *On Becoming a Leader* (Reading, MA: Addison-Wesley, 1989), 98.
30 Burns, *Leadership*, 115; Arthur M. Schlesinger, Jr., *The Politics of Upheaval* (Boston: Houghton Mifflin, 1960), chap. 21 and passim; Jean Edward Smith, *FDR* (New York: Random House, 2007), chap. 17 and passim. Montgomery Van Wart suggests that George Washington falls in the same category of someone who experienced many failures, but persevered and became a great leader; see *Dynamics of Leadership in Public Service*, 473–5.
31 Works of Franklin D. Roosevelt, Address at Oglethorpe University, 22 May 1932, available online at http://newdeal.feri.org/speeches/1932d.htm, accessed 26 July 2012.
32 Warren Bennis and Burt Nanus, *Leaders: The Strategies for Taking Charge* (New York: Harper & Row, 1985), 69ff.
33 Thach and Thompson, "Trading Places," 365.
34 Bennis, *On Becoming a Leader*, 40, emphasis in original.
35 Collins, *Good to Great*, 72.
36 Ibid., 27, emphasis in original.
37 Mouritzen and Svara, *Leadership at the Apex*, 140.
38 McIntosh, "Defining Situational Leadership," 299.

39 Collins, *Local Government Managers at Work*, 7–8.
40 Van Wart, *Dynamics of Leadership in Public Service*, 261.
41 Mats Alvesson and Stefan Sveningsson, "Managers Doing Leadership: The Extra-Ordinarization of the Mundane," *Human Relations* 56, no. 12 (2003): 1435–59.
42 Siegel, "Politics, Politicians, and Public Servants."
43 Bill George, *Authentic Leadership: Rediscovering the Secrets to Creating Lasting Value* (San Francisco: Jossey-Bass, 2003), 12–14.
44 McIntosh, "Defining Situational Leadership," 210 and passim.
45 Ibid., 317.
46 Bennis, *On Becoming a Leader*, 41.
47 Kouzes and Posner, *Leadership Challenge*, 16.
48 Albert J. Dunlap, *Mean Business: How I Save Bad Companies and Make Good Companies Great*, with Bob Andelman (New York: Random House, 1996). A broader discussion of this phenomenon is found in Kotter and Heskett, *Corporate Culture and Performance*, 94ff.
49 Moore, *Creating Public Value*, 292.
50 Kouzes and Posner, *Leadership Challenge*, 387.
51 Collins, *Good to Great*.
52 Ibid., 26.
53 Greenleaf, *Servant Leadership*, 13–14; emphasis in original.
54 Kellerman, *Bad Leadership*, 234, emphasis in original; footnote omitted.
55 Kouzes and Posner, *Leadership Challenge*, 386.
56 Kellerman, *End of Leadership*, 154, 177.
57 Ibid., 169, 172, 183.
58 Ibid., 168.
59 Denhardt and Denhardt, *Dance of Leadership*, 168.
60 Van Wart, *Dynamics of Leadership in Public Service*, 430.
61 Bernard Barber, "Some Problems in the Sociology of Professions," *Daedalus* 92 (1963): 669–88; Morris L. Cogan, "The Problem of Defining a Profession," *Annals* 297 (1955): 105–11; idem, "Toward a Definition of Profession," *Harvard Educational Review* 23 (1953): 33–50; Abraham Flexner, "Is Social Work a Profession?" *School and Society* 1 (1915): 901–11; Corrine Gibb, *Hidden Hierarchies* (New York: Harper & Row, 1966); Everett C. Hughes, "Professions," *Daedalus* 92 (1963): 655–68; idem, "The Professions in Society," *Canadian Journal of Economics and Political Science* 26, no. 1 (1960): 54–61; Ontario, Professional Organizations Committee, *Report* (Toronto: Ministry of the Attorney General, 1980).
62 Louis Brownlow, *A Passion for Anonymity: The Autobiography of Louis Brownlow* (Chicago: University of Chicago Press, 1958).

63 LeRoy F. Harlow, *Without Fear or Favor: Odyssey of a City Manager* (Provo, UT: Brigham Young University Press, 1977).

64 Bill Gilbert, *This City, This Man: The Cookingham Era in Kansas City* (Washington, DC: International City Management Association, 1978).

65 Jocelyne Bourgon, *A New Synthesis of Public Administration: Serving in the 21st Century* (Montreal; Kingston, ON: McGill-Queen's University Press, 2011); Robert B. Bryce, *Maturing in Hard Times: Canada's Department of Finance through the Great Depression* (Montreal; Kingston, ON: McGill-Queen's University Press, 1986); Ole Ingstrup and Paul Crookall, *The Three Pillars of Public Management: Secrets of Sustained Success* (Montreal; Kingston, ON: McGill-Queen's University Press, 1998); Gordon F. Osbaldeston, *Keeping Deputy Ministers Accountable* (Toronto: McGraw-Hill Ryerson, 1989).

66 Gordon Robertson, *Memoirs of a Very Civil Servant: Mackenzie King to Pierre Trudeau* (Toronto: University of Toronto Press, 2000).

67 Crawford, *Canadian Municipal Government*.

68 Edward Glaeser, *Triumph of the City: How Our Greatest Invention Makes Us Richer, Smarter, Greener, Healthier, and Happier* (New York: Penguin, 2011), 227.

69 This seems to be the case in other countries as well; see Annick Magnier, "Beyond the City Hall: Municipal Administrative Leadership and Local Community," in Dahler-Larsen, *Social Bonds to City Hall*, 51–6.

70 Plunkett, *City Management in Canada*, 54.

71 McIntosh, "Defining Situational Leadership," 331.

Bibliography

Alvesson, Mats. "Organizational Culture: Meaning, Discourse, and Identity."
In *The Handbook of Organizational Culture and Climate*, 2nd ed., ed. Neal M.
Ashkanasy, Celeste P.M. Wilderom, and Mark F. Peterson, 11–28. Thousand
Oaks, CA: Sage Publications, 2011.

Alvesson, Mats, and Stefan Sveningsson. "Managers Doing Leadership: The
Extra-Ordinarization of the Mundane." *Human Relations* 56, no. 12 (2003):
1435–59.

American Society for Public Administration. "ASPA Code of Ethics." Washington, DC: ASPA, 2012. Available online at http://www.aspanet.org/
public/ASPA/Resources/Code_of_Ethics/ASPA/Resources/Code_of_
Ethics/Code_of_Ethics1.aspx?hkey=acd40318-a945-4ffc-ba7b-18e037b1a858.

Ammons, David N., and Charldean Newell. *City Executives: Leadership Roles,
Work Characteristics, and Time Management*. Albany: State University of New
York Press, 1989.

Andrew, Caroline, John Biles, Myer Siemiatycki, and Erin Tolley, eds. *Electing
a Diverse Canada*. Vancouver: UBC Press, 2008.

Bal, Mieke. *Narratology: Introduction to the Theory of Narrative*. Toronto: University of Toronto Press, 1985.

Barber, Bernard. "Some Problems in the Sociology of Professions." *Daedalus*
92 (1963): 669–88.

Bass, Bernard. *Bass and Stogdill's Handbook of Leadership: Theory, Research, and
Managerial Applications*. New York: Free Press, 1990.

Behn, Robert D. "What Right Do Public Managers Have to Lead?" *Public Administration Review* 58, no. 3 (1998): 209–24.

Bennis, Warren. *On Becoming a Leader*. Reading, MA: Addison-Wesley, 1989.

Bennis, Warren, and Burt Nanus. *Leaders: The Strategies for Taking Charge*. New
York: Harper & Row, 1985.

Borins, Sandford. *Governing Fables: Learning from Public Sector Narratives.* Charlotte, NC: Information Age Publishing, 2011.

Bosworth, Karl A. "The Manager *Is* a Politician." *Public Administration Review* 18, no. 3 (1958): 216–22.

Boudreau, Julie-Ann. *The Megacity Saga.* Montreal: Black Rose Books, 2000.

Bourgault, Jacques. "Les facteurs contributifs au leadership du greffier dans la fonction publique du Canada." *Canadian Public Administration* 50, no. 4 (2007): 541–72.

Bourgault, Jacques, and Christopher Dunn, eds. *Deputy Ministers in Canada: Comparative and Jurisdictional Perspectives.* Toronto: University of Toronto Press, 2014.

Bourgon, Jocelyne. *A New Synthesis of Public Administration: Serving in the 21st Century.* Montreal; Kingston, ON: McGill-Queen's University Press, 2011.

Brittain, Horace L. *Local Government in Canada.* Toronto: Ryerson Press, 1951.

Brownlow, Louis. *A Passion for Anonymity: The Autobiography of Louis Brownlow.* Chicago: University of Chicago Press, 1958.

Brunet-Jailly, Emmanuel. "Vancouver: The Sustainable City." *Journal of Urban Affairs* 30, no 4 (2008): 375–88.

Bryce, Robert B. *Maturing in Hard Times: Canada's Department of Finance through the Great Depression.* Montreal; Kingston, ON: McGill-Queen's University Press, 1986.

Bula, Frances. "One Tough Broad." *Vancouver Magazine,* 1 October 2008.

Burke, C. Shawn, Stephen M. Fiore, and Eduardo Salas. "The Role of Shared Cognition in Enabling Shared Leadership and Team Adaptability." In *Shared Leadership: Reframing the Hows and Whys of Leadership,* ed. Craig L. Pearce and Jay A. Conger, 103–22. Thousand Oaks, CA: Sage Publications, 2003.

Burns, James MacGregor. *Leadership.* New York: Harper & Row, 1978.

Bussom, Robert S., Lars L. Larson, and William M. Vicars. "Unstructured, Nonparticipant Observation and the Study of Leaders' Interpersonal Contacts." In *Leadership: Beyond Establishment Views,* ed. James G. Hunt, Uma Sekaran, and Chester A. Schriesheim, 31–49. Carbondale: Southern Illinois University Press, 1982.

Campbell, Larry, Neil Boyd, and Lori Culbert. *A Thousand Dreams: Vancouver's Downtown Eastside and the Fight for its Future.* Vancouver: Grey Stone Books, 2009.

Charih, Mohamed, and Lucie Rouillard. "The New Public Management." In *New Public Management and Public Administration in Canada,* ed. Mohamed

Charih and Arthur Daniels, 27–45. Toronto: Institute of Public Administration of Canada, 1997.

Cogan, Morris L. "The Problem of Defining a Profession." *Annals* 297 (1955): 105–11.

Cogan, Morris L. "Toward a Definition of Profession." *Harvard Educational Review* 23 (1953): 33–50.

Collins, Jim. *Good to Great: Why Some Companies Make the Leap ... and Others Don't.* New York: Harper Business, 2001.

Collins, Neil. *Local Government Managers at Work.* Dublin: Institute of Public Administration, 1987.

Collinson, David. "The Dialectics of Leadership." *Human Relations* 58, no. 11 (2005): 1419–42.

Collinson, David. "Rethinking Followership: A Post-structuralist Analysis of Follower Identities." *Leadership Quarterly* 17 (2006): 179–89.

Cooper, Terry L., and Thomas A. Bryer. "William Robertson: Exemplar of Politics and Public Management Rightly Understood." *Public Administration Review* 67, no. 5 (2007): 816–23.

Crawford, Kenneth Grant. *Canadian Municipal Government.* Toronto: University of Toronto Press, 1954.

Culver, Keith, and Paul Howe. "Calling All Citizens: The Challenges of Public Consultation." *Canadian Public Administration* 47, no. 1 (2004): 52–76.

Dagley, John C., and Shannon K. Salter. "Practice and Research in Career Counselling and Development – 2003." *Career Development Quarterly* 53, no. 2 (2004): 98–157.

Dahler-Larsen, Peter, ed. *Social Bonds to City Hall: How Appointed Managers Enter, Experience, and Leave Their Jobs in Western Local Government.* Odense, Denmark: Odense University Press, 2002.

Dalton, Melville. *Men Who Manage: Fusions of Feeling and Theory in Administration.* New York: John Wiley & Sons, 1959.

Day, David V., Peter Gronn, and Eduardo Salas. "Leadership in Team-based Organizations: On the Threshold of a New Era." *Leadership Quarterly* 17 (2006): 211–16.

De Bard Jr., August A. "Council-Manager Government in Halifax." *Canadian Public Administration* 3, no. 1 (1960): 76–81.

Denhardt, Robert B., and Janet V. Denhardt. *The Dance of Leadership: The Art of Leading in Business, Government, and Society.* Armonk, NY: M.E. Sharpe, 2006.

Denhardt, Janet V., and Robert B. Denhardt. *The New Public Service: Serving, Not Steering,* expanded ed. Armonk, NY: M.E. Sharpe, 2007.

Doig, Jameson W., and Erwin C. Hargrove, eds. *Leadership and Innovation: Entrepreneurs in Government.* Baltimore: Johns Hopkins University Press, 1990.

Dukakis, Michael S., and John Portz. *Leader-Managers in the Public Sector: Managing for Results.* Armonk, NY: M.E. Sharpe, 2010.

Dunlap, Albert J. *Mean Business: How I Save Bad Companies and Make Good Companies Great*, with Bob Andelman. New York: Random House, 1996.

Dutil, Patrice, ed. *Searching for Leadership: Secretaries to Cabinet in Canada.* Toronto: University of Toronto Press, 2008.

Enright, Robert, ed. *Body Heat: The Story of the Woodward's Redevelopment.* Vancouver: Blueimprint, 2010.

Fenn, Michael. "Building Effective Council-Staff Relations." *Municipal World* 113, no. 4 (2003): 17–22.

Fenn, Michael. "Emerging Trends in Urban Affairs: A Municipal Manager's View." In *Urban Affairs: Back on the Policy Agenda*, ed. Caroline Andrew, Katherine A. Graham, and Susan D. Phillips, 289–302. Montreal; Kingston, ON: McGill-Queen's University Press, 2003.

Fenn, Michael. "Future Focus: Burlington's Strategic Planning Success." *Canadian Public Administration* 32, no. 2 (1988): 304–10.

Fenn, Michael. "Reinvigorating Publicly Funded Medicare in Ontario: New Policy and Public Administration Techniques." *Canadian Public Administration* 49, no. 4 (2006): 527–47.

Fiedler, Fred E., and Martin M. Chemers. *Leadership and Effective Management.* Glenview, IL: Scott, Foresman and Company, 1974.

Fiedler, Fred E., and Joseph E. Garcia. *New Approaches to Effective Leadership.* New York: John Wiley & Sons, 1987.

Fletcher, Joyce K., and Katrin Käufer. "Shared Leadership: Reframing the Hows and Whys of Leadership." In *Shared Leadership: Reframing the Hows and Whys of Leadership*, ed. Craig L. Pearce and Jay A. Conger, 21–47. Thousand Oaks, CA: Sage Publications, 2003.

Flexner, Abraham. "Is Social Work a Profession?" *School and Society* 1 (1915): 901–11.

Gamberucci, Maurizio, and Annick Magnier. "Italian Local Democracy in Search of a New Administrative Leadership." In *The Anonymous Leader: Appointed CEOs in Western Local Government*, ed. Kurt Klaudi Klausen and Annick Magnier, 204–19. Odense, Denmark: Odense University Press, 1998.

Gardner, Howard. *Multiple Intelligences.* New York: Basic Books, 2006.

Garreau, Joel. *Edge City: Life on the New Frontier.* New York: Doubleday, 1991.

George, Alexander L., and Andrew Bennett. *Case Studies and Theory Development in the Social Sciences.* Cambridge, MA: MIT Press, 2005.

George, Bill. *Authentic Leadership: Rediscovering the Secrets to Creating Lasting Value.* San Francisco: Jossey-Bass, 2003.

Gibb, Corrine. *Hidden Hierarchies.* New York: Harper & Row, 1966.

Gilbert, Bill. *This City, This Man: The Cookingham Era in Kansas City.* Washington, DC: International City Management Association, 1978.

Glaeser, Edward. *Triumph of the City: How Our Greatest Invention Makes Us Richer, Smarter, Greener, Healthier, and Happier.* New York: Penguin, 2011.

Goffin, Stecie G., and Valora Washington. *Ready or Not: Leadership Choices in Early Care and Education.* New York: Teachers College Press, 2007.

Goldsmith, Michael, and Jon Tonge. "Local Authority Chief Executives: The British Case." In *The Anonymous Leader: Appointed CEOs in Western Local Government,* ed. Kurt Klaudi Klausen and Annick Magnier, 49–63. Odense, Denmark: Odense University Press, 1998.

Goleman, Daniel. *Emotional Intelligence.* New York: Bantam Books, 1995.

Goleman, Daniel. "Emotional Intelligence." In *Integrative Learning and Action: A Call to Wholeness,* ed. Susan M. Awbrey, Diane Dana, Vachel W. Miller, Phyllis Robinson, Merle M. Ryan, and David K. Scott, 143–54. New York: Peter Lang, 2006.

Goleman, Daniel, Richard Boyatzis, and Annie McKee. *Primal Leadership: Unleashing the Power of Emotional Intelligence.* Boston: Harvard Business Press, 2013.

Graham, Andrew. "Case Study: The Vancouver Agreement." Available online at http://post.queensu.ca/~grahama/case_studies/VANAGREEMENT CASE-1.pdf, accessed 5 August 2011.

Graham, Katherine A., and Susan D. Philips, eds. *Citizen Engagement: Lessons in Participation from Local Government.* Toronto: Institute of Public Administration of Canada, 1998.

Gray, Henry David, ed. *Thomas Carlyle's On Heroes, Hero-Worship, and the Heroic in History.* New York: Longmans, Green, 1905.

Greater Toronto Area Task Force. *Greater Toronto: Report of the GTA Task Force,* Anne Golden, chair. Toronto: Queen's Printer, 1996.

Greenleaf, Robert K. *Servant Leadership: A Journey into the Nature of Legitimate Power and Greatness.* New York: Paulist Press, 1977.

Gronn, Peter. "Distributed Leadership as a Unit of Analysis." *Leadership Quarterly* 13, no. 4 (2002): 423–51.

Gutstein, Donald. "Vancouver." In *City Politics in Canada,* ed. Warren Magnusson and Andrew Sancton, 189–221. Toronto: University of Toronto Press, 1983.

Harcourt, Mike, and Ken Cameron. *City Making in Paradise: Nine Decisions that Saved Vancouver,* with Sean Rossiter. Vancouver: Douglas & McIntyre, 2007.

Harlow, LeRoy F. *Without Fear or Favor: Odyssey of a City Manager*. Provo, UT: Brigham Young University Press, 1977.

Hickey, Paul. *Decision-Making Processes in Ontario's Local Government; with a Summary of 9 Systems of Local Decision-Making in other Canadian Provinces, the United States and England*. Toronto: Ministry of Treasury, Economics and Intergovernmental Affairs, 1973.

Higgins, Donald J.H. *Local and Urban Politics in Canada*. Toronto: Gage Educational, 1986.

Higgins, Donald J.H. *Urban Canada: Its Government and Politics*. Toronto: Macmillan of Canada, 1977.

Holli, Melvin. *The American Mayor: The Best and Worst Big-City Leaders*. State College: Pennsylvania State University, 1999.

Horak, Martin. "The Power of Local Identity: C4LD and the Anti-amalgamation Mobilization in Toronto," Research Paper 195. Toronto: University of Toronto, Centre for Urban and Community Studies, 1998.

Houghton, Jeffery D., Christopher P. Neck, and Charles C. Manz. "Self-Leadership and Superleadership." In *Shared Leadership: Reframing the Hows and Whys of Leadership*, ed. Craig L. Pearce and Jay A. Conger, 123–40. Thousand Oaks, CA: Sage Publications, 2003.

Hughes, Everett C. "Professions." *Daedalus* 92, no. 4 (1963): 655–68.

Hughes, Everett C. "The Professions in Society." *Canadian Journal of Economics and Political Science* 26, no. 1 (1960): 54–61.

Hummel, Ralph P. "Stories Managers Tell: Why They Are as Valid as Science." *Public Administration Review* 51, no. 1 (1991): 31–41.

Ingstrup, Ole, and Paul Crookall. *The Three Pillars of Public Management: Secrets of Sustained Success*. Montreal; Kingston, ON: McGill-Queen's University Press, 1998.

Institute of Public Administration of Canada. "The IPAC Statement of Principles Regarding the Conduct of Public Employees (1987)." Toronto: IPAC, 1987. Available online at http://www.ipac.ca/OurPrinciples.

Katz, D., and R.L. Kahn. *The Social Psychology of Organizations*, 2nd ed. New York: John Wiley, 1978.

Kaufman, Herbert. *The Administrative Behavior of Federal Bureau Chiefs*. Washington, DC: Brookings Institution, 1981.

Keating, Donald R. *The Power to Make It Happen*. Toronto: Green Tree Publishing, 1975.

Kellerman, Barbara. *Bad Leadership: What It Is, How It Happens, Why It Matters*. Boston: Harvard Business School Press, 2004.

Kellerman, Barbara. *The End of Leadership*. New York: HarperCollins, 2012.

Kellerman, Barbara. *Followership: How Followers Are Creating Change and Changing Leaders.* Boston: Harvard Business Press, 2008.

Kent, Thomas W. "Leading and Managing: It Takes Two to Tango." *Management Decision* 43, no. 7/8 (2005): 1010–17.

Kernaghan, Kenneth. "Politics, Policy, and Public Servants: Political Neutrality Revisited." *Canadian Public Administration* 19, no. 3 (1976): 432–56.

Kernaghan, Kenneth, Brian Marson, and Sandford Borins. *The New Public Organization.* Toronto: Institute of Public Administration of Canada, 2000.

Keyton, Joann. *Communication & Organizational Culture: A Key to Understanding Work Experiences.* Thousand Oaks, CA: Sage Publications, 2005.

King, Gary, Robert D. Keohane, and Sidney Verba. *Designing Social Inquiry: Scientific Inference in Qualitative Research.* Princeton, NJ: Princeton University Press, 1994.

Klausen, Kurt Klaudi, and Annick Magnier. "The Anonymous Leader." In *The Anonymous Leader: Appointed CEOs in Western Local Government*, ed. Kurt Klaudi Klausen and Annick Magnier, 11–30. Odense, Denmark: Odense University Press, 1998.

Kotter, John P. "What Leaders Really Do." *Harvard Business Review* (May/June 1990): 103–11.

Kotter, John P., and James L. Heskett. *Corporate Culture and Performance.* New York: Free Press, 1992.

Kotzé, Martina, and Ian Venter. "Differences in Emotional Intelligence between Effective and Ineffective Leaders in the Public Service: An Empirical Study." *International Review of Administrative Sciences* 77, no. 2 (2011): 397–427.

Kouzes, James M., and Barry Z. Posner. *The Leadership Challenge,* 3rd ed. San Francisco: Jossey-Bass, 2002.

KPMG. "Summary Report to the City of Vancouver, Southeast False Creek Development." Vancouver, 19 January 2009. Available online at http://vancouver.ca/ctyclerk/cclerk/20091006/documents/RR1KPMGreport.pdf, accessed 9 August 2011.

Leighninger, Matt. *The Next Form of Democracy.* Nashville, TN: Vanderbilt University Press, 2008.

Lewis, Eugene. *Public Entrepreneurship: Toward a Theory of Bureaucratic Political Power.* Bloomington: Indiana University Press, 1980.

Lightbody, James. *City Politics, Canada.* Peterborough, ON: Broadview Press, 2006.

Lightbody, James. "Edmonton." In *City Politics in Canada*, ed. Warren Magnusson and Andrew Sancton, 255–90. Toronto: University of Toronto Press, 1983.

Magnier, Annick. "Beyond the City Hall: Municipal Administrative Leadership and Local Community." In *Social Bonds to City Hall: How Appointed Managers Enter, Experience, and Leave Their Jobs in Western Local Government*, ed. Peter Dahler-Larsen, 51–6. Odense, Denmark: Odense University Press, 2002.

Manz, Charles C., and Henry P. Sims, Jr. *The New Superleadership: Leading Others to Lead Themselves*. San Francisco: Berrett-Koehler, 2001.

Manz, Charles C., and Henry P. Sims, Jr. "Superleadership: Beyond the Myth of Heroic Leadership." *Organizational Dynamics* 19, no. 4 (1991): 18–35.

Marini, Frank, ed. *Toward a New Public Administration: The Minnowbrook Perspective*. New York: Chandler, 1971.

Mason, Michael. "Collaborative Partnerships for Urban Development: A Study of the Vancouver Agreement." Research Papers in Environmental and Spatial Analysis 208. London: London School of Economics, 2006. Available online at http://www.lse.ac.uk/geographyAndEnvironment/research/Researchpapers/108%20Mason.pdf, accessed 5 August 2011.

Masson, Jack. *Alberta's Local Governments: Politics and Democracy*, with Edward C. LeSage Jr. Edmonton: University of Alberta Press, 1994.

Maynard-Moody, Steven, and Michael Musheno. *Cops, Teachers, Counselors: Stories from the Front Lines of Public Service*. Ann Arbor: University of Michigan Press, 2003.

McIntosh, Gordon A. "Defining Situational Leadership for the Local Government Chief Administrative Officer." PhD diss., University of Victoria, 2009.

Mintzberg, Henry. "If You're Not Serving Bill and Barbara, Then You're Not Serving Leadership." In *Leadership: Beyond Establishment Views*, ed. James G. Hunt, Uma Sekaran, and Chester A. Schriesheim, 239–59. Carbondale: Southern Illinois University Press, 1982.

Mintzberg, Henry. "Managing on the Edges." In *Managing Publicly*, ed. Henry Mintzberg and Jacques Bourgault, 29–51. Toronto: Institute of Public Administration of Canada, 2000.

Mintzberg, Henry. *The Nature of Managerial Work*. New York: Harper & Row, 1973.

Mintzberg, Henry, and Jacques Bourgault, eds. *Managing Publicly*. Toronto: Institute of Public Administration of Canada, 2000.

Missing Women Commission of Inquiry. "Issues Related to the Structure and Organization of Policing Arising from the Missing Women Investigation." Vancouver, April 2012. Available online at http://www.missingwomeninquiry.ca/wp-content/uploads/2010/10/Issues-related-to-the-structure-and-organization-of-policing-arising-from-the-missing-women-investigations.pdf, accessed 4 May 2012.

Moore, Mark H. *Creating Public Value: Strategic Management in Government.* Cambridge, MA: Harvard University Press, 1995.

Moore, Mark H. *Recognizing Public Value.* Cambridge, MA: Harvard University Press, 2013.

Morgan, David R., and Sheilah S. Watson. "Policy Leadership in Council-Manager Cities: Comparing Mayor and Manager." *Public Administration Review* 52, no. 5 (1992): 438–46.

Mosher, Frederick C., et al. *City Manager Government in Seven Cities.* Chicago: Public Administration Service, 1940.

Mouritzen, Poul Erik, and James H. Svara. *Leadership at the Apex: Politicians and Administrators in Western Local Governments.* Pittsburgh: University of Pittsburgh Press, 2002.

Nalbandian, John. *Professionalism in Local Government: Transformations in the Roles, Responsibilities, and Values of City Managers.* San Francisco: Jossey-Bass, 1991.

O'Flynn, Eamon. "A Position in Flux: Municipal CAOs in Canada." *Municipal Monitor* (Spring 2012): 16–18.

O'Flynn, Patrick Eamon. "The Evolving Role of the Municipal Chief Administrative Officer in Canada, 1985–2010." MA thesis, University of Guelph, 2011.

Ontario. Professional Organizations Committee. *Report.* Toronto: Ministry of the Attorney General, 1980.

Osbaldeston, Gordon F. *Keeping Deputy Ministers Accountable.* Toronto: McGraw-Hill Ryerson, 1989.

Osborne, David, and Ted Gaebler. *Reinventing Government: How the Entrepreneurial Spirit Is Transforming the Public Sector.* New York: Plume, 1992.

Ospina, Sonia M., and Jennifer Dodge. "It's about Time: Catching Method Up to Meaning – The Usefulness of Narrative Inquiry in Public Administration Research." *Public Administration Review* 65, no. 2 (2005): 143–57.

Pearce, Craig L., and Jay A. Conger. "All Those Years Ago: The Historical Underpinnings of Shared Leadership." In *Shared Leadership: Reframing the Hows and Whys of Leadership,* ed. Craig L. Pearce and Jay A. Conger, 1–18. Thousand Oaks, CA: Sage Publications, 2003.

Peters, Thomas J., and Robert H. Waterman, Jr. *In Search of Excellence: Lessons from America's Best-Run Companies.* New York: Harper & Row, 1982.

Plunkett, Thomas J. *City Management in Canada: The Role of the Chief Administrative Officer.* Toronto: Institute of Public Administration of Canada, 1992.

Plunkett, Thomas J. *Urban Canada and Its Government: A Study of Municipal Government.* Toronto: Macmillan of Canada, 1968.

Price, Trevor. "Council-Administration Relations in City Governments." In *Canadian Metropolitics: Governing Our Cities*, ed. James Lightbody, 193–214. Toronto: Copp Clark, 1995.

Punter, John. *The Vancouver Achievement: Urban Planning and Design*. Vancouver: UBC Press, 2003.

Putnam, Robert D. "The Political Attitudes of Senior Civil Servants in Britain, Germany, and Italy." In *The Mandarins of Western Europe: The Political Role of Top Civil Servants*, ed. Mattei Dogan, 87–127. New York: John Wiley & Sons, 1975.

Ridley, Clarence E., and Orin F. Nolting. *The City-Manager Profession*. Chicago: University of Chicago Press, 1934.

Robertson, Gordon. "The Changing Role of the Privy Council Office." *Canadian Public Administration* 14, no. 4 (1971): 487–508.

Robertson, Gordon. *Memoirs of a Very Civil Servant: Mackenzie King to Pierre Trudeau*. Toronto: University of Toronto Press, 2000.

Rost, Joseph C. *Leadership for the Twenty-First Century*. Westport, CT: Praeger, 1993.

Rowat, Donald C. "Do We Need the Manager Plan?" *Canadian Public Administration* 3, no. 1 (1960): 42–50.

Rowat, Donald C. *Your Local Government*. Toronto: Macmillan of Canada, 1965.

Rutter, Laurence. *The Essential Community: Local Government in the Year 2000*. Washington, DC: International City Management Association, 1980.

Sackmann, Sonja M. "Culture and Performance." In *The Handbook of Organizational Culture and Climate*, 2nd ed., ed. Neal M. Ashkanasy, Celeste P.M. Wilderom, and Mark F. Peterson, 188–224. Thousand Oaks, CA: Sage Publications, 2011.

Salovey, Peter, and John D. Mayer. "Emotional Intelligence." *Imagination, Cognition and Personality* 9, no. 3 (1989–90): 185–211.

Sancton, Andrew. "Mayors as Political Leaders." In *Leaders and Leadership in Canada*, ed. Maureen Mancuso, Richard G. Price, and Ronald Wagenberg, 174–89. Toronto: Oxford University Press, 1994.

Savoie, Donald J. *Breaking the Bargain: Public Servants, Ministers, and Parliament*. Toronto: University of Toronto Press, 2003.

Schein, Edgar H. *Organizational Culture and Leadership*, 3rd ed. San Francisco: Jossey-Bass, 2004.

Schlesinger, Jr., Arthur M. *The Politics of Upheaval*. Boston: Houghton Mifflin, 1960.

Self, Peter. *Administrative Theories and Politics*, 2nd ed. London: George Allen & Unwin, 1972.

Shamir, Boas, Hava Dayan-Horesh, and Dalya Adler. "Leading by Biography: Towards a Life-story Approach to the Study of Leadership." *Leadership* 1, no. 1 (2005): 13–29.

Siegel, David. "The Leadership Role of the Municipal Chief Administrative Officer." *Canadian Public Administration* 53, no. 2 (2010): 139–61.

Siegel, David. "Politics, Politicians, and Public Servants in Non-Partisan Local Government." *Canadian Public Administration* 37, no. 1 (1994): 17–30.

Simon, Herbert A. *Administrative Behavior: A Study of Decision-Making Processes in Administrative Organizations,* 3rd ed. New York: Free Press, 1976.

Smith, Jean Edward. *FDR.* New York: Random House, 2007.

Sternberg, R.J. *Successful Intelligence: How Practical and Creative Intelligence Determines Success in Life.* New York: Simon & Schuster, 1996.

Stewart, Kennedy. *Think Democracy: Options for Local Democratic Reform in Vancouver.* Vancouver: Simon Fraser University, Institute of Governance Studies, n.d.

Stillman II, Richard J. *The Rise of the City Manager: A Public Professional in Local Government.* Albuquerque: University of New Mexico Press, 1974.

Stogdill, Ralph M. *Handbook of Leadership: A Survey of Theory and Research.* New York: Free Press, 1974.

Stogdill, Ralph M. "Personal Factors Associated with the Study of Leadership: A Survey of the Literature." *Journal of Psychology* 25 (1948): 35–71.

Stone, Harold A., Don K. Price, and Kathryn H. Stone. *City Manager Government in the United States.* Chicago: Public Administration Service, 1940.

Sutherland, S.L. "The Role of the Clerk of the Privy Council." In *Commission of Inquiry into the Sponsorship Program and Advertising Activities,* Phase 2, *Restoring Accountability, Research Studies, Volume 3.* Ottawa: Government of Canada, 2006.

Svara, James H. "Dichotomy and Duality: Reconceptualizing the Relationship between Policy and Administration in Council-Manager Cities." In *Ideal & Practice in Council-Manager Government,* ed. H. George Frederickson, 53–69. Washington, DC: International City/County Management Association, 1989.

Svara, James H. *Dichotomy and Duality: The Relationship between Policy and Administration in Council-Manager Cities.* Armonk, NY: M.E. Sharpe, 2003.

Svara, James. *The Facilitative Leader in City Hall: Reexamining the Scope and Contributions.* Abingdon, UK: Taylor & Francis, 2008.

Svara, James H. *Official Leadership in the City: Patterns of Conflict and Cooperation.* New York: Oxford University Press, 1989.

Svara, James H., and James R. Brunet. "Finding and Refining Complementarity in Recent Conceptual Models of Politics and Administration." In

Retracing Public Administration, ed. Mark R. Rutgers, 185–208. Amsterdam: JAI, 1989.

Tennant, Paul. "Vancouver Politics and the Civic Party System." In *Problems of Change in Urban Government*, ed. M.O. Dickerson, S. Drabek, and J.T. Woods, 13–37. Waterloo, ON: Wilfrid Laurier University Press, 1980.

Terry, Larry D. *Leadership of Public Bureaucracies: The Administrator as Conservator*, 2nd ed. Armonk, NY: M.E. Sharpe, 2003.

Thach, Elizabeth, and Karen J. Thompson. "Trading Places: Examining Leadership Competencies between For-profit vs. Public and Non-profit Leaders." *Leadership & Organization Development Journal* 28, no. 4 (2007): 356–75.

Toronto Computer Leasing Inquiry: Toronto External Contracts Inquiry. *Report*, vol. 1, *Facts and Findings*, Hon. Madam Justice Denise E. Bellamy, Commissioner. Toronto, 2005.

Trottier, Tracey, Montgomery Van Wart, and XiaoHu Wang. "Examining the Nature and Significance of Leadership in Government Organizations." *Public Administration Review* 68, no. 2 (2008): 319–33.

Urbaniak, Tom. *Her Worship: Hazel McCallion and the Development of Mississauga*. Toronto: University of Toronto Press, 2009.

Useem, Michael. *Leading Up: How to Lead Your Boss So You Both Win*. New York: Crown Business, 2001.

Vance, W. George R. "The Managerial Approaches of Chief Administrative Officers." PhD diss., University of Western Ontario, 1985.

"The Vancouver Agreement." In *Inclusion, Collaboration and Urban Governance: Brazilian and Canadian Experiences*, org. Hugh Kellas, 99–110. Vancouver, University of British Columbia, Centre for Human Settlements, 2010.

Van Wart, Montgomery. *Dynamics of Leadership in Public Service: Theory and Practice*, 2nd ed. Armonk, NY: M.E. Sharpe, 2011.

Vogel, Donna. *Challenging Politics: COPE, Electoral Politics and Social Movements*. Halifax, NS: Fernwood Publishing, 2003.

Watson, Tony J. *In Search of Management: Culture, Chaos & Control in Managerial Work*. London: Routledge, 1994.

White, Graham. "Big Is Different from Little: On Taking Size Seriously in the Analysis of Canadian Governmental Institutions." *Canadian Public Administration* 33, no. 4 (1990): 526–50.

White, Jay D. *Taking Language Seriously: The Narrative Foundations of Public Administration Research*. Washington, DC: Georgetown University Press, 2007.

White, Leonard D. *The City Manager*. New York: Greenwood Press, 1927.

Yerema, Richard. "Top 100." *Maclean's*, 15 October 2007.

Yukl, Gary. *Leadership in Organizations*, 6th ed. Upper Saddle River, NJ: Pearson Prentice Hall, 2006.

Index

The Institute of Public Administration of Canada Series in Public
Management and Governance

Networks of Knowledge: Collaborative Innovation in International Learning, Janice
    Stein, Richard Stren, Joy Fitzgibbon, and Melissa Maclean
*The National Research Council in the Innovative Policy Era: Changing Hierarchies,
    Networks, and Markets*, G. Bruce Doern and Richard Levesque
*Beyond Service: State Workers, Public Policy, and the Prospects for Democratic
    Administration*, Greg McElligott
*A Law unto Itself: How the Ontario Municipal Board Has Developed and Applied
    Land Use Planning Policy*, John G. Chipman
Health Care, Entitlement, and Citizenship, Candace Redden
*Between Colliding Worlds: The Ambiguous Existence of Government Agencies for
    Aboriginal and Women's Policy*, Jonathan Malloy
The Politics of Public Management: The HRDC Audit of Grants and Contributions,
    David A. Good
*Dream No Little Dreams: A Biography of the Douglas Government of Saskatchewan,
    1944–1961*, Albert W. Johnson
Governing Education, Ben Levin
*Executive Styles in Canada: Cabinet Structures and Leadership Practices in
    Canadian Government*, edited by Luc Bernier, Keith Brownsey, and Michael
    Howlett
The Roles of Public Opinion Research in Canadian Government, Christopher Page
The Politics of CANDU Exports, Duane Bratt
Policy Analysis in Canada: The State of the Art, edited by Laurent Dobuzinskis,
    Michael Howlett, and David Laycock
Digital State at the Leading Edge: Lessons from Canada, Sanford Borins, Kenneth
    Kernaghan, David Brown, Nick Bontis, Perri 6, and Fred Thompson
*The Politics of Public Money: Spenders, Guardians, Priority Setters, and Financial
    Watchdogs inside the Canadian Government*, David A. Good
Court Government and the Collapse of Accountability in Canada and the U.K.,
    Donald Savoie
Professionalism and Public Service: Essays in Honour of Kenneth Kernaghan, edited
    by David Siegel and Ken Rasmussen
Searching for Leadership: Secretaries to Cabinet in Canada, edited by Patrice Dutil
Foundations of Governance: Municipal Government in Canada's Provinces, edited
    by Andrew Sancton and Robert Young
Provincial and Territorial Ombudsman Offices in Canada, edited by Stewart
    Hyson